THE KENNEDYS

Amidst the Gathering Storm

WILL SWIFT

Smithsonian Books

Collins
An Imprint of HarperCollinsPublishers

THE KENNEDYS
Amidst the Gathering Storm

A Thousand Days
in London, 1938–1940

HarperCollins books may be purchased for educational, business, or sales promotional use. For information, please write: Special Markets Department, HarperCollins Publishers, 10 East 53rd Street, New York, NY 10022.

FIRST EDITION

Designed by Kate Nichols

Library of Congress Cataloging-in-Publication Data is available upon request.
ISBN: 978-0-06-117356-1

08 09 10 11 12   ID/RRD 10 9 8 7 6 5 4 3 2 1

For my granddaughter EMERSON ELLE SWIFT,
who was born a few days after I finished this book.

AND

for KEVIN JACOBS
who was steadfast throughout.

Only those who dare to fail greatly

can ever achieve greatly.

ROBERT KENNEDY

Contents

1940

Acknowledgments

OVER A FOUR-YEAR PERIOD, I spent countless hours in the John F. Kennedy Library research room, with its magnificent view of Dorchester Bay. I am grateful to the Joseph P. Kennedy Papers Donors Committee for granting me permission to study Joseph P. Kennedy's restricted papers and to the John F. Kennedy Library Foundation for permission to publish private photographs of the Kennedy family.

Megan Desnoyers was extremely helpful in guiding me through the Rose Kennedy papers, showing me Rose Kennedy's marvelously detailed London diaries (with newspaper cuttings pasted in); Kathleen Kennedy's London diaries, which have never been drawn upon before; and newly available family letters. Stephen Plotkin, Sharon Kelly, Michael Desmond, and Frank Rigg were friendly, efficient, and resourceful in solving problems for me (and they tried to help me curtail my bad habit of licking my fingers while thumbing through piles of documents). Mary Rose Grossman went beyond the call of duty in helping me choose a rich selection of photographs and track down their copyrights. Allan Goodrich was able to identify the copyrights of some of the most obscure pictures. Jennifer Quan helped me obtain approval from the John F. Kennedy Library Foundation for photographs and research materials.

Deborah Mitford, the Dowager Duchess of Devonshire, kindly invited me to Chatsworth, and spoke to me at length on several occasions about the Kennedys during the years when the Mitfords lived around the corner from them. Her assistant Helen Marchant was also very thoughtful; they assisted me in finding photographs from that era. The countess of Sutherland shared her memories over lunch at her London townhouse, and Lady Sarah Baring Astor talked to me about her mother-in-law, Nancy Astor, and the Kennedys. Page Huidekoper Wilson, Joe's young assistant at the U.S. embassy in London, who has completed her own memoir, *Shot in the Tail with Luck*, regaled me over tea at her Georgetown home with lively stories from her book.

The community of Kennedy scholars was extremely welcoming and supportive. I could not have written this book without Amanda Smith's brilliantly edited *Hostage to Fortune: The Letters of Joseph P. Kennedy* as a touchstone. Her essay on the ambassadorial period was invaluable. She was exceedingly generous with her time and knowledge. Senator Ted Kennedy was kind enough to take the time out of his extraordinarily busy schedule to talk with me, and sent me a wonderful photograph of himself and his father in London. Melissa Wagoner in his office is one of those delightful people who seems to make everything flow easily. Kennedy speechwriter Ted Sorensen graciously spoke to me about President Kennedy. His comments about the effect of Joe Kennedy's ambassadorship on Jack Kennedy's presidency were extraordinarily helpful. Robert Kennedy, Jr., gave me permission to look at the Lem Billings papers.

David Nasaw, who is writing a Kennedy family–authorized biography of Joseph P. Kennedy, was unfailingly generous and helped me arrange important interviews. Sally Bedell Smith gave me crucial assistance and emotional support along the way, and also inspired me with her books on Pamela Harriman (*Reflected Glory*) and the Kennedys (*Grace and Power*). Discussing the Kennedy family and twentieth-century history with Lance Morrow was a marvelous experience. Charles Higham provided many useful leads and significant encouragement throughout this project. He opened his papers to my assistants and directed me to researchers in England. Bob Self was extraordinarily good-hearted and thoughtful; he answered several difficult research questions for me and painstakingly reviewed the manuscript for minor errors. His superb biography of Neville Chamberlain provided an essential background for this book. Michigan State historian Jane Vieth, who is writing her own book on the Kennedy ambassadorship, kindly read the manuscript and gave me feedback. Anne de Courcy caught several key errors in the text. Allen Packwood of the Churchill archives pointed me to the unpublished correspondence of Unity Mitford and Winston Churchill, helped me shape my early ideas about Churchill, and also read the manuscript. Blanche Weisen Cook was particularly helpful regarding matters related to Jewish refugees. Conrad Black provided insights along the way, and Doris Kearns Goodwin also gave me assistance.

Robert Holmes Tuttle, President George W. Bush's ambassador to the Court of St. James's, spoke with me at the U.S. embassy in Grosvenor Square about the responsibilities and challenges an American ambassador faces in London. His assistant Maureen Malloy was particularly obliging. Peter Hilton arranged for me to have a tour of Prince's Gate, which I greatly enjoyed. Claire Jackson, the college archivist at the Royal College of General Practitioners at Prince's Gate, assisted me with photographs.

I am grateful for conversations and communications with Robert Dallek; James McGregor Burns; Evan Thomas; Stephen Wise's grandson Steve Tulin; Jane Ormsby-Gore Rainey; Burton Hersh; Andrew Roberts; Ed Klein; Laurence Leamer; Ed Renehan; Sylvia Morris; Lynne McTaggart; Angela Lambert; Nigel West; Andrew Parker-Bowles; Christopher Sykes; Sir Ronald Grierson; Pamela, Lady Harlech; Victoria Ormsby-Gore Lloyd; Lady Anne Tree; Lady Elizabeth Cavendish; Katherine MacMillan; Shaul Ferraro at Yad Vashem; Richard Whalen; Lord Astor; William Shawcross; Gore Vidal; Sarah Bradford; Hugo Vickers; and Kenneth Rose. I received valuable assistance from the staff at Cliveden, at the Astor archives, at the Beaverbrook archives at the House of Commons, and from the Department of Special Collections, SUNY Library, Stony Brook, New York. Marvin Russell at the National Archives in Maryland; Christine Kitto at the Krock Papers in the Seeley G. Mudd Manuscript Library in Princeton, New Jersey; Nicholas Scheetz and Scott Taylor at the Special Collections Division of the Georgetown University Library; Lynn Duchez at the Cleveland Public Library Special Collections; and Nancy Fulford at the Astor Archives all went out of their way to help me. Philip Parkinson did research for me in London. And my local librarians Jean Pallis (in Valatie) and Julie Johnson (in Kinderhook) were unfailingly generous to me.

I hope that any contributors I have forgotten to mention will understand how much I appreciate their help despite my temporary memory lapse.

Researching a book is always an adventure: Some uninspiring avenues bear unexpected dividends, while other more promising paths suddenly stop cold. Amanda Smith told me that Joe Kennedy's journalist friend George Bilainkin had written a private memoir about the ambassadorship, *Joseph P. Kennedy: A Fateful Embassy*. Excited about reading this firsthand account, I hired the talented British researcher Philip Adriaan, on Charles Higham's advice, to track down Bilainkin's descendents and recover the manuscript. Working with obituaries, he determined that George was a member of the Royal Commonwealth Society and searched their files for information. He also made use of ancestry websites, and finally located

Bilainkin's granddaughter Jan Dziewulski. She told him that her parents had, indeed, found George's manuscript while they were going through his possessions after he died. Jan's mother told her that the manuscript "wasn't finished and since he was getting ultra-paranoid by that time, the manuscript was rambling and incoherent so she binned it." Tantalizingly, she also told her that her father's intimacy with the Kennedys would have made the manuscript very interesting "if he had still had his marbles while he was writing it." I found it painful that this potentially important document has been lost to history.

I would like to thank Howard Berman; Harold Brown; Jim Wilcox; David Forer; Pamela and David Strousse; Marty Sloane; Jeffrey Young; Ralph Blair; Michael First; Leslee Snyder; Cathy Flanagan; John Locke; Jed, Dianne, Anna, Naomi, and Sara Swift; Paul Swift and Jane Stasz; Anne Schomaker; Rod and DeGuerre Blackburn; Alyne Model; Leslie, Lucas, and Sawyer Maher; Gay and Katie Hendricks; Jacqueline Pomeranz; Brittany Lauer; and Dylan Swift for their support. I am particularly grateful to my intrepid cousins Bill and Betty Swift for making a number of long trips to Charles Higham's archives in California. Betty Swift, a retired librarian, used her considerable skills to plow through mountains of documents. Ruth Randall offered terrific suggestions after reading a first draft of my book proposal. David Groff encouraged me to take on this project, and, with his knowledge of politics and history and his superb judgment, made invaluable contributions along the way.

My thoughtful and resourceful agent Judith Riven found an excellent house for this book. I have thoroughly enjoyed working with Elisabeth Dyssegaard, my editor at Smithsonian Press, and her assistant Kate Antony. I particularly appreciate Elisabeth Dyssegaard's prompt and efficient style, and I respect her outstanding editorial judgment.

My partner Kevin Jacobs, who is working on his own book, proofread every chapter as it came along. His extraordinary love and support made it possible for me to spend these past years happily recapturing that mesmerizing era, three-quarters of a century ago, when the Kennedys were transformed by their time in London.

Will Swift
Valatie, New York
July 2, 2007

Introduction

"The great enemy of the truth is very often not the lie—deliberate, contrived and dishonest, but the myth, persistent, persuasive, and unrealistic. Belief in myths allows the comfort of opinion without the discomfort of thought."

PRESIDENT JOHN F. KENNEDY

"History is argument without end."

DUTCH HISTORIAN PEITER GEYL

T HE UNITED STATES EMBASSY in Grosvenor Square is heavily fortified. Armed guards with machine guns patrol concrete barriers. To enter, I had to go through a series of intense security checks. Eleven months earlier, Islamic terrorists had coordinated two bomb blasts in the London transportation system. Once again, as in 1940, America and Britain were confronting a dictatorial threat from ideologues bent on attacking us. The danger no longer has the visage of fascism; now it emerges from religious fanaticism.

Meeting on June 1, 2006 with U.S. ambassador Robert Holmes Tuttle, President George W. Bush's representative to the Court of St. James's, I was struck by another major difference between then and now. Back then, in a less suspicious era, unbelievably, residents not connected to the embassy lived in apartments on the top floors of the U.S. embassy.

As was Irish-Catholic businessman Joseph Kennedy, who served as the American ambassador to Britain from 1938 to 1940, Ambassador Tuttle is an outsider by birth to the prevailing American establishment: His father was a member of the Chickasaw Indian Tribe. Kennedy served at a defining moment in the histories of the United States, Great Britain, and the West; Tuttle is serving at a similarly historic time. Neither man's ancestry mirrored that of the British elite; both were challenged to fit into the intricate British social and diplomatic mores, while enacting what Tuttle calls "the never-ending responsibilities" of the American representative in London—

duties intensified in a time of crisis when there are constant consultations with British and U.S. government officials and unrelenting requests for intelligence gathering. It is a demanding job at the best of times—despite the fact that today the official U.S. representative, even more so than in Kennedy's era, is a goodwill ambassador rather than a policy enactor.

*T*HE KENNEDYS AMIDST THE GATHERING STORM explores the vital role of America's most enduringly important political family as Britain, and then America, edged into war. At this time when democracy was on the defensive and totalitarian regimes were on the rise, history had its pivotal point in London, where fascist, democratic, and socialist ideologies clashed openly and where the Kennedy family emerged as a political dynasty. It was during this time that future president John F. Kennedy came of age, Rose Kennedy conquered British society, and Joseph Kennedy fought on his own contrarian terms to ally with Neville Chamberlain and Winston Churchill and so safeguard America and protect both the United States and Britain from fascist tyranny. From 1938 to 1940, the Kennedy family served as America's dazzling and bold ambassadors not just to Britain but to the world; they were witnesses and players in a drama involving astonishing upheaval and change.

Threatened by the gathering storm of war, Britain—as experienced by the Kennedy family at the close of the 1930s—was a romantic, anxious, and decadent place of spectacular weekend house parties at grand country estates, nightly debutante balls and dinners amid the floodlit gardens of London townhouses, extravagant charity events, and court presentations at Buckingham Palace. In three of the most tumultuous years of the century, a catastrophic war loomed menacingly on the horizon and slowly but inexorably commandeered this world, culminating with all the fury of the Blitz and the Battle of Britain.

Central to this turbulent era were the intricate and shifting relationships among Kennedy and British prime ministers Neville Chamberlain and Winston Churchill and their personal and political interactions with Franklin Roosevelt, Adolf Hitler, and Benito Mussolini, at a time when the fate of freedom was in doubt.

*T*HE KENNEDYS AMIDST THE GATHERING STORM endeavors to present a fully rounded and empathetic portrait of Ambassador Joseph Kennedy, a man who has become a favorite whipping boy of twentieth-century historians. His story has too often been told from the perspectives of Roosevelt and Churchill, men whose ambitions clashed with Kennedy's own goals. Kennedy's troubled relationships with two of the twentieth century's most venerated leaders have led many of their biographers to cast him in the worst possible light. In his recent magisterial biography *Franklin Delano Roosevelt: Champion of Freedom*, Conrad Black points out that Kennedy was "ultimately widely reckoned to be one of the worst diplomatic appointments in the history of the United States." Was Kennedy really such a bad representative of his country? One of his weaknesses was to see things in black and white, but many of those who have written about him, including authors Ted Schwarz and Laurence Leamer, have fallen into the same trap. In my previous book, *The Roosevelts and the Royals*, I, too, portrayed Kennedy from the Roosevelt point of view, shortchanging him as an opportunistic thorn in the president's side.

The Kennedys came to London at a time when the bruising financial commitments and loss of life during the First World War had not secured a democratic Europe and the American people stood firmly against sending U.S. soldiers into another catastrophic European war. President Roosevelt and the State Department had not yet developed a coherent philosophy of statecraft and diplomacy to deal with the menace of fascism. They failed to provide Kennedy with an agenda to advance or a vision to propound.

Joseph Kennedy and Britain's ill-fated prime minister Neville Chamberlain are easy targets for historians. The myths about Kennedy abound. He has been portrayed as a completely self-centered, anti-Semitic, Nazi-loving defeatist, just as his ally Chamberlain has been depicted as a foolhardy, myopic appeaser. Churchill himself contributed to Chamberlain's negative image by dubbing him "an old town clerk looking at European affairs from the wrong end of a municipal drainpipe."

There is no question that the willingness of Kennedy and Chamberlain to allow Germany to swallow up Czechoslovakia and Austria falls on the wrong side of history. But they have frequently been caricatured by historians and biographers, and the two men's geopolitical motives and philosophies—understandable, and existing within the mainstream of their era—have been denigrated or ignored. Both Neville Chamberlain and Joseph Kennedy deserve fair and comprehensive portrayals of their perspectives and of their exhaustive diplomatic efforts, in the context of the turbulent years from 1938 to 1940. In this book, I will consider Joseph Kennedy in light of recent revisionist scholarship about Neville Chamberlain—most notably Robert Self's 2006 biography and David Dutton's book reviewing Chamberlain's reputation. These authors carefully delineate the military, political, economic, and diplomatic factors that created the context for the Munich agreement.

Like these scholars, I believe we must study and assess Kennedy's and Chamberlain's intentions and decisions in view of what they knew and believed in 1938 and 1939, not just in the context of what we now know about Hitler and the goals of all of Europe's emerging totalitarian regimes. The circumstances of the late 1930s offered a great deal of justification for the arguments made by Kennedy, Chamberlain, and many others that Hitler's territorial ambitions could be appeased and contained, thus avoiding or delaying another calamitous war. They cited the widely presumed superiority of the German war machine, the reluctance of the British dominions to join in the fight, British foreign policy traditions of offering limited concessions when necessary to preserve European peace (a higher priority than maintaining the status quo in Europe), the straits that Europe and America confronted amid the world's worst depression ever, and—especially for Joe Kennedy—the belief, born of the aftermath of World War I, that going to war would economically devastate the West and destroy the very system of democracy that war sought to save.

This book will attempt to do justice to an extremely complex man. Joe Kennedy embodied many contradictions. While raised in an anti-Semitic environment, he did more than FDR's other European ambassadors to assist Jewish refugees. Though shrewd and extremely aggressive in the business world, as a diplomat Kennedy was a tenacious proponent of accommodation with Britain's and America's adversaries. Proud of his realistic approach, he was also a highly emotional man who misread Hitler and Nazism until it was too late. Blunt and outspoken, he could also be extremely secretive. He was optimistic about his personal power to accomplish his aims, yet he would be gloomy about Britain and America's fate in war. At times selfish, he was, nonetheless, often generous, even tenderhearted.

THERE WERE IN ESSENCE three different Kennedy ambassadorships, corresponding roughly to the three years Joe held the post. Two of them were astonishingly successful. In 1938 he was an ebullient, energetic, creative, and amazingly well-connected envoy, providing useful, up-to-date information to the U.S. government. That first year, he appeared to observers to be pro-British in his attitudes in a way that some thought meant he had denigrated his own country and "gone native," but in truth he allied with Chamberlain because his accommodationist policies seemed to offer the best protection for the United States. During 1939 he was perceived both publicly and by the British government to be a pro-American nationalist, as well as a disillusioned pacifist, a maverick who would try almost anything to avert war. By 1940, once Chamberlain's negotiations failed and war had erupted, Kennedy moved painfully but steadily toward advocating limited aid and intervention by the United States, while he vehemently opposed direct American involvement in the conflict. As events overtook him, he would become marginalized, ignored, angry, depressed, and pessimistic. His ambassadorship is remembered like a marriage gone bad—mainly for the last and deteriorating phase. I seek to evaluate it as a more variegated tenure during which Kennedy served his country with a dedication and a conviction that was honestly felt if at times misguided, until he became embittered by the strains of war and diplomatic isolation.

It is time to hear in more depth Kennedy's own words, from his London diaries and his diplomatic memoir, which he never published because he feared, with justification, that it would harm his sons' political careers. Of course, any historian has to approach Kennedy's writing with caution. Joe was, after all, one of the great innovators of political public relations, once declaring, "It is not what you are that counts, but what people *think* you are." The memoir was revised over fifteen years with several ghostwriters, and it can resemble a hall of mirrors. In fact, it begins with a misrepresentation: Kennedy proclaims that he never thought about becoming an ambassador ("The president's suggestion was a complete surprise. Diplomatic service had not suggested itself to me."), but other accounts make clear that he sought out the position.

As revealed in his letters, diary, and memoir, Ambassador Kennedy's flaws were substantial, even tragic. Among them were his failure to see the implications of Nazi ideology; his overemphasis on an economic view of international relations; his failure—very typical of Americans of his era—to acknowledge the importance of maintaining a balance of power in European politics in order to prevent a country like Germany from dominating the continent; his inability to recognize the intangible aspects of spirit that would allow Britain and democracy to triumph in war; his tendency, at times, to confuse his own point of view with that of the United States; and a propensity for reckless behavior in both his professional and personal life, which included some highly publicized extramarital affairs. Joe was more of a tactician than a strategist. A vehement advocate of democracy, he prided himself on being a practical, no-nonsense American businessman who barreled ahead and got things done. Such an attitude had fostered his own fortune. As a diplomat, he based his policy advocacy on the exigencies of the constantly changing conditions he observed. But he was so hyper-realistic that he could not project idealism in an era that demanded vision. He lacked an overarching political view of how to transform America's relations with the world.

Yet without denying his flaws, *The Kennedys Amidst the Gathering Storm* shows Joe Kennedy's genuine patriotism, his desire to serve the United States and safeguard its interests as he understood them, his diligent efforts to forge far-ranging contacts in politics, the press, business, and society and so ferret out the freshest and most acute information for the president and the State Department, his work in fostering British-American relations, his prescience about the economic fate of the British Empire, his compassion for refugees and Americans stranded abroad, his considerable organizational skills, and his personal qualities of generosity, warmth, kindness, and consideration. Kennedy maintained a personal and professional commitment to excellence, which he passed on to all of his children, particularly to his son Jack. Joseph Kennedy was a fiercely protective father, and, as ambassador, he often treated America as if it were another child he needed to shield from harm.

One key to Joe Kennedy's personality was his fierce loyalty, a virtue taught by his father, Patrick, whom he deeply loved. His loyalty was a product of his own insecure identity. Forever the outsider, he could never feel assured of his place in the world. His stubborn loyalty to his own beliefs got him in trouble when he took it to extremes, as he did with his staunch advocacy of U.S. isolationism. During his ambassadorship, his relationship with the president deteriorated, but he stayed in the job when others might have quit. When Franklin Roosevelt circumvented him in the last year of his ambassadorship, Kennedy was deeply wounded. He felt caught between his need to remain loyal to his president and his desire to lash out and break free.

THE KENNEDYS' TIME IN LONDON solidified in America's imagination the story of a family dynasty as compelling as that of the Roosevelts. From 1938 to 1940, the Kennedy family crystallized their own identity as protagonists on the world stage, making public the competitive and clannish intra-family dynamics that would fuel their mythic rise to power. One of the many reasons Kennedy wanted the job in London was to satisfy Rose, an adventurous and highly intelligent woman who longed for the opportunities accorded the wife of an ambassador. Highly social, the daughter of Boston mayor John "Honey Fitz" Fitzgerald, Rose loved traveling and feeling like an actor in the drama of history. In her early twenties, during Honey Fitz's mayoralty, she had substituted for her socially retiring mother as her father's hostess. Now, after a quarter century out of the limelight, she would delight in mingling with the aristocratic, royal, and political leaders of Britain. Rose was an astute diplomat whose advice her husband too often ignored. She later said that had she been born in a different era, she might have become a politician herself.

Rose was a biographer's delight; she took great care to paste into her London diary correctly dated newspaper clippings about significant current events or family outings. In England she would relish the opportunity to teach her children about British and European culture and was eager to witness with them history in action, but she was also often preoccupied by making the right social connections and attending fashionable parties and weekends at grand houses—all events that would enhance her own social status. At times she would leave Joe in charge of the family while she traveled or shopped abroad.

In the privately printed family memoir about their mother, *Her Grace Above Gold*, Ted Kennedy summarized the roles he saw Rose and Joe Kennedy playing in their children's lives: "He was our greatest fan and she was our greatest teacher. We have had our father's drive and our mother's grace, our father's love of action and our mother's love of history and scholarship, our father's gift of athletics and our mother's gift of politics. Dad was our greatest booster, expecting much from us in return. Mother supplied the gentleness, support and encouragement that made Dad's standards reachable."

When the Kennedys arrived in London, they had been married for almost twenty-four years. Eight years before, Joe had cabled Rose, on her fortieth birthday, that she was the Eighth Wonder of the World. By the time of the ambassadorship, Rose and Joe had created a respectful and appreciative partnership focused on raising their children, advancing Joe's political career, and the family's dynastic ambitions. Joe's philandering had become more discreet, and he had long since given up his midlife crisis, a time when he thought of divorcing Rose and marrying actress Gloria Swanson. Rose maintained a willful blindness to her husband's adultery, which would continue during his ambassadorship, when he would have a brief but politically entangling affair with Clare Boothe Luce, the writer and wife of *Time* magazine founder and prominent Republican Henry Luce, and begin a nearly seven-year alliance with the showgirl Daye Eliot, a friend of the entertainment correspondent and author Doris Lilly. Over seventeen years, from 1915 to 1932, Rose Kennedy had borne her husband nine children, who at the start of his ambassadorship ranged in age from twenty-three-year-old Joe Jr. to Teddy, who was nearly six. Their second son, Jack, was twenty-one. Of the middle children, Rosemary was nineteen, Kathleen seventeen, Eunice sixteen, Patricia thirteen, Robert twelve, Jean nine, and Teddy six. In London they would take on a strikingly public presence, projecting a clamoring, headlong vigor to a British people who would become increasingly eager to embrace all things American.

Before joining the family in London, Joe Jr. would first finish his senior year at Harvard, his father's alma mater, and his younger brother Jack would complete his sophomore year there as well. Dashing and bold, Joe Jr. was temperamentally similar to his father and shared many of his political views. Both Kennedy *père* and *fils* opposed U.S. military engagement in Europe; they believed Americans should stay at home and build up the United States as a fortress against world conflict. Father and son perceived Hitler's Germany as a possible bulwark against the spread of the Soviet system they loathed. But as fascist aggression outran the isolationist effort to curtail it, Joe Jr. would be trapped by his need to defend his family's reputation; he would ultimately come to a tragic end trying to prove his mettle as a combatant in the war he and his father had so vehemently fought to avoid.

Joe and Rose saw their oldest son as a model child and gave him responsibility for helping to raise his younger siblings. Having too well absorbed his father's lessons in competitiveness, Joe bullied his thin and sickly younger brother Jack to the point of physical sadism. Joe Jr. must have sensed from early on that Jack's lively intelligence and razor wit made him a serious contender for attention in a large family. The Kennedys' second son would suffer feelings of inferiority after having been so dominated by his older brother. He would handle them by competing with his aggressive and sometimes sarcastic Casanova of a brother to conquer women and be socially brilliant.

Joe and Rose's third child and eldest daughter, Rosemary, consumed much of her mother's attention. She was mildly mentally retarded, just enough to be painfully aware of her inability to keep pace with even her younger siblings. Her frustration led to frequent rages. Pretty, with striking green eyes, she would have been a magnet for men had she not been carefully chaperoned in England, where she would dance with exuberance at London's debutante balls.

The leading light among the girls was seventeen-year-old Kathleen, known as Kick. Petite and dainty like her mother, she was not conventionally pretty, but she was possessed of brilliant blue eyes, perfect skin, ebullience, and a self-deprecating sense of humor, a characteristic she shared with Jack. Kick would be named by London's social press as the "most exciting debutante of 1938." She would remain an American star in the English firmament even after her father departed his post, until tragedy struck her down a decade after she first appeared in London. Bobby, the third son, was the least sociable of the Kennedy boys, and he would have trouble making friends his own age. He could be aggressive and tenacious, but he was also kind and thoughtful. Eunice, gawky and thin, prone to sleepless nights, had a more nervous temperament than her siblings. She and her brother Bobby inherited their father's intensity and, like their mother, were deeply religious. Compassionate and conscientious, taking special care of her retarded older sister, Eunice was the leader of the younger group of children—beautiful and shrewd Patricia; Jean, a bright, reserved, and pudgy late bloomer; and Teddy, who was the most outgoing of them all.

JOE KENNEDY'S AMBASSADORSHIP is a classic American immigrant tragedy. It reveals how the powerful effects of damaging prejudice endured in childhood can reverberate throughout a life and lead, at times unconsciously, to self-destruction. Kennedy, a second-generation Irish-American and a Catholic in a pervasively Protestant nation where immigration remained a volatile political issue, was deeply wounded by the youthful social rejection he suffered at the hands of the WASP establishment in Boston and beyond, and thus was never secure about his place in the world. He labored for thirty years to win a position of prominence from which he could fulfill his dreams of social acceptance and economic and psychic security. His triumphant arrival in London accompanied by his dynamic family promised to defuse his profound sense of being a second-class citizen. For a while, as the Kennedys were welcomed by politicians, aristocrats, and intellectuals, all eager to court America, his dream was realized. In the end, however, Kennedy's adherence to the idea of peace at all costs, his staunch advocacy of American isolationism, and his rebellious behavior cost him the friendship of the British and the admiration of his colleagues at home. As ambassador he would ultimately sabotage himself, painfully consigning himself to the role of outsider that would endure even to the time his son won the presidency.

John F. Kennedy's path to the White House began in London. His father's political fortunes dimmed in those years, as his own star rose. In 1938, Joe Kennedy was widely mentioned as a potential candidate in the 1940 presidential elections; by the end of 1940 he was exiled from government life. During this time Jack was the author of a best-selling book, *Why England Slept*, about the reasons Britain failed to prepare for war; his political career was on the ascendant. The Kennedy children were profoundly affected by their father's ambassadorship; they spent the next half century reacting to his downfall and endeavoring to avoid being tarred by it. Jack carefully studied his father's diplomatic triumphs and failures in London and developed his own independent worldview and a political philosophy that would shape his character, his career, and his presidency. Considering himself an idealist without illusions, Jack surveyed the international political scene and emerged as a man who would balance power with negotiation, brilliant public relations with a complicated private life, and heroic rhetoric with pragmatic action.

Like George W. Bush, the Kennedy sons had to figure out a response to the legacy of a father who was perceived as weak and lacking an optimistic political vision, and who thus had humiliatingly failed. Jack Kennedy used his father's tenure in Europe to travel widely and satisfy his enormous curiosity about other political systems and cultures, which would inspire his book and help him create an identity as an internationalist American.

The father's thousand days as ambassador in London would hover over the son's thousand-day tenure in the White House. Learning from his father's mistakes, Jack would embody hope, flexibility, strength, and visionary optimism. Moving beyond his father's focus on keeping the world secure, Jack Kennedy felt secure enough in himself that he could focus on transforming it. His extraordinary place in our nation's psyche is the greatest legacy of Joe and Rose Kennedy's tenure in London.

Joe Kennedy's ambassadorship may offer some positive lessons for our own time. In an era when it is clear that hasty interventionism can have disastrous consequences, Kennedy's emphasis on using economic incentives and negotiation with dictators can be seen in a slightly kinder light. Might he be remembered a little less as an appeaser, with all the negative connotations the word now carries, and more as someone who, though he failed to articulate a clear moral vision, did explore every reasonable avenue for peace? As Kennedy said in December 1950, "Is it appeasement to withdraw from unwise commitments, to arm yourself to the teeth to make clear just exactly how and for what you will fight? . . . If it is wise in our interest not to make commitments that endanger our security, and this is 'appeasement,' then I am for appeasement.'"

Twisting the Lion's Tail

June to December 1937

I N MID-JUNE, Joseph Patrick Kennedy awoke early at his grand Maryland château and dashed nude into his swimming pool to do brisk laps. As usual, he was at his desk at Marwood before 7:30 A.M., working at his job as chairman of the federal Maritime Commission and calling press barons, politicians, and reporters to trade favors and exchange the latest Washington news and Hollywood gossip.

On this mild June morning, he was also preparing for one of the biggest negotiations of his hugely successful and controversial career. If all went as he was planning, he and his family would be propelled onto the international stage where, as Irish-Catholics, they could finally earn the acceptance and respect Joe had long sought from America's Protestant establishment. Despite being one of the most hospitable and sought-after figures in Washington political and media circles, Joe Kennedy was privately weary of feeling unacceptable to those who mattered. Now he thought he could change all that.

Three years earlier, Joe had come to Washington as Franklin Roosevelt's first chairman of the Securities and Exchange Commission, which terminated corrupt trading practices and regulated the stock exchanges amid the financial uproar of the depression and New Deal. A forty-eight-year-old Irish-American who had made his fortune over the past two decades by investing in the stock market, real estate, movie theaters, a film production company, and a liquor franchise, he had signaled his higher ambitions by renting this French Renaissance estate on 125 wooded acres, complete with an underground movie theater, a vaulted dining hall—copied after the dining room of England's King James I—and twelve bedrooms. The château had been built by a Chicago real-estate mogul to impress his show-girl bride; Joe would use it to court President Franklin Roosevelt and his powerful cronies. He had installed a private elevator to entice the disabled president to leave the White House for a swim, cocktails, dinner, and the latest Hollywood movie, flown in for the occasion. FDR had, indeed, enjoyed bringing his entourage to Joe's launching pad, socializing with the mogul's pals and amusing them with his ribald and jocular stories, all the while keeping his eye on his friend, whom he knew to be ambitious and mercurial.

Joe left his office in the late afternoon and went into the château's dining room to await the arrival of the president's eldest son, James Roosevelt, known as Jimmy, with whom he had an avuncular and arguably exploitative relationship. Jimmy's father had appointed Joe to the chairmanship of the Maritime Commission only last February, but the job of revamping the hopelessly out-of-date merchant marine and battling with the recalcitrant unions was thankless and Joe was discontented. Having championed the president in two elections, today he would tell FDR's son the real payback he wanted—a far more prestigious position.

Jimmy was ushered into the main dining room. Joe was seated at the far end of the imposing dining-room table. Knowing his man, he immediately asked, "What would you like to drink, Jimmy?"

Joe waited until after Jimmy had poured himself a second Scotch. Then he told him, "I'd like to be ambassador to England."

"Oh, c'mon Joe, you don't want that," Jimmy said, as if Joe were only joking. Although he quite liked Joe, Jimmy thought he was too much of a "crusty old cuss" to succeed in the foremost ambassadorial post in the world. He did not want to mediate between Joe and the president about this job. Jimmy did not handle pressure well and was prone to ulcers. He could not have relished disappointing the mentor who had set him up in the insurance business in Massachusetts, included him in a liquor distribution partnership in England, offered his Palm Beach home as a winter retreat, and fixed him up with chorus girls when his wife was not around.

But Joe was deadly serious. In fact, he was hell-bent on becoming the ambassador to Britain. Then, he believed, all of London's social doors—often closed to the Irish—would open for him and his wife, Rose, salving a lifetime feeling of being outsiders. He also thought that as Britain and America's conflict escalated with Hitler's newly bellicose Germany, being in London would put him at the center of the action, test his mettle, prove his patriotism, give him greater visibility, and ultimately advance his own political power—possibly even help him win the presidency. For Jimmy, however, Joe downplayed his motives. "I've been thinking about it, and I'm intrigued by the thought of being the first Irishman to be ambassador from the United States to the Court of St. James's."

"It certainly would set quite a precedent," Jimmy acknowledged. He promised to share Joe's outrageous request with the president.

Jimmy was not surprised at his father's reaction. "He laughed so hard he almost toppled from his wheelchair," Jimmy later reported. An ambassadorship, FDR declared, was out of the question.

But soon the president began to reconsider. Sending Kennedy to Europe would allow Roosevelt to repay his debt for Kennedy's financial backing and for his efforts in writing the campaign book *Why I'm for Roosevelt* during the 1936 election. An ambassadorship might keep Kennedy from inserting himself into the 1940 Democratic presidential nomination process. An appointment to the Court of St. James's could also assuage the strong anti-British sentiments of many isolationist American Catholics, whose support for England might be crucial if war broke out with Germany. Roosevelt knew that Kennedy was wealthy enough to entertain the British in grand style, and was a shrewd bargainer who could facilitate the Anglo-American trade agreement currently being negotiated. Further, FDR assumed that Kennedy's independent-mindedness would allow him to send unbiased political reports from London.

Moreover, by appointing Kennedy, the president could make a little mischief, tweaking the British for their arrogance and their rigid protocol. FDR was already displeased with British prime minister Neville Chamberlain's high-and-mighty ways and maddened by his cavalier dismissal of his invitation to visit the United States. Why not give the prime minister a few headaches by making him contend with the brash and fractious Kennedy? He then told his son that he was "kind of intrigued with the idea of twisting the lion's tail a little, so to speak." After mulling over the idea for several months and querying several advisors, who offered no stern objections, Roosevelt summoned Kennedy for one of history's most notorious job interviews.

When Joe came to the Oval Office to lobby for the job, FDR was seated in his wheelchair behind his imposing desk, constructed from the timbers of the H.M.S. *Resolute* and a gift to America from Queen Victoria. FDR first tried to rattle Joe by telling him that, if he wanted to be ambassador, he would have to give up his movie-star mistress, Gloria Swanson. Conveniently, Joe had already stopped spending time with Swanson, but he was ready with his own riposte: The president should first set an example by giving up his own mistress, his secretary Missy LeHand. Unfazed by his retort, FDR responded by telling Joe to stand by the fireplace so he could get a better look at him. Joe was taken aback, but obliged.

"Would you mind taking your pants down?" the president asked. Shocked, Joe asked if he had heard the president correctly.

"Yes, indeed," FDR replied.

Eager to satisfy Roosevelt, Joseph P. Kennedy—a famous businessman whose fortune in 1937 was worth $9 million—removed his suspenders, dropped his pants, and stood uncomfortably before the president in his underwear.

FDR broke the awkward silence. "Someone who saw you in a bathing suit once told me something I now know to be true. Joe, just look at your legs. You are about the most bowlegged man I have ever seen." The American envoy to the Court of St. James's, Roosevelt explained, would have to wear knee britches and silk stockings during the presentation of his credentials to the king at Buckingham Palace. Then he threw his grenade: "When photos of our new ambassador appear all over the world, we'll be a laughingstock. You're just not right for the job, Joe."

Roosevelt sat back, grinning. Joe was stunned. For a man in a wheelchair, this was no mere jocular hazing: It was a deeply hostile act, born of years sparring with his tricky friend.

After Joe left without being offered the job, FDR had a good laugh with his son. The president thought that the appointment of the Irish-Catholic Kennedy to the British court was "a great joke, the greatest joke in the world." He might end up giving Joe the ambassadorship, but it was fun to humiliate his rival first.

Joe Kennedy also loved to tease his underlings, but he tended to be thin-skinned himself; he did not find any humor in the president's prank. But Kennedy would not be outmaneuvered by the president. He asked FDR to give him two weeks to convince the British government to allow him to wear a cutaway coat and striped pants to the ceremony.

Joe checkmated the president a couple of days later, presenting the official letter of permission he had finagled through connections at the British Embassy.

For months Joe waited impatiently for official word of his selection. On December 2, he was dining at Marwood with an old friend, *New York Times* columnist Arthur Krock, who often served as his personal publicist, when Jimmy Roosevelt arrived unexpectedly. Joe took him aside for a private half-hour conversation.

FDR had had second thoughts, Jimmy reluctantly told him. Although the president's son did not reveal his father's reservations, FDR had been warned off Kennedy by some liberal advisors who were fearful of Kennedy's penchant for criticizing New Deal policies. The president himself had grown concerned that Kennedy's Catholicism would offend diplomats at the British foreign office.

Now Jimmy was caught between his father and his mentor: He had the nerve-wracking task of proposing that Kennedy take the less glamorous position as secretary of Commerce instead. This cabinet position would keep Kennedy too much under FDR's thumb, and it was not the one post he aspired to—Henry Morgenthau's job as secretary of the Treasury. Sniffing another WASP slight, Joe was petulant and resistant. "Well, I'm not going to! FDR promised me London and . . . that's the job—the only one—I'll accept," Joe told him.

After Jimmy left, Joe returned to the dining room, where Krock was waiting. Crafty as always, Joe already had a plan to force the president's hand, and the *Times* columnist was conveniently on hand to help him enact it. He told Krock that the president was about to appoint him ambassador to the Court of St. James's. Krock was eager to break the news, but he knew that he and Joe would have to be careful. The present ambassador to Britain, Kentucky newspaper publisher Robert Worth Bingham, was seriously ill with leukemia and had already returned to the United States for treatment, and it would be politic to spare his feelings. Krock vowed to handle the story delicately and promised Joe he would go through White House channels before saying anything in his *New York Times* column.

According to Arthur Krock, his longstanding friendship with Joe Kennedy was one "in which we were alternatively at peace and war." Krock described the elements of an alliance with Kennedy: "lavish generosity, fierce loyalty, excessive gratitude, harshly articulated candor, and sudden termination—that is without parallel in my experience."

The story played out just as Joe wanted. Claiming that Jimmy Roosevelt had given the go-ahead, Krock infuriated the president by planting a front-page story in the *New York Times* on December 9 announcing that FDR had decided to nominate Joe Kennedy, and that it would be "a complete surprise for Kennedy." Joe had outmaneuvered the president and gotten the job he had longed for. Just before Christmas, the president confirmed Kennedy's appointment at a press conference. He was not happy to do it. That same day, he told Henry Morgenthau that he considered Kennedy a "very dangerous man," and that he had "made arrangements to have Joe Kennedy watched hourly—and the first time he opens his mouth and criticizes me, I will fire him." FDR may have been mollifying Morgenthau, who distrusted Kennedy. The president's warning would turn out to be an idle threat.

SPEAKING OUT of the other side of his mouth, FDR wrote to Rose Kennedy and told her that "it gave me a feeling of real pleasure" to submit Kennedy's nomination to the Senate. While there was considerable hand-wringing at the State Department that the blunt and inexperienced Kennedy would make a troublesome diplomat, Kennedy's hometown Boston newspapers exulted and proclaimed that "the Kennedy family has royal blood antedating the king's." London's diplomats and aristocrats privately expressed disbelief, but British newspapers touted Roosevelt's decision to send his close associate as "the highest compliment Roosevelt could pay to Great Britain." Winston Churchill, who understood the importance of building a strong alliance with America, was pleased to see Roosevelt send a close friend to England—a man with whom he had already discussed building a joint navy strong enough to defeat Nazism.

Kennedy may have been humoring Churchill. Several years after he met with him, Joe, serving as Franklin Roosevelt's Maritime Commissioner, took a different position: He expressed the isolationist view that while America should prepare the merchant marine for any contingency, the nation did not expect to send expeditionary forces abroad to settle central European conflicts of little concern to Americans.

During the First World War, when Kennedy had supervised Bethlehem Steel's Fore River shipyard's effort to build destroyers, he decried to friends the "senseless war, certain to ruin the victors as well as the vanquished." In the 1930s, as he saw totalitarian regimes once again on the rise in Europe and Asia, Kennedy could not abide the possibility of the United States being drawn into another costly and unproductive world conflict; the last war had cost the lives of more than 37 million people, including 360,000 American soldiers. It had ruined four empires, had devastated France, Germany, and Britain, and had led to economic depression and upheaval.

Joseph P. Kennedy would bring his family with him to Britain, a remarkable brood of children who would be exposed, at an impressionable age, to a heady mix of social glamour, aristocratic and royal gatherings, political intrigue, and international crisis. They would play central roles in his dramatic and ultimately tragic tenure as ambassador. The events they witnessed in London from 1938 to 1940—as their father found himself unfairly cast as villain and as Europe slid into a catastrophic war—would profoundly affect their characters and their fates. Their father's ambassadorship would shape history, both in its own time and ultimately in the era that belonged to his children.

The entire clan gathered for Christmas 1937 at their Spanish-style villa in Palm Beach, Florida, which Joe Kennedy had bought five years earlier. The walled compound included a tennis court and a swimming pool, and was located on two acres of private beachfront land where the frenetically sports-minded Kennedy brood could compete against each other as they always had, testing their prowess and winning their father's approbation. For Joe's school-aged children, the prospect of going to England must have been a mixed blessing. Even though they were raised by Joe and their mother, Rose, to believe in the sanctity of public service and the need to make sacrifices for their country, they would not relish leaving behind their school friends, a task not easily contemplated by adolescents, and going to reside in a country alien to them.

That Christmas, with Europe quiescent after several years of aggression by the dictators, Joe Kennedy, seldom one for misgivings or second thoughts, had them. Perhaps defensively, Joe told Harvey Klemmer, whom he had recruited to be his publicist and speechwriter in London, "Don't go buying lots of luggage. We're only going to get the family in the *Social Register*. When that's done, we come back and go out to Hollywood to make some movies and some money." If he didn't create high expectations, there would not be a big letdown if he bungled his diplomatic service to his country. Would he be able to help lead the way, he wondered, in balancing America's need for independence with Britain's call for engagement in Europe while finding a way to accommodate the dictators and fend off war?

Beneath his cocky exterior, Joe Kennedy was uncertain about his suitability for such an important and exalted post, one that put him at the pivotal point of American international relations. Had he finally reached too high? When he received word of his Senate confirmation in mid-January, he sent Roosevelt a surprisingly apprehensive telegram: "I want to say now that I don't know what kind of diplomat I shall be, probably rotten, but I promise to get done for you those things you want done." He trusted his executive skills more than his social graces.

On both sides of the Atlantic, diplomats, government officials, society figures, and the press were doubtful of Kennedy's credentials, temperament, and talents. One writer, the right-wing newspaper columnist Boake Carter, a friend of Joe's, went further, giving him a prescient warning: "[T]he job of Ambassador to London . . . needs skills brought by years of training. And that, Joe, you simply don't possess . . . in so complicated a job, there is no place for amateurs . . . If you don't realize that soon enough, you're going to be hurt as you were never hurt in your life."

1938

CHAPTER I

Into the Lion's Mouth

I T WAS POURING RAIN as Joseph Kennedy boarded the U.S.S. *Manhattan* in New York harbor on Monday, February 23. Joe was completely exhausted. It had been an intense five days since he had been sworn in, in Washington, D.C., as ambassador to Great Britain. Just hours before boarding, Joe had dashed up to Hyde Park, New York, for a secret conference with the president. Now, on this stormy day, he was nearly "suffocated" by the press of "newspaper men, casual well-wishers, old friends and strangers by the thousand," who had essentially cornered him in his cabin, all of them determined to bask in his great success and learn the latest news about Anglo-American relations. Joe could not wriggle through them to reach eight of his children waiting on the top deck to say good-bye.

Jimmy Roosevelt squeezed his way into Joe's cabin and pulled him into the suite's bedroom, but even as they spoke, photographers snapped pictures of the two men sitting together on the bed.

In a brief interview, interrupted by his many friends and associates, Kennedy denied that President Roosevelt had given him any instructions the previous day about how to conduct himself in his new position. Protecting himself and subtly criticizing the president and the State Department, he told the press: "I'm just a babe being thrown into . . ."

"The lion's mouth?" one reporter suggested. Kennedy's vague smile left reporters wondering how he felt about his prospects. For Joe, such an uncontrolled and undignified leave-taking was "a nightmare" and an inauspicious beginning for a man realizing his dream of playing a vital role on the world stage and being, as he told the press, "a staunch believer in peace. . . ."

President Franklin Roosevelt congratulates Joe Kennedy, who has just been sworn in on February 18, 1938 as ambassador to the Court of St. James's. This is the high point of their turbulent and ultimately disappointing relationship. (*Cleveland Public Library Special Collections*)

The president's oldest son, James ("Jimmy"), sitting with Joe Kennedy, who was like an uncle to him, on the U.S.S. *Manhattan* before Kennedy sailed to England, February 23, 1938. James paved the way for his father to appoint Kennedy as ambassador. (*JFK Library Foundation*)

Finally, Joe managed to wend his way up to an upper deck where his sons Joe Jr., Bobby, and Teddy and his daughters Rosemary, Kick, Eunice, Patricia, and Jean had gathered. Joe's second son, Jack, often sickly, had caught a cold training for the swim team at Harvard; it was too risky to his health to see his father off in such inclement weather. Even here, photographers and fellow passengers with cameras intruded on their good-byes. As the ship prepared to depart, Joe's close friend Eddie Moore managed to herd the children off the ship and onto the dock at a place where they could stand, albeit unprotected from the pouring rain, to wave and throw kisses to their father.

Absent from the scene, much to Joe's dismay, was Rose. A month earlier in Palm Beach, while packing for the move to London, she had developed abdominal pains, ignoring them with a characteristic stoicism. When she could no longer tolerate the pain, Joe had her flown by private plane to Boston's Peter Bent Brigham Hospital, where her physician, Dr. Frederick Good, successfully performed an appendectomy. There was reason for such urgency. Rose Kennedy's biographer Charles Higham points out, "In those days before antibiotics came into general use, there was the dread of peritonitis, which killed, among other celebrities, Rudolph Valentino."

On New Year's Day, Roosevelt had written Britain's King George VI that he had chosen a "distinguished citizen" "to reside near the Government of Your Majesty in the quality of Ambassador Extraordinary and Plenipotentiary of the United States of America." With an assurance he would later come to question, FDR told the king, "My knowledge of his high character and ability gives me entire confidence that he will constantly endeavor to advance the interests and prosperity of both governments. . . ." A few days later, the king's representatives informed the president that Kennedy would be "entirely agreeable to His Majesty the King." The inevitable consternation at court about the ambassadorial appointment of a maverick American business mogul who embodied two related issues that remained unresolved in the British psyche—its relation to Ireland and its history of anti-Catholicism—went officially unspoken.

Always clannish, Kennedy would surround himself with a cadre of loyal employees. His handsome and elegant friend Arthur Houghton, a former theatrical manager and an inveterate storyteller, kept Joe amused. The "rough-hewn" Harvey Klemmer, Joe's speechwriter from the Maritime Commission, would provide the ambassador with support on the job, as would Harold B. Hinton, a very sophisticated former *New York Times* reporter Joe had hired to do public relations—a job he anticipated would be extremely important to advance the agenda of both his ambassadorship and his family. Jimmy Roosevelt's friend Page Huidekoper, a very competent nineteen-year-old personal assistant, would serve as Hinton's clerk. Page found Joe to be charming, bright, and self-centered, with "an aberrant sense of humor." She quickly learned that Joe didn't "do nuances."

Kennedy had few close friends, but he could be kind to people in his inner circle. Joseph Kingsbury-Smith, a reporter for the International News Service of the United Press, remembered Joe as a friend who was "warm, kindly, considerate." When Kingsbury-Smith was hospitalized with broken legs, Joe secured for him the services of the royal household's surgeons and specialists, and visited him frequently.

Also accompanying Kennedy were Anthony (Tony) Drexel Biddle and his wife, Margaret. Biddle was the sartorially splendid scion of the banking family that had founded Philadelphia's Drexel University. FDR had made him ambassador to Poland the year before, and he was returning via London to his post. In a curious indication of the power and social proximity of America's most prominent families, Roosevelt's three key ambassadors—Joe Kennedy, Tony Biddle, and William Bullitt, the ambassador to France—would eventually become related by marriage. Tony was a relative of Jack Kennedy's future wife, Jacqueline, and Bill Bullitt's daughter would wed Tony Biddle's son.

As the U.S.S. *Manhattan* sailed toward Britain, Joe finally had time to focus on his mission as ambassador, a job that had taken on increased urgency in recent months as the turmoil in Europe threatened the restless and resentful peace Europe experienced in the nineteen years since the First World War. Viewing himself as Roosevelt's premier delegate not just to Britain but the world, Joe intended to take the lead in keeping the United States from becoming entangled in alliances that could lead it into another European war. On board the ship, when young Page Huidekoper discussed the possibility of war with Joe, he told her, "Include the U.S. out." But as someone profoundly committed to the idea of Western democracy, he recognized the need to contain the rising tide of totalitarianism sweeping Europe. Righteous about protecting America's borders, but no unthinking isolationist, Joe believed the United States could most profitably engage with Europe on economic terms. Increased prosperity for America and for Europe, he believed, would do more than military muscle to rouse and reorder a world that was suffering its eighth year of economic depression.

Joe had his work cut out for him. By early 1938, Western democracies were challenged on all fronts. Hitler's and Mussolini's military posturing and heated rhetoric were becoming increasingly threatening. A civil war raged in Spain, the first large-scale conflict between socialist and fascist movements, and was regarded uneasily worldwide for its possible incendiary effect on democracies in Europe and beyond. Generalissimo Francisco Franco's troops were receiving significant aid from Germany and Italy and were gaining ground against the leftist Popular Front aided by the Soviet Union. In another theater on the other side of the world, the newly aggressive Japanese were attacking China, allying themselves ever more closely with the militaristic regimes in Germany and Italy. Germany had emerged as Europe's most belligerent state. From the time Hitler had taken over in 1933, he had moved to regain its position as a world power. While proclaiming Germany's desire for peace, Hitler had tripled the size of his army to half a million soldiers, begun to re-create an air force, and secretly ordered the construction of a new submarine fleet—all in defiance of the Treaty of Versailles, the 1919 pact concocted by Italy, France, Great Britain, and the United States to punish Germany for starting the First World War by curtailing it economically and militarily.

By the beginning of 1938, British MP Winston Churchill had been out of the government for nine years, monitoring with increasing disgust and alarm Britain's response to fascism. His eloquent attacks on British irresolution left the government, and most of the public, unmoved. Many fellow parliamentarians regarded him as an unstable, hard-drinking adventurer. Churchill had been appalled when London's cloudy, dull, and rainy New Year began with a deception signaling the haughty denial that would suffuse Britain's political climate that year. In the king's traditional New Year's honors list, it was announced that Sir Robert Vansittart, the permanent undersecretary of state, had been promoted to a position as a chief diplomatic advisor. This so-called promotion was British prime minister Neville Chamberlain's way of neutralizing Vansittart, who agreed with Churchill that rapid British rearmament was the only way to counter the increasingly muscular German threat. Chamberlain could not allow pessimistic and prejudiced diplomats to irk Hitler or Italy's Benito Mussolini. Chamberlain was confident that Hitler would listen to reason: Some judicious concessions of territory would keep him in line. Chamberlain would assuage the dictators until Britain had developed superior military power and could negotiate from a position of strength.

In Germany, New Year's Day had also begun ominously, with the announcement that Jewish doctors would no longer possess insurance. This decree was an additional provision of the Nuremberg Laws, first instituted in 1935, that prohibited Jews from joining the army, marrying non-Jews, or holding professional jobs, stripping them of their citizenship and, thus, their right to vote.

Early in the new year, Hitler's nephew William (Willy) Patrick Hitler, a twenty-six-year-old London bookkeeper, told reporters, "My uncle is a peaceful man," adding, "He thinks war is not worth the candle." War may not have been worth a candle, but Hitler was preparing to light a fuse. By early February, he had taken personal charge of Germany's armed forces and was in full control of Germany's foreign policy. Germany needed lebensraum ("living space"), he declared, and he was determined that no one would deny the fatherland what he believed it deserved. German "living space" was to be found in Austria. Threatening a German invasion, Hitler intimidated Austrian chancellor Kurt Schuschnigg into ceding him control of Austria in mid-February.

The peril of war preoccupied the new ambassador as he sailed on the U.S.S. *Manhattan* to Britain. According to Joe's later accounts, war also dominated his parting consultations with Roosevelt when the two men met at Hyde Park on February 22. Two other dramatic events that occurred on February 20 would also preoccupy them. In London, Sir Anthony Eden, British foreign secretary, had suddenly quit the cabinet in protest over what he believed was Prime Minister Neville Chamberlain's autocratic and foolhardy policy of accommodation with Mussolini. And in Berlin, Hitler had announced in a theatrical speech that he would protect the ten million Germans who lived in the areas surrounding Germany—a pronouncement that Roosevelt told Joe "forebode ill to Austria and Czechoslovakia."

After the "usual light and cheerful banter and gossip at lunch," the two men retired to the president's study to discuss the international situation. FDR did not chronicle any of his recollections about this crucial meeting, whereas over the next seventeen years Joe revised his memories of this talk three times in various drafts of his diplomatic memoir before settling on a final version. Joe's granddaughter Amanda Smith, the editor of his letters, points out that in one early draft, written by Joe's PR man Harold Hinton, the statement "The president had given me no instructions" and "I was on my own" had an editorial annotation by Hinton: "(amplify—there must have been some)." This suggests Joe may have fudged the president's mandate to justify the actions he would take in London. It is also possible that FDR did not give Joe a mandate, thinking he would pump him for information, get him out of the way, and pursue his own agenda with Britain through other channels.

According to Joe's revised memory, FDR asked him to safeguard America's isolationist stance: "Be careful about one thing, Joe. Don't forget that this country is determined to be neutral in the event of any war." Roosevelt, Joe recounted, considered the situation too uncertain for the United States to do anything but "mark time until the present crisis was past." A time would come where the nation could, FDR supposedly said, "play an important part in initiating an overall peaceful settlement . . . It was important for us . . . to remain in a position where our sincerity of purpose to help them all working for peace could not be doubted." Joe agreed with the president's emphasis on neutrality.

According to Joe, FDR did not seem to resent the position Chamberlain had taken of trying to make deals with Germany or Italy to fend off a crisis, but in fact Roosevelt did have serious reservations about Britain's prime minister. The American president had gotten off to a bad start with Chamberlain after he became prime minister in May 1937, and Chamberlain had haughtily turned down his offer to visit the United States and thus shore up Anglo-American relations. Just a month before his meeting with Kennedy, the president had made a top-secret offer to Chamberlain to host a wide-ranging diplomatic conference in Washington, D.C., that November to mark the twentieth anniversary of the end of the First World War. Roosevelt wanted an international conference to reaffirm principles of international conduct, reduce armaments, and promote economic welfare. Chamberlain wrote FDR that he needed to wrest concessions out of the two totalitarian regimes before doing anything that would give them an excuse to balk. Joe recalled that FDR seemed bitter about Chamberlain's "cold reception" of his plan.

Roosevelt was also angered by Chamberlain's appeasement of Italy. In 1936, Mussolini had used modern weapons and poison gas to win a lopsided victory over the barefoot warriors of Abyssinia (the nation now known as Ethiopia) and had annexed the country. Chamberlain planned to offer Italy full recognition of the annexation, in exchange for Italy's pledge to join with Britain in an alliance that could provide a check on Germany's ambitions. FDR had written the British prime minister that acceptance of Italy's conquest of Abyssinia was a serious mistake, causing Americans to lose faith in Britain and suggesting to Japan that Western forces were spineless.

After intense and fruitless cabinet discussions in which Eden insisted that Italy be required to make concessions as part of any agreement, the foreign secretary resigned. Edward Wood, Viscount Halifax, a fox-hunting aristocrat who had less interest in foreign affairs, was immediately appointed to replace him. Halifax, who had visited with Nazi leaders in Germany the previous fall, was more sympathetic to Chamberlain's attempts to appease the dictators.

Eden's resignation caused worldwide consternation. In the first of his great speeches of 1938, Churchill lamented the coddling of Italy and the ominous power plays in Austria: "This has been a good week for Dictators," he told the House of Commons. "It is one of the best they ever had. The German Dictator has laid his heavy hand upon a small but historic country, and the Italian Dictator has carried his vendetta to a victorious conclusion against . . . the late Foreign Secretary [Eden] . . . There can be no doubt who has won . . . Signor Mussolini got his scalp."

But according to Joe's account, Roosevelt continued to have faith in Chamberlain's policy. "To tell you the truth, Joe," he supposedly told his brand-new ambassador, ". . . I still have not lost heart. If Chamberlain succeeds in pacifying the dictators the time may soon come when my [peace] plan can be put into effect. The United States, of course, cannot participate in any political settlements, but it can, and I believe it will be able to lead the world out of the economic morass in which it is floundering."

K ENNEDY'S IMMEDIATE SUPERIOR AS AMBASSADOR was Cordell Hull, a former Tennessee congressman who had served Roosevelt as secretary of state since 1933. The dependable and highly respected Hull was in many ways the opposite of Joe Kennedy. Hull claimed to be an intellectual and a disciple of "Locke, Milton, Pitt, Burke, Gladstone, and Lloyd George." In contrast to Joe Kennedy's bright smile and brash charm, Hull was a dour and at times smug character with "slumped shoulders and downcast eyes." He tended to be cautious, set in his ways, and unimaginative. The two men shared one characteristic, however: Each was determined to get his own way.

Hull had not offered his new ambassador much information or guidance, which left Joe resentful and frustrated. The briefings he did receive contained no clear statement of American foreign policy toward Britain or Europe, primarily because the era's American foreign policy did not seek to shape international events, but rather reacted to them. Joe received short briefings about the key Anglo-American matters needing resolution.

But Joe knew that if he were to succeed as an American diplomat with a political future, he would have to do it on his own terms, working from his political strengths. Right after being confirmed, he wrote South Carolina newspaper editor William Gonzales, who had defended his nomination, "I have no misgivings about my training as a diplomat. If whatever success I have for the country is to be determined by the standards of a regular diplomat I am afraid it looks rather hopeless. . . . All I can promise is to do the best I can, and if I feel that I cannot deliver, then . . . I will be back on a boat." A little more accommodation to his lack of diplomatic training, however, would have done Joe some good.

As the U.S.S. *Manhattan* approached England's southern coast, Joe knew that he would have to thread a thin needle to satisfy his two constituencies—wary Americans and expectant Englishmen. Even before he left Washington, D.C., Joe had begun to grapple with a thorny and deep-seated issue that, he knew, would color perceptions of his entire ambassadorship—for good or for ill. In 1938 America had not claimed her full power in the world, and the adolescent country was anxious about her independence from Great Britain. In his memoir, Joe explained, "[The British] sense of social prestige has bred a wide-spread belief in this country that we, as a younger and more impressionable people, follow—rather than lead—in the formation of foreign policy."

"Friend after friend in high office" warned Kennedy about the perils of kowtowing to the British. One of his close friends, Senator James F. Byrnes, quoted Woodrow Wilson's exasperated remark about his ambassador in London during the First World War: "'You can send an American to London, but it is difficult to keep an American there.'" Byrnes added that British government officials are both "able and attractive . . . It is difficult to resist them."

A lifelong outsider, Joe had struggled with his own identity as an American, hating being perceived primarily as an Irishman. Now his predicament would be compounded. Would he appear too British, and thus too weak, or too American, and therefore too insensitive to the needs of his British hosts, whose social ranks he hoped to scale?

The issue of the knee britches was Joe's first effort to tread his own path. Wearing the expected court dress for ambassadors was, for Joe, an effeminate act that might compromise his masculinity. FDR's astute needling about his unattractive legs compounded his discomfort. Consequently, the new ambassador formulated a plan to turn his personal discomfort into a political statement that would play well at home. His unwillingness to wear the knee breeches would represent what he called in his memoir "a gesture of independence in no way hinting at discourtesy but quietly maintaining the right of the United States within reason to insist on her own traditions."

Joe had concocted a second strategy to signal, politely, his independence from British standards of conduct. He would limit the number of presentations of American women at court. "This race to gain social prestige at home by having the opportunity, for no particular reason, to bend the knee abroad, had the making of what we Americans know as a 'racket' without any real purpose or real benefit," he wrote. Before leaving the United States, he had obtained assent from the president and British ambassador Lindsay to enact his significant gesture.

Aware of the historic nature of his mission, Joe began a diary, which he would keep during his entire ambassadorship.

Soon after he arrived in London, in what Kennedy said was "a bantering postscript to one of his early letters to me," FDR wrote, "When you feel that British accent coming upon you, and your trousers riding up to your knees, take the first steamer home for a couple of weeks' holiday." Roosevelt planned to use his volatile friend as an independent source of intelligence, but he didn't take into account his new ambassador's predilection for autonomy.

CHAPTER 2

A Hole-in-One

JOE DISEMBARKED at Plymouth on the evening of March 1, a drizzly and dispiriting night. A small cutter brought him to shore through high, wind-whipped waves. The *New York Times* noted that Kennedy, arriving without his family, seemed "uncharacteristically nervous." After an overnight train ride in the company of Winston Churchill's son Randolph, who represented his pro-American father; Tony Biddle; and Herschel Johnson, who would serve as a counselor at the American Embassy, Joe arrived in London's Paddington Station at 7:00 in the morning. According to Page Huidekoper, Herschel, worried about Joe's sense of propriety, was "terrified that Joe would chew gum upon his arrival." London was, in 1938, the most important metropolis in the world. The city was the royal, financial, judicial, and social nexus of the British Empire, a globe-spanning entity in which approximately one-quarter of the world's population lived in one-fifth of its territory. During the 1930s the Empire had been ceding power to independent dominions that were still allied to the crown, and its hegemony was fading, but it was still a formidable force.

Joe's new post was in the world's largest, wealthiest, and most alluringly energetic city—a perfect spot for the hyperkinetic new ambassador. With its rapidly expanding suburban sprawl, Greater London had over eight million residents, easily topping the world's second-largest city, New York, where fewer than seven million people resided. London, with its many ethnic communities—Chinese, Greek, Cypriot, Italian, Middle European, and Middle Eastern among them—was a far more vibrant and cosmopolitan city than Paris or New York. Already more than fifty thousand Jews from Germany, Austria, and Czechoslovakia had fled there as refugees from fascism. This great world center was, however, an extremely anxious city. With over one-fifth of Britain's population within its 750 square miles, it would be a prime target for a massive air assault from the much-feared German Luftwaffe.

Joe's first day in London was cold but sunny. He had had little sleep. He stopped off at his official residence at 14 Prince's Gate for breakfast with his aides Jack Kennedy (later called London Jack or Ding Dong to differentiate him from the ambassador's son) and Bill O'Brien.

Joe's six-story, thirty-six-room eighteenth-century home was nothing short of a palace, albeit a decrepit one. From the residence's top floors, he could see all the way to Hyde Park and Kensington Gardens. The mansion was once the London home of financier J. P. Morgan, who had given it to the United States. The large first-floor reception room, with its gilded moldings and marble plaques, was an exact replica of an assembly room at Versailles. A grand staircase led from an imposing oval reception hall to the Louis XVI ballroom, which featured French panel wall paintings, Aubusson carpets, and Empire furniture. Mrs. Kennedy would soon take the adjacent Pine Room, its paneling hung with an early French tapestry, as her reception room. For all its fixtures, the building was a faded duchess of a structure. The façade was cracking, and its balustrades were falling apart. Inside, the curtains were threadbare and the Louis XV antiques were in disrepair. Even worse, the chimneys and flues were faulty, the floors and walls were cracked, the pipes were not fully functional, and the doors were warped. Joe, whose new job paid $17,500 annually—a step up from the $12,000 he had earned as chairman of the Maritime Commission—would spend at least $250,000 a year out of his own pocket to refurbish the official residence and maintain the lavish schedule of entertaining expected of a wealthy ambassador.

Even with the company of his cronies and a staff of twenty-four, Joe's new home—with its twenty-seven bedrooms—must have seemed lonely without his rambunctious family to bring it to life.

It was only a half-hour walk from the residence at 14 Prince's Gate to the American embassy at 1 Grosvenor Square. Besieged by photographers and reporters, Joe first entered the embassy to be greeted by 195 staff presented to him in relays, including twenty-five consular officials and many secretaries, security guards, and cooks. Joe would alienate the professional diplomats on the embassy staff with his informal ways and his failure to make an effort to invite them to his parties. In sharp contrast to the diplomatic situation in a later, security-conscious era, in the 1930s the embassy was housed in the bottom floors of four newly renovated Georgian brick townhouses, whose upper level contained living quarters for private indi-

Joe Kennedy's U.S. embassy was located in what is now the Canada House at 1 Grosvenor Square. Amazingly, residents, unconnected to the embassy, lived on the upper floors in that less suspicious time. (*photo by Belal Ashraf*)

viduals not connected to the embassy. (It is now the headquarters of the Canadian High Commission.) Kennedy's large second-floor office looked out on the handsome central gardens of Grosvenor Square. However, Joe found the office's décor to be threateningly precious: "I have a beautiful blue silk room and all I need to make it perfect is a Mother Hubbard dress and a wreath to make me Queen of the May. If a fairy didn't design this room I never saw one in my life."

The United States has been associated with Grosvenor Square in London's Mayfair section since the late eighteenth century when John Adams, the first United States representative, then called a Minister Plenipotentiary, lived from 1785 to 1788 in a house, which still stands, on the corner of Brook and Duke streets. His son John Quincy Adams was posted to London after an extraordinary career as a minister in Russia and Europe. Early in the American Civil War, when Britain appeared ready to recognize and aid the Confederate states, John Quincy's son Charles Francis Adams, in London from 1861 until 1868, played a crucial role in keeping Britain neutral.

An article in the *Western Newspaper Union*, which Joe clipped for his scrapbooks, summarizes the formidable ambassadorial lineage Joe would confront in London: "Joseph Kennedy is placing his sturdy business shoes in the footsteps where formerly walked philosophers, poets, historians and members of the social elect. He is not America's first businessman ambassador, but he is the first businessman to get the job without first showing his listing in society's 'Who's Who.'"

Emblematic of that pedigree was a fellow Massachusetts native and Harvard graduate, Joseph Hodges Choate, whose lordly portrait eyed Kennedy in the ambassador's office. The popular and aristocratically urbane Choate, ambassador to Britain from 1899 to 1905, was credited with significantly improving Anglo-American relations and, coming from a prominent WASP family, possessed all the establishment credentials Kennedy lacked. As a lawyer he had argued some of the most important legal cases of his era, helped expand the Carnegie Endowment for International Peace, and fostered the Metropolitan Museum of Art. This ultimate American WASP "watched me daily as I began and closed my work," Kennedy recounted. "At times it seemed to me that I could hear him say, 'You are a cad, sir!'"

In a meeting with Ambassador Kennedy, Rabbi Stephen Wise, founder of the World Jewish Congress and head of the American Jewish Congress, pointed to the portrait and reminded Joe of Choate's frequent and vehement anti-Irish sentiments. Joe replied, "I'll ring for the porter and have the portrait removed at once." Although Choate seemed to be frowning at Wise as well, "on general principles as a Jew and Rabbi," Joe ultimately decided to give "the earlier Joe a chance to hang on the wall if he adapts himself to his new Irish-American surroundings."

Kennedy's ambassadorial forebears were intimidating but also promising. The twenty-four American representatives who preceded him included five future presidents (the two Adamses, James Monroe, Martin Van Buren, and James Buchanan), four future vice presidents, and ten future secretaries of state.

THE DAY AFTER HIS ARRIVAL, Joe paid his first visit to Sir Sidney Clive, the marshal of the diplomatic corps. Sir Clive, according to Joe, was "plainly horrified" when the new ambassador "sprang on him" the idea that presentation of American debutantes at court that year might be radically curtailed. The entire court was still highly sensitive about the uncertain status of King George VI, who had ascended the throne fifteen months earlier, after the scandalous abdication of his older brother, the charismatic Edward VIII. Although the British people had begun to warm up to the new royal family, many top economic, political, and social leaders doubted whether the stammering new king had the requisite confidence and ability to unite and animate the country in increasingly fractious times. Sir Clive thought the court presentations enhanced their image abroad and at home.

That afternoon Kennedy began his diplomatic rounds with an initial call on Britain's foreign secretary, Viscount Halifax, a "tall, spare, and aesthetic-looking man" known as the "Holy Fox" because of his fondness for fox hunting and High Anglican church services. Halifax had negotiated peace with Gandhi while he was the viceroy of India. Practical and shrewd, he would become one of Joe's closest contacts and one of his better friends in England.

When Joe spoke frankly to him about how Britain "must not get in a mess counting on us to bail them out," Halifax was not surprised; he understood how strongly isolationist American public opinion was. Like the prime minister who had just appointed him foreign secretary, Halifax believed that Britain could win peace by accommodating Germany.

One of Kennedy's first meetings was with Rabbi Stephen Wise, who was worriedly monitoring not only Hitler's ever-fiercer war against the Jews but the British response to it. Disturbed by the British government's lack of interest in providing a safe haven for endangered German Jews in the British colony of Palestine, Wise expressed his concerns to Kennedy. The ambassador would later be criticized for anti-Semitism, but Wise wrote directly to Roosevelt saying, "JK is going to be very helpful . . . he is keenly understanding, and there is just enough of the Irish in him to make him sympathetic to those of us who resent the British promise [of help to us] that is in danger of being broken." Rabbi Wise's grandson Steve Tulin told the author that Wise always had positive things to say about Kennedy.

On Friday, March 4, after a relaxed morning horseback ride along Rotten Row, which bordered Prince's Gate, Kennedy was unexpectedly summoned to 10 Downing Street to meet Prime Minister Chamberlain. Joe loved powerful men. With Chamberlain he would become entangled with one of the most authoritarian prime ministers of the modern era. Possessed of a self-confidence that more than bordered on arrogance, Chamberlain dominated his cabinet like no other prime minister since William Gladstone, who had stamped his moral authority on his era while heading four governments under Queen Victoria from 1868 to 1894.

Both Kennedy and Chamberlain prided themselves on being realists who gathered facts and based their decisions on current realities rather than on high-flung theories. Both products of the business world—the prime minister had started his career in the copper-brass business—they were natural allies who viewed war in general and communism in particular as the provocateurs of world chaos. Kennedy saw economic policies as the key to preserving world peace, while Chamberlain saw the world largely in political terms. "Politics in international affairs," he wrote, "governs actions at the expense of economics, and often of reason."

Like Kennedy, Chamberlain was an extremely proud and complex man, whose competence and sheer hard work won the loyalty of close associates but whose overconfidence could freeze a whole room. MP Sir Arthur Salter wrote, "In manner he is glacial rather than genial. . . . his expression often tends to something of a sneer, and his manner to something like a snub, even when there is nothing in either his intentions or feelings to correspond . . . To a somewhat exceptional extent he regards unquestioning loyalty, obedience, pliability, as giving better claim to his favors than signs of personal initiative or judgment . . . he prefers the even running of his craft to the vigor of the individual oar."

Chamberlain was not counting on the United States to send troops to help defend Britain if war broke out. He planned to appease Germany and Italy until Britain's belated military buildup had enough muscle to checkmate Hitler and Mussolini. Joe reaffirmed the U.S. commitment to neutrality and to building up its own defensive capacity. "I talked to him quite plainly," Joe wrote in his diary, "and he seemed to take it well."

At a news conference at the embassy, Kennedy made a show of informality, putting his feet up on his desk while deflecting a bevy of questions about international affairs. "You can't expect me to develop into a statesman overnight," he told them. But in an implicitly isolationist argument about the average American's engagement with the world beyond national borders, he declared that "right now he is more interested in how he is going to eat and whether his insurance is good, than in foreign politics. Some, maybe, even are more interested in how Casey Stengel's Boston Bees are going to do next season." This attitude was the first public indication that Joe's independent thinking would give FDR headaches.

Joe's isolationist remarks were soon subsumed in a literal stroke of good fortune. The next day he played golf with London Jack and Arthur Houghton on the new Stoke Poges course in Buckinghamshire. On the second hole he hit an iron shot 128 yards; it bounced off the side of a ditch, landed on the green, and trickled into the cup. It was Kennedy's first-ever hole-in-one. Knowing that the British perceived the ideal American as vigorous and sporty, Joe realized that he had scored a public relations coup. He proclaimed his good luck "the triumph of my diplomatic career to date." Writing James Landis, a future editor of his diplomatic memoir, Kennedy said, "I couldn't have done anything better to make a hit in England if I had twenty-five years to discover the best answer."

Joe noted with satisfaction in his diary that the British newspapers were "filled with accounts of my golfing triumph." London's Sunday *Observer* created a contest for the best poem about the ambassador's achievement. With his unerring eye for opportunity, Kennedy would later use in his speeches this clever line: "I am much happier being the father of nine children and making a hole in one than I would be as the father of one child making a hole in nine." His sons Jack and Joe Jr., used to his masterful manipulation of the media and seeing a good opportunity to pull his tail, sent him a telegram: "Dubious about the hole in one."

SINCE THE ACCESSION of Queen Victoria in 1837, all ambassadors have presented their credentials to the monarch at Buckingham Palace. On March 8, preparing to present his letters of credence to King George VI, Joe was barely able to conceal his excitement. "It's a quarter past nine on Tuesday morning," he wrote U.S. senator James Byrnes, "and I am sitting in a bathrobe at the Embassy and am supposed to dress in about an hour to get ready to be drawn to the Palace in a carriage with white horses to present my credentials to the king." Just after eleven in the morning, coaches with "scarlet-coated drivers and footmen" picked up Kennedy, sartorially splendid in a tailcoat with white tie, and wearing not knee breeches but full-length trousers.

In the half-hour ceremony at Buckingham Palace, the king, dressed impressively as an Admiral of the Fleet, stood with Foreign Secretary Halifax at his side and received the credentials of America's tense and excited ambassador. Joe recorded that the king was "almost boyish looking," while Halifax "looks and acts like a Cardinal or Abraham Lincoln (without a beard)." After the formal presentation, the king set out to win over the new American ambassador, surprising him with his relaxed manner. Knowing that many Americans saw the British monarchy as rigid, old-fashioned, and condescending, King George was determined to mend Britain's increasingly strained relationship with the United States. The king had long been fascinated with America, and he recognized the key role the nation could play in defending democracy.

The king commended him for his recent hole-in-one. He confided that he was currently out of commission with an infected hand. Just as Franklin Roosevelt had exulted in meeting King George V in 1918, Kennedy delighted in his royal debut. "The show . . . was set up to expectations," Joe reveled in his diary. He wrote Arthur Krock that the king had been "much more nervous than I was." The king, Joe noted, "was most gracious . . . a very pleasant chap who acts to me like a fellow that was doing all he could to keep people loving 'the king.' "

Afterward, at a luncheon at the Savoy for the American Correspondents' Association, Kennedy told its members that he was "by no means sure that an American ambassador could accomplish anything here" and that he would return home promptly if that were the case. He also made his first diplomatic faux pas. He broke an unwritten rule by revealing to a *Daily Telegraph* reporter details about his meeting with the king. The king, he boasted, wanted to see the ambassador's children when they arrived in England. Tradition dictated that presentation of an ambassador's credentials to the king became official only after it was announced in the Court Circular. Protocol required that no foreign envoy reveal anything the king had said; the most any diplomat could offer was that the king looked well.

Back at the embassy, Kennedy repeated this indiscretion with several wire-service reporters. According to biographer Richard Whalen, an embassy secretary chased after the reporters as they rushed out to file their story, trying to convince them not to publish the ambassador's comments. The *Daily Telegraph* gave good play to his remarks. Perhaps even more woundingly, Joe's recent escort to London, Randolph Churchill, wrote in the *Evening Standard* that Kennedy and the "less important waiters were the only civilians at the presentation in trousers." Joe must have cringed at this kind of attention.

Compounding the uproar was the first of many incidents of presidential backstabbing. At a lunch that included London University's political science professor Harold J. Laski, whom Joe had chosen to educate both Joe Jr. and Jack, Laski repeated some rather critical comments FDR had written to him about Joe. "It is both unfair and unjust to an ambassador," Joe wrote in his memoir, "for the Chief of State without his knowledge to maintain a line to persons in the country which will be used for political purposes." Joe complained to Jimmy Roosevelt, but had no reply from the president. "But, as I look back, it was symbolic of much that was to come." Joe reported this incident in the second chapter of his diplomatic memoir, perhaps setting the stage for showing that FDR was the more responsible party in the ruin of their relationship.

On March 9, Austrian chancellor Kurt Schuschnigg flouted Nazi bullying by calling for an immediate plebiscite on Austria's independence. Joe declined to see the conflict as a prelude to battle. He wrote in his diary, "In my mind, no general war is visible in the immediate future."

The next day Joe went to lunch with Winston and Randolph Churchill.

He had pursued Churchill, the leader of the interventionist group in the Conservative Party, to gather intelligence for the president. Joe wanted to understand Churchill's strenuous objections to Chamberlain's foreign policy and to know how far he would go in challenging the dictators. According to Joe, Churchill gave him an earful. Mussolini "had been headed for a fall," and only Chamberlain's policies and Eden's resignation had saved him, Churchill claimed. "The smaller countries by this action had been led to believe that the dictatorships are getting somewhere and are more inclined to want to play with them than they were heretofore, and the fact that the Lion has had his tail wrung has lost them prestige," Joe reported. An Anglo-Italian agreement would gain Britain nothing, and an Anglo-German alliance was unlikely, given German ambassador Joachim von Ribbentrop's pronouncement that "England must close its eyes to the procedure in the East." Churchill was emphatic that Britain's plan to delay "all action until they got stronger is a fallacy" because the German army and air force were growing at faster rates.

Kennedy transmitted Churchill's comments to the State Department, but without mentioning his own contributions to the conversation or his reactions. In 1935, during a visit to Britain, after Joe and Rose had had lunch with the Churchills at Chartwell, Rose Kennedy called Churchill "the greatest living Englishman." Joe had concerns about Churchill's drinking and his bellicosity. Had Joe begun to see Winston as an antagonist who would try to drag America into a war it did not want? Neither his diary nor his diplomatic memoir answers this question, and Churchill left no record of their March 1938 meeting. Did Joe stubbornly insist that America would never come to Britain's aid? Randolph Churchill would grow to scorn Joe, and his misgivings may have begun during that lunch.

Joe was relieved that war did not seem imminent. "Nobody is going to fight a war over here unless Germany starts shooting somebody," he wrote FDR. "Nobody wants it." Britain's "top-side people" were mainly interested in having the United States "stay prosperous and build a strong navy," he said. The time would come for FDR to "make a worldwide gesture and base it completely on an economic stand. . . ."

IN NEW YORK on March 9, Rose Kennedy and Kick, Pat, Bobby, Jean, and Teddy boarded the U.S.S. *Washington* to sail to Britain. After the avalanche of publicity about the family, arranged no doubt by Joe, it was not surprising that the Kennedys were mobbed by journalists, photographers, and newsreel cameras. For the first time, the Kennedy children were treated as celebrities, their every word recorded. Even considering her early training as the daughter of a Boston mayor, Rose was making a huge leap from Bronxville, New York, to an international fishbowl where she would entertain some of the world's most polished social and diplomatic celebrities. Although she was a highly sophisticated and well-educated woman, she was intimidated by being plunged into the Irish-distancing hereditary British establishment. She had also lost some confidence in her social skills after decades focused on child rearing. Sister Mary Quinlan of the Manhattanville Sacred Heart convent confided in Kennedy biographer Laurence Leamer that Rose asked Mother Patterson, a brilliant, quick-witted schoolteacher, for help with her conversational skills. "She said that she had spent so many years looking out for her children and led such a retiring life that she didn't feel she was up to socializing with adults," Sister Quinlan recalled.

In the torpor that followed the abdication of their glamorous former king, the British press "seemed fascinated by the idea of a large and lively Boston Irish family descending on the London diplomatic scene," Rose acknowledged. These energetic American arrivistes made an intriguing contrast with Britain's staid if proper royal family.

Joe was eager to see his family and to establish his clan as a force to be reckoned with in London. "Hurry that boat up," he cabled Rose, "terribly anxious to see all of you."

In mid-March, Hitler replaced his foreign minister, Baron Konstantin von Neurath, with his current ambassador to Britain, Joachim von Ribbentrop. The new foreign minister, a wealthy former champagne salesman, was utterly dedicated to Hitler. The Fuhrer, eager for acceptance in upper-class British circles, was impressed with Ribbentrop's connections with titled foreigners, but Ribbentrop had alienated Britain's upper crust by giving a Hitler salute to the king, posting SS guards outside the German embassy, and flying swastika flags on official cars. His defiantly undiplomatic reputation led him to be dubbed Herr Brickendrop. On March 10, Ribbentrop gave himself a farewell tea party. He still had enough clout to attract not only Kennedy and other members of the diplomatic corps, whose presence was required, but also some London political and society figures. MP Chips Channon chatted up the American ambassador and in his diary made a famously snide evaluation of Joe: "I talked to Mr. Kennedy, the new American ambassador, whose chief merit seems to be that he has nine children."

On March 11, the Chamberlains gave a grim farewell luncheon for the Ribbentrops at 10 Downing Street. Guests included Winston and Clementine Churchill, the Halifaxes, and Lord and Lady Londonderry (Londonderry, the former air minister, had consorted with the Nazi leaders in Germany, hoping that keeping cordial personal relations would help restrain them). During lunch, Chamberlain was talking to Ribbentrop about easing tensions between their two countries when a Foreign Office messenger delivered a telegram for the prime minister. Churchill noticed that Chamberlain, reading it, suddenly looked disturbed. German troops were crossing the border into Austria and heading toward Vienna.

After finishing the meal, Chamberlain took Ribbentrop aside and implored him to prevail upon Hitler to stop his invasion and talk with Britain about Germany's needs. Meanwhile, Churchill told Frau von Ribbentrop, "I hope England and Germany will preserve their friendship."

"Be careful you don't spoil it," she retorted. The Anschluss had begun; Hitler had long believed that Austria should be reunited with Germany and was about to realize his goal. Churchill noted in his history of the Second World War that this was "the last time I saw Herr von Ribbentrop before he was hanged."

The next day, from the balcony of the Hofburg Palace in Vienna, Hitler told a quarter of a million cheering Nazi supporters that it was God's will he bring his homeland back into Germany. Later he met with his friend Unity Mitford, the scion of one of England's most prominent literary families, who had become obsessed with him. One of six politically diverse Mitford sisters, Unity and her twenty-seven-year-old sister Diana had embraced fascism. Diana had wed the British fascist leader Oswald Mosley in Joseph Goebbels's drawing room with Adolf Hitler in attendance. Their father, Lord Redesdale, denied the rumors rampant about Unity's romantic interests: "There is not, nor has there ever been, any question of engagement between my daughter and Herr Hitler. The Fuhrer lives only for his country and has no time for marriage."

Unity wrote her cousin Winston Churchill to tell him how joyfully the Austrian people had welcomed Hitler's takeover—one day "the entire population looked pathetically oppressed and hopeless, as they had done for years; on the next, everyone looked happy & full of hope for the future." After carefully gathering facts from the British ambassador in Vienna, Churchill sent Unity a blistering reply that ended their correspondence forever: "A large majority of the people of Austria loathes the idea of coming under Nazi rule. It was because Herr Hitler feared the free expression of opinion that we are compelled to witness the present dastardly outrage."

Kennedy went to the House of Commons to hear the debate on foreign affairs following Hitler's annexation of Austria, arriving after Chamberlain promised a renewed look at British defense programs. There he encountered Churchill, and certainly heard from him the gist of the speech he would shortly give: "The gravity of the [annexation] cannot be exaggerated. Europe is confronted with a program of aggression, nicely calculated and timed, unfolding stage by stage, and there is only one choice open . . . either to submit, like Austria, or else to take effective measures while time remains to ward off the danger." Kennedy did not stay for Churchill's speech.

With Czechoslovakia next in Hitler's sights, Churchill urged a Grand Alliance bringing the small states of Europe into a collective defense, with adherence to the covenant of the League of Nations whereby member nations could take any appropriate action to counter aggression. But Neville Chamberlain's cabinet had already rejected the air minister's plan for achieving British air parity with Germany and shirked from the possibility of an alliance to confront Hitler's aggression.

In what would be the beginning of a problematic friendship, Waldorf Astor soon visited Joe Kennedy at the embassy. Astor, who would become, along with his American-born wife, Nancy, a key supporter of the Kennedy family, startled Joe by telling him that "some of the leading men believe that immediate war is a greater danger than they like to let the public know." As soon as Lord Astor left, Joe phoned Secretary of State Cordell Hull and urged him to cancel his upcoming National Press Club speech warning the dictators that a failure to accept their international responsibilities would lead to trouble. Joe did not want him to say anything that would provoke Hitler and Mussolini.

Joe noticed that Hull sounded unwell (probably distressed by his presumptuous suggestion) and that he was noncommittal. Knowing that Kennedy could easily go over his head to talk with FDR, who listened to the friends he had placed in ambassadorial positions more than he did to the State Department, Hull probably placated his new ambassador. On the seventeenth, Hull would announce that although the recent lawlessness in Europe and the Far East made it necessary for the United States to rearm, there would be no change in the U.S. policy of neutrality.

After talking to Hull, Joe made his way to Plymouth to greet the U.S.S. *Washington* and collect his wife and five of his photogenic children. Thanks to his publicity efforts, the Kennedys' arrival was widely anticipated—especially the advent of Rose, whom one British publication had dubbed "as vivacious as a screen-star, as wise as a dowager." Amid the menace of war, London's social season was about to commence. Whether intrigued, amused, or invigorated by the advent of the American ambassador's family, Britain's aristocrats would willingly open their doors; the Kennedys would not have to crash the gates.

CHAPTER 3

Pilgrims from the New World

A S JOE KENNEDY ENDEAVORED to master his ambassadorial duties in Britain, his charismatic older sons Joe Jr. and Jack were biding time before venturing into the political intrigues and aristocratic delights of London. Joe, a hard-working Harvard senior, and Jack, coasting though his sophomore year, were close friends, living and often dining together among many of Harvard's top athletes at Winthrop House, set on the Charles River with a fine view of the city of Boston. They were also the fiercest of rivals on the playing fields and in the sport of bedding women. One evening after Joe Jr. had wangled a date with actress Katharine Hepburn, Jack tried to outdo him by showing up at a nightclub with movie actress Gertrude Niesen, who was just starting her film career in *Top of the Town*. Joe Jr. cleverly arranged for Jack to be summoned to take a phone call, while he rushed off with Gertrude before his brother noticed he had been bushwhacked.

During his harried first days in London, the ambassador was very worried about Jack, who had to be hospitalized in the Harvard infirmary, and later New England Baptist Hospital, after his weight plummeted—due to what only years after the fact was understood by historians and doctors to be irritable bowel syndrome. Nonetheless, Jack sneaked out to swim in the college pool for an hour each afternoon and was barely beaten in the final heat for a place on the varsity swim team. In a family raised to prize athletic prowess and finishing first, Jack must have been tormented by his continued failure to match Joe's accomplishments until he found a way to trump his older brother. Neither his father nor Joe Jr., blocked by WASP elitists, had won admittance into Harvard's much-coveted social clubs, but

Joe Kennedy greets Rose, Kick, Pat, Bobby, Jean, and Teddy upon their arrival at Plymouth on March 17, 1938. Joe and Rose had a temporary scare when Teddy went missing, but he was found on the far side of the ship looking for the "dredger." (*Photofest*)

Jack was very popular among his friends in the university's Protestant establishment; they banded together and insisted he be accepted in the prestigious Spee Club. Tellingly, Jack would write all his letters to his family in London on Spee stationery.

To his father's great pride, Joe was busy that spring working on his senior thesis, *Intervention in Spain*, which sympathetically chronicled the efforts of an American isolationist organization, the Hands Off Spain Committee. Loyal to his anti-communist father, Joe Jr. surely favored Franco and the Catholics who were fighting to depose the Soviet-supported Loyalist government.

The ambassador was eager to bring his sons to London; he believed they would serve as useful lieutenants and, like John Quincy Adams and Charles Francis Adams before them, would not just witness history in action but help to make it.

After a difficult trip with "mountainous seas," Rose and five of her younger children arrived at Plymouth and were met by Joe. She and Joe underwent a momentary scare when Teddy went missing. After a frantic search, he was found leaning off the other side of the ship. "I want to see the dredger, Daddy," he explained to his father. Joe teased Kick, telling his daughter he had been reading all about her in the papers. Kick blushed and asked why. Joe explained that earlier that day the press reported she had become engaged to her boyfriend back in the United States, Peter Grace, the Grace Lines shipping heir—and within minutes after the family disembarked, reporters ambushed Rose and eighteen-year-old Kick with questions about her reported engagement.

Placing his hand on Rose's shoulder, and looking over at his five children, Kennedy exclaimed, "Now I've got everything," and added, "London will be just grand."

The Kennedys instantly became major celebrities. The day after their arrival, the *Daily Express* headlined KATHLEEN, AGED 18, IS IN LOVE. Rose began to receive the kind of fawning publicity associated with top-tier film stars. *Vogue* magazine romanticized her as a "remarkable woman responsible for much of that rare harmony and unity which is both the central theme and the leitmotif of the Kennedys." The British press called Joe "Jolly Joe," "The U.S.A.'s Nine-Child Envoy," and "The Father of His Country."

Joe put his Hollywood public relations experience to good use. His PR team soon had the British press treating all the Kennedys as transatlantic stars. Kick was a particular focus of media attention. In the late 1930s London's debutantes were treated as celebrities worthy of significant press coverage, and before Kick had even arrived in England, the aristocratic social chronicle *Queen* featured her as one of the stars of the upcoming social season.

Almost daily in the next few months, the London morning papers would feature pictures of one or more Kennedy children exploring the city: Teddy and Jean watching the changing of the guard at Buckingham Palace; Bobby and Teddy on their first day of school; Teddy taking a picture with his camera upside down; Kick delivering home-baked cookies to London's Great Ormond Street Hospital for Children, or riding horseback with her father on Rotten Row.

The American press joined in the adulation. In April, Henry Luce celebrated the Kennedy family in *Life* magazine, declaring, "There are only five Dionne Quints and the Kennedy kids are nine . . . His bouncing offspring make the most politically ingratiating family since Theodore Roosevelt's." FDR, *Life* gushed, "got eleven ambassadors for the price of one. Amazed and delighted at the spectacle of an Ambassadorial family big enough to man

Almost daily in the spring of 1938, London morning papers would show pictures of one or more Kennedy children exploring the city. Bobby and Jean take photographs, while Teddy mugs for the camera. (*JFK Library Foundation*)

a full-sized cricket team, England has taken them all, including extremely pretty and young-looking Mrs. Kennedy, to its heart. As a family act in the British press, the Nine Kennedy Kids are rapidly outstripping the Quints."

Such rapt, even rapacious, press attention must have made Rose nervous. After the 1932 kidnapping and murder of the son of famed aviator Charles Lindbergh, Rose had asked their friend Henry Luce to curtail publicity of her family in *Time* and *Life* magazines. Just after Joe had arrived in England, a deranged Londoner named George Buchanan had written letters threatening to kill the Kennedy family. He was arrested. Joe's public promotion of the Kennedy clan, while augmenting the family's power and prominence, came at a cost to its comfort and security.

WHEN ROSE ARRIVED at Prince's Gate, she wasted no time organizing her staff of twenty-four to shape up the run-down residence. The younger children delighted in running about the mansion, sliding down the banisters on the great staircase, and calling each other from phones in the many bedrooms to arrange meetings in the hall. Teddy commandeered the elevator, taking giggling housemaids up and down, stopping to announce each floor as if he were a department-store elevator operator.

Bobby and Teddy, in maroon blazers and gray flannel shorts, were enrolled at Gibbs School for Boys, and Jean and Pat, soon to be joined by Eunice, were sent outside London, to the Sacred Heart Convent at Roehampton, where they were, according to a fellow student, "like birds of paradise, bringing a glamour and worldliness that contrasted with the attitude of the dour daughters of displaced European aristocrats and English girls in tweeds."

Bobby's London classmate Cecil Parker told author David Heymann that Bobby, who had difficulty making friends, was not happy at the Gibbs School: "He particularly hated Latin, did poorly in the subject and eventually dropped it. He also never quite got the hang of cricket, although he did his utmost to keep up with the rest of us . . . I remember his refusing to

---

The Kennedys' London home at 14 Prince's Gate, across the street from Hyde Park, was a badly deteriorated structure. Joe Kennedy spent $250,000 of his own money to refurbish and furnish the home to make it suitable for elegant entertaining. Today it is the Royal College of General Practitioners. A plaque on the façade notes that John F. Kennedy lived there. (*Archives of the Royal College of General Practitioners*)

join the English Boy Scouts because he would have had to say a pledge of allegiance to the throne. He didn't want to appear unpatriotic to the United States."

CLEMENTINE CHURCHILL'S COUSINS David and Sydney Freeman-Mitford, the second baron and baroness Redesdale, maintained a home just around the corner from Prince's Gate. The Kennedys became friendly with this eccentric couple, whose six daughters variously championed the era's prevailing political ideologies. Unity and Diana had embraced fascism, and Jessica, twenty-one, had taken up communism and eloped to Spain with Winston Churchill's cousin Esmond Romilly. The youngest daughter, Debo, who went on to become the duchess of Devonshire, says, "I was never in the least bit interested in politics. I had too much of it at home."

Along with Kathleen Kennedy, Debo was one of the celebrated debutantes of the 1938 season. "Of course, everybody loved her," she would say of Kick. "It was the effervescent energy, all the things that go with—not beauty—but a kind of liveliness which is very rare." Joe Kennedy's bright young assistant Page Huidekoper adored Kick, even though she believed that Kick "did not have an intellectual bone in her body." They would become good friends.

ON ST. PATRICK'S DAY, Joe got in trouble with his Irish-Catholic supporters in Boston when he accompanied other diplomats and dignitaries to a full-dress court levee at Buckingham Palace. A Boston friend phoned to inform him there was talk of burning him in effigy in South Boston. It was a sober reminder of how carefully he was being watched at home, and of how many constituencies he had to satisfy.

The next morning Joe was back at Buckingham Palace, presenting Rose to the queen, who came forward with a "happy, natural smile" to greet her. In their conversation, Rose noticed how keenly the queen understood politics. Dressed in her most chic two-piece blue suit, the ambassador's wife hid her anxiety and made small talk with the queen about raising their children: Princess Elizabeth was close in age to Bobby, and Princess Margaret was only slightly younger than Jean.

Rose had arrived in England six weeks before the official beginning of the London Season. According to protocol, she would have to meet the mothers of the year's debutantes before any of them could attend the parties she would throw for her daughters Kathleen and Rosemary. On

March 25, Lady Malcolm, the daughter of Edward VII's famous mistress Lily Langtry, had Rose to tea to meet all the mothers. The women, who looked, Rose thought, conservative with "little make-up" and "hardly any lipstick," were ushered up separately to meet her. Rose found them to be cordial, but proper in a way that chillingly reminded her of Boston Back Bay society.

Joe, meanwhile, had his own impending encounter with the British establishment. American ambassadors traditionally delivered their first major speech before the high-level political, diplomatic, and business members of London's Pilgrim's Society. The new envoy's speech was typically a non-controversial paean to Anglo-American unity. Kennedy's speech, coming at this time of increasing anxiety about the possibility of war, would be carefully scrutinized on both sides of the Atlantic.

On March 14, four days before the speech, Joe received a diplomatic dispatch from Hull, who told him that its tone was too rigid and that the content made America appear more isolationist that she was. Hull made clear that his changes had been reviewed and approved by the president. Politely downplaying his orders as "suggestions for your consideration," he asked Kennedy to omit comments about the American people's lack of interest in foreign affairs and their unwillingness to go to war.

At the Pilgrims dinner, held at Claridges, Lord Halifax joked about Joe's athletic prowess, his hole-in-one, and the fact that Britain's weather had been surprisingly sunny ever since the ambassador's arrival. Britain was lucky, Halifax said, that the new ambassador was "so representative of modern America." The feeling in the room was so convivial, Kennedy wrote his friend Arthur Krock, "that it was difficult to let them have the unpalatable truth I had to offer." He wrote his speech with an eye to reassuring Americans that, as he said to Krock, "he had not gone over to the British."

Extolling bluntness, Kennedy told his British hosts, "we should always be able to speak plainly, knowing that there can arise no misunderstanding that plain speaking will not clear away." Of the attitudes of his fellow citizens, he told them, "The average American has little interest in the details of foreign affairs . . . [and] today has two worries. He fears he may lose his job and he fears his country may get into a war . . . It must be realized that the great majority of Americans oppose any entangling alliances . . . We cannot see how armed conflict can be expected to settle any problem or to bring happiness or contentment to any nation. There certainly was no winner in the World War, we can all see now."

He gave words of encouragement for both isolationists and interventionists: "In some quarters," he said, the U.S. attitude has "been interpreted to mean our country would not fight under any circumstances short of actual invasion. That is not accurate, in my opinion, and it is a dangerous sort of misunderstanding to be current just now. Others seem to imagine that the United States could never remain neutral in the event a general war should unhappily break out. That I believe is just as dangerously conceived a misrepresentation as the other." Afterward, Joe noted in his diary that parts of his speech "fell flat."

On March 21, assessing his first weeks on the job, Kennedy sent Arthur Krock the first of many "Private and Confidential" letters that he would dispatch to many friends and American opinion leaders, among them columnists Walter Lippmann and Boake Carter; anti–New Deal columnists John O'Donnell and Hugh Johnson; William Randolph Hearst; T. J. White of the Hearst organization; Felix Morley of the *Washington Post*; Russell Davenport of *Fortune*; J. Pierrepont Moffat, the European section head at the State Department; diplomat Bernard Baruch; Jimmy Roosevelt; assorted senators, and the chairmen of the House and Senate Foreign Relations Committees. Inexplicably, the president was not included. Roosevelt became increasingly annoyed at Joe's eagerness to inform everyone but the one man to whom he was beholden.

Joe's first two letters to Krock showcase his isolationist views. "The march of events in Austria made my first few days here more exciting than they might otherwise have been," he wrote, "but I am still unable to see that the Central European developments affect our country or my job." Economic factors were crucial, he went on to say. "An unemployed man with a hungry family is the same fellow, whether the swastika or some other flag floats above his head." He was worried about the effect of continued economic doldrums: "A few more months of depression of values will have us and the rest of the world so deeply in the doghouse that war might seem an attractive out. Pressure is brought to bear on those in authority to do something drastic to better the economic lot of their subjects . . . Britain . . . can't go on much further unless there is a general pick-up. After all, the armament program will have to be financed with borrowed money. They have practically reached the limit of taxation, they seem to think."

Joe thought the British were working on a "general appeasement" until they were "strong enough to stand up to the bargaining table with a few aces in the hole . . . That is a long shot, perhaps, but at least they think they know what they are doing. Are any of the rest of us conscious of what we are doing, if anything?"

Joe was convinced that "[n]obody is prepared to talk turkey to Messrs.

Hitler and Mussolini" and risk war. He, however, made the mistake of assuming that "none of these various moves has any significance to the United States, outside of general interest . . ."

O N MARCH 24, Neville Chamberlain delivered a long-awaited speech, telling the House of Commons, "the fundamental basis of British foreign policy [is] the maintenance and preservation of peace," but made clear that "that does not mean that nothing would make us fight." Britain would not give a direct guarantee to protect Czechoslovakia. Nor would she guarantee to fight with France to defend the Czechs. Such a promise would leave Britain no control over the circumstances that might precipitate a war, Chamberlain said. Britain would not fight over an area "where our vital interests are not so concerned as in France and Belgium." Joe told Arthur Krock that Chamberlain's speech was a "masterpiece." "I sat spellbound in the diplomatic gallery," he continued. "It impressed me as a combination of high morals and politics such as I had never witnessed." The speech, he said, "simply slew the Opposition." Other, more experienced, politicians did not agree with the greenhorn ambassador.

Winston Churchill's speech was as prescient as it was eloquent: "After a boa constrictor has devoured its prey it often has a considerable digestive spell . . . Now after Austria has been struck down . . . there may be another pause . . . then presently we will come to another stroke. For five years . . . I have watched this famous island descending incontinently, fecklessly, the stairway which leads to a dark gulf. It is a fine broad stairway at the beginning, but after a bit the carpet ends." The nation, "rising in its ancient vigor, can even in this hour save civilization."

Two days later, as if to confirm Churchill's foreboding, Hermann Goering told Jews that they should leave Austria, and Hitler cranked up his propaganda campaign to undermine the Czechs by convincing Konrad Henlein, leader of the large Sudeten German minority in Czechoslovakia, to ratchet up tension by making unrelenting and unreasonable demands on the Czech government.

On the afternoon of Tuesday, March 29, the dowager Queen Mary received Joe and Rose in a small sitting room in her home, Marlborough House. Rose was impressed that "[s]he sat very straight, [and] was meticulously groomed." Attuned to power, Joe noted in his diary that the queen struck him as "one to rule the roost." Queen Mary's willingness to receive the Kennedys was part of a concerted effort by the royal family and the upper classes to make America's representatives feel welcome in England.

THE VIRGINIA-BORN NANCY ASTOR, a passionate collector of interesting people and a vigorous proponent of British-American friendship, could not wait to meet the new ambassador and his family. In 1918 she had succeeded her husband Waldorf Astor as a member of Parliament for Plymouth, becoming the first woman to serve in the House of Commons. Among her intimates were Mahatma Gandhi; George Bernard Shaw; Philip Kerr, the eleventh marquess of Lothian, who would soon become British ambassador to the United States; Lady Alexandra Metcalfe, whose easygoing and dim husband "Fruity" was a notoriously close friend—some say romantically close—of the duke of Windsor; Geoffrey Dawson, editor of the London *Times*; Rudyard Kipling; Charlie Chaplin; and T. E. Lawrence. They all visited the Astors at their London townhouse and at Cliveden, their huge Italianate mansion, which had been designed by Charles Barry, architect of the Houses of Parliament. Situated on an idyllic bend in the Thames River, it offered panoramic views of the Berkshire countryside.

Nancy Astor was often brilliantly witty but could also be tactless. According to Debo Mitford, "there was a fearsome uncertainty as to what Lady Astor might say or do." She was known to interrupt Churchill's speeches at the House of Commons by yelling, "Rude," or "Shame." Once at a party, Churchill, wanting to get attention, called, "How many toes are there in a pig's foot?" Nancy retorted, "Take off your shoes and count."

Fearless, big-hearted, and sometimes muddle-headed, Lady Astor—and her taciturn husband—championed Kathleen Kennedy and her parents as vibrant new faces on the London scene. The support of the era's leading social and political hostess was a coup for the Kennedys, especially given Lady Astor's previous expressions of anti-Catholicism.

It would also prove to be a mixed blessing. Joe Kennedy was soon branded a "Cliveden set appeaser" by the leftist journalist Claud Cockburn, who claimed that the guests at Cliveden were an influential, Hitler-adoring cabal plotting to make British foreign policy pro-Nazi. In reality, Lady Astor's gatherings were populated by a mix of pro- and anti-appeasement politicians and celebrities. Cockburn hit a nerve, however, exploiting intense fears on both sides of the Atlantic about people in power kowtowing to the Nazis. When reports of Kennedy's "Cliveden sympathies" reached the American press, Joe sent Nancy Astor a playful note: "Well, you see what a terrible woman you are, and how a poor little fellow like me is being politically seduced. *O weh ist mir!*" Ultimately, Cockburn would do significant damage to the international reputations of Kennedy and the Astors.

Before her first visit to Cliveden, Kick wrote her friend Lem Billings she was "scared to death not knowing any of them," but she enjoyed herself. According to Rose, Nancy Astor thought of Kick as a "kindred soul, a younger version of herself . . . they would both talk about anything with great spirit and intelligence." Kick was also introduced to Nancy Astor's favorite after-dinner entertainment, charades and musical chairs, and found the evening "very chummy and much gaiety. Dukes running around like mad freshmen."

Rose had first met Lady Astor on March 30, at the American Women's Club luncheon. Lady Astor, who had five sons and a daughter, told Rose over lunch that she "quite envied me the last three youngsters." Right from the start, Rose, emotionally inhibited and very proper in public, was drawn to Nancy, who was her opposite, the kind of freewheeling woman who would chew gum while wearing a $75,000 tiara. "She is great fun any-place, talks about everything, anything, intelligently and with gusto and with an inexhaustible sense of humor," Rose wrote in her memoir. "Also she is a clever mimic, and when she puts in a pair of false teeth she changes her whole facial expression and is marvelous." By contrast, Rose said of herself, "Well, I am just an old-fashioned girl. I don't drink, I don't smoke and I have a lot of children."

On April 4, the Astors entertained the new ambassador and his wife at a star-studded dinner at their Victorian townhouse in St. James's Square. Joe crowed in his diary that Clementine Churchill, sitting next to him at dinner, had told him that "her husband liked me very much and would see me any time that I cared to see him," and that the Archbishop of Canter-bury told him that "he knew of no one who met the success I had since my arrival and wanted to have me for lunch." Joe took an immediate liking to Lady Astor. With their blunt and at times reckless manners, the two were worthy sparring partners.

DURING THE LATE 1930S, London was a menaced and menacing city. Oswald Mosley's black-shirted fascists marched through heavily Jewish neighborhoods. Communist, fascist, and democratic values were at war amid a realm where aristocratic power was fading and social classes clashed. On April 10, tensions over British support of fascism boiled over in Hyde Park when Unity Mitford, smartly dressed and sporting her swas-tika badge, showed up at a Socialist Party event, "Save Peace, Save Spain," and was attacked by the crowd. Police officers had to rescue Unity when the angry Socialists started pushing her toward the Serpentine River.

That same day Joe Kennedy also made news, with his decision to end the presentation of U.S.-residing debutantes at the court of King George VI. The *New York Times* reported that he had been "driven almost to distraction by a flood of applications from home." Joe also released a letter he had written to Senator Henry Cabot Lodge of Massachusetts explaining why he would not present a young lady from his home state at the British court: It was "undemocratic" to choose, merely on the basis of the number and quality of their recommendations, a small selection of women from a large pool of applicants. Kennedy had received three hundred letters from young women living in the United States and abroad. One Midwestern applicant had submitted references from six governors, five senators, and thirteen House members. Joe declared that only Americans living in England, or family members of American officials in Britain, would be presented. Cynical observers could not help but note that Joe's decision allowed his own daughters to be presented at court with less competition for attention.

In her memoirs, Rose Kennedy called the weekend of April 9 "one of the most fabulous, fascinating events" of her life. When the Kennedys arrived for their visit to Windsor Castle, the master of the household took them to their rooms in a castle tower. While sipping their cordial and savoring their dizzying rise to the highest ranks of society, Joe reportedly told his wife, "Well, Rose, it's a hell of a long way from East Boston." His words, perhaps apocryphal, have passed into legend as part of the Kennedy story.

The Kennedys dined in the Garter Throne Room, with its spectacular chandeliers and tables with floral centerpieces so tall that the king could barely see the queen across the table. Joe sat next to Queen Elizabeth, and Rose shared the king with Mrs. Chamberlain. Conversing with the queen during dinner, Kennedy propounded the American isolationist position about involvement in Europe's affairs: "When they remember 1917 and how they went in to make the world safe for democracy and then they look now at the crop of dictatorships, quarrels, and miseries arising out of that war they say to themselves, 'Never again!' And I can't say I blame them. I feel the same way myself."

"I feel that way too, Mr. Kennedy," the queen answered. But, according to Joe, she did not hesitate to challenge him: "But if we had the United States actively on our side, working with us, think how that would strengthen our position with the dictators."

Joe may not have taken the queen's words to heart, but he found her very appealing: "Fired by an idea, speaking rapidly, her face acquired a charming animation that never shows in photographs." Kennedy told her that a visit by the king and queen would greatly improve Anglo-American relations. As he put it to the queen that night, "You could charm them as you are charming me." He broached the same idea privately with the king. Their Majesties, who had long wanted to come to the United States, were enthusiastic.

Lady Halifax asked Joe what his friend Franklin Roosevelt was like. Joe told her about Roosevelt's heroic struggle against his disability and his doughty will: "If you want him in one word, it is gallantry. The man is almost paralyzed, yet he ignores it and this forces others to overlook it. He dominates a room. I have seen him, when he is determined to win an argument, rise to his full height and, bearing his weight solely upon his arms braced against the desk, make the point to bring him victory." Joe's praise for Roosevelt would redound against him; the president did not appreciate anyone talking about his disability.

After dinner the women joined the queen, who stood alone in front of a fireplace so that she could have a private audience with each of the wives. During Rose's fifteen minutes with her, she mispronounced "Ma'am"—the correct form of address for the queen—until Her Majesty took pity on her and released her from that formal obligation. Discussing the difficulties of sleeping in noisy London, the queen was amused when Rose confessed to sleeping with wax in her ears.

Rose studied the queen as Lady Halifax, her lady-in-waiting, brought Mrs. Chamberlain and the other ladies up for their private conversations. She was standing under Van Dyck's famous portrait of the five older children of King Charles I. Rose was captivated by this portrait and had a premonition: "There was something about seeing those children frozen for that moment in time, blissfully ignorant of all the pain of the years ahead, that made me shudder inside and suddenly feel afraid." Despite her public image as an unfailingly optimistic individual, Rose was privately fatalistic, "believing that tragedy had to follow triumph, as surely as night follows day—that Providence allows no perfect, happy families."

The following afternoon, while out for a walk with Halifax, Prime Minister Chamberlain and Ambassador Kennedy began to bond. Chamberlain explained that every time he tried to address the German government's incessant complaints about having been deprived of their rightful territories, they refused to become specific as to what territory they wanted back and when.

On April 16, he got his Anglo-Italian pact. The agreement, known as the "Easter accords," was signed in Rome—and with it, Chamberlain hoped, would come peace in the Mediterranean and a wedge against Hitler in Eastern Europe. Despite a barrage of criticism, the British would recognize Italy's sovereignty over Ethiopia in return for the cessation of Italy's anti-British propaganda in the Middle East, and for Italy's agreement to reduce its troop fighting in Libya and in the Spanish Civil War. Lord Halifax asked Joe to press Roosevelt to issue a statement supporting the agreement. But the most FDR was willing to say publicly was that the treaty was "proof of the value of peaceful negotiations."

Any optimism about the Anglo-Italian agreement was tempered by a fresh crisis brewing in Czechoslovakia. The Nazi propaganda machine was spreading stories that the Czechs were torturing and mistreating its Sudeten German minority. Feigning outrage, Hitler claimed that he had to defend his maltreated compatriots. On April 21, Hitler ordered secret plans for an invasion of Czechoslovakia. Five days later, the German Reich withdrew from the New York World's Fair. Germany's willful alienation from the community of nations further portended war.

CHAPTER 4

A Season of
Unprecedented Abandon

LESS THAN TWO MONTHS into his ambassadorship, Joe's unorthodox and freewheeling style had become the subject of stinging criticism back in America. Joe smarted over Drew Pearson and Bob Allen's April 22 "Washington Merry-Go-Round" column suggesting that he had been taken in by the Astors' "Cliveden charm," and that he was allied with their pro-Nazi politics. He expressed his pique directly to Pearson in a telegram: "Your story on the Cliveden Set is complete bunk. There is not a single word of truth to it and it has done me great harm . . . the repercussions over here have been quite bad."

Two days later, Joe and Rose showed up for a luncheon at the Astors' London townhouse. Their fellow guests were buzzing about the "Cliveden Set" propaganda, and Kennedy's decision to choose a small number of American debutantes for presentation at court. Provocative as ever, Nancy Astor asked eighty-two-year-old Nobel Prize–winning playwright and journalist George Bernard Shaw whether he approved of the ambassador's changes. "Certainly not," Shaw replied. "We don't want the court to have only selected riff-raff." This was the kind of jibe Nancy cherished.

Fatefully, Nancy and Waldorf introduced Joe and Rose that afternoon to Charles Lindbergh and his wife, Anne Morrow Lindbergh, a bestselling author and the daughter of the former U.S. ambassador to Mexico. After the nightmare of their young son's abduction and murder, the Lindberghs had fled America and taken up residence in Kent with diarist and MP Harold Nicolson and his wife, the writer Vita Sackville-West.

Charles, normally reticent, and Joe immediately connected. Lindbergh

American-born Nancy Astor and her British husband, Lord Astor, championed Kathleen Kennedy and her parents as fresh faces on the London scene. The Astors' friendship would be a mixed blessing. (*Astor Archives*)

had been following Kennedy's speeches and spoke "most intelligently" and approvingly of his beliefs, Joe noted happily in his diary. He told Joe he was taken by his warning that democracies needed to look inward for help. Anne also liked Joe, finding him "clean-cut, humorous, and intelligent."

The previous day, with his triumphant entry into Rome at the beginning of a state visit to Italy, Hitler had challenged the very sentiments Kennedy and Lindbergh shared. Having determined that Mussolini would be indifferent to any move he made on Czechoslovakia, unbeknownst to Chamberlain, Hitler now felt free to discard any agreements with the British prime minister.

THE PROSPECT OF WAR propelled Londoners into the 1938 social season with unprecedented abandon, even as the scene had changed significantly over the previous several years. With their propensity for bending the rules, the Kennedys were charging into a social world that had recently grown significantly more conservative. "Society had been dominated for two decades by rich, smart, sometimes vulgarly ostentatious and decidedly *American* hostesses," wrote Angela Lambert, a chronicler of London society in the 1930s. "Now their reign, too, was over. The loosening of mores and morals which had started during the First World War and had continued throughout the hysterical twenties was now decisively halted. The mood of Society—emphasized by the wholesomeness of the new royal family and underscored by the growing fears of war—was one of rectitude. People continued to entertain lavishly; but it was the lavishness of old family houses with old family retainers serving traditional English food on old family silver."

Eunice and Rosemary Kennedy arrived in London just after the beginning of the Season, which typically started at the end of April with the opening of the private viewing of the art at the Royal Academy's Summer Exhibition and the spring Newmarket races. This full-throttle Season included four court presentations. Presentation at court was, in Rose Kennedy's words, "the most utterly simple, and intensely complicated event[s] imaginable." Although the actual presentation was nothing more than a brief introduction of each of several hundred women and girls to the monarchs, it required elaborate preparations and adherence to longstanding and often arcane protocols. Presented in pairs before the seated king and queen, each woman had to perform a slow, sweeping curtsy to the king, then take three gliding steps to her right and curtsy again to the queen, then slide farther to the right and exit judiciously out a side door.

Gladys Scanlon, wife of the embassy air attaché, took Rose to Paris to shop for her gown; Rose wore a white lace dress embroidered in tiny silver and gold beads created by the trendy British designer Molyneux. Both Kick and Rosemary (Eunice was too young to be presented) wore white net gowns trimmed with silver.

Kick managed the tricky maneuver in spite of her nerves. "My train not fastened on—only put on at last minute. Walked by very quickly," she wrote in her diary. Rosemary was not so fortunate. According to Kennedy biographer Laurence Leamer, who interviewed an embassy staff member off-the-record, Rosemary suddenly tripped and nearly fell over. Her mother must have been hugely embarrassed. She had taken a big gamble by including her beautiful but clumsy and mentally slow daughter in such a high-profile and high-pressure event. The king and queen smoothed over the moment with smiles and Rosemary recovered her balance, and then sidled after her protective younger sister. Despite the mishap, Rose found the whole process "glamorous beyond belief."

The next day Kick joined her father for a lunch at the home of Sibyl, Lady Colefax, who was noted for entertaining a good mix of literary, political, and society figures. Lady Colefax remained a supporter of former King Edward VIII and Wallis Warfield Simpson, the American divorcée he had forsworn the throne to marry, and had thus slipped a rung in the social hierarchy under the new monarch. Her great society rivals were the extravagantly generous American-born Laura Corrigan, a former cocktail waitress who inherited her money when her older husband died suspiciously soon after she married him, and the witty, charming, and yellow-haired Emerald Cunard, who was called a "canary of prey" for her opportunistic mixing of sparkling beauties, literary sages, aristocrats, and politicians, and who had also lost standing by allying with the former king. The only renowned London hostesses who had kept on the good side of the royals were Lady Londonderry, the extremely wealthy and well-connected wife of the former air minister, and Lady Astor, whose status as an American divorcée did not dispose her more favorably toward the Duchess of Windsor.

The three months of the London season—May, June, and July—averaged ten dances a week. Almost every evening young men in white tie, tails, and white gloves would join debutantes in ball gowns at dinner parties at elegant homes in the chic Belgravia and Mayfair sections of London, and would then attend balls starting at 10 P.M. Kick found the dinner-dance at the Dorchester Hotel "more fun than the dances at the houses or rented houses for the evening," but she decried the "beastly" dance card system: "No boy will dance with a girl until a formal introduction has been obtained. Many girls standing around with no partners."

The debutantes' hectic schedule was hard on their mothers. "All the mothers say it is rather difficult to sit night after night and watch the young things dance until two or three in the morning, but most of them do it at the beginning of the season," Rose confided to her diary. By the end of the three months of dances, the mothers would "send the car with the chauffeur and it is supposed to be all right for the girl to come home in her own car, but she must never invite a young man to accompany her and the worst possible offense is to go on to a night club afterwards." Of course, the most adventurous young ladies and their escorts sneaked out regularly to dance unsupervised at the dimly lit and fashionable 400 Club or the Café de Paris. They crept back to the balls in the early morning before the orchestra played "God Save the King."

In this era, the *New York Times* would chronicle London society news regularly on its own society pages. According to the *Times*, Kick attended the ostentatiously wealthy Lady Baillie's coming-out party for her daughter Pauline Winn, a granddaughter of American financier William Whitney. In one of Lady Baillie's two ballrooms, the stylish duke and duchess of Kent led the crowd gyrating to the tune of the "Big Apple," "in which everyone formed a circle and ended with a 'bumpsadaisy,' and the popular dance *Lambeth Walk*."

Henry Luce, the founder and publisher of *Time*, *Life*, and *Fortune* magazines, had arrived in London in mid-May in order to study how European diplomats, politicians, and intellectuals were planning to handle challenges from the totalitarian dictators. His wife Clare Boothe Luce accompanied him, hoping to work out wrinkles with British censors over her new play *The Women*, which she planned to stage in the West End. They arrived in time for the Kennedys' dinner for foreign secretary Lord Halifax and his wife. In honor of his guests the Lindberghs, Joe screened the film *Test Pilot*, starring Myrna Loy and Clark Gable. With her typical attention to character, Rose carefully observed the Lindberghs. She wrote, "He acts very shy, smiles in a boyish sort of way and seems to retire to the corner where he stays most of the time. Anne is all poetry and light, simple, natural, lovable with an enchanting smile." The Luces were soon honored with their own dinner. According to her biographer Sylvia Morris, Clare "won the libidinous interest of the American ambassador."

T HE LONDON SEASON was darkened by the surprise visit to London of Konrad Henlein, the head of the Sudeten German minority in Czechoslovakia, who had alarmed Britain by demanding that Prague set up and recognize a separate state for ethnic Germans and repay the Sudeten Germans for the injustices the Czechs had inflicted upon them since the end of the First World War. Churchill met with him to discuss Henlein's plan for a federal system for Czechoslovakia. Bluntly, and without authority to make such a declaration, Churchill told him if Czechoslovakia were attacked, Britain would join France in declaring war against Germany. Chamberlain did not corroborate the renegade Churchill's warning and missed an opportunity to send Hitler a stern signal when he declined to appoint Churchill secretary of state for air—an appointment that would have evidenced conviction about building air parity with Germany.

By mid-May, the British received reports of German troop movements near the border of Czechoslovakia, just as local elections were due to be held in the Sudetenland. The British cabinet, always reluctant to fight, felt they had to issue a warning that if France were forced by treaty to defend the Czechs, Britain might not stay its hand. Then the British military attaché in Berlin raced to the German-Czech border and determined that the whole thing had been a false alarm; Germany had not garnered troops for an invasion. Chamberlain became convinced that the German government had "made all the preparations for a coup, that in the end they decided after getting our warnings that the risks were too great . . . ," as he wrote his sister at the end of May. Chamberlain's optimism would soon prove itself unfounded. Hitler was merely holding off his plans for "Operation Green," the invasion of Czechoslovakia, until the Reich's Siegfried Line defenses were strengthened to protect against an Anglo-French invasion of Germany.

On June 4, the day after the Nazis issued a decree to confiscate "degenerate art," Sigmund Freud left Vienna for London. The exile of the eighty-two-year-old Austrian psychiatrist and psychoanalyst had taken months of negotiation and the payment of a large ransom to the Reich. Arriving by train at Victoria Station on June 6, Freud was welcomed to England by family members who had already fled the Nazi occupation of their homeland. His son Martin told the press that Dr. Freud planned only to rest: "He is a very old man and what he wants most is peace and quiet for the rest of his days." His fellow European Jews would find no peace at all.

The brief Czechoslovakian crisis, and the British cabinet's resulting panic, brought the menace of war to Kennedy's doorstep for the first time. Writing to Jimmy Roosevelt at the end of May, he expressed a freshly somber view of the incendiary danger Europe faced: "We seem to be living through one crisis after another these days, and no one appears to have any idea of how long this fumbling can go on without getting out of hand." Joe was worried. "The momentary lull in Central Europe has not caused anyone here to think that the Czechoslovak business is settled. The hard part lies ahead, of course."

Secretary of the Interior Harold Ickes, visiting London with his new wife, Jane, corroborated Joe's evolving perceptions: "Joe Kennedy was . . . greatly afraid that hell might break loose at any time over Czechoslovakia." Bill Bullitt, Kennedy's counterpart in Paris, went farther than Joe, predicting a catastrophic war, Ickes reported to the president.

Trying to relax after the Sudeten crisis was over, Joe accompanied Kick and Rose to Lady Astor's dance for the king and queen. According to Kick, "everyone had decorations on, but no knee breeches—No hard drinks—

and rather staid, but house quite lovely. White gloves for all." Kick noticed Charles Lindbergh sitting with the queen on a couch and conversing. She did not know that Lindbergh, who had never set foot on the dance floor, had turned down the queen's request to dance—a major but understandable breach of protocol.

THE NEXT SOCIAL EVENT the Kennedys had to negotiate was the Epsom Derby, Britain's premier thoroughbred horse race for three-year-old colts and fillies. Accompanying Edward George Villiers Stanley, the seventeenth earl of Derby, whose ancestor had founded the Derby, and his wife Alice, Joe, Rose, and Kick arrived at Surrey and were forced to walk in pouring rain to the racecourse. Rose was put off by the "carnival atmosphere" with "mobs of people out for a holiday." Wearing a tweed suit and a felt hat, Rose noted self-consciously that all the other ladies were dressed in "printed dresses and navy blue coats—fox fur pieces and even lavender coats and dresses (a color accented this year) rather than tweed." For Rose, the "sartorial elegance" of the Derby seemed to "be a sort of tryout for Ascot," the most elite of Britain's social events.

Joe, Rose, and Kick were among one thousand guests invited to the Royal Derby Night Ball at Buckingham Palace that evening. They arrived back in London late, and Kick was "forced to leave in the middle of dinner to go to [the] court ball which was terrific." Kick, dressed in white lace with "a shocking pink bodice," was struck by the "beautifully bejeweled" women, and in particular Mrs. Ronald Greville, a brewery heiress and Edwardian-era hostess. The king, the queen, and the dowager Queen Mary sat on the dais at one end of the room. Kick noted that "Daddy was the only man without knee breeches. He looked so funny sitting up with old Queen Mary trying to force a smile out of her." The highlight of the evening was when "platinum blonde Evelyn Dall"—an American cabaret singer—"appeared in blue satin rocking the rafters with her crooning." She sang "Nice Work If You Can Get It."

In spite of such a long and eventful day, Kick got up the next morning and, with the help of her friend Jean Ogilvie, set the place cards at the tables for the coming-out party her parents were giving at the embassy that night. Figuring out who would sit next to whom at the dinner dance was "quite a sweat as there are so many petty jealousies in London." It was understood by many of the guests that although both Kick and Rosemary were making their social debut, the party was more for Kick than for Rosemary, who took an unruly, childish delight in such events.

The evening began with a dinner for sixty of the capital's most socially prominent debutantes, noblemen, and visiting foreign royalty. Kick sat next to her friend Prince Frederick of Prussia, who was entangled with heiress Barbara Hutton—much to the dismay of Hutton's husband Count Reventlow. Also seated with her were Lord Robert Cecil, the son of the marquess of Salisbury; John Stanley, grandson of the earl of Derby; Jean Ogilvie; and Debo Mitford.

Afterward, over three hundred guests entered the embassy through corridors of multicolored lupines, sailing up the stairway to the French-paneled ballroom, which was strewn with purple and pink flowers. Ambrose's Band, which ordinarily played at the Mayfair Hotel, provided the swing as Kick danced with, among others, the duke of Kent and Prince Frederick. Rosemary, carefully chaperoned by her father's aide "London Jack" Kennedy, was a tireless and gifted dancer, staying on the floor the whole evening. American nightclub favorite Harry Richman's rendition of "Thanks for the Memories" brought down the house. The dance broke up around 3 A.M.

Kick did her best to lend her vivacious, informal style to the heady evening. "Our brawl went off very well," she wrote her friend Lem Billings. "Tried to get everyone to cut in but it was the most terrific effort. They all acted as if it was absolutely the lowest thing in life to tap someone on the shoulder . . . but otherwise everything was wonderbar." Kick took the formal Brits to the edge of impropriety without seeming crass. Her father would have done well to study her style.

At the final dinner party Joe and Rose hosted before his sojourn home, film director Darryl Zanuck and his wife, American film star Rosalind Russell, hobnobbed with ambassadors, aristocrats, and politicians including Major John Jacob and Lady Violet Astor; Randolph Churchill; the Edens; Sir Thomas Inskip, the minister for Coordination of Defense; and the former Lord Viceroy of India, the Marquis of Willingdon.

Visiting the German embassy, Joe hoped to impress upon the new ambassador, Herbert von Dirksen, that he appreciated the Reich's economic progress and improved living conditions for the German people but was concerned about Germany's treatment of its Jews. Joe had tired of the State Department bureaucracy and its lack of direction about how to handle Germany and the issue of German Jews. He had been a successful mediator in tough situations in the past, and he wanted to see if he could find common ground between the United States and the Reich. In his maverick actions, he was insubordinate, creatively assertive, or both.

What did Kennedy tell von Dirksen? In Joe's own account of their meeting, he explained to the ambassador that the difficult situation of the Jews in Germany stood in the way of improved U.S. relations with the Reich, and "something should be done about it." Moreover, Axis efforts to spread fascism in South America had become a major impediment to trade with Germany, Italy, and Japan. In a mid-May address at the University of London annual dinner, Joe had already spoken out against restrictions of thought in totalitarian countries.

Von Dirksen's account of their meeting is quite different, even damning. According to von Dirksen's report to the German foreign ministry, Joe had told him "it was not so much the fact that we wanted to get rid of the Jews that was harmful . . . but rather the loud clamor with which we accompanied this purpose." He claimed Kennedy said he "understood our Jewish policy completely; he was from Boston and there, in one golf club and in other clubs, no Jews had been admitted for the past 50 years . . . such pronounced attitudes were quite common, but people avoided making so much outward fuss about it." According to von Dirksen's account, trying to soften the German view of Roosevelt's pronouncements, Kennedy supposedly suggested that the president had been poorly advised on Germany and that Roosevelt's advisors and the East Coast press had been unduly influenced by fear of Jewish opinion.

When von Dirksen's dispatches regarding his meetings with Kennedy were published in the 1940s, Joe would proclaim that they amounted to "complete poppycock." However, the mention of Boston golf clubs does bring authenticity, if not accuracy, to the German ambassador's account. In a thorough review of those documents in the 1990s, Amanda Smith, the editor of her grandfather's letters, would find "some muddling of the verifiable facts" in von Dirksen's accounts, and noted that Joe's own diaries claimed that the German ambassador was not fluent in English. According to German foreign policy documents, von Dirksen's own bosses at the foreign ministry discounted Kennedy's comments; they saw them as casual remarks or an attempt at political advancement.

No matter whose account is to be relied upon, if Kennedy encouraged von Dirksen to believe that there were real opportunities for compromise on the treatment of Jews in Germany that would ensure better relations with the United States and the Western powers, he made a serious mistake.

However, even as Kennedy was cozying up to von Dirksen, he was also taking action against the Nazis. In mid-April he had sent Roosevelt a report detailing how the Germans and Italians were spreading totalitarian propaganda by shortwave radio throughout South America, and urging

FDR to set up rival networks to counter them. Kennedy also passed on to FDR a letter written to him privately by his friend Cardinal Eugenio Pacelli, the Vatican secretary of state and soon to be Pope Pius XII, denouncing Hitler's betrayal of Christian values.

In addition, Kennedy attempted to have Nazi agent Werner Georg Gudenberg arrested when his ship, the *Hamburg*, docked in Southampton. According to William Breuer's book *Hitler's Unknown War*, Gudenberg had provided Nazi spy William Lonkowski with private information about American aviation plants. The *Hamburg*'s captain claimed Gudenberg was ill and would not allow him to be taken off the ship. Over the next year, Kennedy would at once decry and accommodate German transgressions.

KICK'S JUNE DIARY captures a debutante's progress: at Cambridge for the annual food fight at Whitsun; to Glyndbourne, near Brighton on the south coast, to see the opera and the gardens; a cocktail party at the Ritz, and dinner at David Rockefeller's flat; watching the regiments at the Trooping of the Color; at Cliveden for Ascot week; at Hatfield, the home of the marquess of Salisbury and his grandson Robert Cecil, where Kick took their anti-Catholicism in stride; and to Wimbledon for tennis. On June 22, Kick attended Laura Corrigan's party at Marlborough House, where the aristocrats went wild: "The Duke of Kent doing the Big Apple for all he's worth . . . Diana and Duff Cooper hopping about with a shoe on her head." Two days later she joined Billy Hartington and his cousin David Ormsby-Gore at the dance hosted by the speaker of the House of Commons, at Parliament, on a "romantic spot overlooking the Thames and the bridge."

The four days of Ascot races in mid-June are the centerpiece of the English Season, and they capture the essence of English society. As Lady Sarah Churchill archly summarized it, "The debs, too, were under starter's orders: just like fillies at a race track, y'know, being wandered around for sale to the best bidder." Rose, having resolved to forgo tweed, had meticulously visited many of the most exclusive dressmakers from London and Paris to assemble her Ascot outfits. She recognized many of the smart frocks in every shade of pastel from lavender to pink. After the first race, Joe and Rose were escorted up to the royal box, where they lunched with the king and queen; the Gloucesters; the Kents; Mary, the Princess Royal; and former Queen Ena of Spain. Rose, in her glory, was escorted to lunch by the handsome duke of Kent on one side and the bejeweled maharajah of Rajpipla on the other. Rose noted in her diary that the maharajah wore a "black homespun coat with five buttons of diamonds and rubies and a turban of a mixture of green with yellow stripes swathed around his head." Joe was relegated for once to a less glamorous position than his wife's; he escorted the duchess of Gloucester. For Rose it was "the most perfect day . . . an atmosphere of contentment, of joy, of interest and satisfaction. . . ." Joe, for his part, regarded the scene from a more American perspective. Spotting the royal procession, he exclaimed, "Well, if that's not just like Hollywood."

In late June, John ("Honey Fitz") and Josie Fitzgerald visited their daughter Rose during a six-week tour of the British Isles. As a treat for Boston's former mayor, Rose wangled an invitation to tea with the Chamberlains. Mrs. Chamberlain delighted Honey Fitz by telling him that her father was Irish, and, further, that her family name was Fitzgerald. At Wimbledon, Rose introduced her parents to Queen Mary, who invited them to join a group of dignitaries and royals for tea.

For Rose, Queen Mary's invitation "was a heart-warming example of how well trained the royal family was." But despite Rose's compulsive need for order and her eagerness to gain approval by following protocol, her family was happily breaking through the rigid conventions of pre-war London society. With her American informality, Kick had infused a fresh element into the hidebound rituals of the Season. Visiting Blenheim Palace in mid-May with her parents, she got away with calling the duke of Marlborough "Dukie Wookie." In the residence at Prince's Gate, Rose must have winced watching eleven-year-old Bobby "flicking cherry stones across the table" at his grandmother. Josie herself cheerfully sabotaged her daughter by encouraging Bobby to hide all of Kick's left shoes. Kick came down to dinner wearing a black and white dress, and one black and one white shoe. Even Rose was amused.

The ambassador's wife could also risk impropriety, at least when it came to showing off her connections with aristocracy. On June 27, while Kick represented the Kennedy family at the memorial services for the queen's mother, the countess of Strathmore, Rose entertained her parents at Berroc End, the large country home near Ascot the Kennedys had recently rented, and then took them down to Cliveden. They entered the estate through a mile-long drive lined with blooming rhododendrons. Lady Astor was not home, but perhaps Nancy's characteristic boldness rubbed off on Rose. She talked the butler into allowing them to walk through the house so that they could look down through a terrace of boxwood and contemplate a beautiful vista stretching to the Thames.

A S JOE SAILED HOME on the *Queen Mary* with his aides London Jack and Arthur Houghton, he had a chance to discuss Nazi activities in South America with his fellow passengers, the anti-Nazi diplomats Carraciollo Parra-Perez, who was the Venezuelan ambassador to Switzerland, and Raoul Martinez Vegas, from the Bolivian embassy in Paris. Joe was concerned that FDR had not yet set up a program to counter the Germans' use of shortwave radio broadcasting in the southern hemisphere, and was determined to lobby the president to renew efforts to make such broadcasts happen. Joe was now refining his freelance-portfolio style of diplomacy, mixing superb intelligence-gathering for the president with autonomous forays into murky and dangerous diplomatic waters. He had no idea what punishments awaited him at home—from his alma mater and his president.

CHAPTER 5

Honor and Humiliation

JOE RETURNED to the United States in early June to attend Joe Jr.'s graduation from Harvard and to consult in Washington, D.C., with the president and government officials increasingly anxious about the advance of fascism. After he set sail from Britain, the State Department exacerbated tensions by demanding that Germany pay off Austria's First World War debt to the United States because the Third Reich had essentially taken over the country, and the day he arrived in the United States, eighteen people were indicted in Washington for being German spies.

When Joe entered New York harbor on the *Queen Mary* on June 20, Jimmy Roosevelt joined reporters on a cutter out to the ship. He took Joe aside and warned him that the press was going to badger him about his interest in being a presidential candidate in 1940. FDR had left open the possibility that in two years he would run for an unprecedented third term, but he had made no commitment, hoping to be drafted by his nation and party. Speculation was rising that other Democrats, including Kennedy, would be all too happy to replace their leader in the White House.

In mid-March, right after Joe had arrived in London, *Washington Post* columnist Harlan Miller celebrated the "beguiling" image of "all the kinetic Kennedys" holding court in the White House, declaring that of all known contenders to FDR's throne, Joe possessed "the nearest to the Rooseveltian personality." The ambassador's assiduous cultivation of the press paid off further when *Liberty* magazine headlined an article "Will Kennedy Run for President?" Journalist Ernest Lindley wrote that a few political analysts were betting that Kennedy, a long shot, would be the next Democratic nominee. Soon newspapers in Boston, Washington, and New York began speculating about a Kennedy presidential run. As for Joe's ambitions, "No one can lightly turn away a serious suggestion from his friends," he would write disingenuously in his memoir, "that he is worthy of succeeding to the presidency of the United States."

According to Joe, the press "nearly stormed" him when the *Queen Mary* docked. Pressed about his presidential aspirations, he spoke with the tactful loyalty of a true politician: "I enlisted under President Roosevelt to do what he wanted me to do . . . If I had my eye on another job it would be a complete breach of faith with President Roosevelt."

Joe knew that publicly he had to proceed with great care; Roosevelt did not take kindly to anyone eager to assume the mantle of crown prince. In his memoir, he wrote, "Mr. Roosevelt also had a quality—a failing, some have called it—of resenting the suggestion that he was to be succeeded."

After a night at the Waldorf-Astoria in Manhattan, Joe went straight to Hyde Park. He protected himself by recording that the president "did not then or later express any particular criticism of Chamberlain's objectives or techniques," all of which Kennedy was being roundly criticized for supporting.

Joe traveled from Hyde Park to Cambridge a proud, bitter, yet hopeful man. His oldest son was about to graduate from Harvard, which was reason to celebrate, but he still smarted over his failure two years earlier to win election to the Harvard Board of Overseers. He had finished tenth out of the twelve candidates nominated for the five positions. That was not good enough for a man for whom winning was everything—you were either in the "castle or the outhouse," as he put it. Now, in a fresh attempt to win recognition from his alma mater, he was seeking to be awarded an honorary Harvard degree at Joe Jr.'s commencement ceremonies. Such a tribute would signal that his position as ambassador to the Court of St. James's had garnered him the respect of the American establishment; it might also clear the road for significant positions at home—perhaps even the presidency. Joe believed he deserved an honorary Harvard degree, but he always denied to others it was a possibility, even as newspaper reports circulated that spring—to his delight—that he was being considered for the honor. Traditionally, Harvard maintained strict secrecy about its honorees until just before the commencement ceremony itself. On the way to Boston, Joe learned the devastating news that the film industry, in which he had been a player, would indeed be recognized, but it was Walt Disney who would receive the honor. To add insult to insult, another, more illustrious diplomat, also with connections to the film industry, was among Harvard's thirteen honorees: Canada's governor general John Buchan, who had written the novel *The Thirty-nine Steps,* the basis of Alfred Hitchcock's acclaimed 1935 movie. Joe was devastated.

Later, denying he had sought out the degree, he wrote that the "action of my well-intentioned friends" caused him "considerable personal embarrassment." Joe moved quickly to limit the damage, declaring that there would be only one "honors" degree—Joe Jr.'s. His son was graduating cum laude—and "that would be pretty good for one family, I think." But Joe went even further to protect his pride—and at considerable cost to his family. He sent out a press release indicating that he had actually turned down an honorary degree because a family medical crisis kept him from attending commencement. He said he would have to spend the day of the ceremonies with Jack, who was bedridden at their home in Hyannis.

Joe did have legitimate concerns about Jack, who had just returned home after "holding court up here at the New England Baptist Hospital," as he wrote to his best friend, Lem Billings. His gastric problems had been exacerbated when Dr. Sara Jordan of the famed Lahey Clinic in Boston prescribed a diet rich in milk products, to which Jack was allergic.

Joe accompanied his oldest son to the colorful Harvard Class Day activities the day before graduation, but then immediately departed to Cape Cod. At the Wianno Yacht Club, near their home in Hyannisport, Joe Jr. and Jack competed for Harvard in the MacMillan Cup Regatta, where the top collegiate sailing team was determined. Both of the Kennedy boys' boats placed second in their races, helping Harvard stay close to the lead. The next day, after Joe Jr. had gone back to Cambridge to graduate, Joe Kennedy watched the seven-man Harvard team boat, with Jack aboard, place second, thus ensuring Harvard the MacMillan Cup. The triumph pleased him, but Jack's participation on the winning Harvard team exposed his father's face-saving fib.

"He would be damned," Joe told those closest to him, "if he would sit and watch Disney take *his* honors." His unwillingness to participate in one of the key days in the life of his devoted first son, upon whom he placed such hopes, highlights his profound humiliation. "It was a terrible blow to him," Rose later admitted. "After all those expectations had been built up, it was hard to accept that he wasn't even in the running. . . . suddenly he felt as if he were once again standing in front of the Porcellian Club, knowing he'd never be admitted."

A few days later the president asked Secretary of the Interior Harold Ickes, "Can you imagine Joe Kennedy declining an honorary degree from Harvard?" FDR was not only amused but piqued; Joe, he believed, was scheming behind his back to establish himself as a presidential candidate.

The president handled the situation poorly. Instead of setting limits on what he considered unacceptable behavior from a subordinate, he undermined Kennedy secretly, eroding what trust still existed between the two men. FDR had the White House press secretary plant a story with the anti-Roosevelt *Chicago Tribune* and elsewhere, saying Kennedy had included confidential information about British debt and trade negotiations in the "Private and Confidential" letters he sent to his political allies, providing copies of the letters as proof.

Two days later, while Joe was sequestered at his Hyannisport home, the *Chicago Tribune* published this damaging article on the front page, headlined "Kennedy's 1940 Ambitions Open Roosevelt Rift." The paper claimed, according to "unimpeachable sources, Mr. Roosevelt has received positive evidence that Kennedy hopes to use the Court of St. James's as a stepping stone to the White House in 1940," and, thus, "the chilling shadow of 1940 has fallen across the friendship of President Roosevelt and his two-fisted trouble-shooter, Joseph Patrick Kennedy." The *Tribune* quoted a "high Administration official" who declared, "Joe Kennedy never did anything without thinking of Joe Kennedy . . . And that's the worst thing I can say about a father of nine kids. He'd put them in an orphanage one by one to get himself into the White House."

Joe was incensed. Later, back in London, he wrote the editorial director of the *Detroit Free Press* to complain that the entire article was malicious and libelous. Joe was enraged about aspersions cast upon him as a father: "The statement that I [would] put my children in an orphanage is, of course, so scandalous that I won't even pretend to answer it."

Some historians have said the antagonism between Kennedy and Roosevelt went deeper than the threat of Joe's presidential hopes. According to biographer Richard Whalen, the "president's real concern was that the ambassador would become not a rival, but a critic. The faltering New Deal was vulnerable to the business-oriented opposition that a disaffected Kennedy could mobilize." With his increasing prestige, the ambassador could cause the president real problems if he attacked the "sluggish recovery program." Kennedy could also mobilize Catholic voters, whose support for Roosevelt was tepid, to vote against the president. When Joe dined with the president at the White House on a Friday night in late June, he still had no idea that his wily boss was behind the attacks on him. Later, when he was finally told who had leaked the *Chicago Tribune* story, he was furious: "It was a true Irish anger that swept over me." Joe wangled a final meeting with the president, "with whom it was not my habit to mince words." Roosevelt denied any involvement, but Joe sensed that FDR had turned on

Anthony (Tony) Drexel Biddle, the scion of the banking family that had founded Philadelphia's Drexel University, was FDR's ambassador to Poland. Tony and Joe were returning to Europe by ship in June 1938. Roosevelt's three key ambassadors—Joe Kennedy, Tony Biddle, and William Bullitt, the ambassador to France—would eventually become related by marriage. (*JFK Library Foundation*)

him: "In his way he assuaged my feelings . . . but deep within me I knew that something had happened."

Back in Washington, Kennedy presented Cordell Hull with a report critical of Foreign Service intelligence gathering. He reported, "Far too much time was spent [by Embassy staff] in attending teas, receptions and other gala occasions and then picking up chit-chat about affairs" that was then forwarded to the State Department as if it were verified information. Informal diplomacy required keeping close contact with sources and double-checking stories as any good reporter would do, he told Hull. In his first months on the job Kennedy had performed brilliantly—enhancing America's image in Britain, making all the right contacts to obtain the freshest political and economic information Washington had seen in years, improving embassy efficiency, and requiring that embassy reports present hard facts.

After the embarrassment of the never-offered Harvard honorary degree, Joe was more than eager to get back to London, but just as he prepared to leave, a scathing article, headlined "Jimmy's Got It," appeared in the *Saturday Evening Post* claiming that Kennedy owed his ambassadorship and his success as a liquor mogul to his manipulation of the president's oldest son. Jimmy had been involved in a multitude of shady business deals, the *Post* reported, one of which allowed Joe Kennedy to make a fortune selling Scotch whisky. Joe was left to wonder which of his enemies had encouraged the story.

Joe could have been completing his sojourn back in the United States well positioned to press his case for the presidency. Instead, his political stock had fallen, and so had his mood. Two of the most prestigious institutions in the United States—Harvard and the White House—had turned on him. On the voyage back to Britain on the S.S. *Normandie* with Joe Jr. and Jack, Arthur Krock, and financier Bernard Baruch, none of Joe's prototypical ebullience was in evidence. He also had no idea that Roosevelt had secretly asked Baruch to undertake a mission assessing the European situation and double-checking Kennedy's reports of Nazi strength.

Retreating to his cabin, Joe tried to impose a midnight curfew on his irrepressible sons. Joe loved showgirls and actresses, but he was irritated at Joe Jr.'s pursuit of a fellow passenger, a very appealing actress. According to Krock, Joe assumed his namesake was "a little too impulsive and the girl was making a play for a youth of . . . prominence and wealth." Joe insisted on early bedtimes for his sons. Jack, of course, "had a girl that I think his father didn't know too much about," reported Krock. Late one night the boys figured out how to sneak out of the ambassador's suite through a service door. Krock enjoyed their ingenuity and said nothing to their father.

WITH THE ARRIVAL in London of Joe Kennedy's dashing older sons, the Kennedy allure would grow even more powerful. Both young men would engage themselves not only in society events but in policy—in ways that evidenced their increasing insight into world affairs, but also sometimes caused controversy for their father.

As soon as Jack and Joe Jr. arrived at 14 Prince's Gate, they dressed for the annual Fourth of July dinner and ball of the American Society of London at the Dorchester Hotel. They would spend their first night in London listening to their father and former foreign secretary Anthony Eden speak at the dinner about Anglo-American relations. Joe addressed the need for Britain to resolve quickly the tensions with Germany and Italy, hinting that America wanted the fascist countries to make concessions over their territorial ambitions. Both Eden and Kennedy indicated that although the American people and their British counterparts had many common goals, their governments would not necessarily have identical policies.

Eden said pointedly that "racial and religious tolerance" had now become "almost rare in this troubled Europe." Kennedy was gratified to hear Eden say that the United States should not be "asked or expected to pull British chestnuts out of the fire, though there are beginning to be quite a few chestnuts that concern us both." Among the chestnuts were Britain's relations with Czechoslovakia, Poland, Japan, France, Italy, and Germany.

When Joe visited Chamberlain late in the afternoon of July 5 at the House of Commons, the prime minister was in a foul mood. His political difficulties at home, along with his problems with Mussolini and with the French over Czechoslovakia, weighed heavily upon him. Joe was happy to boost Chamberlain's spirits, telling him his stock was rising in America—based on his conversations with a wide variety of American corporate, political, and press sources—and relayed Roosevelt's offer to employ his moral authority to support the prime minister when crises arose. Chamberlain was cheered. He wrote in his journal that Kennedy had returned to England with "the most roseate accounts of the change of American opinion in our favor and of the president's desire to do anything to help."

JOE'S MOTHER, Mary Augusta Kennedy, had refused to name her only son Patrick Joseph, after his father; she did not want the boy too closely associated with Ireland and things Irish. Honoring his mother's wishes, Joe identified fervently with his family's new country. But now, in the aftermath of the insults to his reputation from Harvard and the press, Ireland beckoned to him with the promise of the recognition that the American WASP establishment and the Roosevelt administration withheld. Joe had been back in London for only two days when he set off with Joe Jr., Eddie Moore, and the sympathetic American journalist John B. Kennedy for an official visit to Ireland—the first ever by a U.S. ambassador to Britain. Rose had originally planned to accompany them, but at the last moment she declined to go; there were heavy rainstorms that day, and she had a phobia about flying in inclement weather.

That spring, on Joe's behalf, real estate magnate John Cudahy, the American ambassador to Ireland, had arranged with the American-born Irish prime minister Eamon de Valera for him to receive an honorary degree from the National University in Dublin. The British Foreign Office found it odd that the U.S. ambassador to Britain would receive a formal tribute from the Irish prime minister, but knew that opposing it would only inflame tensions at a delicate time. Only a year before, the southern part of Ireland, known as Eire, had been granted status as a "sovereign independent state." Fulfilling President Roosevelt's mandate to assist Britain and Ireland in establishing a treaty to end the long-running disputes between Eire and its British occupiers, Joe had worked to soften Eire's demands. During those negotiations, Chamberlain gave up rights to three naval bases in Eire—a deliberate instance of his policy of appeasement and a message to Hitler that the British could be reasonable about territorial accommodation. Winston Churchill had objected strenuously about relinquishing bases that were a gateway to Britain. "Who would want to put his head in such a noose?" he demanded.

According to several of his biographers, including the Irish writer Thomas Maier, as Joe visited the birthplaces of his grandparents in the Irish countryside, he began to feel a surprisingly strong upsurge of sentiment for the land of his forebears. His affinity with Ireland deepened when de Valera, who also served as chancellor of the National University, presented him with a doctor of laws degree.

De Valera toasted Kennedy that evening at a state banquet in the historic Dublin Castle, where British viceroys had held dazzling levees in years gone by. "We are proud that men like you not merely do honor to your country, but honor our race," de Valera said. Experiencing what for him was a rare emotion of deep belonging, Joe was on the verge of tears when he spoke. "My parents and grandparents talked ever of Ireland," he said. Somewhat disingenuously, he went on, "and from my youth, I have been intent on this pilgrimage. I did not dream I should come."

Upon his arrival in London, Jack was reunited with his sister Kick, the sibling with whom he felt the most affinity. They shared an enormously appealing, self-deprecating sense of humor and a subtle sense of detachment that made them all the more attractive to British society—and the opposite sex. Only a few weeks after he arrived, Jack stunned the lunchtime crowd at the Ritz Hotel by showing up with the astonishingly beautiful model Honeychild Wilder, the Cotton Queen of Louisiana. Honeychild was in Britain promoting the cotton industry and doing quite a good job of it. According to Jack, she was also "quite necessary to keep around" because she was "remarkably talented at providing aid and comfort to Americans abroad, relieving their stress, and rendering them every service for the good of God and country."

Jack and Kick were "very generous in outlook, and very funny," remembers Debo Mitford. "That was what was so marvelous about Jack—he was able to laugh at himself. No politician I've ever known was like that." Mitford recalls how her mother observed Jack at a party and declared that "'that young man will be president of the United States' . . . She saw some-

Jack on the lawn behind Prince's Gate. After Joe Jr. and Jack arrived in England in July 1938, the future U.S. president blazed a seductive path through social and aristocratic London. (*JFK Library Foundation*)

thing in him which was unlike anybody else. Like Kick, he was an absolute fount of energy, enthusiasm, and fun, and intelligence, all the things which make people want to become them."

But it was Joe Jr. who his father had anointed to become president. He would spend a year in London as his father's political aide at the embassy and would go on fact-finding trips throughout Europe. Joe also was a habitué of the exclusive 400 nightclub, where he cavorted with the Argentine ambassador's daughters, Turkish pashas, Greek ship owners, and other members of the international elite. That first summer in London he competed for women with his boyish and skinny younger brother, and was frustrated when British females seemed to prefer Jack's deft and humorous style. Joe was possessed of an aggressive manner; he could flare in anger when challenged, and he needled people. He did, however, win the affections of the vivacious Virginia Gilliat, later Lady Sykes of Sledmere House, who had been a debutante a few years before and was often described in the British press as "Popular Girl Number One."

On Jack's second night in London he accompanied Kick to the palatial Londonderry House in Park Lane, where British prime ministers had long joined Winston Churchill's cousins, the Londonderrys, at the top of their legendary double-wide staircase, welcoming the top political and aristocratic figures of the British establishment. On such lavish evenings, the nation's policymakers would debate the issues dominating the era. This heady setting was the perfect place for Kick to introduce Jack to London's political intrigues. Thoughtful and seductive, Jack Kennedy began that night to blaze his beguiling path through London.

Londonderry House, however, was not neutral political or social ground. It was the London seat of Winston Churchill's politician cousin, Charles Vane-Tempest-Stewart, the seventh marquess of Londonderry, and his formidable and statuesque wife Edith, who was known as "Circe," and who, according to historian Anne de Courcy, was said to possess "a tattoo of a snake winding up her leg." The couple were two of the era's wealthiest, best-connected, and most pro-German British aristocrats. As minister of air in the pacifist mid-1930s, Lord Londonderry had failed to convince the British to accelerate the rebuilding of the Royal Air Force.

Kick also introduced Jack and Joe Jr. to a group of cousins at the heart of Britain's political aristocracy—the Cavendishes and Salisburys, who had been in power so long that they acted as if they ruled the world. Kick's close friend Jean Ogilvie, daughter of the earl of Airlie; the duke of Devonshire's sons Billy Hartington and his brother Andrew Cavendish; and David Ormsby-Gore, the heir to Lord Harlech, were all descended from the Cecil family of Hatfield House. Among their forebears were the first Lord Salisbury, Robert Cecil, who was secretary of state to Queen Elizabeth I, and Queen Victoria's three-time prime minister Lord Salisbury. The Cecils were notorious for their rapid-fire manner of speech. Andrew and his cousin David "never drew breath—they talked all the time," according to Ormsby-Gore's daughter Jane Rainey. "At Hatfield they would talk all night. They would go into chapel next morning in their evening clothes because they had never been to bed."

Jack had long been fascinated with British political society, its love of debate, and its confident, detached, and dryly witty style. He found its embodiment in David Ormsby-Gore, Hugh Fraser, and Billy Hartington and Andrew Cavendish, and he joined the other young men in arguing foreign policy and the role of honor, pragmatism, and power politics in world affairs. Chamberlain's politics of accommodation, Churchill's insistence on setting limits, Hitler's and Mussolini's masterful manipulation of public opinion, and the Czech government's uncertain fate were foremost on their minds.

David Ormsby-Gore would play a crucial role in Jack Kennedy's political development. Ultimately, as Lord Harlech, he would serve as the British ambassador to Washington during the JFK presidency. Like Jack, David was a late developer. According to Debo Mitford, he had been "sent down from Oxford and lay on his couch listening to jazz," and he was "without doubt one of the most charming people I have ever met . . . rambunctious company and a high spirited leader of the group." David and Jack both appeared to be the classic slacker second sons, but they were intellectually gifted, avid readers, and addicted to politics. Pamela Harlech remembers that her late husband "took things very seriously, but could also see the lunatic or ludicrous side of things." In later years David, who entered politics before Jack, would act as a wiser older brother, cautioning his friend against impetuous responses in foreign matters. After Jack's death, Rose would advocate for David, whom she found to have integrity and charm, to marry his widow, Jacqueline Kennedy.

Jack had admired Winston Churchill since he was a boy, studying the man's career, speeches, and books: He read about the origins of the First World War in *The World Crisis*, the concept of honor in *Great Contemporaries*, and the questions of rearmament and appeasement in Churchill's recently published *Arms and the Covenant*. On July 11 he got to witness his hero in action, when he joined David in the House of Commons visitors' gallery as Churchill defended the conduct of his son-in-law, MP Duncan Sandys. Sandys had used secret information, obtained in his capacity as a territorial army officer, to ask embarrassing questions in Parliament about the inadequacies of London's anti-aircraft defenses.

Two days later, on July 13, Kick had a fateful first outing with the man she would marry. After selling programs at a benefit garden party at the Tower of London, she was whisked off to a dinner at the home of the duke and duchess of Kent by Billy Hartington. Also in attendance was Adele

Astaire Cavendish, the former vaudeville dancer and entertainer—and Fred Astaire's sister—who had married Billy's uncle Lord Charles Cavendish. Although her encounter with Billy was only glancing, the two of them would soon embark on a romance that would arouse Britain's suppressed prejudices around Americans and Catholicism.

Now that the entire Kennedy family was reunited in London, they would all gather for dinner at Prince's Gate. According to Ted, "it was a formal concept; everyone showed up at the table at the same time—not like now when children are accustomed to eating whenever they want." Ted recalls that the family meals where they discussed current events "led to familiarity and strong relationships. The tremendous advantage of a large family was that we were always reinforcing each other." Joe read to Teddy at dinnertime, shared the Sunday-morning funnies with him, took him riding along Rotten Row, and included him in many adult activities.

A S GERMANY GREW MORE BELLICOSE and rabidly anti-Semitic, Europe and America were increasingly beset by a difficult moral and political question: What would it take to help Germany's Jews? Speaking at Konigsberg that March, Hitler had made clear that he would be delighted to allow German Jews to move to the Western democracies. Roosevelt initiated a July conference of thirty-two nations at the French resort Evian-les-Bains, its goal to help German and Austrian Jews emigrate. He named George Rublee, a high-energy Washington lawyer, a superb negotiator, and, as a retired diplomat, a man with a wide range of contacts in Europe, as the head of what became known as the "Evian Committee," and appointed Joe Kennedy as "vice-chairman." Although Joe did not attend the conference, he monitored the progress the delegates made. Many of the reports from Evian were sent to the American embassy and then forwarded to Washington.

As Joe looked on, the Evian conference did find places for approximately 100,000 new refugees. However, the assembled nations did not agree to raise immigration quotas to admit more Jews to their countries. According to Britain's Imperial War Museum, Jews soon came to believe that there were in this world "two kinds of countries: those where Jews could not live and those where Jews could not enter."

While Joe Kennedy agreed with Chamberlain's top priorities—maintaining peace and a stable economy, and rearming Britain—he did perceive a major human disaster looming and wanted to do his part to ameliorate the situation. At the same time, he was afraid that American indignation about Germany's persecution of the Jews might be the tinderbox that would set off American public opinion and bring America into war with Germany.

Even though Kennedy would be criticized for failing to help refugees effectively, he took an early stand on the problem. While the Evian conference was meeting, he spoke about the plight of Jewish refugees at a ceremony at Winchester Cathedral. Kennedy condemned anti-Semitism even as he balanced his vehement remarks with his typical economic concerns, focusing on the massive costs to Western democracies of relocating refugees. "Certain nations," he said, "have attempted to relieve the suffering of some of their people at the expense of others of their inhabitants." Delegates at the Evian conference, he continued, were working to develop means "to see that these refugees do not perish cruelly and hopelessly . . . Tolerance, concern for the under-privileged, innate sense of fairness—these are the qualities we must cultivate collectively as well as individually if we are to pass safely and happily through the years of transition that lie ahead of us." Kennedy had set a moral tone, but it remained to be seen whether he could follow up with effective action.

At the same time, Kennedy was involved with another refugee rescue mission. The mother superior at the Sacred Heart Convent, where his daughters attended school in Roehampton, had asked for his help in rescuing twenty-eight Catholic nuns from the strife of the Spanish Civil War in Barcelona. Kennedy successfully lobbied Chamberlain and Halifax, who was himself a Catholic, to arrange an evacuation. On July 21, a British destroyer brought the nuns to Marseilles, France.

IN A LONG FOLLOW-UP MEETING with German ambassador Herbert von Dirksen, Kennedy told his counterpart that the president stood ready to support Anglo-German negotiations over Germany's grievances about the Treaty of Versailles. Von Dirksen, in turn, explained to Kennedy if the United States could encourage Britain to include Russia, Poland, and Czechoslovakia in an arms agreement with Germany, France and Italy could be involved as well—serving as a European safety wall for the United States. Kennedy did warn von Dirksen that if the Czech situation deteriorated into war, the United States would enter the conflict on England's side. In an enthusiastic dispatch to Cordell Hull, Kennedy relayed von Dirksen's request for American intervention: "This morning his manner was a revelation to me. Definitely he gave me the impression that Hitler was decidedly in the mood to start negotiations with the English." But Hitler, as the world would discover within the year, would use negotiation only as a wedge toward war. The German dictator would remain unappeasable in his territorial aggression and his anti-Semitism. Even as Kennedy and von Dirksen spoke, the German government was busy issuing special identity cards for Jews.

ON JULY 18 at the Buckingham Palace garden party, Kick Kennedy had an intense personal encounter with Billy Hartington. On a sunny and breezy day, twelve thousand guests walked alongside the lake and the royal gardens. They socialized with members of the royal family, who walked informally amidst ambassadors and debutantes, charity workers and other invited guests. Rose noted that the queen, who was in mourning after the recent death of her mother, appeared "rather smart looking" in black organza and a black hat, and that black was "a welcome change from pastel colors which she usually wears and which nearly always looks the same." The Kennedy family was invited for tea under the striped canopy in the royal enclosure. The ambassador and his wife watched their daughter Rosemary carefully as she mingled, without incident, among the other royal guests. Joe had hoped that Joe Jr. and Jack could be formally presented to the king and queen, but the king was recovering from gastric flu and was too weak to accommodate the ambassador.

Kick, dressed in a pastel summer dress, had arrived with Jack, dashing in a gray suit and his father's gray top hat; Joe Jr.; and her new Catholic friend Sissy Lloyd-Thomas, the daughter of the former private secretary to the Prince of Wales. Rose recalled that her daughter looked her most beautiful that afternoon. At some point during the party, Kick and Billy began to sense a special affinity—although she failed to mention him in her diary entry for the day, which was a terse description of a "very hot day and very dull procedure. King and queen stood with rest of royal family while different foreign princes came and bowed." According to Debo Mitford, the six-foot-four marquess of Hartington "was a charmer of great intelligence. He had great presence . . . and he was loved by everybody . . . He and Kick were about the two most popular people you could imagine." His sister Lady Anne Tree described him as "a fairly formed character who would have made a serious politician." They were an odd pair—the diminutive Catholic-American heiress, socially brilliant and flighty, and the tall, diffident, deeply thoughtful and bookish Protestant scion of the British establishment—the genuine opposites that often attract each other. The soft-featured Billy would have been an excellent match for Princess Eliza-

On July 13, 1938, Kick had a fateful first outing with Protestant Billy Hartington, the man she would eventually marry. He whisked her off to a dinner at the home of the duke and duchess of Kent. Billy Hartington belonged to a group of powerful cousins at the heart of Britain's political aristocracy—the Cavendishes and Salisburys were all descended from the Cecil family of Hatfield House. (*JFK Library Foundation*)

beth had she not grown up to be more attracted to bold, outspoken men like Prince Philip of Greece.

Billy's family owned 180,000 acres of farmland and had eight homes including an Irish castle, a Scottish abbey, and the magnificent Palladian mansion Chatsworth, the family seat, with its famous gardens, in Derbyshire. His father, Edward Cavendish, the tenth duke of Devonshire, was undersecretary of state for Dominion Affairs, and came from a long line of anti-Irish and anti-Catholic politicians. For Kick and Billy, however, several hundred years of family history meant little in the face of their powerful attraction.

Still hoping that Kick would agree to marry him, Peter Grace had sailed to England during his summer break, Kick having assented to his trip. Lem Billings had already warned Kick that Peter "is wildly in love with you and is heading to England . . . in order to clinch the romance—so watch it, Kick." Not to her credit, Kick heeded his warning. When the butler greeted Grace at the front door, Peter introduced himself and eagerly announced, "I'm here to see Miss Kathleen Kennedy."

The butler had bad news. "I'm afraid that's quite impossible, sir," he said. "Miss Kennedy is in Sussex at the races." At around the time of Peter's arrival, photographers for society's *Queen* magazine snapped a picture of Kick enjoying the races with Billy Hartington.

In her diary, Kick noted coolly that "Peter Grace arrived." In her next sentence she returned to her main focus: "Jakie [Lady Astor's son] drove me to Compton Place to spend Goodwood with the Devonshires." Compton Place was the Devonshires' exquisite, modest, ivy-covered mansion near the sea in Eastbourne. While staying there, the Devonshires and their guests attended the Goodwood Races, held in one of the most beautiful racetracks in the world, set amid the Sussex Downs on the estate of the Duke of Richmond.

This would be Kick's first meeting with her future in-laws, the very silent and bookish tenth Duke of Devonshire and his loquacious wife, Lady Mary Alice Gascoyne-Cecil Cavendish. Kick would have much to over-

---

Kick Kennedy picnics with friends at the Goodwood races on July 26, 1938. Kick (far right) sits between Billy Hartington (leaning into picnic basket) and her new friend Debo Mitford. Debo's future husband, Andrew Cavendish, is stretched out on the ground at the far left. (*ILN Picture Library*)

come. "She is very sharp, very witty, and so sweet in every way," the duke wrote his friend Lady Astor. "The Irish blood is evident, of course, and she is no great beauty, but her smile and her chatty enthusiasm are her salvation. I doubt, of course, she'd be any sort of match for our Billy even if we managed to lure her out from under the papal shadow." The duke's comments were mild considering that he had recently published a pamphlet warning of a plot to marry Catholic girls into the upper levels of the British aristocracy, thus bringing Catholicism more into the mainstream of the kingdom. As a man responsible for appointing approximately forty Church of England clergymen to the parish churches on his land, he could not fathom the idea that his eldest son would consider marrying a Catholic woman.

When she returned five days later from Compton Place, Kick and Peter had a tense reunion. Kick, like her brother Jack, had an offhand way of treating those who succumbed to her charm. She admitted to him that she was involved with someone else. Perhaps one of Billy Hartington's charms was that he, too, treated his women in a slightly dismissive way—at least at first, an attitude that contrasted seductively with Peter's overeager attentions.

OCCURRING AMID GREATER TENSIONS than any time since the days preceding World War I, King George's state visit to France revived the Anglo-French relationship as a bulwark against the saber-rattling European dictators. At the end of the king's visit to France, to mollify the Nazis, the British government asked Czechoslovakia to grant concessions to the Sudeten Germans. Lord Halifax sent Lord Runciman, who had formerly been the president of the board of trade, to serve as a mediator between Czech president Edvard Benes and Sudeten Nazi leader Konrad Henlein.

As Hitler made his secret preparations for attacking Czechoslovakia, Europeans held their breath, and tried to distract themselves with their regular August and September rituals of summer and its ending. Many British aristocrats continued their annual social progress as if nothing were unusual: They headed north to Scotland for the grouse hunting and the fall social season. Rose chose the warmer beaches of Cannes for the Kennedy family vacation. There, Joe Kennedy would need all the rest he could muster in the hot August sun; he was soon to face the first major test of his ambassadorship.

CHAPTER 6

"Grave Danger in the Air"

IN A RESPITE from the social scene and political turmoil of London, Rose and her children took up residence in a rented house at Cap d'Antibes on the celebrity-laced French Riviera, where Elsa Maxwell, known as "The Hostess with the Mostest," and the exiled duke and duchess of Windsor summered, entertaining the likes of Somerset Maugham. In August, Joe Kennedy would dismay Britain's king and queen when he joined the duke's yachting party out of Nice.

Staying in the hills near Cannes, about a half hour from the beach and the shopping district, Rose and her children bathed at Eden Roc, a swimming club set on a rocky height above what she described as the "azure blue, clear, deep sea." They visited country churches and historic villages, including St. Paul de Vence, and hunted celebrities. Rose had encouraged the younger Kennedy girls to collect autographs as a way of documenting their European stay. Walking along the beach, the children discovered actress Marlene Dietrich strolling with Elsa Maxwell and begged for her autograph. Dietrich, with "her hair thrown to the winds and no worry about make-up," according to Rose, was gracious, lively, and accommodating. Later, Jack would claim that during that same August she gave him much more than a flourish of her pen.

When Joe and the older children arrived, they enjoyed the "Blue Mediterranean and the sun-drenched sands, the casualness of people in a holiday mood, luncheons, teas, dinners, and golf," as Joe recalled in his memoirs.

Joe's children relished spending time with their father. "His broad smile and wholehearted laugh were infectious," Teddy remembered. "His welcome was warm and genuine—a special one for each of us." Teddy also found his

dad to be "generous to a fault." Bobby was struck by his father's active interest in whatever they were doing and his helpfulness at times of crisis: "The
greater the disaster, the brighter he was, the more support he gave."

Rose was less of a playmate and more of a teacher for her children. As
a young mother, she had wondered, "Why did I spend time learning to read
Goethe or Voltaire if I have to spend my life telling children why they should
drink their milk . . . But then I thought raising a family is a new challenge
and I am going to meet it." Realizing that motherhood would be her legacy,
she had chosen to look upon "child rearing as a profession," and decided
that "it did not have to keep a woman tied down and make her dull or out
of touch." Rose constantly challenged herself and her family to grow intellectually. Walking by her room late at night, Ted would hear her listening to
records in French. Ted remembers her as an "acute grammarian as well as
reader." When she took her children on walks, she would drill them on gram-
mar and on math skills: "When do you use 'I' and when 'me'? What's two
and two plus three take away four?" she would ask. She insisted that her children write daily diaries during their time in England, where "the British are
very good at that." She would read their diaries and comment on them. She
wanted them "to take issues seriously, but not ourselves." She taught them
that politics was not merely serious; it could be "fun, joyous, and upbeat."

Joe Jr. romped on the beach with his younger sisters and especially
with young Teddy, who, though chubby, shared his eldest brother's striking
Fitzgerald looks. At Eden Roc, the best competitive, eleven-year-old Bobby
could manage was a swim with the forty-four-year-old widow Lady Peel,
otherwise known as the great comedic actress Beatrice Lillie. Jack brought
his friend Claiborne Pell, a Rhode Islander and a future Democratic senator; the two young men water-skied, sunned on the beach, and sampled the
swanky nightclubs of the French Riviera. With great pride, Jack confided
in Claiborne that he had had an affair with Dietrich, and Claiborne shared
with Jack his desire to date Kick.

Tensions in Europe took no respite that summer. Hitler called up one
million reservists and the German army began war maneuvers. Roosevelt
responded forcefully to the German aggressiveness; at the University of
Ontario, in what became known as his "defense of Canada" speech, he declared that the United States would defend Canada against attack—making
it clear to Hitler and Mussolini that the United States would defend its
hemispheric ally, a nation that was a part of the British Empire the fascist
powers were threatening.

Rose chose not to focus on war; her August diary deals with diets, sour
milk, and sightseeing. "As usual, Jack is trying to put on pounds, while

Joe Jr., Kathleen, Rosemary, Eunice are all trying to shed what they put on during the British season. Pat is seesawing between gaining and losing." Jack fell ill again briefly, and Rose was concerned enough to contact his doctors in Boston. It was urgent, she believed, that Jack regain the weight he had lost during Harvard's spring term, but she was afraid to serve him the unpasteurized milk available in Cannes. After Joe joined his family, he was able to convince Rose that unpasteurized milk would not give her children typhoid.

From Cannes, Joe and his older sons followed the latest anti-Czech diatribes of Hitler's propaganda machine, in which the German dictator fabricated Czech insults and instances of persecution against the Sudeten Germans. Joe sensed that a climax was approaching. When Joe Jr. returned to London to prepare to work under Bill Bullitt at the Paris embassy, Rose noted that "his father thinks there may be a crisis in the government at any minute and so it is a grand opportunity for him to be on the spot." Joe was eager for the intelligence his son could provide about the efficient running of an embassy during a time of crisis.

During Jack and Kick's ten-day sojourn with friends at Worthsee Lake in Austria, Kick went out to a bar with two friends, one an Austrian Jew named Rudi, the other an Englishman, who got into a fight with some Nazis "over the fact that . . . [Rudi's] suspenders were showing." Kick noted in her diary that Rudi, the son of the former Austrian minister to Rome, was "scared to death as Nazis would probably have killed him" had they known he was Jewish. "I suppose that one must behave in a foreign country," Kick wrote, "but everyone says that Austria has lost its gayness and carefreeness." After this brief encounter with prejudice made personal, Kick and Jack spent a night dining with ex-king Alfonso of Spain, "a small man and rather sallow looking," who wore extraordinary golf trousers "like women's culottes," and who bragged how much he was doing to direct the Loyalist forces in the Spanish Civil War.

Back in Cannes, Kick went to the beach with her siblings and, after swimming alone for forty-five minutes, was caught in the surf and nearly drowned. She was brought to recover in the bedroom of Marlene Dietrich's daughter Maria in the Cap d'Antibes Hotel. Just back from death, Kick ogled the signed photographs on which Marlene had written to her daughter "my love in French, German, and English."

IN MID-AUGUST, Prime Minister Chamberlain, suffering from acute sinusitis, returned from Scotland to London for treatment, where he received intelligence reports suggesting that the Germans were about to attack the

Czechs. Churchill, meanwhile, was publicly declaring that the British were still capable of defending the basic rights of mankind.

Kennedy, after a stopover in Paris to discuss with George Rublee, Myron Taylor, and Bill Bullitt where Jewish refugees could be relocated, arrived back in London and met with Chamberlain, after which he concluded in a dispatch to Cordell Hull that the British prime minister "is still the best bet in Europe against war, but he is a very sick-looking man; he is worried but not jittery." Kennedy wrote that he told Chamberlain that if Hitler seized Czechoslovakia, "It will be Hell." The prime minister was concerned that "very little of the proper information gets to Hitler any more, so far as world peace is concerned: he is kept high up on a mountain peak . . . by a ring around him." Chamberlain saw a fifty-fifty chance of war. If the French went to war against the Reich, Chamberlain would keep Britain out until public opinion forced him to fight. As of late August, the British public opposed going to war on behalf of the Czechs, but that could change, Chamberlain thought, if and when France declared war.

At times both the American ambassador and the U.S. president promised Great Britain more than they should have. According to a letter Lord Halifax wrote to British ambassador Lindsay in Washington, Kennedy overstated America's readiness to help the beleaguered prime minister, telling Chamberlain that if France and Britain went to war against Germany, "the United States would follow before long." Without FDR's permission, Kennedy had said that the president had decided to "to go in with Chamberlain; whatever course [he] desires to adopt he would think right." Roosevelt hinted at future U.S. involvement in a meeting with Lindsay in mid-September, but this was a prerogative he reserved for himself in private conversations.

THROUGHOUT SEPTEMBER, world peace, not to mention the future of many political careers, seemed to depend on the fate of one small Central European state. On September 2, Hitler mobilized his troops, cynically declaring that Germans living in the Sudeten section of Czechoslovakia required protection from their own government.

But in early September the English were still lethargic with summer. Jack Kennedy found London to be surprisingly dull. He joined his father at Aberdeen Cathedral in Scotland for the dedication of a memorial to Samuel Seabury, America's first Episcopal bishop. With his son beside him, Joe Kennedy had planned to speak of the bloody folly of war: "I should like to ask you all if you know of any dispute or controversy existing in the world which is worth the life of your son, or of anyone else's son? Perhaps I am not well informed of the terrifically vital forces underlying the unrest in the world, but for the life of me I cannot see anything involved which could be remotely considered worth shedding blood for." Hull vetoed these words. Kennedy, the State Department felt, would not only be encouraging Nazi territorial avarice but making a direct appeal to the British people over the heads of their own leaders.

Joe was angry. In the revised speech, rather than minimize the conflict between Germany and Czechoslovakia, Kennedy delivered a powerful and thinly veiled attack on Germany and Italy for their persecution of the Jews: "In certain parts of the world, the profession and practice of religion is being called a political offense. Men and women are being deprived of their natural-born citizenship. They are being thrown out of the land of their nativity because they profess a certain religion which political authorities have decided to uproot." But he did not swallow his opposition to armed conflict. Young people, he said, should be given something to hope for other than "a short life carrying a gun." Calling for a "spiritual war on war," Kennedy declared, "Every road to peace must be explored." For the next year, the American ambassador would expend all his prodigious energy to forestall war. He would maintain, as he did when he spoke at a luncheon that same day, "the issues over which governments make such a fuss are generally small ones . . ."

Kennedy made a gaffe in early September when he appeared to be taking foreign policy into his own hands, telling the Boston *American* in an exclusive telephone interview that its readers should "keep cool—things aren't as bad as they seem." He had met with Foreign Secretary Halifax that morning, he said, intimating that nothing the British foreign secretary had said suggested the current situation was deteriorating. "No war is going to break out during the rest of 1938," Kennedy predicted.

Roosevelt, incensed, told Cordell Hull to inform Kennedy that U.S. ambassadors should not grant an exclusive to newspapers. When Kennedy defended himself—"I manage to get along reasonably well with the agencies and have not heard of any complaints, and it is my custom to answer any telephone call that comes from Boston because that is where my family is. I am sorry if everybody was disturbed"—Roosevelt responded with unusual directness:

> As you know, we were all greatly disturbed by the appearance of an "exclusive" message of advice from you which was published as having been given to the Boston *American* and then passed on to the other Hearst papers.

I know that the Secretary wired you about it and the other day I saw what you sent to the Secretary. It is not a question of "getting along reasonably well with the agencies"—for, of course, you do that but it does involve the use by an American newspaper or single news agency of a "special interview" or "special message of advice" to people back here.

I know you will understand.

Expressing his frustration to Treasury Secretary Henry Morgenthau, whose job Kennedy had coveted, FDR said, "The young man needs his wrists slapped rather hard," but in truth, Roosevelt rarely bothered to reprimand or even to guide his most prominent, important, and volatile ambassador. FDR hated direct confrontation, and was thus far too lax about setting limits for his creative and wily emissary. Joe Kennedy has long borne more than his fair share of blame for the dysfunctional dance that the president created with him. Roosevelt bears his share of responsibility for not exercising leadership and giving clear and usable instructions to an ambassador whose place on the front lines of world conflict allowed him to be a forceful advocate, mediator, and messenger for American interests and world peace.

Rather than spending his first six months in the London capital "flitting around like a hummingbird in flight," in Michael Beschloss's disparaging words, Kennedy had employed his prodigious vigor and appetite for hard work to cultivate an extensive range of contacts throughout the government, the business community, and the aristocracy. These contacts would become remarkably useful as war loomed. Few ambassadors, before or since, would ever supply their governments with the level of extraordinarily detailed inside information Kennedy produced during September 1938. By nature a fixer, he also envisioned ways for the United States to take an active role in preserving peace—this at a time when the State Department and the president were consumed by their own caution.

On September 5, Kennedy was summoned to the Foreign Office, where Lord Halifax briefed him on Hitler's recent meeting with Sudeten leader Henlein at the dictator's Berghof retreat in the Bavarian Alps. Hitler had ordered Henlein to incite more anti-government incidents and make impossible demands to the Czech government. The German dictator would seize upon fabricated incidents as an excuse to subvert Benes's attempt to salve the situation. Halifax told Kennedy that Hitler would likely act against the Czechs sometime during September. The U.S. government would need to determine how to support Britain while still honoring the American people's desire to stay out of war.

A S THE SUMMER OF 1938 ENDED, many in Europe were partying and vacationing as if peace were not desperately fragile. Rose Kennedy, for one, seemed oblivious. Her diary focused on sightseeing, shopping, and attending the dog races in Paris with Kick. While she certainly knew of the rising tensions on the continent through visiting Joe Jr. at the Paris embassy under Bill Bullitt, she also would confide in her diary that she had shampooed her hair and "arranged it on top of my head which is the way a great many smart people are wearing it now." At Versailles, she marveled at the gardens and especially the fountains—"nothing more delicate, evanescent, shimmering as fountains." What was truly evanescent that early autumn was peace.

The ambassador celebrated his fiftieth birthday on September 6. Rose called him from Paris at 8:45 in the morning, but he was already out riding. His family had scattered. Joe Jr. was in Paris, and Jack was sailing home for his junior year at Harvard. Fearing that there might be a sudden air attack on London, Joe Kennedy had packed off Rosemary, Pat, Bobby, and Eunice on a two-week trip with their governess to Ireland and Scotland. Teddy and Jean, the youngest, remained on the Riviera with their governess. It seems odd that Rose did not come back to London to celebrate Joe's birthday, and some may see it as a sign of distance in their relationship. Doris Kearns Goodwin points out, though, that with nine children and constant travels, the Kennedys did not treat birthdays as special events. Rose did buy Joe "terrifically expensive" diamond cuff links that were "more elegant than anything in Paris . . . and the most exclusive design" in the capital.

Never a man for self-analysis, Joe spent the day working "instead of indulging in the philosophic reflections a man presumably ought to have on attaining the half-century." Rose later recalled how glum and fearful he sounded that day.

When Jack arrived in New York harbor, he was greeted by his friend Lem Billings and a crowd of reporters peppering him with questions. Jack minimized the brewing European crisis, saying there would not be a war and American citizens would not have to be evacuated, pointing out the ambassador's decision to keep eight of his children in Europe for the next year. This would be Jack's first informal press conference, a medium he would learn to dominate.

Joe Kennedy carefully monitored every nuance of the developing crisis and reported back to Cordell Hull how the restive British cabinet first agreed to send Hitler a stern signal that Britain would actively stand up to Germany if it would not accept a negotiated settlement with the

Czechs—and then promptly backed down. The British ambassador in Berlin, intimidated by Hitler's tirades, insisted that the cabinet warning would inflame the situation. This gave Hitler one more reason to believe that Britain would not check his aggression—a belief immediately compounded when an editorial in the avidly pro-Chamberlain London *Times* strongly encouraged his designs on Czechoslovakia, suggesting the Czech government consider "making Czechoslovakia a more homogeneous state by the cession of that fringe of alien population who are contiguous to the nation to which they are united by race." Neither Hitler nor Heinlen had yet demanded cession. Taking notice of the editorial, Hitler, according to his biographer Allan Bullock, then moved up his timetable for conquering the Czechs and took his generals to task for their tentativeness. At the same time, Roosevelt, maintaining his strategy of delicately nuanced neutrality, said that the United States was not allied with Europe against Hitler. After the Sudeten Germans held large demonstrations for reunion with Germany, on September 10, Hitler ordered his troops to mass along the Czechoslovak border. Winston Churchill marched into 10 Downing Street and insisted that the government deliver an immediate ultimatum to Hitler threatening war. Chamberlain resisted him, wanting to defer his response until after the Fuhrer's anxiously awaited speech in Nuremberg. He wanted to keep Hitler guessing about his intentions; he was seriously concerned about playing into the hands of extremists in Germany he perceived as being more bellicose than Hitler himself. Moreover, Chamberlain did not want to threaten actions he could ill afford to carry out. His chiefs of staff had advised him that, pitted against the German war machine, Britain would lose.

Churchill did not know that Chamberlain had already decided, after consultation with the cabinet, to seek negotiations with Hitler without the Czech leaders. Having already written his sister that he was "racking my brains to try and devise some means of averting catastrophe," he had in mind a plan to visit Hitler in Germany—a move "so unconventional and daring that it took Halifax's breath away."

The day before, Kennedy met with the managing editor of the *New York Times*, Edwin James, who had just visited Prague, Vienna, and Berlin. James had concluded from talking to his sources that Hitler did not expect France and Britain to force war over Czechoslovakia. According to James, Hitler hoped that the Sudeten Germans could get their demands met without fighting, but believed it would take only three months to subdue the Czechs if they chose to fight. Kennedy noted in his diary that James's information did not confirm what British sources were saying, and added wisely about Hitler: "How can he tell when they [the British and French] don't know themselves?" He did not reckon, however, with Hitler's shrewd assessment of Chamberlain as desperate for peace.

After meeting with both the permanent undersecretary of state and Halifax, Ambassador Kennedy wired Hull with a startlingly incisive, moment-by-moment view of events unfolding within the British government—including the current secret information the British were using to determine their policy. The British sources were telling him that Hitler was, indeed, prepared to march on Czechoslovakia, that he could not wait long, and that his generals were disturbed by the direction in which he was taking the country. There was a possibility they would revolt. This intelligence had been corroborated in his meeting with Edwin James.

Kennedy provided Hull his own analysis of the situation: "My own observation is that much against their will, the British are veering away from the stand of keeping out . . . I feel they sense great danger in the air, but they are quite calm." He also noted, "If they were doing business with a normal man, they all reiterate that they would have some idea what might happen, but they are doing business with a madman." It was difficult for him, he said, to provide consistent daily bulletins "as with shifting events and information the top-side people are changing their minds every few hours as to procedure."

Halifax wanted to know how America would react if Hitler took over Czechoslovakia. Astonishingly, the State Department had not prepared Joe for this possibility. Joe told Halifax that he had "not the slightest idea; except that we want to keep out of the war." Halifax then asked—according to Joe, not in a nasty tone—"why *his* country should defend all the ideals and values of democracy by itself." Joe told him that the British had made Czechoslovakia their business, and "where we should be involved, the American people just failed to see."

The United States in fact had no response prepared for Germany's impending invasion of Czechoslovakia. Roosevelt suspected that the British government was looking for a clever way to shift some of their awful responsibility onto American shoulders. The secretary of state wired Kennedy that the president did not believe it would be practical to "be more specific as to our reaction to hypothetical circumstances." The leader of a persistently isolationist America, FDR chose to dodge accountability; he would be supportive of the British in a general way, but he was determined that the decision to take on a potentially devastating war or to destroy a small, innocent European country would be for the British to make on their own.

Halifax wired to Ambassador Lindsay in Washington his own version of his conversation with Kennedy. Intriguingly, Halifax's report suggests that Kennedy, operating with a paucity of guidance from the State Department, had engaged in some adventurous foreign-policy brainstorming, seeking ways to break the impasse: "[Kennedy] wondered whether over the weekend it might not be possible for the Soviet government to make some movement that would compel attention, such as concentration of aeroplanes near the frontier." Despite his abhorrence of U.S. involvement, Kennedy told Halifax, "If . . . London was bombed, he thought there would be a strong revulsion of feeling . . . leading a good deal more rapidly than in the last war to American intervention."

Every September since Hitler had taken power, the Nazis had held their weeklong party congress and rallies in Nuremberg, a hypnotic frenzy of pageantry, speeches, and spectacles for crowds of several hundred thousand Nazi supporters. Unity Mitford had never missed a congress, and this year she brought her parents, Lord and Lady Redesdale, and her brother Tom, also avid admirers of Hitler. On September 9, they listened to Hermann Goering call the Czechs "this miserable pygmy race without culture—no one knows where it came from—[which] is oppressing a cultured people, and behind it is Moscow, and the eternal mask of the Jew Devil."

Reporter Virginia Cowles noticed that during this Nuremberg week Hitler had appeared unusually "grave and preoccupied," and, atypically, had refused to meet with his own advisors and declined to give audiences to foreign diplomats. In honor of Hitler, Ribbentrop held a tea for seventy guests, including top Nazi officials Hermann Goering and Heinrich Himmler, at the Deutscher Hof Hotel. According to Cowles's book *Looking for Trouble*, Unity Mitford was in attendance, "surrounded by officials who kissed her hand and bowed and scraped . . . Hitler's gaze wandered over the gathering and his eye suddenly lit on Unity. His face broke into a smile, he nodded and gave her the Nazi salute." Hitler then sent an aide to invite her to join him in his suite after the party. At the time, Cowles was amazed that Hitler, poised on the precipice of war, would spurn encounters with important officials but agree to see this twenty-four-year-old blond English girl. Cowles did not realize what a fervent friendship the two had forged, and how much Hitler still wanted the approval of a British aristocrat, not to mention one who was related to Churchill—who continued to speak out against him. After Unity had met privately with Hitler, she dined with a group that included Cowles. When asked if Hitler wanted war, Unity said, "I don't think so. The Fuhrer doesn't want his new buildings bombed."

On Sunday, September 11, Joe awoke to editorials in Waldorf Astor's

Observer and in the *Express* suggesting that war could be morally necessary. For the American ambassador, the moral imperative was to protect the United States by avoiding war. If he had to break the rules of diplomacy, and make his own decisions on the spot, he would do it, and shoulder any blame. That Sunday, to add muscle to his pacific intentions, Joe called Roosevelt and asked him to move two cruisers into a position that would signal Hitler that the United States might throw their might into the equation. Roosevelt readily agreed.

Kennedy then went straight to 10 Downing Street, as the police cleared him a path through thousands of anxious bystanders. There he told Halifax that the two American ships were on their way to Britain and that the British could make effective propaganda out of that.

By now Kennedy had formulated a strategy all his own for affecting the world situation and, by his very physical actions, influencing Germany. The American ambassador had taken it upon himself to make frequent trips to Downing Street; such visits would give the impression that the United States and Britain were in close collaboration. The press paid attention to his frequent "consultations," which Kennedy hoped would give the Nazis pause. He would later announce to Charles Lindbergh and the king, among others, "I go sometimes only to read the newspapers." The king found this amusing, Joe noted in his diary. The ambassador's assertive if largely symbolic actions contrasted with the State Department's delicately neutral stance.

Kennedy soon went one step further in his personal campaign to check Germany's aggressive designs. He met with the German counselor of legation Edvard von Selzam and endeavored to convince him that Britain's newfound strength and resolve were formidable: "There was a new glint in Chamberlain's eyes and in those of Samuel Hoare [the British home secretary] and of the others which I have never noticed before." Britain was now willing to join France, if necessary, in fighting the Germans, and Roosevelt would be sympathetic, Kennedy told him, saying, "This time they mean business." Kennedy made clear that if there were a war, the United States would eventually fight alongside their allies. Von Selzam quoted Kennedy as saying, "It depended on Hitler whether there was to be chaos, from which no country in the world could remain immune." With an adept mixture of flattery and warning, Kennedy posited that "[f]eeling in America had never yet been more anti-German as was the case at present, and in his personal opinion very wrongly so as Hitler had done wonders in Germany." A memo carefully quoting Kennedy in English was forwarded to the German foreign office in Berlin.

JOE KENNEDY LISTENED from Prince's Gate as Hitler delivered his Nuremberg speech on September 12. For the first time, Americans heard Hitler speaking live to a large political gathering. Jack, recuperating from another bout of ill health, listened over the radio at Hyannisport. As Hitler spoke at the rally, framed with one thousand lighted swastikas, his rants sent a shiver around the world. Kennedy thought that Hitler's "shrill, almost whining" speech was "boastful, offensive and threatening," but that he "held out to the democracies the hope that . . . European peace was a possibility." The Fuhrer had made no specific demands. But the next day, pro-Nazi forces incited violence throughout the Sudeten area. Martial law had to be declared. Chamberlain sent a letter off to Hitler proposing an immediate meeting in Germany. Hitler accepted.

Just as Chamberlain was preparing to make his dramatic flight to Germany, a plot against Hitler was brewing. Both the commander of his general staff and the head of the Berlin area were poised to unleash the German Officer Corps in a coup to depose Hitler before he launched an attack on Czechoslovakia they expected to be disastrous. Though the British prime minister did not know it, his offer to meet could not have been worse; the coup had been dealt a fatal blow.

Kennedy kept up his constant rounds between the Foreign Office and 10 Downing Street, trying, he said, "to keep up my contacts so we would know what really was going on before it actually happened so that we would not be caught unprepared and contemplating the possibility of the bombing of London with eight children as prospective victims. . . ." Rose proudly pasted in her diary of September 10 front-page newspaper photos of Joe, "looking calm," as the paper put it, arriving at 10 Downing and being shown into the prime minister's home by a black cat, whose eerie appearance on this and future occasions did not bode well.

Kennedy was called to Downing Street on September 14, where Chamberlain told him the cabinet had approved his secret plan to fly to Germany. When Kennedy asked Chamberlain to assess the meeting's greatest potential pitfall, the prime minister replied that it would be Hitler's request for a plebiscite in the Sudeten regions, which would force the Western democracies to counter what would appear the will of the people for secession. Kennedy sent a dispatch to Hull explaining that Chamberlain planned to offer Hitler local self-government in the Sudetenland in exchange for his agreement to terminate the mobilization of his troops. After five years' time, the Sudeten Germans would be reunited with the Reich or would be able to hold their own elections in their territories. Presciently, Kennedy wrote, "If the German Chancellor . . . wants immediate action, the prime minister will suggest that it might possibly be done in six months. The great trouble with this is that Herr Hitler will be winning a victory without bloodshed [making] the next crisis . . . much easier for him to win out. This is realized by Mr. Chamberlain but he plans to say that he is ready to talk economics, colonies or any other big plan for the peace of the world . . ."

O N THE EVENING OF SEPTEMBER 13, Joe had called Rose, who was back on the Riviera, and told her that things were "terribly agitated" in London. Even though she was looking forward to spending a few days socializing without her children, he insisted she get back to England immediately. Teddy and Jean would be sent to London the next morning on a previously scheduled flight. Because of the crisis, Rose could not get a plane reservation for herself, so she made her way back to London via Paris, where she arrived by sleeper-train on September 15.

When Rose heard, on her stopover in Paris, that Chamberlain was on his way by air to Berchtesgaden, she noted in her diary, "Everyone ready to weep for joy and everyone confident that issues will be solved." She also proudly recorded that people were telling her that "Joe has been on hand constantly and has aided [Chamberlain] by his presence. Feel that he has given great moral support." By the time Rose got back to London, the crisis had temporarily abated. After spending more than a month with the children in France, she took one of her frequent breaks from parenting, staying at Prince's Gate just long enough to gather her wardrobe and then departing for the social season that was then beginning in the north. In Scotland she checked in to the elegant Gleneagles Hotel, where she could play golf and walk in the highlands. Kick, newly svelte after eating little on the Riviera in anticipation of a September reunion with Billy, also went to Scotland, where she stayed with her friend Jane Kenyon-Slaney at Lord and Lady Glenconner's turreted home, the Glen. The younger Kennedy children were sent back to school in London.

O N THE MORNING OF SEPTEMBER 15, Neville Chamberlain, dressed in a prim black overcoat and sporting the furled black umbrella he would make infamous, took his dramatic flight to meet with Hitler at Berchtesgaden in the Bavarian Alps. Foreign correspondent William Shirer noted in his journal that Hitler was "astounded but highly pleased that the man who presided over the destinies of the mighty British Empire should come pleading to him . . . Hitler had not had even the grace to suggest a meeting place on the Rhine, which would have shortened the trip by half." Contrary to myth, it was not Chamberlain's first flight; he had flown briefly with the future King George VI in 1923.

Chamberlain's childhood experiences with a dominating father and bullying peers had created within him a dynamic of subjugation. He dominated those beneath him, but he did not always know how to command respect from powerful men like Hitler. For instance, he did not seem aware that he had undermined his entire bargaining stance by flying seven hours to meet Hitler without seeking a compromise location. Naïvely, he failed to surround himself with the trappings of power. Accompanying the prime minister were only his most trusted and intimate advisor, Sir Horace Wilson, a former civil servant who had virtually no experience in foreign affairs; two foreign-office diplomats; two typists; and a detective and bodyguard from Scotland Yard. "We should have traveled with about 50 secretaries and an imposing array of bodyguards," Wilson acknowledged later. "Instead we had this tiny delegation, and for a great power we looked puny. We didn't know any better." As they were driven up the mountain to Hitler's alpine retreat, both sides of the winding and mist-shrouded road were lined with jackbooted SS troops, all dressed in crisp, severe black, their authoritarian presence as foreboding as the day's rainy sky. Wilson wondered to himself whether they would come out of this experience alive.

As Chamberlain told Kennedy several days later, Hitler "thoroughly convinced [me] that he would be completely ruthless in any of his methods and aims, and that he is cruel, overbearing, and has a hard look." A tired Chamberlain, who had been traveling since dawn, listened to Hitler rant about Czechoslovakia. Interrupting, the British prime minister presented his plan for ceding to Germany all Czech districts with a German population over 50 percent. Hitler countered with an angry outburst, declaring he would "solve the problem one way or the other." Chamberlain replied in anger, as he recalled to Kennedy, asking Hitler why, if he was unwilling to negotiate, he had "bothered to have him come to Berchtesgaden because if that was all there was to say the sooner the conversation stopped the better." Hitler backed down. He asked that Chamberlain give a guarantee of self-determination for the Sudeten Germans.

Chamberlain biographer Bob Self points out that a careful reading of the transcripts of the meeting shows the prime minister skillfully cornering Hitler on a number of points where the Fuhrer had been vague. Chamberlain told Hitler that he had no trouble with ceding the Sudeten-dominated areas to Germany, and would discuss with his cabinet the question of rapid transfer of those areas. Hitler promised that he would not attack the Czechs in the meantime. Yet this was no concession; Hitler had not planned to march until the beginning of October.

Playing to the prime minister's need for approval from powerful people and his inflated sense of his own skills, Hitler's advisors convinced Horace Wilson that the Fuhrer had been "very favorably impressed" with Chamberlain. According to Chamberlain, Hitler had told them that he "had had a conversation with a *man* and one with whom [he] can do business and he liked the rapidity with which I had grasped the essentials. In short I had established a certain confidence, which was my aim." In a burst of vanity, Chamberlain boasted, "I am the most popular man in Germany." Chamberlain seemed more concerned that Hitler follow a protocol in tearing apart Czechoslovakia than whether or not the Fuhrer should be chopping up a country. Graham Stewart, in his book *Burying Caesar*, quotes military historian Williamson Murray: "As usual British leaders were more concerned with Germany's bad form than with the actual event."

On the same day that Chamberlain went to meet Hitler, Winston Churchill famously wrote to a friend, "We seem to be very near the bleak choice between War and Shame. My feeling is that we shall choose Shame, and then have War thrown in a little later on even more adverse terms."

Although Chamberlain told the cabinet that Hitler was "the commonest little dog he had ever seen," he was taken by the Fuhrer's air of power. As he wrote to his sister, "In spite of the harshness and ruthlessness I thought I saw in his face, I got the impression that here was a man who could be relied upon once he had given his word." His whole career would flounder on his failure to recognize Hitler as a bully who would betray him. Joe Kennedy, too, would suffer mightily for his alliance with Chamberlain's miscalculation.

CHAPTER 7

Jubilation and Shame

R OSE ARRIVED AT PRINCE'S GATE in mid-September to find Joe under greater pressure than ever. "The telephone still rings constantly and insistently for Joe—sometimes from London and sometimes from the U.S.A.," Rose noted in her diary. Calling her parents to congratulate them on their forty-ninth wedding anniversary, Rose found herself the subject of rumors that reflected international tension: She was overheard telling her parents about the children's recent trip to Ireland, which led to stories in several American papers that the Kennedys would send the children to school in southern Ireland when war, presumably inevitable, came.

Ambassador Kennedy, monitoring the disputes in the British government over policy toward Germany, wrote Hull that "[t]he whole plan [to carve up Czechoslovakia] has been objected to by some members of the British Cabinet and Chamberlain appreciates that the rape of Czechoslovakia is going to be put on his shoulders. Nevertheless, since war is the only alternative, he says he can see no justification in fighting for a cause which would have to be settled after the war was over along more or less the same lines as he is trying to settle it at the present time." However, Kennedy told Hull that "the British government are deceiving themselves by believing that a war at some time in the future is not inevitable."

In Washington, D.C., at a confidential meeting at the White House with British ambassador Lindsay, Roosevelt told Lindsay that if Germany invaded Great Britain, Americans would send their troops to defend her. He would later be furious when he heard that Kennedy had occasionally suggested the same thing in London in private. The president did not want anyone else running ahead of American public opinion. Kennedy's constant visits to 10 Downing Street and his many meetings with Halifax and the British Foreign Office, as effective as they were in providing the latest information, rankled some Washington officials. On September 19, the *Washington Star* declared that "while Kennedy is loved in London, he is no longer popular at the White House." The article was a warning: Kennedy's all-too-apparent bond with Chamberlain could cost him in support at home.

Haunted by the threat of an air attack on London, Kennedy was alarmed when he read a report from William Bullitt about Lindbergh's belief that German air power was superior to that of the British. Kennedy cabled Lindbergh, asking him to hurry to London from France for consultations. On September 21, after meeting six of the Kennedy children, Charles and Anne lunched alone with Joe and Rose. With her usual keen eye, Rose captured their miens: "He was rosy cheeked, fresh looking with very wavy hair . . . [and] has a wonderful smile which comes easily and lights up his entire face. She is small, gentle, terribly sweet in looks and manner with a wistful expression, all of which makes you seethe to know that anyone had hurt her so tragically."

In what Rose would call a "rude awakening," Lindbergh declared that Germany could "turn out dozens of planes to England's one." Lindbergh, however, had been deceived. During a 1936 visit to Germany, in what would become a hugely effective act of propaganda, Hermann Goering, the head of the Luftwaffe, led the celebrated flyer to believe that German airplane production was almost ten times what it actually was. Kennedy was shaken. In his diary entry for that day, Lindbergh would summarize what he told Kennedy: "The English are in no shape for war . . . They have always before had a fleet between themselves and their enemy, and they can't realize the change aviation has made. I am afraid this is the beginning of the end of England as a great power. She may be a 'hornet's nest' but she is no longer a 'lion's den.' "

Joe asked Lindbergh to write up his military appraisal, which he made sure reached Chamberlain, Roosevelt, Halifax, and Hull: "For the first time in history a nation has the power either to save or ruin the great cities of Europe . . . she can bomb any city in Europe with comparatively little resistance," Lindbergh stated. "England and France are far too weak in the air to protect themselves."

Churchill would see the German military threat in a more complex way, and he would disapprove of Chamberlain's announcement that he would return to Germany to negotiate the partition of Czechoslovakia.

What Roosevelt had told Ambassador Lindsay was "the most terrible remorseless sacrifice that has ever been demanded of a State," Churchill said "amounts to the complete surrender of the Western democracies." He pointed out that the evisceration of Czechoslovakia would liberate twenty-five German divisions massed at its borders, which could then threaten the West. Churchill added, "The belief that security can be obtained by throwing a small state to the wolves is a fatal delusion."

As Chamberlain's final round of negotiations began, for Kennedy, "few days in my life have been so crowded as those of the week beginning with Chamberlain's flight to Godesberg and his final return from Munich," he would recall in his memoir. "Night after night it would be three or four in the morning before I could get to bed. Dispatches with a recent turn in the news were tapped out to the State Department almost every hour on the hour. Preparations had to be made to protect our staff from air raids . . . Thousands of Americans . . . clamored for transportation back to the United States."

On September 24, Chamberlain returned empty-handed from the Godesberg talks. Hitler had shocked the prime minister by demanding immediate cession of Sudeten territory. Pretending to present a special concession, Hitler had offered to hold off the date for the handover from September 28 until October 1, the day he had initially intended to invade. "You are the first man for many years who has got any concessions from me," he told the prime minister. Sir Alexander Cadogan told Kennedy that Hitler's responses to Chamberlain's negotiation points were so absurd that they reinforced the idea that the Fuhrer was insane.

At 2:30 in the morning of September 26, according to his memoir, Joe called Roosevelt and Hull urging them to take action; war was imminent. Roosevelt appealed to Hitler, Chamberlain, Mussolini, French statesman Edouard Daladier, and Benes to keep negotiating until they resolved the Czech situation. The American president sent an additional message to the Fuhrer suggesting an international conference to determine a workable compromise. Hitler wrote back that Germany lacked neither patience nor a desire for peace. Later that morning, Kennedy called Hull and reported that if Hitler did not hint at any compromise in his speech that evening at the Berlin Sportpalast, it was likely he would invade, sparking war. Kennedy would need considerable help evacuating American citizens from Britain.

That night, twenty thousand people gathered in New York's Madison Square Garden for a rally expressing solidarity with the Czech people. At a Nazi rally at Berlin's Sportpalast that same evening, Hitler, cocking up his shoulder in a nervous tick, appeared to lose control of himself, "shouting and shrieking in the worst state of excitement I've ever seen him in," according to journalist William Shirer. Hitler declared that Germany would take over the Sudetenland by October 1 ("It is our holy will"), and claimed that Czech chancellor Benes had burned down villages and attacked Germans with hand grenades and gas. As Roosevelt wrote to his cousin Daisy Suckley, the Fuhrer's audience "did not applaud—they made noises like animals."

The Czech crisis led to an escalation of war preparations and heightened anxiety, verging on panic, in England and France. Fearing that London would soon be subject to unimaginably savage air attacks, hundreds of families began moving to the countryside. Former prime minister Stanley Baldwin predicted that sixty thousand Londoners would die during the first Nazi air strike.

"All over London people were fitted with gas masks," Joe Kennedy noted in his memoirs. "In the churches, the theaters, at the sports matches, announcements were made of the depots to which they should go. A motor van slowly cruised through Grosvenor Square with a loudspeaker attachment urging people not to delay in getting their masks. It carried posters pleading for more recruits for the air protection services." Air-raid trenches were now being dug in Hyde Park, and anti-aircraft guns were being put in place along the Embankment and the Horse Guards Parade area. Cellars and basements were commandeered as air-raid shelters, and the British air force patrolled the skies over London.

The British cabinet declared a state of emergency and mobilized the Royal Navy, but Chamberlain tried to hedge his bets by announcing that it was only a precautionary measure that did not mean war was inevitable. The American embassy issued an advisory that all American citizens should leave Britain and return home, and long lines of agitated Americans, hoping to get visas, formed in front of the embassy. The waiting list for the *Queen Mary* had already swelled to eighteen hundred. Ambassador Kennedy, worried about finding enough ships to transport his countrymen home, asked the British government to commandeer the *Normandie* and other ships for an evacuation.

Kick was staying with a group of Billy's friends and cousins at Cortachy Castle—the tenth-century Scottish seat of the Earl of Airlie—to celebrate the earl's daughter Jean Ogilvie's twentieth birthday. Billy Hartington and David Ormsby-Gore were so obsessed with "listening to the radio for news flashes" and discussing the Czech crisis that Kick, who normally loved to talk about politics, was exasperated. She wanted to enjoy her romantic Scottish holiday with Billy and resented that it was overshadowed by war. "All you can hear or talk about at this point is the future war which is bound to come," she had written Lem Billings on September 23. "Am so damn sick of it."

On September 27, Joe was having lunch alone with six-year-old Teddy when 10 Downing Street called to inform him that the peaceful resolution of the crisis was impossible; Sir Horace Wilson was returning to England after a morning meeting with Hitler, who had remained explosive and obdurate. If his ultimatum was not accepted, Hitler told Wilson, "I will smash the Czechs." Kennedy called Hull and urged him to send ships immediately to Britain to evacuate the Americans who would soon be besieging him with demands to get them home. That same day, he met with King George and, annoyed to be a mere messenger, presented him with a sealed letter from Roosevelt inviting the king to come to the United States for a goodwill tour in 1939. The invitation, with its intimations of a stronger British-American alliance, had to be kept secret lest it rile American isolationists and Europe's fascist dictators. Continuing his policy of intermittently humiliating his ambassador by keeping him in the dark, FDR had ordered Kennedy to present the letter to the king in person but did not reveal its contents. Kennedy found out about the president's invitation when the king read the letter aloud to him.

In an eleventh-hour attempt to avert war, Roosevelt went beyond his invitation to the king and his generally ignored entreaties for an international conference. Through Sumner Welles, he asked Joe to pass on several suggestions for the prime minister to consider before he gave a radio address that same evening. Chamberlain, FDR said, should personally appeal to Hitler for a resumption of negotiations, and if the opportunity arose, he should suggest that Hitler widen the negotiations to include all interested nations, which could meet in a neutral country. Chamberlain ignored the suggestion.

In Scotland, Rose listened to the prime minister on the radio as he gravely addressed the British people that evening. "How horrible, fantastic, incredible it is," Chamberlain said, "that we should be digging trenches and trying on gas masks here because of a quarrel in a far-away country between people of whom we know nothing. It seems still more impossible that a quarrel which has already been settled in principle should be the subject of war." The British Empire would not necessarily dive into a war when a small nation was challenged by a powerful neighbor, Chamberlain said, unless that neighbor sought to dominate the world by force, as Germany did. "War is a fearful thing, and we must be very clear that it is really the great issues that are at stake, and that the call to risk everything in their defense . . . is irresistible."

Even as he urged everyone to stay calm and hold out hope, Rose found his voice full of sadness and discouragement. She described the mood in Scotland in her diary: "Today individual, brooding, silence was as general as un-smiling, un-emotional faces. Everyone unutterably shocked and depressed." Alone in London, Joe wrote Arthur Krock that he was feeling "very blue" because he had begun seriously contemplating sending Rose and his children back to America—"maybe never to see them again." He would have to stay in Britain "alone for how long God only knows."

Like all of Europe, Joe Kennedy was dreading what would happen the following day, already dubbed "Black Wednesday," when at 2 P.M. Hitler's deadline for Czechoslovakia's submission arrived.

Joe busied himself trying to arrange for a Swedish-American liner to stop at a British port to pick up anxious Americans and transport them to the United States. With telephone lines jammed, it was not an easy task. He called Rose that morning to tell her to return to London so they could make plans to get the children safely out of Britain. Joe made sure that everything was packed for the family to go back to the United States. None of the kids liked the idea of returning, except Teddy, "who wants to go to North America to have his tonsils out," Rose wrote in her diary, "because he thinks if he does he can drink all the coco-cola [sic] he wishes and all the ice cream." Rose visited briefly with Kick and gave her the unsettling news that she might have to leave England and Billy Hartington.

Ten-year-old Jean wrote her parents from the convent at Roehampton expressing her awareness of the frightening situation. Mixed in with her tale of playing a game of netball, Jean reported that one of the nuns had told her that she was safe as long as she stayed at the convent. "I hear that the war is very bad," she added.

Just before leaving for the House of Commons to hear Chamberlain's speech in response to the passing of Hitler's deadline, Ambassador Kennedy received a bucking up from the president. A cable arrived: "I want you to know that in these difficult days I am proud of you." Kennedy, who had been working nonstop with little sleep, needed the support and, fortunately, was not immediately aware that Roosevelt had sent the same cable to his fellow ambassadors in Berlin, Paris, and Prague.

Breaking with precedent, Queen Mary, dressed in black, made her first-ever appearance in the House of Commons, sitting with the duchess of Kent in the Ladies Gallery. Kennedy was seated in the cramped Strangers Gallery with his fellow ambassadors from France, Czechoslovakia, and Italy. As diarist and MP Chips Channon dramatically recorded, "the solemn House . . . filled every seat, and everyone was aware of the momentous hour and the gravity of the situation, which was beyond anything perhaps the House had ever known." There was a hush in the House as Chamberlain stood to speak before microphones that were supposed to carry his words to the overflow crowd in another room and out to 100 million people, the largest radio audience ever up to that point in history. They would hear a broadcaster repeat the text of his speech. "We were all conscious that some revelation was approaching," Harold Nicolson noted in his diary. An audible shudder passed through the House when Chamberlain acknowledged that he was now convinced that Hitler was willing to risk a world war.

A messenger suddenly rushed up to the peers' gallery and said that he had an important message for Lord Halifax. The peers passed the letter over their heads to Halifax, who skimmed it and smiled broadly. Halifax jostled his way out of the crowded gallery and passed it to Sir John Simon, who was right at Chamberlain's side.

As Chamberlain related his final appeals to Hitler and Mussolini the previous night, Simon interrupted to give him the letter. Chamberlain stopped, adjusted his pince-nez, and read it. There was a long pause. Then, "his whole face, his whole body, seemed to change," wrote Nicolson. "He raised his face so that the light from the ceiling fell full upon it. All the lines of anxiety and weariness seemed suddenly to have smoothed out; he appeared ten years younger and triumphant." The prime minister declared, "That is not all. I have something further to tell the House. 'Herr Hitler,' he said, 'has just agreed to postpone his mobilization for twenty-four hours and to meet me in conference with Signor Mussolini and Signor Daladier at Munich.'" The prime minister paused briefly. "I need not to say what my answer will be."

After a moment of stunned silence, there was an extraordinary roar of approval, "like the biggest thunderstorm you ever heard," Chips Channon said. "We stood on our benches, waved our order papers, shouted until we were hoarse—a scene of indescribable enthusiasm." Some of the audience wept.

Euphoric, Kennedy joined in the shouts of relief. "I never was so thrilled in my life," he wrote in his diary. He wired Hull, "[N]ever again did I expect to be entertained in a theater after . . . being present at the finish of this dramatic speech. . . ." The normally stoic and undemonstrative Queen Mary wept and reached out to touch those near her. Anthony Eden left the chamber. Churchill stayed glumly in his seat on the floor of the House of Commons. Afterward, he told Chamberlain, mobbed with congratulatory supporters, "I congratulate you on your good fortune. You were very lucky."

Anxiety turned to jubilation on the streets of London. When Kennedy returned to the U.S. embassy, he announced, "Well boys, the war is off." Rose went off to a cocktail party at Lord Forteviot's castle in Scotland, where she shared the news with Kick. Kick wrote in her diary that when "the news came through that he was going to Munich, I have never seen such happiness." Joe Kennedy optimistically ended his diary entry for that day, "[I]t may be the beginning of a new world policy which may mean peace and prosperity once again." Others were not so sanguine. That night Harold Nicolson went to bed still gloomy, knowing that honor had not triumphed and war would come.

Immediately after the speech, FDR cabled Kennedy that he should urgently and confidentially transmit a simple message to Chamberlain: "GOOD MAN," with the president's signature. Still being exquisitely careful to tread the line between encouragement and involvement, Roosevelt sent Kennedy a further cable to pass on to Chamberlain: "I fully share your hope and belief that there exists today the greatest opportunity in years for the establishment of a new order based on justice and law." Kennedy would later claim that he read the cable aloud rather than hand it to Chamberlain—"I had a feeling that the cable would haunt Roosevelt some day, so I kept it."

At Munich, during the four-power conference among France, Italy, Germany, and England, which Chamberlain called a "prolonged nightmare," he and French prime minister Daladier extracted only a slight concession: The Czech withdrawal from the Sudetenland would occur over a ten-day period, not immediately as Hitler had demanded. The four parties agreed that the remainder of Czechoslovakia would be spared unprovoked aggression, and that Britain and Germany would work out their differences by consultation rather than war.

In what would become infamously known as the Munich Agreement, the parties agreed to strip Czechoslovakia of most of its resources (iron and steel, electrical power supplies, timber, railway services and fortifications), and the Czech air force was ordered to leave 1,350 planes for the Germans in Sudeten territory. To complete the humiliation, Poland and Hungary were allowed to carve up small areas of the country where their ethnic populations lived. The fleeing Czechs could not take anything with them but the clothes on their backs. Even their cows would have to be left behind.

Before returning home, Chamberlain met privately with Hitler and got him to sign an agreement declaring that neither country wanted to go to war with each other again. The Fuhrer told Ribbentrop, "[T]hat scrap of paper is of no significance whatsoever," and he would later tell his generals that he had realized at Munich that "our enemies are small worms." In one of the many unanticipated side effects, the Munich agreement thwarted the plot of army officers—including his military chief of staff—to topple Hitler if he went to war with the Czechs. After his victory, no organized opposition to Hitler would exist for another five years.

CHAMBERLAIN ARRIVED at Heston aerodrome outside London, sporting his umbrella and waving the piece of paper Hitler had signed. A huge crowd gathered along the Mall and roared their approval when the king and queen joined the prime minister on the balcony of the palace. Rose wrote optimistically in her diary, "We all feel that a new psychology for settling issues between different countries has been inaugurated and that henceforth war may be out of the question."

Relieved at the prospect of peace, Charles Lindbergh noted inaccurately in his diary, "Kennedy has taken a large part in bringing about the [four power] conference. . . ." Yet the responsibility for arranging the summit at Munich, like its outcome, belonged mainly to Chamberlain. The prime minister did value all Kennedy's advice and his intervention with Roosevelt. Kennedy recorded in his diary that he had been thanked by both Mrs. Chamberlain and the prime minister: "He was kind enough to say that on nobody had he depended more for judgment and support."

At 10 Downing Street, Chamberlain committed an act of rhetorical overreaching that would haunt him for the rest of his life. In his exuberance, he told the crowds that "this is the second time in our history that there has come back from Germany to Downing Street peace with honor. I believe it is peace for our time." His description of the outcome of his negotiations would become his ironic epitaph.

AS THE INITIAL RELIEF AND EUPHORIA FADED, many people in London, Washington, and Paris began to express their doubts, distress, and sense of disgrace about the morality and the geopolitical effectiveness of carving up a country to assuage a madman. Conservative MP Leo Amery had written prophetically in late September in the *Times* that "it is not Czechoslovakia but our very soul that is at stake."

Britain's anguished argument about how to balance honor and pragmatism, and power and negotiation in foreign relations, was laid out in four days of parliamentary debate about Munich. Rose returned from

Scotland in time to join Joe in the House of Commons gallery, where they would witness some of the twentieth century's most dramatic parliamentary skirmishes and oratory, pitting the proponents of containment and confrontation against the advocates of accommodation. Highly protective of Chamberlain, Joe thought that Duff Cooper, the First Lord of the Admiralty, gave "a most ordinary defense" of his decision to resign from the government over the Munich agreement. Cooper pointed out that Hitler had agreed to go to Munich only after learning that the British had mobilized their fleet, declaring, "The Prime Minister has believed in addressing Herr Hitler through the language of sweet reasonableness. I have believed that he was more open to the language of the mailed fist." Joe noted in his memoir that Chamberlain "sat quietly slouched upon the front bench with his feet on the Speaker's table as others hurled at him both criticism and blame." He thought the greatest weakness in Chamberlain's argument was that he promised to protect Czechoslovakia, and then did little to help.

Rose paid particular attention to the jousting between Neville Chamberlain, thin and exhausted from his September ordeal, and Winston Churchill, freshly emboldened by his conviction that capitulation to Hitler was a disastrous mistake. Rose knew about Churchill's reputation as a brilliant orator, and this was her first opportunity to hear him speak. She was not disappointed. When Churchill, who had only a handful of allies in the House, rose to attack the government's policy, he was frequently drowned out by cries of protest. When he declared "that we have sustained a total and unmitigated defeat," Nancy Astor shouted, "Nonsense."

Churchill declared that Chamberlain's accord allowed "the German dictator, instead of snatching his victuals from the table," to "have them served to him course by course." He warned Britain of the dire consequences of their capitulation to Hitler: "All is over. Silent, mournful, abandoned, broken, Czechoslovakia recedes in the darkness . . . we have sustained a defeat without a war . . . We are in the presence of a disaster of the first magnitude." When Churchill mocked Chamberlain's recent comments that Czechoslovakia was a faraway country about which "we know nothing," Lady Astor shouted out, "Don't be rude about the Prime Minister."

"No doubt the Noble Lady has been receiving very recently a finishing course in manners," Churchill retorted.

"From von Ribbentrop," shouted a Labor member.

Churchill closed by saying, "This is only the first sip, the first foretaste of a bitter cup which will be proffered to us year by year unless . . . we arise again and take our stand for freedom as in the olden time."

Profoundly partisan, Joe would note in his diary that the debates were

Joe Kennedy and Lord Halifax leave the British Foreign Office. The practical and shrewd Viscount Halifax, the British foreign minister, became one of Joe's closest contacts and one of his better friends in England. (*Corbis*)

"singularly unimpressive," but Rose found Churchill's great speech to be "fascinating, delightful, and easy to follow." Jack Kennedy, following the debates from Harvard and beginning to develop his own theory of the causes of Britain's capitulation, must have been very envious of his mother, who shared his love of history.

Rose took Kick to Parliament to attend the final session, which would culminate in a vote supporting the government. When the prime minister closed the debate, Rose noted appreciatively the "quiet, unhurried, deliberate way" the young-looking but seventy-year-old Chamberlain addressed his colleagues. Despite all the fiery rhetoric, the House gave a nearly three-to-one vote of confidence in Chamberlain's government. Rose bid good-bye to an exhausted and strained Mrs. Chamberlain, on her way to Scotland for a holiday with the prime minister, who, it would be revealed later, had felt close to a nervous breakdown in the last weeks.

Hitler, speaking on October 10 at Saarbrucken, on the French border, attacked Churchill as a warmonger. Joe Kennedy watched warily as NBC offered Churchill a chance to respond to the dictator on October 16, in a radio broadcast to the United States. Churchill would use his seductive oratory to embrace Americans and bring them to his cause. His words were dramatic and uncompromising. He told Americans, "The stations of uncensored expression are closing down; the lights are going out; but there is still time for those to whom freedom and parliamentary government mean something, to consult together."

The battle for the hearts and minds of Americans had begun in earnest. Joe Kennedy and Lord Halifax were disturbed by what Joe called America's "virtuous idealism" while "sitting comfortably on the sidelines" and Americans' inability to see that "England's frail resources" necessitated averting or postponing war. Joe helped Halifax prepare a countervailing radio broadcast to America. A week after Churchill made his case to the United States, Halifax told Americans, "We have learnt by bitter experience that, however righteous the cause, war is likely to leave a legacy of greater difficulties than it can resolve, for the heat of conflict is fatally apt to blur the issues, and the evils of war drag on into the peace that follows. . . ." In choosing Halifax, Kennedy would lose more than he could imagine.

CHAPTER 8

Outrage

THE DAY AFTER THE MUNICH DEBATES CONCLUDED, Rose and Joe celebrated their twenty-fourth wedding anniversary. After attending the opening of the play *Bobby Get Your Gun*, Rose accompanied Joe to a late supper at the Savoy Hotel in the company of cast members and other show business people—Joe's favorites. The dinner's atmosphere killed the romance for her. She did not like listening to the theater crowd call each other "darling," even though Joe explained that this was a standard form of greeting in entertainment circles. "I was sick to death of it and worse, I remember him using it to someone over the phone occasionally," Rose wrote in a rare fit of pique. This unusually personal diary entry betrays her jealousy and disappointment over her husband's waywardness. Rose had shut Joe out of the bedroom long before—with rare exceptions for procreation—and Joe had enjoyed the company of showgirls as well as a long attachment to actress Gloria Swanson.

Examining the trenches being dug in Hyde Park (across the street from her residence) and walking by streetlamps recently painted black, Rose pondered how to protect her brood from potential German attacks. British gas masks did not seem to fit Bobby, she noted, pasting a comparative photo of British and American gas masks in her diary. Joe had tried to order masks for the younger children from the U.S. State Department, but was turned down. Angry, he informed the department that he was going to put on public record that the government would not spend $10 to outfit citizens in harm's way. Eventually they did get the masks.

Rose monitored her children's safety carefully, bringing Teddy back to

Prince's Gate from a convalescent facility where he had been recovering from having his tonsils removed and paying a call on Jean, Eunice, and Pat at their convent in Roehampton, chronicling proudly in her diary that Jean had been selected head of her class. She worried, though, about Pat, who was never as happy at boarding school as her sisters. Seeking to arrange for Kick to take courses at Queen's College, she discovered that half of the teachers and students had been moved to the country in preparation for war. Kick never attended. During the September crisis, Bobby and Teddy's school, Gibbs, had relocated one hundred miles out of London, but the boys had stayed at home with their father. Now that the school had reopened in London, the two boys revolted and demanded a vacation of their own in the countryside. Their minor rebellion made for an item in the newspapers but did not impress their parents, and the two sons returned to school as planned.

The protection of children in wartime was a concern Rose shared with other women in her circle. At a luncheon in mid-October, she heard from one of England's most prominent Anglo-American aristocrats, Irene Curzon, the first Baroness Ravensdale, about her experiences helping to move children out of London. Irene was miffed that some of the owners of the big estates outside London had been reluctant to open their gates and take in city youngsters. The baroness was one of three celebrated daughters of the first Marquess Curzon of Kedleston, a former viceroy of India, and his wealthy American wife. Casting aside her interest in pursuing married men, Irene was now devoted to charitable causes. Her new passion for service signaled a shift in the focus of high society; partying would become secondary to serving the public welfare.

JOE VIGOROUSLY CONTINUED to explore every possible opportunity to ameliorate relations with Germany. When John Clarence Cudahy, the U.S. minister to the Irish Free State, and his wife came over for supper in mid-October, Joe told them how much he wanted to go to Berlin to help reconcile Germany with Britain and the United States, but Cudahy cautioned Kennedy that Roosevelt would not want him interfering. As usual, Joe resisted this kind of constraint. As Rose explained in an understated way in her diary, "At times Joe becomes restless and chafes at restraint necessarily surrounding his position."

Kennedy recognized he had a singular opportunity to promulgate his particular vision of peace in his upcoming speech at the British Navy League's annual Trafalgar Day dinner on October 19, only three weeks after Munich. As the first foreigner ever to be chosen to deliver the annual speech, he had received a unique tribute, one that reflected the new ambassador's expertise on naval and maritime issues and his popularity in a country increasingly eager to court America.

If the Pilgrims Club speech in March marked Kennedy's emergence as a blunt and powerful proponent of America's independence from Britain, this Trafalgar Day speech, only six months later, was intended to signal his own pragmatic alignment with Chamberlain's policies as the best strategy for maintaining peace. For all his staunch advocacy of American isolationism, Kennedy would now emerge as an interventionist in British politics, inserting himself into the middle of the still roiling debate over Britain's policy toward aggressive fascism. His speech would prove more combustible than he could have imagined, occurring as it did between the Munich agreement and Kristallnacht that November, when Nazi violence against Jews became shatteringly evident to the whole world.

Preparing, Joe asked Rose, who had a finely honed sense of social and political diplomacy, to give him feedback before sending the speech on to the State Department for approval. Following her advice, he set up the speech as a dialogue between the ambassador who tossed out provocative themes and Rose herself, who told him why it would be a mistake to discuss such controversial or easily misunderstood topics. (Diplomatically facilitating her husband's efforts, Rose gave evidence of how she might have made an interesting ambassador.) Dialogue or not, the speech still sounded incendiary themes, and Joe's beliefs were plain to anyone who looked for them. But because Joe had made clear that his controversial comments were "a pet theory of my own," Jay Pierrepont Moffat, the chief of the State Department's European Division, saw no major problem with the speech, and forwarded it to Secretary of State Hull and Undersecretary of State Sumner Welles without sounding any alarms. Welles was preoccupied by a negotiation with Mexico and distractedly signed off on the speech. Assuming that Welles or Moffat would alert him if there were a problem, Hull assented as well. According to Kennedy's memoir, Hull cabled him, "I think you have been successful in avoiding many pitfalls." Their acquiescence to the maverick ambassador's key speech would have major international ramifications and would diminish Kennedy's reputation and influence in Britain. But it is possible that Hull, Welles, and Moffat knew exactly what they were doing—deliberately allowing Kennedy to suffer a maelstrom of criticism that would undercut his effectiveness.

That night, in a room full of politicians and navy officers, some of whom had fought in World War I, Joe declared of Chamberlain, "He was forced to make one of the gravest decisions of our time. It is not for me to comment on his decision—history will show whether or not he made the right decision. . . . But . . . his all but superhuman efforts in behalf of peace should command the respect of all." He told the crowd how Rose had objected to his judgment of the prime minister. "'Have you thought about how this would sound back home?'" he quoted her as saying. "'You know, dear, our ambassadors are supposed to lose all powers of resistance when they get to London and only see things through English eyes.'"

Praising Chamberlain for making a difficult decision might not have been so provocative in itself, but Kennedy went on to make a personal pitch for peaceful coexistence with the dictatorships. In doing so, he dove headfirst into a ferocious U.S. foreign policy debate between the values of idealism and the demands of pragmatism. In the international misgivings already arising after Munich, both world opinion and American foreign policy were shifting from Kennedy's live-and-let-live strategy to Wilsonian moralism. Even as he quoted Rose's caution that "if you want to talk about that idea in any useful way . . . you will find yourself discussing issues which a diplomat should not raise," he uttered these incendiary thoughts: "It has long been a theory of mine that it is unproductive for both the democratic and the dictator countries to widen the division now existing between them by emphasizing their differences, which are now self-apparent. Instead of hammering away at what are regarded as irreconcilables," he told the audience, they can solve "their common problems by an attempt to re-establish good relations on a world basis.

"It is true that the democratic and dictator countries have important and fundamental divergences of outlook, which in certain matters go deeper than politics. But there is simply no sense, common or otherwise, in letting these differences grow into unrelenting antagonisms. After all, we have to live together in the same world, whether we like it or not."

Kennedy would hold fast to these ideas and expound on them, even in the face of fierce criticism. Several weeks later, in a letter to T. J. White, the general manager of Hearst Enterprises, Kennedy wrote that the democracies should stay consistently on the sidelines rather than "one minute kicking the dictators' heads off and the next suggesting that they cooperate along certain lines." When you were doing business with nations, he believed, you should either stay away from them altogether or "if you are going to stick your tongue out at them or slap them on the wrist, you had better be prepared to punch them in the jaw." Kennedy was buttressed in these beliefs by his conviction—one he shared with many of Chamberlain's military advisors—that Britain and France did not have the military power to defeat the Nazis. And he saw no evidence that the United States military was prepared to ensure victory.

Kennedy also told White, "I have no more sympathy with Hitler's ideas than anyone in America . . . [and] I don't know whether trying to get along with him [Hitler] is going to bring good results or not," but he declared "my heart is almost broken watching us gradually lower ourselves into an abyss it will be very difficult to get out of." However, in his speech, Kennedy gave no expression to his profound and personal worries or his abhorrence of Hitler. If he had, he might have softened the international outrage he incited.

And outrage there was. While the British press gave respectful coverage to the speech, American newspapers howled in unison. The *New York Post* lambasted Kennedy for suggesting that the United States "make a friend of the man who boasts that he is out to destroy democracy, religion, and all of the other principles which free Americans hold dear . . . that passes understanding." Journalists, diplomats, and government officials besieged Hull and his deputies, demanding to know whether the administration's foreign policy had changed. Immediately, FDR and the State Department hung the ambassador out to dry. Roosevelt rebuked Hitler and admonished Kennedy in a radio speech. "Peace by fear has no higher or more enduring quality than peace by the sword," he declared. "There can be no peace if national policy adopts as a deliberate instrument the threat of war." Kennedy felt stabbed in the back, and rightfully so.

America's columnists took dead aim at him. Walter Lippmann, in his influential "Today and Tomorrow" column in the *New York Herald Tribune*, chastised the ambassador for failing to use proper diplomatic discretion in airing his personal views in a public forum. "Amateur and temporary diplomats take their speeches very seriously. Ambassadors of this type soon tend to become each a little state department with a little foreign policy of their own," he wrote.

However, it was fellow Harvard graduate and newspaper columnist Heywood Broun's attack in the *New York World Telegram* that particularly got under Kennedy's thin skin: "It must be that the British have some secret drug which they slip into the tea of visiting celebrities. And in the case of our Ambassadors they give them double dosage . . . The craving to serve his country and defend democracy leaves him almost overnight . . . A group of distinguished Americans should board the boat and drop him in the harbor to rest awhile amid the alien tea. He needs the hair of the dog."

In his diplomatic memoir, Kennedy was forthright about how the criticism stung him. He was "hardly prepared, despite years in public office, for the viciousness of this onslaught." Kennedy vented his rage to U.S. senator James Byrnes: "I am so god-damned mad I can't see. Of all the insidious lying I have ever read in my life I have read in these columns in the last two weeks." Kennedy would come to believe that Jewish elements—in his view, the Jewish influence in Washington newspapers—were the cause. Early in his life WASP prejudice against Irish-Catholics had damaged his self-view, and now he would invert that to suggest that another ethnic group was out to ruin him.

These angry columns and newspaper editorials stoked blistering indignation among the American public. Kennedy received many sharply written rebukes from ordinary American citizens. Among the many letters found in folders marked "Trafalgar Day Speech" at the John F. Kennedy Library in Boston, several cried shame: "It is unbelievable the way you have misrepresented your country, and forsaken your country . . . by suggesting that the United States of America should submit itself to Nazism! Shame, Shame, Shame! . . . Go deep within yourself and think, think, think! your way back! We wonder what it is that begets our diplomats over there. Is it fear, flattery, or is it the Boston Irish going grand in St. James Court! We wonder!"

To Miss Margaret Wolffen, who had succinctly written, "Shame on you! Shame on you!" Kennedy summoned a conciliatory tone, replying, "We are all striving for the same things—peace, prosperity, and an opportunity to live decent lives in a free country." Joe was deeply disturbed by how roundly Jewish Americans thrashed him. He wrote T. J. White that "75% of the attacks on me by mail were by Jews and, yet, I don't suppose anybody has worked as hard for them as I have or more to their advantage."

Joe Kennedy's attitudes toward Jews are extremely complex, and any attempts to elucidate them are confounded by his diligent efforts to project a favorable political image and to use his memoirs to erase any stains on his ambassadorial tenure. Raised as an Irish-Catholic in Boston, he was exposed to the common Irish-Catholic prejudice of the time against the Jews, a more recently arrived ethnic group who competed with them for an economic and social place in America. Even though Joe staunchly maintained that he reacted only to criticisms from individual Jews and had no categorical prejudice against Jews, there did exist a strand of anti-Semitism in him. It tended to surface when he felt criticized, misunderstood, or threatened—as he was when he feared that Jews in America and Europe would urge America into a war it would lose. Reflecting on her grandfather's years as ambassador, Amanda Smith noted, "The belief that he was under attack in influential Jewish circles for his reported anti-Semitism, indifference to the refugee issue and support of appeasement seems to have prompted him, curiously, to record his views on Judaism and on some of his Jewish colleagues far more explicitly and pejoratively than he had ever done before."

Yet Page Huidekoper recalls that Joe "was appalled that there was no Jew in the embassy." Alan Steyne, an expert on economics, was Jewish, but he worked on the consular side. Joe insisted that Alan be made a Foreign Service officer on the diplomatic side. George Bilainkin noted in his diplomatic memoir that senior officials were very upset when Joe demanded that Alan's name be included on a list of diplomatic officers to be presented to the king. "Steyne, provided with suitable regalia," Bilainkin wrote, "thus broke through the ranks, broke through traditions and all strict precedent for a bow to Britain's monarch."

At times Joe took strong stands against anti-Semitism. For instance, he became incensed when Cape Cod's Wianno golf club rejected Kennedy's proposal of Henry Morgenthau, Jr., as a guest member for the summer in the 1930s. Twenty years later, Joe would say, "I haven't been in the place since." While Joe's occasional anti-Semitic comments (documented in his letters) are understandable given his background and the prejudiced attitudes pervasive in America at that time, and while there is no solid evidence that he was any more anti-Semitic than many other leaders of his era, some of his comments are still disturbing.

Amid the calumny following his Trafalgar Day speech, Joe's two oldest sons loyally backed him up. Joe Jr., a great admirer of Germany, had been traveling through Eastern Europe when the controversy over the speech erupted. He fired off to his father a memorandum challenging Walter Lippmann's condemnation, calling it the "natural Jewish reaction." To counter claims that an ambassador could be "taken in" by his host country, he sarcastically suggested that the United States "recall all our ambassadors and rely for information on the daily press." He praised his father's courage in espousing views that might not be popular at home, and suggested that the natural result of Lippmann's stand against ambassadorial outspokenness would be to substitute ambassadors with "third rate clerks." Although it would be "hard for the Jewish community in the U.S. to stomach," getting along with the dictators would offer them the best results, he declared.

Jack, who could be as dispassionate as his brother was vociferous, also wrote to soothe his father. "While it seems to be unpopular with the Jews, etc . . . [it] was considered to be very good by everyone who wasn't bitterly anti-fascist." Like his brother, Jack had yet to understand why the Jews were desperately vehement about confronting Nazism.

J ACK'S SUMMER IN EUROPE had jump-started his emotional and intellectual maturation. That fall of 1938, entering his junior year at Harvard, he began to exhibit the scholarly self-discipline and intellectual rigor that would characterize his maturity. He also deepened his interests in government and foreign policy. Even as he took six courses—in order to take the spring semester off for a return trip to Europe—he would raise his grades from Cs to Bs that fall semester. In a bold move that would lead him to establish his own analysis of recent events, Jack decided to use his senior thesis to explore how the British policy of appeasement during the 1930s had led to Munich.

Harvard's Russian specialist Bruce Hopper, a charismatic scholar who was advising Jack, introduced him to British historian John Wheeler-Bennett, who would later be the official biographer of King George VI and who became Jack's intellectual mentor. Wheeler-Bennett, an expert on Germany, was beginning a book on Munich. Recognizing Jack's talents, he made special trips to Harvard from the University of Virginia, where he was a guest lecturer, to tutor the young man on what he called "the imponderables of the human spirit," and to debate ideas about the balancing of power with upholding honor in foreign relations that challenged his father's rigid beliefs. Jack thrived on the contradictions.

Jack was thriving physically as well. Dr. Sara Jordan, who was the head of gastroenterology at Boston's Lahey Clinic, wrote Joe in early November with the encouraging news that Jack "is looking better than I have ever seen him look, and having relatively little difficulty." Although it is not commonly mentioned by historians, the fact that Joe and Jack both had stomach problems led Joe to have a unique and vulnerable bond with his second son. Revealingly, he wrote her back: "I worry a good deal more about him than I do about international affairs or anything else, so your letter came as especially good news . . . while we haven't got to the point where everything is quiet, we are hoping it will be very soon." But there would be no relief.

In mid-November, public opinion hardened against Joe Kennedy and Neville Chamberlain's peace efforts after Hitler launched "a series of hideous Jewish persecutions, confiscation of Jewish businesses and the imposition of a fine of one billion marks upon the Jewish community," as the ambassador described it in his memoir. On the night of November 9, gangs of Nazi youth rampaged through Jewish neighborhoods, attacking and killing Jews, smashing windows in their homes and businesses, stealing property, and burning their synagogues. This pogrom became known as "Kristallnacht." Within days of Kristallnacht, Hitler talked to his top leaders about his "Final Solution" to the Jewish problem, and over eighty thousand Jews fled Germany, seeking refuge in countries across the globe.

Newspaper photographs of the destruction of Jewish stores stoked unprecedented worldwide outrage. In the face of this terrible setback to his efforts at reconciliation with the Nazis, Joe tried to maintain hope. He wrote to Charles Lindbergh on November 12, "[T]his last drive on the Jews in Germany has really made the most ardent hopers for peace very sick at heart . . . It is more and more difficult for those seeking peaceful solutions to advocate any plan where the papers are filled with such horror. So much is lost when so much could be gained."

Joe worried that Jewish outrage over Kristallnacht would precipitate the catastrophe of world war but was horrified by the attacks on the Jews. Regrettably, he did not make his reaction public. He was already in plenty of trouble with the White House for speaking out of turn, and he shared Chamberlain's concern that criticism of Nazi mistreatment of the Jews would only lead to increased persecution of them. When Joe arrived back in the United States in December, he would tell reporters that the anti-Jewish campaign was the "most terrible thing he had ever heard of." He added, "I'll probably lose my job for saying that, but let it stand . . . Oh, how I would like to say a lot more."

Later, in his diplomatic memoir, Joe made partial amends for his unwillingness to express greater moral outrage at the time. He declared that the few Jewish publishers and writers—here he was thinking of columnists such as Heywood Broun and Walter Lippmann—who had wanted war "should not be criticized for their objective. After all, the lives and futures of their compatriots were being destroyed by Hitler. Compromise could hardly cure that situation; only the destruction of Nazism could do so." He did note, however, that the "tactics of this group may some day be analyzed. Some of them in their zeal did not hesitate to resort to slander and falsehood to achieve their aims . . . I received my share of it."

At a November 15 press conference, Franklin Roosevelt delivered a statement expressing shock at the Nazi rampage, saying that "I myself could scarcely believe that such things could occur in a twentieth century civilization." The United States and Germany each recalled its ambassador; they would not return until after the war. When he was asked directly if he would relax immigration restrictions for Jewish refugees, the president said that a change in the quota system was "not in contemplation." He remained unwilling to buck American resistance to increased immigration. Public opinion polls were showing that 94 percent of American citizens disapproved of the Nazi treatment of Jews, but 72 percent of them did not want to increase immigration quotas for Jewish exiles.

ON NOVEMBER 8, Joe and Rose attended the opening of Parliament and heard the king's announcement that he and the queen would be making a goodwill visit to the United States the following June. This was bittersweet news for the Kennedys, who had been major proponents of the benefits of such a trip, but who were not included in the plans and had to hear the news when everyone else did. The president was conducting the negotiations for the June 1939 royal visit through British ambassador Sir Ronald Lindsay in Washington, D.C. Joe felt humiliated. He worried, not without cause, that Roosevelt's circumvention of him signaled a loss of faith in him. "If the president wanted me to be aware of any discussions he is having I suppose he would inform me," he wrote Cordell Hull with undisguised resentment. "Because I imagine my contacts and prestige here would be seriously jeopardized, I hate to admit knowing nothing about it. Although it is difficult, I can continue to look like a dummy and carry on the best I can."

On November 15, Joe accompanied Rose, decked out in "diamond tiara, diamond ruby necklace, and diamond ruby bracelets," to the grand royal event of the fall season—the king and queen's Buckingham Palace reception for their cousins King Carol of Romania and his son Prince Michael. This royal visit was an important one, allowing the British government to explore the effect of the recent Czech crisis on the security of southeastern Europe. For the occasion Rose had ordered a white satin dress worn with a crinoline underneath, which "made it very full and glamorous." She was "the only one, except [the] Queen to wear a crinoline under my dress," she wrote in her diary, and she was disappointed that the newspapers did not comment on her distinctive outfit, but recognized that "the Queen was to stand alone in launching that style." The next day, however, she had herself photographed in the same dress before heading off to Paris to shop for an even more eye-popping ensemble.

During the reception, Queen Elizabeth laughingly said to Joe that she knew only three Americans, "You, Freddy Astaire and J. P. Morgan," but that she wanted to know more. She told Rose how much she would like to see America "as just a simple visitor without people suspecting she was going there with the intention of forming a political alliance. . . ." When Joe conversed with the king, the monarch fretted over a recent Walter Lippmann article suggesting that the royal couple should not visit America. He worried that American isolationists would thwart his goal of forming an alliance with Roosevelt. According to his diary, Joe cornered Chamberlain to discuss the Jewish refugee situation. The prime minister told him that he was taking seriously his requests to speed up the immigration process for German Jews seeking entrance into Britain and would act to "ease the public conscience."

As Rose noted with pride in her diary, the next day Kick and Rosemary were the only young people among six hundred guests invited to a reception in the Picture Gallery and the Bow Salon in Buckingham Palace for King Carol and his son. Kick noted in her diary that she found King Carol to be "rather fat but very gallant." The Duke of Kent pressed her to talk with young Prince Michael ("For God's sake say something"), who was "good looking with nice dimples." Secretary of War Leslie Hore-Belisha teased Kick that he was going to announce her engagement to the Romanian prince, which no one took seriously because Kick had become ever more publicly enamored of Billy Hartington that fall. As Kennedy presented his two daughters to Queen Mary, they looked entranced, thought Chips Channon.

Secretary of State Cordell Hull was committed to the idealistic vision that economic cooperation could eradicate the root causes of political conflict. Joe Kennedy had arrived in London advocating Hull's optimistic conviction that peace could be gained through economic adjustments and trade pacts and determined to make the yearlong trade negotiations evidence of that belief. Taking into account Britain's dominions and the colonies, the two countries accounted for about 40 percent of the world's trade. The British cabinet had resolved not to make any significant concessions to a trading partner who exported twice the amount of goods to Britain that England sent to the United States. Since he had arrived in London, Joe had been the key salesman for freer trade between the two nations. He stressed the positive political and social impact of an Anglo-American trade pact and sold Chamberlain on the idea that the more the United States and Britain were seen to be working together, the less they would have to spend on armaments; increasing trade would itself prove disarming to their enemies.

Now Kennedy was sidelined. Despite his expertise in business negotiations and his concerted efforts to bond with key British cabinet ministers,

Hull dominated the negotiations, held in Washington, as they approached resolution that November. Kennedy was allowed to handle only the part of the trade agreement related to the movie industry. He complained in his memoir that "no attempt was made to keep us conversant with even the broadest details."

After the Anglo-American Trade Agreement was finally signed in Washington, D.C., on November 16, Joe embraced it as if he had negotiated it himself. With characteristic exaggeration, he called the agreement "one of the greatest contributions to world stability ever made. . . . This is the sort of thing that really counts in preserving the peace of the world." However, he acknowledged, "No one will contend that the liberalization of trade is a panacea for the ills of the world."

CHAPTER 9

Praying for Peace

A FTER THE TRADE AGREEMENT WAS FINISHED, largely without him, Kennedy turned his attention to a cause where he felt an ambassador could make a difference: the resettlement of the German Jews. There were an estimated 330,000 Jews in Germany and Austria that would need new homes.

George Rublee, FDR's appointee as head of the Intergovernmental Committee on Refugees, had been frustrated by the worldwide reluctance to offer refuge to German Jews, even as nations everywhere professed concern for their welfare. At Rublee's insistence, shortly after the Munich agreement, FDR asked Kennedy to push Chamberlain to intercede directly with Hitler. Chamberlain had been so absorbed and exhausted by the debate over Munich that Kennedy could only send him a note about the issue, and then mention it briefly as the weary prime minister prepared to vacation in Scotland.

American Jews were growing increasingly agitated about recent rumors that Britain would curtail their support for the Jewish refugees in a partitioned Palestine, which had been under a British mandate after World War I. One Joe Weingarten wrote Ambassador Kennedy on behalf of the Jews of Houston, Texas, expressing "how deeply grateful we are for your energetic sincere efforts in behalf of German refugees," but suggesting that the "real hope lies in the opening of Palestine to as many refugees as possible." Nathan Rosenstein cabled Kennedy asking him to "help avert threatened tragedy to destitute Jews by interceding in favor of a homeland in Palestine." I. Instone Bloomfield suggested a radical alternative: "a self-supporting, autonomous Jewish state in Alaska," while a Miss Cooper wrote of her plans for a settlement of refugees in lower California.

When a British commission declared that the partition of Palestine was not feasible, U.S. citizens flooded the State Department with letters and telegrams strenuously protesting the possible curtailment of Jewish immigration to Palestine. The State Department asked Kennedy to address this complex and incendiary problem. The U.S. government could not appear to be interfering with British policy making, so Joe spoke privately to Alexander Cadogan, the permanent undersecretary of state, and Malcolm MacDonald, secretary of state for the colonies. They agreed to act in consultation with U.S. officials, but little progress was made. Joe grew impatient. "If political and personal considerations could be gotten out of the way," he wrote in his memoir, "if the plight of the Jews would only not continue to be subordinated, particularly in American Jewish circles, to the destiny of Palestine, progress could be made with rapidity provided that funds could be supplied."

He also pressed British officials to find a solution. Dining with Rose and Joe Jr. at MacDonald's country estate on November 13, Joe queried his host about why England, where there was much talk about the Jewish refugees, did not show more interest in finding space somewhere in the Empire for the German Jews to live. Once Britain had allocated land for the refugees, Joe felt that the "problem of financing the emigration of Jews to that area could be put as a challenge before those persons of Jewish and non-Jewish extraction who felt sufficiently touched in their pocketbooks as well as in spirit" to help raise a fund of $50 million to $100 million. Kennedy told Hull he had said to MacDonald "that it looked to me like everyone was feeling sorry for the Jews, but that nobody was offering any solution." According to Rose, Joe thought "countries like Australia" might be likely havens for Jewish refugees, and "some concrete thing should be attempted instead of everyone deploring the conditions but nothing definite volunteered." At around this time, the State Department began investigating the possibility of getting Britain to cede British Guiana to the United States so it could be used as a home for German Jews fleeing Nazi persecution, but nothing would come of the idea.

Kennedy also paid a call on the prime minister to discuss the issue, writing years later that "I was both disturbed and indignant over the situation." (He did not record such feelings at the time.) Responding at least in part to U.S. pressure applied by Kennedy, Chamberlain announced that resettlement of the persecuted German Jews would be necessary to preserve peace in the world. He made no specific proposals, however. On November 15 the *New York Times*, probably encouraged by Kennedy's public relations team, reported that the U.S. ambassador "talked earnestly of the need for action by Britain and all nations of the British Commonwealth." According to the *Times*, Kennedy, Chamberlain, MacDonald, and Halifax met to work out a resettlement plan, which the press called the "Kennedy Plan," for moving large numbers of Jews from Germany to less populated areas in North and South America and Africa.

Did the Kennedy Plan ever really exist? In her exhaustive study of her grandfather's papers, biographer Amanda Smith could not find any verification of the plan. "Among the extensive collection of papers, clippings, memorabilia that he took home from London, curiously little information would survive about his plan or its proposed implementation," she has said. Smith hoped that the diary of Malcolm MacDonald would cast light on this plan, but found instead that during this crucial period it dealt "exclusively with the subject of bird-watching." I was not able to find any evidence of the plan in the papers of the American Zionist leader Stephen Wise, nor in those of Chaim Weizmann (president of the World Zionist Organizaton) at the Yad Vashem memorial to Holocaust survivors in Jerusalem. No one at the Simon Wiesenthal Center in Los Angeles nor at the Association of Jewish Refugees in London was able to provide any viable leads. It remains unknown whether Kennedy ever presented a formal plan or if he used the press to pressure the British to accede to such a plan.

FDR had asked Kennedy to intercede with the British government to advocate Jewish resettlement within the Empire, but when the State Department and the president read about his efforts in the newspapers without hearing from him for several days, they grew uneasy. The State Department sent a wire asking for clarification. Joe cabled back that "[i]f any contribution has been made by me," it is that "I urged speed to get someplace." Joe pointed out that he had been pushing the British government for the last four months. With barely concealed irritation, he added, "If I had any news . . . which I thought would be of interest to you, you would have had it as you always do from me."

At the end of November, the *New York Times* crowed about the "Kennedy Plan" in an editorial, "What Mr. Kennedy has managed to do is the talk of diplomatic circles in London at the moment." Such public praise of his ambassador stoked FDR's suspicions that Kennedy was using the Jewish situation and a "Kennedy Plan" to win attention for a 1940 presidential run. Surely, Joe, furious about recent attacks on him, was interested in generating positive publicity for himself, but he was also a fixer who loved tackling a major world problem.

Rose claims in her autobiography that Joe worked tirelessly to forge an escape plan for the Jews: "For months he poured much of his energies into developing this plan, getting the permissions, transportation, facilities, trying to cut through the endless red tape and details" and trying to organize the millions of dollars needed for the plan. Rose also claimed that he "was active, behind the scenes, in helping many individual Jews escape." After the Nazi government allowed Jewish children to leave Germany in return for British and Dutch trade concessions, Joe worked feverishly to facilitate their departure. One hundred and ninety-six children were moved to Britain, some staying at makeshift Boy Scout camps and some housed at Lord Balfour's Scottish estate. Larger numbers of children were sent to France, Liberia, and the British and French colonies in Africa. The approximately fifteen hundred children saved at this time would be among the few who would escape Hitler. Most of their parents were not as fortunate.

In the Joseph Kennedy correspondence files at the Kennedy Library there is ample evidence of the pressures the ambassador, Eddie Moore, and the rest of the staff faced while helping Jewish refugees. Mr. Grover Loening asked for preferential status for Herbert Klotz and his Jewish wife, Gertrude, as they tried to get American immigration visas under the German quota. Even though Mr. Klotz's wealthy son had given money to help the victims of the *Athenia*, which was torpedoed by a German submarine, Moore explained that while they would do all they could to help, "favoritism was out of the question." Joe Kennedy was able to help Mr. and Mrs. Isaak Kaufmann and Mr. and Mrs. Meyer Kaufman, elderly citizens of Viernheim, Germany, get visas to enter Britain. Kennedy wrote Geoffrey Lloyd of the British Home Office to express his gratitude: "I never got such quick action out of any government department in my life."

Kennedy's Harvard classmate Arthur Goldsmith wrote frequently in 1939 and 1940 asking the ambassador to help expedite visas for his friends and acquaintances. In March 1939, Eddie Moore was extremely upset when a Miss Sophie Marie Egger arrived at the embassy with an introductory letter from Goldsmith and the expectation that the ambassador's staff could provide quick and effective action to rescue Mr. and Mrs. Ignaz Hirschl, who had been ordered by the police to leave Vienna within four days. Moore wrote Goldsmith that while he did everything he could to help, "he didn't like being put in that position" of being unable to assist a helpless woman who had been led to believe she could count on him.

ON NOVEMBER 21, in the House of Commons, Prime Minister Chamberlain announced that Nyassaland, Kenya, and Northern Rhodesia were willing to set up limited settlement areas for German Jews. Ten thousand miles of forests and savannahs could be developed in British Guiana, Chamberlain said, with fifty thousand more acres in Tanganyika. He stated, however, that he did not believe that Palestine could increase its current quota of refugees. Kennedy did not win accolades for the British change in policy. American Jews made him aware that they felt that the resettlement plan was "a political trick" of the British government, "timed to soften a blow" of restricting further Jewish immigration to Palestine.

As Joe well realized, one of the biggest issues of resettlement was money. Germany had confiscated huge sums from Jewish citizens, but resisted providing funds to assist Jews in repatriation. The U.S. State Department vetoed a plan to increase trade with Germany and use the additional German capital to finance the resettlement, fearing that it would lead to an increase in anti-Semitism. The best solution seemed to be to raise private funds. According to Joe Jr., the ambassador wondered "whether the righteous indignation aroused all over the world . . . will be backed up with cold cash."

IN THE AFTERMATH of his Trafalgar Square speech, the ambassador welcomed Joe Jr. back at Prince's Gate, glad for a sympathetic listener. Joe was returning after his stint working for Bullitt at the Paris embassy and his informational tour of key cities in continental Europe, Russia, and Scandinavia. In the mornings father and son rode horses on Rotten Row along Hyde Park, and on weekends they would take Teddy to sail his toy boat in the park's pool.

Kick continued to spend as much time as possible with Billy Hartington in spite of the unease it caused her staunchly Catholic mother and the virulently Protestant duke and duchess of Devonshire. The day before Thanksgiving, she dined with Billy at the popular Ciros club and then accompanied him to a coming-of-age party for his cousin Richard Cavendish. Kick was very much aware that she was under scrutiny, being coolly evaluated by her boyfriend's family. She noted in her diary, "All Billy's relatives [were] sitting around getting an eyeful." She then joined all the other Kennedys except Jack for their first Thanksgiving in London, with a traditional dinner at 2:00, followed by a family trip to the movies. A few weeks later, on December 9, Kick dined with the entire Devonshire family for Billy's twenty-first birthday, an encounter she found "rather frightening with the Dowager Duchess and Lord and Lady Harlech giving me dirty looks." She had, however, gained a foot up on the duke of Devonshire before Christmas when she and Billy ran into the duke, who was celebrating with his mistress Lady Dufferin at Ciros. The awkward encounter did not seem to fluster Billy or his father, nor the worldly Kick.

IN EARLY DECEMBER while Rose was confined to bed with the first bad cold of her life, Joe visited their daughters at the convent, reporting to his wife that Eunice was "going wild as it becomes nearer to the time for her to receive her Child of Mary's Medal" for her exemplary devotion. On December 8 at the convent, Rose and Joe watched Jean, Eunice, and Pat carrying white lilies in a procession for the Feast of the Immaculate Conception of Mary, which Rose thought was "always the most mystic, most beautiful, most inspiring ceremony" of the year at Sacred Heart. Joe, once an altar boy in Boston, was allowed by the Mother Superior to light the altar candles.

By contrast, in mid-December, Lady Redesdale and her daughter the Honorable Unity Mitford were busy eating plates of sausages at an Anglo-German friendship party in Bloomsbury. Published accounts suggested that Hitler was giving Miss Mitford a valuable camera for Christmas.

Before attending the convent ceremony, Joe had spoken at a dinner of the Plymouth Chamber of Commerce at the invitation of Lady Astor. Joe Jr. noted that Lady Astor "is hipped on the idea of Anglo-American cooperation and would like us to come into the war at the beginning to save lives." During her speech that night, he reported, "She pretended that Dad and she were only friends for the evening, that really the southerners had no use for the Yankees and it is only on conditions like these that the U.S. showed a united front. She ballyhooed the press, spoke indirectly about letting the Jews in, and really got away with wholesale murder."

Joe discussed the recently completed Anglo-American trade agreement, but then challenged those who would call him defeatist (accepting or expecting defeat), saying, according to the *Times*, that "he was inclined to believe that we are making things worse for ourselves by adopting a defeatist attitude." Kennedy asserted, "I am one of those who dare to hope we shall be able to solve the difficulties of the present."

A few days before he was to depart for a two-month trip to the United States, Joe wrote to Charles Lindbergh, "I don't know just what England can do to satisfy Hitler. If ever a man was willing to work out a deal, it was Chamberlain, but I do not doubt that he is rather despondent about the outlook now." Since the Munich agreement, British hopefulness for peace had faded, thanks to the increased belligerence of the dictators and the lack of any tangible fruits of appeasement. Chamberlain had bitterly attacked Winston Churchill's "lack of judgment" in the House of Commons, provoking Churchill to retaliate with an overall condemnation of Chamberlain's judgment in foreign affairs. When Joe paid his final call on Chamberlain before leaving, he found him depressed over Germany and Italy's persistent belligerence. The prime minister told Kennedy that his secret sources were suggesting that Germany would attack England soon, adding, "If I believed all that the secret service told us, I would never be able to sleep at night." Although he was not optimistic it would work, Chamberlain told Kennedy he was going to make one final bid to persuade Germany to act in "a rational manner" in European affairs.

Chamberlain entreated Kennedy to seek support in Washington to "firm up our attitude in the Far East," where Britain needed help in providing financial relief for General Chiang Kai-shek, whose Chinese Nationalist forces were "in severe straits" and on the verge of having to "come to terms" with Japan or even Russia.

Joe boarded the *Queen Mary* on December 10, exhausted from a year of intense work, frustrated with the constraints inherent in diplomacy, and infuriated by the attacks on him. Before he left, he vented to Joe Jr., setting himself up as a self-sacrificing parent, complaining once again about Jewish journalists, and chafing—with considerable justification—about his treatment in Washington and in the media. His son recorded Joe's reactions in a memorandum:

> Dad . . . claims that he would give it [the ambassadorship] up in a minute if it wasn't for the benefits that Jack and I are getting out of it and the things Eunice will get when she comes out next Spring. He doesn't like the idea of taking orders and working for hours trying to keep things out of his speeches which an ambassador shouldn't say. He also doesn't like the idea of sitting back and letting the Jewish columnists in America kick his head off. The papers have made up a pile of lies about him . . . he claims that he is going to let off a few blasts when he gets back there in a couple of days.

Bobby missed his dad so much that he wrote to him the day after Joe's departure, "I hope the waves aren't as big as in the Popeye short we saw the other night."

Before leaving Liverpool for his trip home, Joe told reporters, "I am going home to face the president and tell him what I think—and what I think won't please him." He also made clear that he was going home to "do some thinking about America."

According to Joe's memoir, he was preoccupied during his voyage home with thinking about the Jewish refugee problem and the need for improved Anglo-American policy coordination regarding the Far East. He fretted about the American perception that Chamberlain was "a weak and easily deluded man, even sympathetic to Nazi ideals," and the assumption that England and France were militarily stronger than Germany despite Charles Lindbergh's observations about the powerful German air force.

Arriving in New York, Kennedy admitted to the press that "nothing has been accomplished in the way of appeasement. But we must keep trying for peace or we shall have only two alternatives . . . economic chaos, and second-war." He made clear his position: "I am pro-peace, I pray, hope, and work for peace." He then went straight to the White House to report to FDR.

Kennedy presented the president with a memorandum that, more than he had ever done before, laid out his vision of impending calamity and how to avoid it. He offered a far-reaching strategic analysis of what war between Britain and Germany would mean, predicting Britain's defeat and detailing how the collapse of the British Empire would affect the United States. There were, in his view, two unpalatable options: an America "ringed with totalitarian enemies," or a United States that fought alongside Britain and ultimately would have to assume the "responsibility of running the world," insisting that it be made "safe for democracy." If the world were to be divided into totalitarian and democratic spheres, then the United States would have to rearm to keep that balance of power. "Live and let live was [the] key, and not a Pax Britannica or a Pax Americana for which too many would have to die." Adamant about the menace of Nazism, FDR would toss aside his ambassador's analysis.

Appeasement had failed to appease, Kennedy believed. It was probable that war would break out in the spring. With Hitler promising to be more bellicose than ever, Kennedy was adamant that America be able to protect herself without going to fight in Europe. To that end, he agreed with the president that it was crucial to revise the Neutrality Act so that the United States would be freer to provide arms and support to Britain and France, which could serve as a bulwark against the dictators.

After FDR reassured him that he indeed wanted to keep him at his post in London, Joe headed to Florida for a vacation, the latest instance of what biographer Amanda Smith calls a pattern Kennedy employed: He "had seemed to thrive upon the cycle that he had repeated throughout middle age: intense, relatively short-term round-the-clock focus and activity followed by period of recuperation in Palm Beach or Hyannis Port." Jack flew down from Boston to join him for the Christmas holidays.

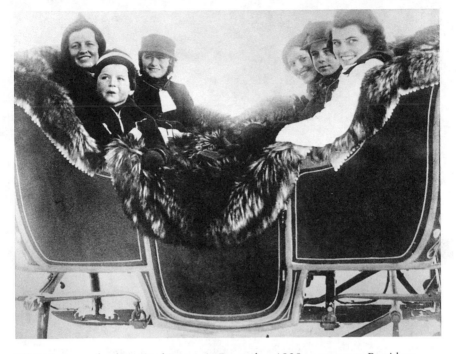

While Joe went back to Washington in December 1938 to report to President Roosevelt on his first year in London and to celebrate the Christmas holidays with Jack, Rose took the rest of the children to St. Moritz, Switzerland, a ski resort featuring "sleighs filled with fur rugs looking cozy and luxurious with the tassels bobbing on the horse's heads," she wrote in her diary. (*JFK Library Foundation*)

Ensconced at his North Ocean Boulevard home in Palm Beach, Joe reacquainted himself with American public opinion firsthand. One of his Palm Beach neighbors, Colonel Robert Rutherford McCormick, was the editor and publisher of the strongly Republican *Chicago Tribune*. Its slogan "The American Paper for Americans," the *Tribune* was rabidly isolationist and heavily biased against the British, the French, and FDR's New Deal programs. Not the most objective observer, McCormack reassured Kennedy that the American people still staunchly favored isolationism.

Kennedy invited columnists Walter Winchell, Boake Carter, and Arthur Krock to Palm Beach to discuss the nation's mood and political outlook. He also gave Winchell a scoop, telling him he had submitted Charles Lindbergh's reports on the strength of the German air force to Chamberlain and others in the British government, and that this had influenced their readiness to appease Hitler at Munich. Joe had no idea that his role in disseminating Lindbergh's views would soon be cited as evidence of his

Kennedy children (left to right) Patricia, Eunice, Robert, Joe, and Rosemary taking skiing lessons. The Kennedy boys all injured themselves. Bobby sprained his ankle, Teddy wrenched his knee, and Joe Jr. fell and broke his arm. (*JFK Library Foundation*)

poor judgment, nor that historians would judge him harshly for helping to undermine Britain.

In London, Rose represented her husband at a farewell luncheon at Claridges for Jan Masaryk, who had resigned as the Czech ambassador to Britain after his country had been partitioned and overrun by Germany. Rose's busy holiday schedule included a visit to Cliveden and a dance at the home of the former Netherlands minister to Great Britain, where her dinner partner was the fourth Lord Fermoy, who would become the grandfather of Diana, Princess of Wales.

Rose and eight of her children arrived in St. Moritz on Christmas Eve for their winter break. The ski resort featured "sleighs filled with fur rugs looking cozy and luxurious with the tassels bobbing on the horse's heads," she wrote in her diary, "and the skiers gliding skillfully in and out between the hotel buses, the sleighs." The family exchanged a few presents and then went to a midnight mass and communion at a church overlooking a skating rink.

On Christmas Day, Joe and Jack called from Palm Beach. The next day the children wrote to their father. "We had a grand Christmas . . . Everything is beautiful," Rosemary wrote. "I hope mother is getting a rest. I will try not to worried [sic] her." Pat explained that Rosemary was working with a private ski instructor and "is getting along quite well." Eunice detailed to her father Joe Jr.'s efforts to find a girl—"He had gone to almost every hotel in St. Moritz"—and wrote that "it really would have been perfect if you and Jack had been here." Rose was pleased with Teddy's physical dexterity, writing Joe that he was "a riot on skies and skates . . . and a better kid never lived," and that "If you want a partner to go around the world on a two-wheeled bike with, he's the baby . . . I could tell you a million stories about him."

With typical recklessness, the Kennedy boys all injured themselves. Bobby sprained his ankle and six-year-old Teddy wrenched his knee on the beginner's slope. During a long skiing hike, Joe Jr. fell, lacerating and breaking his arm. Setting an example for his brothers, he shook off the pain, used his scarf as a tourniquet, and skied back to the hotel from the slopes. He called the family's longtime governess, Louella Hennessy, and asked her for a Band-Aid. When she got a look at his arm, she immediately called in the family fixer, Eddie Moore, who got Joe Jr. sent by sleigh to the nearest hospital, three hours distant. Once his arm was set, he told Louella, "Look at this. It sure looks awful doesn't it?" Soon he was photographed, with his arm in a sling, skating tenaciously with Megan Taylor, the attractive, eighteen-year-old world figure-skating champion. Looking for ways to capitalize on the Kennedys' escalating celebrity, the newspapers reported that Megan and Joe Jr. were engaged. The press also paid Rose a special honor. On December 28, Joe sent her a congratulatory telegram:

ASSOCIATED PRESS TODAY PICKED YOU AS OUTSTANDING WOMAN OF THE YEAR FOR SELLING THE WORLD THE AMERICAN FAMILY JACK AND I ARE BASKING IN YOUR REFLECTED GLORY HE HAS GAINED FIVE POUNDS MY LOVE TO ALL—JOE

Having advanced the cause of the Kennedy family over the last year, Rose wrote President Roosevelt to thank him for "all the interesting and stimulating experiences which we had enjoyed during 1938. We appreciate the fact that it had all been made possible through the honor which you had conferred upon Joe."

Joe could take solace in evidence that over the past year his dynasty's story had become part of current American cultural lore. Cole Porter's hit new musical *Leave It to Me*, starring Sophie Tucker and featuring the celebrated debut of Mary Martin, got its biggest laughs from jokes about the

Kennedys. The show, which would run from November 1938 until July 1939, told the story of a naïve and dyspeptic Mr. Alonzo Goodhue, a U.S. businessman with remarkable similarities to one Joseph P. Kennedy. He was awarded the ambassadorship to Russia after his social-climbing wife made significant donations to FDR's reelection campaign. Upon hearing that her husband had been given the job in Moscow, Goodhue's wife says, "If only those sneaky Kennedys hadn't grabbed London first." Later she asks her husband why they don't have nine children the way the Kennedys do. "Because I am tired!" the ambassador replies. The audience roared. During festivities celebrating the ambassador in Red Square, Mrs. Goodhue is so pleased that she exclaims, "I bet the Kennedys are boiling!" Another big laugh.

The musical, for all its froth, carried a warning: Ambassador Goodhue is recalled home when he gives a speech insisting that countries get along with each other.

Jack was already aware of the peril that came with his family's new fame. After attending the opening night in New York, he wrote to his mother in St. Moritz, "It's pretty funny and jokes about us get by far the biggest laughs, whatever that signifies."

On New Year's Eve, Rose, Joe Jr., Bobby, and Kick joined Kick's friend Charlotte McDonnell and her family for dinner and dancing. As the new year approached, the children sang along as the band played "Auld Lang Syne" and kissed their mother at midnight. Joe Jr., Kick, and Charlotte stayed up all night and then went to the small chapel below the hotel, where Joe served a 6 A.M. mass.

In England, the New Year inspired dread. MP Harold Nicolson made his final 1938 diary entry: "It has been a bad year. Chamberlain has destroyed the Balance of Power . . . A foul year. Next year will be worse."

1939

CHAPTER 10

A Jittery Winter

F EW YEARS have been so disliked in advance as 1939," wrote London's *Observer* on New Year's Day. The Kennedys were cosseted from the brunt of London's jitters, however. At St. Moritz, Rose Kennedy and her children began the year by attending a 10 A.M. mass before going skiing, while in Palm Beach, Joe Kennedy and his son Jack were lathered in cocoa butter and lounging at poolside, probably enjoying some female companionship.

Hitler made the year hateful from the start. In a decree published on the first day of the year, Jews were required to carry a police identity card. Already banned from attending entertainments such as concerts, movies, and theaters, they now were forbidden to drive or own cars. In a cynical New Year's message, Hitler asserted that Germany hoped to contribute to the maintenance of world peace, but it would also further build up its armed forces.

Joe listened very carefully on January 4, as Roosevelt responded to Hitler within his State of the Union message. In what became known as his "Methods Short of War" speech, FDR essayed to educate the American people about the escalating international danger and to direct their anger at the dictators: "There comes a time in the affairs of men when they must prepare to defend, not their homes alone, but the tenets of faith and humanity on which their churches, their governments and their very civilization are founded . . . This generation will 'nobly save or meanly lose the last best hope of earth.'" In Joe's view, FDR's ringing words seemed like the first clarion call of war.

Ten days later in Washington, Kennedy and William Bullitt testified, at

FDR's behest, before a secret joint meeting of the House and Senate Foreign Affairs committees. Kennedy described the European situation as "gloomy" and "dismal," and both ambassadors asserted that the German military's strength was superior to the combined forces of Britain and France. After his testimony, Kick wrote her father with the ominous news that the British were carefully monitoring the statements he made in America, and they were frustrated with him: "People feel you rather let them down over here & caused a great deal of unnecessary jitters in America by your statement about 'war is inevitable' even though it was denied." Kennedy had made his pessimistic comments during a visit to Roosevelt in Washington.

Isolationists such as North Dakota senator Gerald P. Nye suspected that FDR was using Kennedy's and Bullitt's alarmist testimony to buttress an effort to surmount the nation's economic difficulties by expanding his armaments program. Roosevelt was indeed secretly preparing for war, but he was cleverly repositioning the issue of rearmament as a means to create a protective shield for isolationist America.

I N MID-JANUARY, Rose and the children returned to London from Switzerland. That same night Kick rushed off to dinner with Billy. "The weather is awful, rain and fog," Pat wrote her father, "and everybody is sniffling all over the place." For Rose, settling back in London where "it is rainy—dull and bleak" was "a come down," she wrote Joe, "so stay there [in Florida] as long as you can—darling." Rose managed the miserable weather by buying antiquarian books and by attending lectures on painting and furniture at the Wallace Collection and the Tate Gallery. "Mother runs to two or three art lectures a day," Kick warned her father, "so it won't be long before Papa will be paying for every picture in Christies."

Kick also reported that "Joe is teaching us all to play bridge which is quite a struggle." During a late January weekend that Kick and Joe Jr. spent at the Norfolk home of their father's close friend the liquor distributor Sir James Calder, Kick's inept card play caused her brother to suffer "extreme anguish," she said. Young Joe was a fierce adherent of his father's credo that winning is everything. Meanwhile, Rose escaped wintry London by dashing off to Paris to shop. As Kick explained to her father, "Mother left for Paris in a rush . . . She is the busiest cup of tea." Taking on her mother's role, Kick went up to Roehampton to visit her sisters, bringing them a chocolate cake.

During that winter, Kick would grow closer to Billy and her friend Debo Mitford. In early February, Kick visited Debo's small private cot-

tage on Lord Redesdale's property near Oxford. Debo insisted on doing
all the cooking. Kick and Billy, David Ormsby-Gore, and his girlfriend
Sissy Lloyd-Thomas went to Lady Ravensdale's dance for her niece Vivien
Mosley, whom Kick found "very nice, but enormous." Vivien was the
daughter of Lady Ravensdale's late sister Cynthia and Oswald Mosley; the
girl's father had since taken up with Debo's older sister Diana. A week
later, Kick and Debo went up to Cambridge to watch Andrew Cavendish
ride in a steeplechase, dining in Billy's rooms under the strict eye of chap-
erone Lady Ravensdale. Kick complained in her diary about the double
standard ("What about Unity I ask myself"). Unity didn't seem to require
much chaperoning when she was meeting with Hitler, and Lady Ravensdale herself was fond of drink and chasing married men.

On Valentine's Day, Kick and Debo went to Brompton Oratory for the
wedding of Derek Parker-Bowles. Billy was one of the ushers and would
later be godfather to Derek's son Andrew Parker-Bowles, whose ex-wife
Camilla would marry Charles, Prince of Wales. Rose carefully monitored
how much time Billy and Kick spent together, and held out hope that Kick
was not taking seriously her romance with the glamorous but Protestant
and thus unsuitable Billy, and that she still kept an eye out for an appropriate American husband. Kick "goes out with Billy," she wrote Joe, "but
watches the U.S. Lines for mail." Nice Catholic American boys remained
among her regular correspondents.

Joe Jr. spent two weeks that winter working in banks and brokerage
houses learning about foreign exchange, the discount market, and the different types of bills. He joined his mother for tea with the Lindberghs,
who were spending the winter in Paris after the international outrage over
Kristallnacht derailed their plans to move to Germany. The Lindberghs
"inquired most solcitiously [sic] after you," young Joe wrote his father.
Summarizing the mood in London, he wrote, "Everyone seems to be getting jittery again . . . I suppose they will feel surer of themselves after Hitler
speaks next week. . . . One of the great dangers will be if the Italians continue to insult the French they may have trouble on their hands before they
know it . . . Nothing much is going on in the Embassy except the Jewish situation . . . Angola and the Philippines seem to be the places of the moment
[for emigration] . . . Herschel [Johnson] is running over to the Foreign
Office constantly. . . . He is rather pessimistic. . . ." Having decided that
its plan to partition Palestine between Arabs and Jews was not feasible, the
British government had invited Jewish and Arab representatives to London
in early February for consultations with the government. The Arabs would
refuse to speak to the Jews.

On January 30, Adolf Hitler made his annual speech commemorating his coming to power, appearing before the Reichstag in the Kroll Opera House in Berlin. He condemned Winston Churchill, Duff Cooper, Anthony Eden, and Harold Ickes as agitators against the truth (Hitler's lies about Germany's intentions), and jeered the Western democracies for their failure to resolve the Jewish refugee problem: "It is a shameful spectacle to see how the whole democratic world is oozing sympathy for the poor tormented Jewish people, but remains hard-hearted and obdurate when it comes to helping them." He made a public threat against the Jews, predicting that a world war would mean "the annihilation of the Jewish race in Europe!"

He ended his speech on a racist yet mollifying note that sent stock prices soaring in a New York and London eager for any positive news: "Germany has no territorial demands against England and France apart from that for the return of our colonies. . . . millions of American citizens who, despite all that is said to the contrary, by the gigantic Jewish capitalistic propaganda . . . cannot fail to realize that. . . . Germany wishes to live in peace . . . with America." But even if businesspeople were temporarily encouraged, the unease and tension persisted unabated that winter. British ambassador Lindsay told Sumner Welles, the undersecretary of state, that "the nervous strain under which they were all living in England was appalling." Herschel Johnson, who headed the embassy in Joe's absence, passed on disquieting reports to the ambassador: Hitler remained resentful about having to postpone his plans to commandeer Czechoslovakia the previous fall, and blamed Britain for the perceived humiliation. Intelligence reports suggested that the most perilous time yet for war would begin at the end of February. Rumors had Hitler making an air attack on London, invading Holland, and encouraging Italy to attack France. The British government accelerated their military buildup so that by June, Britain would be in a somewhat stronger position to negotiate for peace.

In response to such anxiety-inducing intelligence, Neville Chamberlain sent word to Roosevelt that Kennedy should cut short his two-month working vacation and return immediately. Chamberlain wanted to hear firsthand about Kennedy's meetings with Roosevelt. Joe was due to leave the United States on February 23; instead he boarded the *Queen Mary* on February 9.

According to Joe's memoir, at his final meeting with Roosevelt before his return, he offered to resign his post unless the president directly restated his full confidence in him. "I never say anything privately," Joe reminded FDR, "that I have not said to you face to face." FDR told him to ignore "those cracks at you, some people just like to make trouble." But while the president gave his ambassador the oral reassurance he sought, he said nothing to Joe that hinted further at his strategy for Europe. Kennedy would tell Chamberlain, as the prime minister later reported to his sister Hilda, that he was "totally unable to find out what his [Roosevelt's] policy was or whether he had any policy at all."

According to FDR's biographer Conrad Black, the president already had an incomparably "ambitious plan for making over the world." He wanted to arm America "to complete the conquest of the Depression . . . arrange a virtual draft to a third term as the candidate of peace through strength . . . complete the acquisition of an overwhelming level of military might," set up the dictators as the aggressors, and conquer them "leading the world to a post imperial Pax Americana, in which, . . . Woodrow Wilson's goals of safety for democracy and international legality would be established by some sort of American-led international body."

Since Munich, any alliance between the president and his ambassador had clearly unraveled. FDR was no longer willing to trust Kennedy, nor would he set firm limits on Kennedy's policy making. By employing Kennedy's skills as an able embassy administrator and often useful conveyor and communicator of information but leaving him out in the cold as a strategist and negotiator, Roosevelt did his diplomat and his diplomacy a disservice. If he wasn't willing to rely on Kennedy, he should have found a kind way to reassign him to a post at home. But Roosevelt's judgment was affected by his concern that Kennedy might spearhead a movement of business leaders and isolationists to block his effort to win a third term. However, as a man of convictions as well as cunning, Roosevelt himself might argue he was serving a higher good—isolating and disabling a potential opponent to further his conviction that the nation needed him as it faced a cataclysmic war.

"The fog and gray skies and chill of the English winter were beginning to stimulate my wanderlust," Rose wrote in her autobiography. She did not linger in London long enough to greet her returning husband. As was her practice, she waited until Joe was on his way and could take over supervising the children before she fled Britain with her friend Marie Bruce for a tour of the Riviera, Genoa, Naples, the Greek Islands, Athens, Turkey, Palestine, and Egypt. Rose wrote Joe from Athens, where she said she had spent a "thrilling day . . . with plenty of climbing about. It was so wonderful to think we were standing at the spot where St. Paul preached—where Pericles spoke. All my love Rosa."

His wife was not the only one absent when Joe arrived at Prince's Gate on February 16. He was greeted by a sobering cable from Joe Jr.: "Sorry

I missed you. Arrived safely Valencia, Going to Madrid tonight. Regards. Joe." Departing before his father had a chance to stop him, young Joe had gone to Paris, where he exchanged his diplomatic passport for a regular American one. He did not want to trouble the U.S. State Department if he encountered danger during his adventure with the Spanish Civil War, a conflict that retained its romantic political associations among young Americans and Europeans even as Franco's fascists were nearing victory. Joe arrived in Barcelona as it fell to Franco, caught a ride on a British destroyer to Valencia, and lingered a day before wangling his way onto a crowded military bus—smoothing his passage by handing out cigarettes to the troops—headed for Madrid.

In the frequently bombarded port of Valencia the "damage is beyond description," Joe wrote in one of many letters in which he essayed to give a truthful—if not literary—depiction of the last throes of the Spanish Civil War. "There are many days when the bread ration is cut off, and the lines form to buy whatever may be offered in its place. It's a mystery to me how the scrawny dogs, which prowl around the garbage cans in vast numbers, manage to exist." Joe underwent his first bombardment while he and the city's residents took refuge in "rough tunnels or dug-outs under the tumbled bricks and masonry." The noise from the bombing of the port was so intense that it made his ears ache: "The buildings vibrated like drums." Joe found himself developing a shield of fatalism: "The thing that got me was the feeling of absolute helplessness."

Arriving in Madrid, he wrote his alarmed and worried father from the abandoned U.S. embassy, which was manned by one skinny Spaniard who safeguarded an assortment of refugee cows, sheep, hens, and lambs. "Hundreds of people are starving to death every day, and everybody's hungry all the time," he wrote. Joe survived on the meager rations of bread, lentils, and salt fish. Homes had no heat. When a large tree was chopped down, "about fifty people let out a screech and rushed for it, some with tiny hatchets. A guard tried to push them off with the butt of his gun, but he hadn't a chance. The tree was literally torn to pieces and disappeared in no time."

The ambassador had decidedly mixed feelings about Joe's escapade. He was proud of Joe's physical courage and his passion to observe the front lines of a historic conflict, but he feared what might happen to him. Rose was also anxious. She knew her son had always been drawn to danger. In Switzerland in early January, he had plunged fearlessly down the perilous Cresta bobsled run at seventy miles per hour. The ambassador worried that if Spain's Loyalist forces (an uneasy alliance of Communists and liberals)

On March 16, 1938, Ambassador Joseph Kennedy departs from the American embassy to present his credentials to King George VI at Buckingham Palace. He is flanked (right to left) by Sir Sidney Clive, the marshal of the Diplomatic Corps (in full regalia and plumed hat); the counselor of the American embassy, Herschel Johnson; and his military and naval attachés. (*JFK Library Foundation*)

Photographers besieged the Kennedy family on the lawn of their residence. From left to right: Kathleen, Joe, Teddy, Rose, Rosemary, Jean, and Bobby. (*JFK Library Foundation*)

June 1938. Teddy and Bobby getting acquainted with an elephant at the opening of the London zoo. (*Corbis*)

Teddy peeks at the camera as Joe and Rose dine with their seven youngest children at Prince's Gate. Jack and Joe Jr. were in America finishing their studies at Harvard. (*Peter Hunter/Nederlands Fotomuseum*)

This picture of Ted and his father "working" together at the ambassador's desk in London is one of Senator Kennedy's favorite photographs. (*From Senator Kennedy*)

May 11, 1938. Rose Kennedy and her two oldest daughters. The international press goes into a frenzy as Kick and Rosemary prepare to be formally presented to the king and queen at court. (*JFK Library Foundation*)

Rose serves a formal English tea to Teddy, Bobby, Rosemary, and Kick at their new home, 14 Prince's Gate. (*Estate of Tom Hustler/National Portrait Gallery*)

Ambassador Kennedy flanked by Joe Jr. (left) and Jack (right) as they travel onboard the S.S. *Normandie* to England in June 1938. The boys defied their father by engaging in secret late-night romantic assignations onboard the ship. (*Photofest*)

RIGHT: Jack cut an enthralling path through London's social and political scene. Here he joins his brother Bobby on a balcony overlooking the gardens at Prince's Gate. (*JFK Library Foundation*)

LEFT: July 4, 1938. Bobby Kennedy and his school chum John Sheffield eat strawberries and cream at an Independence Day party for 1,500 people given by Joe and Rose Kennedy at the American embassy. (*Corbis*)

After Jack and Joe Jr. arrived in July 1938, the family gathered for a formal portrait by Dorothy Wilding. Standing (left to right): Kathleen, Joe Jr. with hands on Jean, Eunice, Joe Sr., Rosemary, and Jack. Seated: Patricia, Teddy, Bobby, and Rose. (*Estate of Tom Hustler/National Portrait Gallery*)

RIGHT: David Ormsby-Gore and his future wife Sissy Lloyd-Thomas were close friends of Jack and Kick. David later became an important advisor to Jack Kennedy, and served as the British ambassador to the United States during Kennedy's presidency. (*Illustrated London News Picture Library*)

LEFT: Tony Loughborough, the sixth earl of Rosslyn, Baron Loughborough (left), and Jack became fast friends. They thought of themselves as the girl-catching team of "RossKennedy." Tony is seated with Kick's close friend Jean Ogilvie, who was the daughter of the Earl of Airlie and a cousin of Billy Hartington and Andrew Cavendish. (*Illustrated London News Picture Library*)

August 1938. The entire Kennedy family gathered at a rented house in Cap d'Antibes on the French Riviera and bathed at Eden Roc swimming club. Joe recalled that they enjoyed the "Blue Mediterranean and the sun-drenched sands, the casualness of people in a holiday mood." (*JFK Library Foundation*)

recognized his son, they might punish young Joe for his father's vigorous and public efforts to strangle their ability to fight. Kennedy had actively lobbied President Roosevelt to extend the Neutrality Act to cover countries in civil war, and he had recently battled to keep that amendment in force. His efforts, and those of other fervent Catholics backing the pro-Church Franco, had cost the Loyalist military forces the arms shipments that might have helped them turn back Franco's Nationalists. Nonetheless, the ambassador bragged to the press about his son's exploits, and the London newspapers began referring to young Joe as the "Crisis Hunter." By the end of February, Britain and France would recognize Franco's government, and Joe Jr. would stay on in Madrid to witness the denouement of Spain's civil war.

Lonely without his wife in London, Joe took Rosemary to a concert. Later, writing several letters to her father, Rosemary strained to please him by reciting her accomplishments: "Thank you for taking me to the concert. It was very nice of you. I have been very busy making an Album for Dr. Montessori when she comes in March. I have been taking Alouquation [elocution] lessons . . . But it is wonderful to get a deploma [sic]. Then I will be a school teacher. I got a deploma for being a Child of Mary . . . I have been taking First-Aid also . . . Practising bandages . . . I did it last term also. *very interesting.*" Rosemary also told her father she was following an Elizabeth Arden diet. "I have gone down between 5 and 7 pounds already living on salads, egg at night." She ate meat once a day, she wrote, adding, "I will be thin when Jack sees me."

BACK AT HARVARD, Jack had been battling to integrate and refine the political ideas that animated the conflicts in which his father was a player and his older brother an adventurer. He had written a masterly study of the politics and legislating of upstate New York congressman Bernard Snell, and had thereby become well acquainted with the workings of Congress. Highlighting his freshly serious intentions, he had taken six courses during the fall semester and had made the Dean's List for the first time. He accomplished all this despite a stay in the Mayo Clinic for tests after his bowels became blocked, and despite spending every other spare moment ignoring his health and pursuing a highly eligible, accomplished, and very Protestant heiress, Frances Ann Cannon. Cannon, a brilliant graduate of Sarah Lawrence College, had taken advanced studies in business administration. She was one of the last debutantes presented to the king and queen in London before Jack's father ended the practice.

For the first time, Jack, who had grown proficient at operating from behind a protective psychic shield, found himself taking a woman seriously, as his equal. He fell in love with Frances Ann and asked her to marry him. Unaccustomed to the prejudice that had wounded his father so deeply, Jack was genuinely stunned and hurt when her staunchly Presbyterian father insisted she could not marry a Catholic and her mother promptly whisked her off on a four-month round-the-world cruise. Taking off the spring semester, Jack left for London depressed and unnerved. He would take his brother's place as his father's secretary-companion.

A S SOON AS HE RETURNED TO LONDON, Kennedy had long sessions with Lord Halifax and Neville Chamberlain, whom he warned against saying anything publicly that would suggest that Britain was counting on American help in an impending war. Kennedy cabled Hull with the news that Chamberlain seemed more optimistic that Hitler, though an "impractical and fanatical" tyrant, was not showing any signs of readiness to strike either in the east or west: "He still feels that the only hope of doing business with Hitler is to take him at his word. . . . he realizes that it is by no means certain that the word will be kept, but up to date he has no reason personally to disbelieve it." With a combination of credulousness and informed optimism, Chamberlain hoped that if Britain could help Hitler solve Germany's economic problems, the dictator would not be impelled to make war. Hitler was in fact making contact with various leaders of British industry and had even signed a coal contract with Britain. The prime minister also told Kennedy that America's stronger stand and the escalation of British defense spending had given Hitler pause. Even though the Italians were making blustering threats to France, Chamberlain professed not to be worried. During the prime minister's visit to Italy in early January, Mussolini had charmed Chamberlain, who characteristically misread him as a sincere and reasonable man. Mussolini, however, was privately contemptuous of Chamberlain and Halifax. "These men are not made of the same stuff as the Francis Drakes," he said. "[They] are the tired sons of a long line of rich men and they will soon lose their Empire."

Over lunch with Kennedy, Churchill was equally and surprisingly sanguine about prospects for peace. Churchill was "vociferous in his belief that Germany had been bluffing [at Munich] and would continue to do so," according to Joe's memoir. "If Chamberlain had shown more strength at Munich," Winston told Joe, "he was certain Germany would have been crushed."

On February 24, Stephen Wise and Louis Lipsky, American Zionist leaders, met with Kennedy and asked him to convey to the British government their strong objections to Britain's plans for appeasing Mideast Arabs by reducing Jewish immigration into Palestine. Kennedy agreed, and three days later met with Halifax to tell him that this reduction would be unfavorably received in the United States. At the same time, Neville Chamberlain wrote his sister Hilda that the Jews "are behaving admirably, most reasonable, and pathetically patient in the face of brutal realities." Kennedy cabled the State Department to say that the British were "giving the Arabs the better of it" (only 75,000 Jews would be allowed to enter Palestine in the next five years). His efforts on behalf of the Jews led the Arab National League to denounce him as a "Zionist Charlie McCarthy." Being compared to a ventriloquist's dummy was perhaps a welcome change for a man so often attacked for being anti-Semitic.

Much to Joe's relief and excitement, George Rublee had succeeded in getting Germany to agree that all of the Reich's Jews would leave within five years and would be given a cash allotment to help them resettle. Joe called Rublee to congratulate him on the extraordinary agreement. "Why hadn't they done something like this before?" he asked Rublee. But the clock was running out on the Jews, and still ticking toward war.

CHAPTER 11

Blitzkrieg Against Denial

J ACK LOVED HIS NEW JOB as a "glorified office boy" at the American embassy in London. On March 2, his first day at the office, the *Daily Mirror* gave him the celebrity treatment, complete with a flattering photograph of him in a beautifully tailored blue pinstripe suit, sitting at his desk and manning the telephone. "Been working every day and going to dinners etc. with Dad," he soon wrote to Lem Billings, "feeling very important as I go to work in my new cutaway." He relished the social perks as well, dressing in white tie and tails for his formal introduction to King George, Queen Elizabeth, and Queen Mary: "Met the king this morning at a Court Levee," he told Lem. "The king stands and you go up and bow." Afterward he had tea with twelve-year-old Princess Elizabeth, "with whom I made a great deal of time," he boasted to Lem. On the night of March 9, he returned to the palace for the first court of the season "in my new silk breeches, which are cut to my crotch tightly and in which I look mightily attractive." Jack knew how to make fun of himself and how to tease and titillate his gay friend.

Jack and his father flew to Paris, where the ambassador had consultations with French officials before joining the younger children on an overnight train to Rome for an even more meaningful event—the coronation of a family friend as the new pope. After Pope Pius XI had died in mid-February after a seventeen-year reign, the Vatican secretary of state, Cardinal Eugenio Pacelli, had been chosen to replace him. During Pacelli's 1936 tour of the United States, Joe had arranged for him to meet President Roosevelt at Hyde Park. To Rose's great delight, the cardinal then visited the Kennedys at home in Bronxville. Rose roped off the couch on which the cardinal sat, and treated it as a relic.

Jack and his best friend, Lem Billings, in The Hague in August 1937. Throughout 1939 Jack wrote Lem, who was gay, many provocative and thoughtful letters detailing his conquests and expressing his opinions about the situation in Europe. (*Photofest*)

As cardinal, Pacelli had expressed distaste for the Nazis' anti-Christian stance and their barbaric treatment of minority groups. While the cardinals were convening to elect Pacelli, the German government had tried to intimidate the College of Cardinals into voting against him. Hitler would say that this new pope was the "only human being who has always contradicted me and who has never obeyed me." As Pope Pius XII, Pacelli would reign from a Vatican state surrounded by Hitler's great ally, fascist Italy. His papacy would be controversial; he would be accused of having overly accommodating relations with the Axis state and with Hitler's regime. Joe and Rose could barely contain their excitement at his election.

Kennedy wanted to officially represent the United States at the pope's coronation almost as badly as he had wanted the ambassadorship to Britain. He lobbied for the position with Sumner Welles at the State Department and called the president directly. Although FDR was watching Kennedy warily for signs that he was parlaying public exposure into a 1940 run for the presidency, he rewarded him with this prominent position as an easily bestowed bonus for his diligent intelligence-gathering in London. While Joe always courted publicity, this papal event had far greater meaning for him than self-advancement. The coronation was "overwhelming in its memory, in its magnificence, in its universal appeal," he told the *New York Times*. Indeed, he would find the new pope "awe-inspiring, majestic, kindness personified and with the humility of God."

The night before the coronation, Joe and the children were greeted in Rome by Rose, who had arrived earlier from her travels in Egypt. Joe Jr. did not join them; he was monitoring the triumph of the Spanish fascist army, as Colonel Segismundo Casado Lopez, the commander of the Loyalist forces in central Spain, overthrew Republican prime minister Dr. Juan Negrin, setting off a week of street fighting between Communists and Casado's forces in Madrid. "Everyone seemed relieved to see soldiers on the streets," Joe wrote his father on March 8, "and I am sure most people thought the war was over in spite of a declaration by Casado that the Loyalists will fight until they get a worthy peace."

But, as Franco's Nationalist forces approached Madrid, Joe Jr. nearly lost his life. In his role as an observer, he was traveling with members of the Nationalists underground in a car when they were stopped by Communist sympathizers, forced out of their car, and lined up against a wall. Just as it appeared the men were going to be shot, Joe turned around and presented his American passport and visa. After furious, whispered discussions, the Communists decided it would be prudent to let the group go.

On Sunday, March 12, at 7:30 A.M., Joe and Rose Kennedy, their staff, and eight of their children arrived at St. Peter's Basilica in a caravan of four cars flying the papal and U.S. flags. As the Kennedys entered, Joe noticed Mussolini's son-in-law, Count Ciano, the Italian minister of foreign affairs, strolling around the enormous basilica and giving everyone the fascist salute. Ciano threw a fit when he found that his seat in the gallery of the official missions was taken. He was quickly seated next to Joe.

Seventy thousand people were stuffed into the basilica. The Kennedys sat directly in front of the altar where the pope celebrated the mass. Joe had wangled seats in the first row for his family, displacing other invitees into less desirable seats in the gallery. For Joe, "the beauty of it that day was beyond belief . . . To us kneeling in the hollow of the Dome" the pope's intonations and the "responses of the Sistine Choir were a never to be forgotten experience."

The next day, the new pope held a private audience with the Kennedy family in his small papal apartment. Joe entered first. He genuflected, knelt, and watched with amazement as the pope broke with tradition by rising and walking to the American ambassador, offering his hand so that Joe

could kiss the papal ring. Formal diplomatic relations between the Holy
See and the United States had been severed after King Victor Emmanuel
had seized the Papal States in 1867 and annexed them to Italy, leaving only
Vatican City as a tiny, independent state. Bowing to strong anti-Catholic
sentiment in America, the U.S. Congress refused to send an official representative to the Vatican. Discussing the pope's efforts to have relations
restored, Kennedy recommended that the Vatican persistently lobby Catholics within the Roosevelt administration. Joe offered to advocate for an
official representative to the Holy See. The pope wanted to make him a
papal duke, but Joe declined; such an honor might not go over well during
a presidential campaign. He settled instead on receiving the Order of Pius
XI, normally reserved for heads of state.

Rose came next, wearing her black veil set off with a smart tiara, accompanied by her children and staff. Joe recalled that Rose nearly fainted
because the pope "talked to her so much and so kindly and intimately."
The pope "seemed pleased to see everyone, especially Teddy, whom he remembered fondly as the little boy in his lap who had been so curious about
the crucifix." After the papal audience, seven-year-old Teddy held his first
press interview. "I told my sister Patricia I wasn't frightened at all," he said
to reporters. "The pope patted my head and told me I was a smart little
fellow. He gave me the first rosary beads from the table before he gave
my sister any." Feeling first in such a large family was, indeed, a special
moment for the boy. Outside the church, flanked by two Swiss guards, the
smiling Kennedys posed for a famous photograph.

Two days later in a small and private, red-walled chapel filled with the
scent of lilies and candles, Pius celebrated his first papal mass, a private one
attended by the Kennedys. Surprisingly, Rose missed this mass; she chose
to hurry off to Paris for a scheduled appointment with her exclusive Paris
dressmaker. While his father, Jack, Pat, and Eunice watched, Teddy, wearing a blue suit with a white rosette on his left arm, had his first communion from the new pope. The pope made the Sign of the Cross on Teddy's
forehead and said, "I hope you will always be good and pious as you are
today." Rose would ruefully say years later she had hoped that "with such
a start he'd become a priest or maybe a bishop, but then one night he met
a beautiful blonde and that was the end of that."

Jack found the experience of receiving communion from the pope "very
impressive," but he could not resist poking fun at the family's social climbing in his letter to his friend Lem: "Pacelli is now riding high, so it's good
you bowed and groveled like you did when you first met him [in Bronx-
ville] . . . They want to give Dad the title of duke which will be hereditary

and go to all his family which will make me Duke John of Bronxville and perhaps if you suck around sufficiently I might knight you."

His father the ambassador, however, had been heartened that this "most saintly man" with an "extensive knowledge of world conditions" might just be the ballast that Western civilization needed in such parlous times. "If the world hasn't gone too far to be influenced by a great and good man, this is the man," he wrote to Jay Pierrepont Moffat at the State Department. By contrast, Joe was particularly unimpressed with Count Ciano: "A more pompous ass I have never met in my life," he wrote Cordell Hull. At the U.S. embassy, Ciano "spent most of his time rushing girls into the corner for conversation and at the dinner he could not talk seriously for five minutes for fear that the two or three girls, who were invited to get him to come, might get out of sight . . . I came away with the belief that we would accomplish much more by sending a dozen beautiful chorus girls to Rome than a flock of diplomats and a fleet of airplanes."

Even as the new pope ascended the papal throne, Nazi propaganda was inciting considerable unrest among the Slovak minority in Czechoslovakia. The brewing crisis escalated on March 10, while the Kennedys were still in Rome, when the Czechs dismissed the Slovakian cabinet and placed the Slovak premier, the pro-fascist Catholic priest Josef Tiso, under house arrest in Bratislava. Hitler pounced on this opportunity to swallow up the Czech state. He arranged with Tiso to have the Slovak assembly proclaim independence and ask for German protection, then brutally intimidated Czech president Dr. Emil Hacha into signing a declaration handing his country over to Hitler's "protection." In the early morning of March 15, Hitler sent his troops across the Czech border into Moravia and Bohemia. They met no opposition. That evening, Hitler announced to the world that Czechoslovakia had ceased to exist. He told his secretaries, "I will go down as the greatest German in history." A couple of days later, Unity Mitford touted Anglo-German friendship in an article in the *Daily Mirror*, then left for Germany, taking over an apartment from which a Jewish family had recently been ousted.

The *New York Times* London correspondent described London's initial reaction to Hitler's aggression as a kind of shell-shocked apathy, both in "the House of Commons, where the general attitude was a helpless shrug of the shoulders, [and] among the general public which seemed to care more about a cricket match in far-off South Africa than about the transformation of the map of Europe." By the next day, reality began to set in. The *Daily Telegraph* described the Nazi invasion as the "most flagrant and impudent act of unprovoked aggression that has been witnessed in Europe in modern time."

The Czech crisis put an abrupt end to Joe's Roman idyll. He took the overnight train to Paris, where he found Rose praying at the Madeleine church. He then had a quick breakfast with Ambassador Bullitt, his anxieties stoked when Bullitt told him he believed that the Nazi incursion indicated the end of our civilization. Bullitt had just spoken on the phone to the president, who had expressed outrage about Nazi treachery and Chamberlain's mild response to it: "I have the evening papers in front of me with headlines 'Chamberlain washes his hands,'" FDR fumed. The president asked Bullitt, "You know the last well known man about whom that was said?" Bullitt replied that it was Pontius Pilate. Like his boss, Bullitt was rapidly abandoning his isolationist predilections; he would soon write FDR suggesting the president ready several million troops for action.

Immediately, Joe and Rose flew separately, as was their habit, from Paris to London. Joe quickly sought out Lord Halifax, who told him that Nevile Henderson, the British ambassador to Germany, had been recalled. It was rumored in London that Hitler would soon pounce on Romania. Kennedy met with an agitated Viorel Tilea, the Romanian minister to London, who wondered whether his country should rush to make their best deal with the Nazis.

While Kennedy was frantically gathering information in London, Chamberlain agonized over his limited options. He was humiliated and insulted by Hitler's betrayal, and he knew that the whole world was nervously awaiting his next move. An astute politician, he had been sobered by the growing outrage among the public, Parliament, and the Dominions.

Feeling the weight of history as he spoke on March 17, in Birmingham, Chamberlain focused on the absence of justification for Hitler's actions: "Is this the end of an old adventure or is it the beginning of a new? Is this the last attack upon a small State, or is it to be followed by others?" Was the takeover of Czechoslovakia not "a step in the direction of an attempt to dominate the world by force?" Hitler and Mussolini would be mistaken to assume, he declared, that "the nation has so lost its fibre," that Britain would not vigorously commit itself to resisting further aggression. But he still was not ready to draw a firm line. Chamberlain wrote to his sister Hilda that he needed further time to think and answer the question, "as Joe Kennedy puts it, 'Where do we go from here?'" He was relying increasingly on his bond with Kennedy to buttress his diplomatic efforts to thwart Hitler's aggressions while averting war.

The next day was Chamberlain's seventieth birthday, but he was not in a mood to celebrate. Joe sought to bolster his friend by sending him "affectionate" birthday greetings, reminding him that "I count upon your courage never failing and your strength increasing . . . I have been one with you in your striving for peace and have nothing but admiration for the convictions you so eloquently expressed last night. Opinions may change but underlying conviction changes only to deepen."

The next day, Kennedy was summoned off the golf course for an urgent meeting with Lord Halifax. Fears about a Nazi invasion of Romania had intensified, and, according to his record, he told Halifax, "I didn't see how they could expect to have any world standing if they permitted Hitler to move into Romania and England do nothing," given the warnings to Germany contained in the prime minister's Birmingham speech. Yet "I was dead set against the United States getting into [the] war," Kennedy said he told Halifax. Asked by the foreign secretary if there were any circumstances under which the United States would go to war, Kennedy said, "Possibly, but not until it was definitely for our own selfish reasons." Ever the realist, he wanted to make clear that no sudden infusion of Wilsonian idealism would motivate the United States into making a quick intervention in the European morass.

On March 21, amid grave uncertainty about Hitler's intentions, French president Albert Lebrun and his wife arrived in London for a state visit, showcasing the strength of the Anglo-French alliance—a needed tonic for the British public. As the Lebruns arrived in London, Nazi activists seized Memel, a port town on the Baltic Sea, and Hitler annexed this formerly German region, which had been ceded to Lithuania after World War I. The takeover raised fears that Germany would soon devour Poland as well. Chamberlain worried that the Germans might bomb London from the air during the French president's visit; he called out the anti-aircraft battalions, positioning soldiers with guns and searchlights around the capital.

Joe and Rose joined 180 people at Buckingham Palace for a state banquet that night in honor of the French president. Joe mentioned in his diary that "Rose looked beautiful in her new dress" (featuring a jewel-laden hooped skirt of aquamarine satin) during an evening that was "alive with color." The gala was a tonic for Rose, who had arrived back from her southern travels to find London once again dreary and anxiety-ridden. Joe talked so excitedly about the political situation that a flustered Lord Sidney Clive admonished him not to raise his voice.

At dinner when Joe looked over at the queen, she raised her glass in a toast to him. Not knowing whether he was violating protocol (he was), he returned the toast. He was reassured when he noticed that the duke and duchess of Kent, at the other end of the table, "smiled sweetly" at him. The king privately believed Chamberlain had done an excellent job rallying the world behind him, but with the Germans rumored to be massing twenty divisions on the Western front, and Poland failing to respond to Britain's attempt to build an alliance against Germany, Chamberlain was miserable; he likened this state banquet to the Brussels Ball in 1815 when Wellington learned of Napoleon's movements on the eve of Waterloo. Jack, adding a postscript in a letter to Lem that night, wrote, "Everyone thinks war inevitable before the year is out. I personally don't, though Dad does."

When the king stood up to toast the French president, he hesitated for several moments before being able to speak. Joe looked over at Queen Elizabeth, whose face was "crimson running away down her throat. . . . her hands . . . were absolutely clenched. The poor girl suffers the torment of the damned when he speaks." Later, Joe would advocate that the king's state visit to the United States be managed so that he would not have to give a public speech.

The India Office reception, with Lord and Lady Halifax as hosts at the Foreign Office in Whitehall on March 23, was the last great official event in pre-war London. In a room hung with magnificent old tapestries, Joe and Rose enjoyed a seven-course dinner (with eight wines) served on splendid plates by waiters in "scarlet waistcoat, bright blue coat with gold trimmings and dark plush breeches, worn with the usual white stockings." The glamorous crowd was decked in jewels. Lady Londonderry wore the spectacular Londonderry diamonds, and, amid a party twinkling with tiaras, the duchesses of Devonshire and Buccleuch stood out with two "of the largest ever seen." The Foreign Office itself was festooned with lilies, azaleas, magnolias, Japanese cherry trees, and pillars entwined with climbing roses.

Chamberlain during this time was trying to arrange a four-part agreement wherein Poland, Russia, France, and Britain would resist further aggression from Germany. Poland balked, resisting any alliance with its adversary Russia that might also provoke Hitler to attack. Russia was willing to sign an agreement, but as Kennedy told Hull, Halifax believed that "Poland is of much more value to the tie-up than Russia because their latest information on Russia shows their air force to be very weak and old and of short range, their army very poor and their industrial backing for the army frightful." Kennedy worried whether Britain and France could forge agreements with Poland and Russia strong enough to keep the Allies from finding "it necessary to wash their hands of the whole of Southeastern Europe" if Hitler attacked Poland or Russia. Halifax replied that he was confident that Britain could lay down a firm line with Hitler.

Hitler kept up pressure on the Poles to give Germany access to Danzig and the Polish Corridor, which separated East Prussia from the rest of the

German Empire. Danzig and the Polish Corridor had both been taken from Germany in 1919 at the Treaty of Versailles to allow Poland access to the Baltic Sea. Fearing an imminent attack on Danzig, a free city administered by the League of Nations, the Poles mobilized. In response, Germany broke diplomatic relations with Poland. But Hitler backed off from attacking Poland; he wanted to calm Western nerves with a strategically quiet period. He did, however, complete an economic agreement with Romania, providing Germany with access to that nation's petroleum supplies.

Right after the French state visit to London, Rose rushed back to Paris, where she acted as her friend William Bullitt's hostess at a dinner dance for President and Mrs. Lebrun on March 25. It was "an unusual move for one ambassador's wife to help out a colleague in another country," her biographer Charles Higham wrote, "but she and Joe were very fond of Bullitt, and approved of his action against the Soviet Union in breaking the Franco-Russian pact."

R ESPONDING TO INTELLIGENCE REPORTS that Hitler might be ready to move on Poland, Halifax and Chamberlain decided that only tough limits might avert war. As soon as Kennedy learned about Britain and France's impending decision to guarantee Poland's Western borders against aggression, he called Roosevelt. FDR approved of Chamberlain's resolve and willingness at last to confront Hitler, but thought "it probably means war." Kennedy told the president how determined the British were to broadcast Chamberlain's House of Commons speech to the German and Italian people despite their governments' attempts to block it. Chamberlain still held out hope, as did Kennedy, that Britain could change the attitudes of the peoples of these totalitarian countries, if not those of their leaders.

On March 31, Neville Chamberlain proclaimed a dramatic reversal in British foreign policy: "In the event of any action which already threatened Polish independence, and which the Polish government accordingly considered it vital to resist with national forces, His Majesty's government would feel themselves bound at once to lend the Polish government all support in their power. . . ." Reversing Britain's centuries-old policy of going to war only when it saw fit and not as a result of a binding alliance, Chamberlain had effectively placed the decision for war in the hands of a foreign power. It was a remarkable transformation, perhaps causing Britain to see itself as less of an autonomous and imperial power, with the fate of war and peace contingent on the actions of enemies, not its own authority. Britain had also pledged to protect Romania from attacks in order to prevent Germany from taking over Romania's oil fields and protecting itself from the negative effects of any future British naval blockade.

Hitler, for once, had been blocked by Chamberlain and that "dastardly" Churchill, who he assumed was egging the prime minister on. The Fuhrer had expected that intimidation would work wonders on Poland, as it had on the Czechs and the Austrians. Now he would have to grab Danzig and the Polish Corridor by force. Hearing the news of the British pledge to defend Poland (France already had an alliance with Poland), he fell into a rage, pounding his fist on the hard marble surface of a table in his Reich Chancellery study. "I'll brew them a devil's potion," he yelled.

In an April 1 speech at the launching of one of the many German battleships whose deployment was intended to overtake the British navy, Hitler summed up his bellicose philosophy: "He who does not possess power loses the right to life." Two days later he directed his senior military commanders to prepare Operation White, the invasion of Poland, for action by September 1.

CHAPTER 12

Encirclement

O N MARCH 28, Franco's forces seized Madrid. "The entrance of the Nationalist troops into Madrid was not a glorious one, accomplished with a fanfare of trumpets," Joe Jr. reported. "The city was taken prematurely by Franco sympathizers within the city. Some daring ones raced through the streets with the Nationalist flag in their cars." Soon he saw Nationalist flags, planted by Fifth Columnists, in almost every building. "The city came to life," Joe wrote, with "pretty women appearing from nowhere . . . women and men weeping for joy."

Joe turned down an offer of safe passage out of Spain aboard a U.S. warship because he wanted to experience Palm Sunday that weekend, in a city where priests had been murdered and many churches had been desecrated by Loyalist partisans angry that the Catholic Church had sided with the fascists. He attended mass at one of the few reconsecrated churches, and then watched as forty thousand citizens celebrated mass in the streets with olive sprigs substituting for palm leaves.

The ambassador was proud that his son had taken the risk required to witness the death throes of Republican Spain. He read aloud Joe Jr.'s discerning letters to politicians and reporters alike. During one late February weekend at Cliveden, the Astors invited him to read his son's letters during tea to the Lindberghs, Lord Lothian, and Geoffrey Dawson, editor of the London *Times*, who was impressed with the prose, and again after dinner in the presence of Neville Chamberlain, who appreciated Joe Jr.'s anti-Communism.

Always a man striving to overcome his feelings of inadequacy by acquiring emblems of success and social acceptance, Joe encouraged his son to publish. Authoring a book had won him respect and fostered his political advancement; he thought the same approach could work for his namesake. After failing to get the editor of the *Saturday Evening Post* and the Hearst newspapers to commission Joe Jr. to write a series of articles on communism, and receiving no interest from Geoffrey Dawson of the *Times* for his son's account of the fall of Madrid, Joe asked his speechwriter Harvey Klemmer to fashion his son's letters into a book. Page Huidekoper remembers that Joe dumped a pile of Joe Jr.'s letters on Harvey's desk and said, "Turn those into a book and you'll make enough money to send both of your girls to college." By the time Klemmer finished a draft a year later, the outbreak of war had dated young Joe's pro-fascist opinions and made them less fashionable, and the book was unpublishable. Unfortunately, many of Joe's letters to his father from Spain have disappeared.

On Saturday, April 1, Bobby Kennedy carried out his first official diplomatic engagement, representing the United States at the laying of the foundation stone at the Clubland Temple of Youth in South East London. The next day Rose pasted in her scrapbook a *New York Herald* story, headlined "Bobby Kennedy, 13, Proves Chip Off the Old Diplomatic Block: Ambassador's Son Prevents Childish Sino-Japanese Flare-Up." When the Chinese ambassador's eleven-year-old daughter Doris met seventeen-year-old Rosa, who was representing Japan, with which China was at war, there was an uncomfortable silence. The tension was dispelled by Bobby, who jumped in to engage the girls in a discussion of the official opening of the temple with Queen Mary in May. Bobby, the sons of the premier of France and the consul-general of Belgium, the daughters of the Norwegian and Swiss ministers, and the niece of the Chinese ambassador gave speeches. As Ambassador Kennedy, Teddy, and one thousand guests looked on, Bobby read his comments forcefully from a crumpled piece of paper that he pulled out of his pocket: "All the temples I've read about in history books are very old—and they've lasted a long time. But this 'Temple of Youth' is awfully young. . . . When I'm a man—it will be grown up too . . . Many years from now, when we are old, this Temple of Youth will still be standing to bring happiness to many English children."

On April 4, three days after the Spanish Civil War officially ended with the surrender of the last of the Republican forces, Rose and Joe swept past photographers at 10 Downing Street as they arrived for lunch with the Chamberlains. The prime minister "looked very worn down, compared with last spring," Rose wrote in her diary. Chamberlain hoped to rest over the Easter holiday in Scotland, he told them, but wondered warily "what Hitler had in view" regarding further expansion of German territory in Europe. Would he be confident about the prospects for peace if Hitler were to die? Rose asked him. Chamberlain said he would. That night at the Brazilian embassy, the Kennedys attended a glittering dinner party honoring Queen Mary. The dowager queen told Rose how amused she had been by Teddy's behavior at Nancy Astor's recent children's party. Even though his hat kept falling off, Teddy tried to hold onto it tightly as he bowed and bowed to her.

I N MID-MARCH, on his way back to London from Rome with his father, Jack had stopped in Paris for lunch with Carmel Offie—or "La Belle Offlet," which was one of Jack's affectionate nicknames for him. Offie was William Bullitt's secretary at the Paris embassy, and had been his lover beginning with their joint tenure in late 1933 at the U.S. embassy in Moscow. Bullitt invited Jack to stay with "him and the Offer [as Jack called him], but think I shall graciously decline," Jack told Lem, but he provocatively wrote him, "Offie . . . and I are now the greatest of pals and he is really a pretty good guy though I suppose it will make you ill to hear it . . . Offie has just rung for me so I guess I have to get the old paper ready and go in and wipe his arse." He wanted to keep his social options open. Jack returned to London to attend the Grand National steeplechase. He did little work "but have been sporting around in my morning coat, my 'Anthony Eden' black Homburg and white gardenia smelling slightly like George Steele."

Not long after his brother's heroic return from Spain, Jack set off on his own independent intelligence-gathering tour in Europe. He spent a month working alongside William Bullitt at the Paris embassy, where he obsessively studied all the diplomatic cables. Offie remembers him "listening to telegrams being read or even reading various things which were actually none of his business but since he was who he was we didn't throw him out." Jack was passionate about assimilating vast amounts of political information, and he loved watching the day-to-day unfolding of foreign affairs.

O N GOOD FRIDAY, Joe and Rose were finishing an unpenitential round of golf at their local club when a staff member interrupted Joe with a news bulletin. Rose watched as his face tensed up. Mussolini, piqued that Hitler had not given him advance warning about his invasion of Czechoslovakia, and tired of being overshadowed by the German dictator, had just ordered an invasion of the small mountain kingdom of Albania. After weeks of threats, the Italians had crossed the Adriatic and had captured several key Albanian ports. Five days later, the Albanian parliament voted under duress to unite the country with Italy. Britain and France might have no choice but to go to war. Albania was an easy stepping-stone for an Italian invasion of Greece and the whole Balkan Peninsula. Joe rushed back to the Foreign Office to monitor events. He asked Chamberlain about whether Britain would abrogate the Anglo-Italian agreement that had traded British acceptance of Italian sovereignty over Ethiopia for a pledge of friendly relations between the two countries in the Mediterranean, North Africa, the Middle East, and Spain, but the prime minister told him that he needed to ensure the Italians would leave Spain by May 2, as they had agreed to when the Loyalists surrendered. Otherwise, Italy could use Spain as a base for an attack on France.

"Everyone stunned and shattered by news of Italians advance, especially on Good Friday," Rose wrote. "It seems their technique always calls for their coups [invasions] taking place over the weekends." She felt sorry that the Chamberlains would have to cut short their holiday weekend, but that was the least of the prime minister's travails. He was badgered by his two opposition parties and, as he wrote his sister Ida, "Winston who is the worst of the lot, telephoning almost every hour of the day." He wondered whether Churchill, if included in the government, would wear him out "resisting rash suggestions" for calling Parliament in session on a Sunday to conduct important business or seizing Corfu as a hedge against Axis incursions.

On April 11, Kennedy cabled Hull that, according to Halifax, the British government was about to offer both Greece and Romania a guarantee of protection, thus extending their policy of encircling Germany and fending off Italy. The Italian paper *Correre della Sera* posited that because Britain "seemed to have a mania for guaranteeing countries which no one was likely to attack, she might like to guarantee the moon." Illustrating his plans for encirclement of the fascist countries, Chamberlain showed Joe a map and wryly declared, "If this continues much longer, I will need a new map." The spring of 1939 seemed a race to see whether the Western democracies could encircle their totalitarian adversaries before they were encircled themselves. A few days later, Kennedy cabled Hull to say that Chamberlain was falling apart: "He has failed more in the past week than he has in the past year. He walks like an old man and yesterday talked like one."

FURIOUS AT THE NEW FASCIST AGGRESSION, FDR came up with an ingenious plan to put Hitler and Mussolini in a box. Calling himself a "friendly intermediary" speaking "with the voice of strength," he sent them a letter, which he read at a press conference, asking if they would give a ten-year guarantee not to attack or invade any of a group of thirty independent countries that included all of Scandinavia, Western Europe, Eastern Europe, as well as Syria, Palestine, Egypt, and Iran. "Heads of great governments in this hour are literally responsible for the fate of humanity," Roosevelt declared. "History will hold them accountable for the lives and happiness of all—even unto the least. I hope your answer will make it possible for humanity to lose fear and regain security for many years to come."

Mussolini replied to FDR in a speech celebrating the opening of two huge new buildings that were part of his World Exhibition outside Rome: "If we had any intention of setting the world ablaze, we should not be harnessing ourselves to a task [building the World Exhibition] so enormous." Hitler was incensed—no surprise at all—at what he viewed as the president's arrogance. On April 28, in a globally broadcast speech listened to by several hundred million people, he mocked Roosevelt's call for a guarantee and used Orson Welles's *War of the Worlds* radio narrative, which had caused such panic in America the previous fall, to suggest that the American press was causing the current hysteria by fabricating lies. "Unbridled agitation on the part of the press," he said, "and an artificial spreading of panic goes so far that interventions from another planet are believed possible and cause scenes of desperate alarm." During this tense exchange, Kennedy was thankful when FDR agreed to move part of the U.S. fleet to the Pacific to support the British Royal Navy there, allowing Britain to focus on containing the Italian navy in the Mediterranean.

In the midst of this crisis, on Friday, April 14, Joe and Rose accompanied James Roosevelt, who was representing his father, to Windsor Castle to spend a weekend with the royal family. They presented the king and queen a copy of the president's speech, whose words of support for Britain the king read so avidly that the royal couple was late for dinner. In less than two months they would visit the United States to do their part in Britain's advocacy campaign, spearheaded by the Foreign Office, to stir moral, political, and practical support for Britain's cause.

At dinner Joe sat to the right of the queen, who, clad in a gold dress, was as "lovely and charming as ever," he thought. As she sat down next to him, the queen laughed and said, "I have a hard time fitting into these chairs with these new dresses, but tonight I don't seem to overflow." Stung by public sniping about her plumpness, she had lost weight in anticipation of her North American visit. The queen noted that the previous April she and the British court had all been abuzz about curtailing court presentations, but now they were discussing invasions of countries. "She wanted still very much to go to the U.S.A. no matter how dangerous it was because not to go would give satisfaction to the enemies," Joe wrote in his diary. "What a woman." The queen laughed about the possibility that she and the king might get stuck in Canada or America if war broke out. "I suggested moving to the U.S.," Kennedy recounted. "We would love to have her."

To counter this serious talk of war, Kennedy brought the queen a nugget of gossip he knew she would relish: The previous spring, while in Paris, Rose had declined to dine with the duke and duchess of Windsor because they were out of favor in royal circles. A few weeks later she felt obligated to accept Bill Bullitt's invitation to a dinner with the disgraced royal couple, but she did not curtsy to the duchess. Her slight was not taken lightly. That summer in Cannes, an American newspaper reporter showed Mrs. Kennedy the draft of an article she had written in coopera- tion with the duchess. In it, Wallis Simpson called the Kennedys "undemo- cratic snobs, only concerned to lick the boots of royalty," neglecting to point out her pique at Mrs. Kennedy's inattention to her own ducal boots. When the reporter asked Rose for her reaction, Joe insisted that the article include his own comment: "I know of no position that I could hold which would involve my wife in any obligation to dine with a tart." The duchess quickly quashed the article. According to Joe, the queen laughed when he told her the story and said "that it served her right."

Earlier that evening, Princess Beatrice, Queen Victoria's youngest daughter, now in her early eighties, had stoked Joe's anti-Soviet senti- ments with a tale about a recent Russian catfight in Buckingham Palace. The previous Soviet ambassador's wife encountered one of the old czarina's ladies-in-waiting at a palace reception and spat at her. The lady-in-waiting spat back. Such were the primitive complications of international Soviet- Russian relations.

After attending Catholic mass that Sunday morning at Windsor, Joe and Rose went out for a walk, encountering the royal couple. Joe told them he would write an account of the last six months of world events and dedicate it to the king, "the man who has the most to lose and shows it the least." Blushing, the queen slipped her arm through the king's and said, "That would be most kind of you."

Arriving for lunch that day, Neville Chamberlain greeted the Kennedys enthusiastically, buoyed by Roosevelt's message to the dictators and deci- sion to shore up the U.S. Pacific fleet, and told Joe that he was delaying any agreements with the Russians until he had lined up agreements with the Balkan states. Joe sat between Princess Elizabeth, whom he thought "handles herself beautifully," and the queen. The princess talked about Snow White and her favorite dwarf, Dopey, while the queen discussed how difficult it was to make any definite plans for her family that summer with war looming. When a ladybug was discovered at the table, Princess Elizabeth proclaimed it good luck and offered the tiny insect to the prime minister. Gingerly, it was ladled from one gold spoon to another down the table until it reached the queen, who made several attempts to place it on the prime minister. Finally the ladybug began to climb up his shoulder. The stiff-necked Chamberlain was uncomfortable. "It will probably go down my neck," he said. The queen removed the good luck symbol from the beleaguered prime minister and sent it to the other end of the table. This would not be Chamberlain's lucky year.

That afternoon the Kennedys, the royal couple, the Chamberlains, Princess Beatrice, and her older sister, Princess Helena Victoria, went to Surrey to inspect several balloon squadrons, an expedition that the *New York Times* declared indicative of Britain's "interest in tightening her defenses." Viewing these kinds of photographs in their daily newspapers, Americans were slowly absorbing the possibility that the Nazis would attack England, perhaps sooner than they expected.

In another venture into the heart of British aristocracy a week later, Rose, Joe, Joe Jr., Eunice, Pat, and Kick spent what Kick told Lem Billings was an "exciting weekend" with Lady Astor at Cliveden. The king and queen, their daughters, and Queen Mary arrived unexpectedly. Rose, a dynamo herself, had met her match in her weekend's hostess. "Nancy Astor has the most amazing energy of anyone I have ever seen," Rose recorded in her diary. "She went to Christian Science church, had a huge lunch with about twenty-eight to thirty, went off to play eighteen holes of golf." Rose was drawn to Nancy Astor because she saw aspects of herself in the other woman: "I think she is inherently good, works hard to help out others, strives to do the right thing, is passionately devoted to her family." But while she shared personality traits with Lady Astor, Rose lacked her playfulness, which could have allowed her to impart her moral convictions in a lighter and more effective fashion.

ON APRIL 20, in celebration of Hitler's fiftieth birthday, the German propaganda minister Joseph Goebbels choreographed the largest display of military might in the history of Germany. The five-hour parade in Berlin was designed to intimidate the Western powers, giving them second thoughts about bucking Hitler's will for national expansion. "There is no one on the globe who can remain indifferent to the name of Hitler," Dr. Goebbels declared. "The great German Reich has now been brought to pass in the broadest sense, and the Fuhrer has brought peace to central Europe." With his typical focus on the financial imperatives underlying political situations, Kennedy told Cordell Hull that he feared that Hitler would be forced into war to keep his economy from falling apart. Still hoping against hope or willfully blind, Chamberlain urged King George to send Hitler birthday greetings—an act of good will the king would come to regret.

Kennedy still felt that the United States should remain a hegemon in North America but should stay out of Anglo-European conflicts. He counted on the Soviet Union and Germany to weaken each other in their struggle for power in the East. If worse came to worst, he was willing to see America become a garrison state, reducing personal liberties in the short run to defend itself against aggressive empires in Europe and Asia. The day after Hitler's birthday, Kennedy was scheduled to make a speech in London, but Adolf Berle, the assistant secretary of state, was so disturbed by his planned comments "urging England not to support a war" that he convinced FDR to approve a cablegram insisting he refrain from any such incendiary statements. Kennedy got the point, but sent Cordell Hull a tongue-in-cheek dispatch saying that for his next public appearance, when he received his doctor of laws degree from the University of Edinburgh, he would, as ordered, omit all references to international affairs, "talking about flowers, birds, and trees. The only thing I am afraid of is that instead of giving me the freedom of the city [a municipal award honoring an esteemed individual] they will make me the queen of the May."

It was a sour preamble for the ceremony at Edinburgh University, where Kennedy was formally capped by the vice chancellor. Next he went to Usher Hall in Edinburgh, where he was given the freedom of the city. As he was being honored for his "weighty responsibilities," several of the three thousand citizens in the hall had to be removed when they protested against his isolationist policies. The press praised Kennedy's speech, which called on world leaders to be cognizant that their actions could undermine society itself. Declaring that "war was not inevitable," he challenged his audience that amid their anxiety they not forget their many blessings, which included freedom, faith, and friendship. The calm courage with which people were going about their business was, for him, one of the most hopeful aspects of the current situation, and "as long as we could rise above self and dedicate ourselves to the service of our fellow men . . . the future was not without hope."

On April 27, Parliament enacted the Military Service Act, reinstituting compulsory military service. In a huff, Germany pulled out of the 1935 Anglo-German naval accord. Kick was struck by the equanimity of the British populace toward the accumulating auguries of war: "People over here are absolutely calm compared to the Americans," she wrote her friend Lem Billings in the States. "It's rather odd as England is so near and exposed and America so far away and comparatively safe." Lem had recently noticed a change in American attitudes toward the military and the possibility of armed conflict. He wrote Kick, "Last night at the movies they showed the newsreel pictures of our air force and army maneuvers and everyone hysterically got up and cheered," and he added ominously, "even brother John's flat feet and bad stomach won't keep him out of this one."

JOSEPH STALIN'S MURDEROUS EXCESSES in Russia and the Loyalists' atrocities toward the Catholic Church in Spain had intensified Kennedy's antipathy to communism. He had watched with unease as Britain and France began negotiations with Russia in mid-March on a tripartite alliance, as a bulwark against further Fascist aggression in Europe. In April, Soviet foreign minister Maxim Litvinov had convinced Stalin to put an offer of an alliance with Britain in writing, but Chamberlain proceeded cautiously. He worried that a pact with the Russians would alienate Spain and drive it into the Axis camp—costing the British far more than he thought they would gain from a Russian alliance. However, on April 12, Spain signed an anti-Comintern (against both the Soviet Union and international communism) pact that allied it with Japan, Germany, and Italy. Spain would, a few weeks later, withdraw from the League of Nations. In spite of these events, in mid-April, Britain and France rejected the first Russian proposal for an alliance against Germany. Kennedy and Chamberlain knew what a treacherous opponent Russian leader Joseph Stalin could be. He had executed more than half of his central committee members, and had ordered his secret police to kill millions all across Russia.

Churchill was pushing hard for such a pact. "Without Russia there can be no effective Eastern front," he said in the House of Commons. "If the government, having neglected our defenses for a long time, having thrown away Czechoslovakia [and its] military power, having committed us without examination of the technical aspects to the defense of Poland and Rumania, now reject and cast away the indispensable aid of Russia and so lead us into the worst of worlds, into the worst of wars, they will ill have deserved the confidence . . . [of] their fellow-countrymen. . . ."

Kennedy remained wary of such an alliance. He believed that Russia would fight to stop a Nazi thrust through Poland and Romania whether or not Stalin made a pact with the West. He wanted Germany and Russia to pounce on each other and destroy themselves.

Joseph Davies, the U.S. ambassador to Belgium—and formerly to the Soviet Union—visited London and debated the Russian situation with Kennedy. He strongly disagreed with Kennedy's position. Russia's over-riding need for security, Davies felt, would actually push it into an alliance with Germany if it could not forge a suitable pact with the other Western powers. The entire process of Anglo-Russian rapprochement was abruptly plunged into jeopardy in early May when the Jewish and pro-British for-eign minister Litvinov was unexpectedly replaced by Vyacheslav Molotov, a relatively unknown political figure. Hitler was reportedly delighted to see Stalin remove from power the government's last Russian Jew. MP Chips Channon deftly summed up the ambivalence of his government: "I gather that it has now been decided not to embrace the Russian bear, but to hold out a hand and accept a paw gingerly." Chamberlain was exasperated with the Soviets. "I can't make up my mind whether the Bolshies are double crossing us," he wrote his sister Ida, "or whether they are only showing the cunning and suspicion of the peasant . . . I incline toward the latter view."

WITH THE SUPPORT OF KENNEDY and other figures in diplomatic circles, Chamberlain continued his race toward encirclement. Two weeks after the invasion of Albania, Britain announced that it would pro-tect the independence of the Netherlands, Switzerland, and Denmark. On May 12, in an effort to secure the Balkans, Britain and Turkey signed a mutual assistance pact to protect against German and Italian aggression in the Mediterranean. Some experts were now predicting that Germany would respond with a preemptive strike against Britain, unleashing mas-sive air raids and gas attacks to destroy British cities. Posters were placed throughout London warning how to recognize mustard gas and giving in-structions on how to decontaminate oneself. Silver barrage balloons, de-signed to deter enemy aircraft, appeared in the London skies. Parliament passed a Civil Defense bill requiring adequate air-raid facilities and com-pulsory blackouts in buildings, and the government proceeded with plans to evacuate to the country some two million London children at the first sign of war.

In this fraught climate, Joe Kennedy saw a possibility to ratchet down tensions with the Nazis—a scheme in which he would be a central player. James Mooney, president of General Motors Overseas, had called him on May 4, inviting him to come to Paris for a dinner party that would include Hermann Goering's assistant, the American-educated economist Dr. Helmut Wohltat. Mooney told Kennedy that Nazi officials would agree to a general disarmament and steps toward peace in exchange for an Anglo-American gold loan of $500 million to $1 billion, which would help finance Goering's ambitious Four Year Plan to build a self-sufficient and independent German economy, as well as restore German colonies and remove embargoes on German goods. Joe cabled Cordell Hull to ask what special financial or political information he should obtain from Wohltat, who had influence with the Reichsbank and with Foreign Minister Ribbentrop.

Hull ordered Kennedy not to go to Paris. Sumner Welles cabled him that his attendance at such a dinner might create a false impression and incite "unfortunate comment." Kennedy went over the head of the State Department to talk to the president. Roosevelt insisted that he have nothing to do with Wohltat. While Kennedy thought these negotiations held genuine promise, Hull and Roosevelt considered them to be potentially damaging pipe dreams. They had already concluded that Hitler was set on an aggressive course meant eventually to encircle America.

Kennedy defied the State Department. Determined to explore all avenues—especially economic ones—for accommodation with Germany, he met secretly at London's Berkeley Hotel, on May 9, with Mooney and Wohltat, who had quietly flown to Britain. According to Mooney's unpublished manuscript, "Each man made an excellent impression on the other. It was heartening . . . to witness the exertion of real effort to reach something constructive."

Several days later, the *Daily Express* uncovered the "special mission" and, no doubt, gave Kennedy a chill by announcing Wohltat's appearance in London under the front-page headline "Goering's Mystery Man is Here." The Nazi banker fled London before reporters could catch up to him and discover who his contacts in London were. Mooney suspected that MI5, the British domestic Counter Intelligence Service, had deliberately leaked Wohltat's name to the press. It is very possible that the British were now worried enough about the U.S. ambassador to put him under surveillance. Joe's transgressive meeting with Wohltat would mark a pivotal point in his ambassadorship—thereafter he would increasingly lose the confidence of President Roosevelt and the British government.

CHAPTER 13

The Last Whirl

IN EARLY MAY, the Irish Republican Army detonated tear gas bombs in two London movie theaters. Since the beginning of the year the IRA had waged a terror campaign, acts that would soon include blowing up the statue of King Henry VII at Madame Tussaud's waxworks and the explosion of acid bombs in post offices and letter boxes across Britain, in protest of the partition of Ireland, in 1922, into Northern Ireland and the southern Irish Free State. Scotland Yard was understandably worried when the Irish-American ambassador invited the king and queen to a dinner party at the American embassy on May 5, the day before the royal couple were to leave on the first tour of North America ever undertaken by a reigning monarch. Security was pervasive and probing; detectives interviewed the embassy butler, who reassured them he was employing only staff that had served at Buckingham Palace.

Rose was obsessed with creating the perfect evening for the royal couple. As a final decorative touch, she asked Carmel Offie to send "unusual flowers" from Paris, but the flowers did not arrive until a couple of hours before the dinner. "Everyone was rather nervous until they arrived because it always takes a long time to arrange them, and get the right colors for the right room," Rose noted in her diary. She chose "particularly lovely moth-orchids" for the table. Fearful that reporters covering the event would consider orchids as "too nouveau riche or too extreme" for table decorations, she used their botanical name, fillanopsis, when speaking to the press. Rose had fresh strawberries flown from Paris for an old-fashioned shortcake, but the meal would otherwise be all-American—including Baltimore shad roe and mousse of Virginia ham flown over from the United States, Georgia pickled peaches, and Uncle Sam savory.

Just after 8 P.M., William Bullitt arrived, "very elegant and very happy-looking, as usual," Joe wrote. Among the carefully chosen guests were Nancy and Waldorf Astor; Lord and Lady Halifax; the Foreign Office undersecretary, Viscount Cranborne (the future marquess of Salisbury), and his wife; the queen's brother David Bowes-Lyon and his wife, Rachel; and the dukes and duchesses of Devonshire and Beaufort. Just before 8:30 P.M., Joe and Rose, who was wearing an elegant turquoise satin dress and a tiara in honor of the queen, went downstairs to welcome the royal couple. As required by protocol, Joe met them at the foot of the stairs. The queen, in a "beautiful pink satin gown with paillettes, a crinoline style which she wears," led the way—by order of the king—upstairs to the Louis XVI reception room overlooking the garden. The royal couple declined cocktails, with the queen telling Rose that they "never lifted her up."

Jack flew back from Paris for the historic evening. At dinner, Rose seated her six youngest children at a small table in view of the royal couple. When the queen joined Rose upstairs for a "little powder," she inadvertently embarrassed her hostess. Elizabeth asked Rose if she got up in the morning to see her children off for school. "I used to in . . . the good old days," Rose replied, "but now [that] I am usually up late at night and [I] rest in the morning." To Rose's dismay the queen explained that she got up, "half-dressed," to see off her two daughters, and then went back to bed.

After dinner the king and queen spoke privately with some of the American guests about their upcoming trip to the United States. The Kennedys then screened two films—a Walt Disney short film, followed by *Goodbye, Mr. Chips*, during which the queen had a "little weep."

The next day, May 6, the royal couple left on a seven-week visit to the Western Hemisphere. This parting dinner would be as close as Joe got to the royal tour; Roosevelt deliberately excluded his potential presidential rival from this highly publicized Anglo-American event.

That same weekend, in Munich, Unity Mitford was photographed having tea with Hitler. "Hitler, unsmiling, looks overweight and menacing while Unity—also overweight, also unsmiling—seems ill at ease in the presence of her hero," social chronicler Angela Lambert concluded. At this same time, 330,000 German Jews were losing their last remaining freedoms: They were no longer allowed to live in buildings with Aryan tenants.

DESPITE THE MENACE of the IRA bombings, and the absence of the king and queen on their vital and much-ballyhooed tour of the West, the London Season proceeded with its highly publicized and sometimes tedious rituals. The Season featured an average of ten dances a week, which Jessica Mitford described as "[e]ndless successions of flower-banked ballrooms filled with very young men and women, resembling uniformly processed market produce at its approximate peak."

The Season's May centerpiece was the annual birthday ball in aid of Queen Charlotte's Maternity Hospital, hosted by five of Britain's most esteemed duchesses, at Grosvenor House. Eunice Kennedy was one of 228 girls who swept down two staircases in pairs and curtsied with martial precision—staving off their giggles—first to Queen Victoria's granddaughter Princess Helena Victoria and then to a cake honoring Queen Charlotte, the queen consort of King George III, against whose government the American colonies had revolted. Guests were required to wear tiaras, white gloves, and decorations. "In this way we expect to get people to dress up again and get away from their present gas-mask mood," said a *Daily Mail* columnist.

Rose faced a fresh round of social anxieties in presenting her third daughter that season. Her children were sneaking off to nightclubs, as the duke of Kent would accidentally tell her—"he had seen Kennedys at every table at the 400 Club which is supposed to be rather gay and not a place for Kathleen." Joe would reprimand his daughter, and the duke apologized to Kick for ratting on her.

Accorded the highest social status were families holding a coming-out ball in their own homes, such as Lady Astor, who, on May 9, brought her niece Dinah Brand out into Anglo-American society at 4 St. James's Square. Nancy's sister Phyllis, Dinah's mother, had helped Nancy captivate British society in the Edwardian era. Nancy had been absolutely devoted to Phyllis, who had died in 1937. Lady Astor, as a divorcée, was forbidden to present Dinah at court, but she compensated by launching her niece with unparalleled style. Rose and Joe arrived before the dance that night, mingling with debutantes, dukes, and duchesses at a dinner for fifty, served by footmen resplendent in livery and wearing white gloves. Rose was escorted to dinner by Billy Hartington's father, Edward Cavendish, the tenth duke of Devonshire. The Astors' ballroom was redolent with spring flowers brought up from Cliveden, interspersed among gardenia trees in full bloom. As the band serenaded the guests with "Anything Goes" and "Cheek to Cheek," Rose watched Joe dance with the duchess of Kent and admired her light "pink frock with a parture of light blue turquoise"—a wedding gift from Queen Mary. Such events would be London society's last dance before the advent of world war.

SIGNALING HIS GROWING AFFECTION for the Kennedys and his increasing reliance on the ambassador as an ally, the prime minister invited Joe and Rose to spend the weekend of May 13 at Chequers. Two days earlier, Chamberlain had publicly dismissed Hitler's claims that Britain wanted to isolate Germany, and made clear he would not tolerate any further Nazi interference with Europe's autonomous states. The use of force in Danzig, he declared, would incite war. After lunch, on a magnificent spring day when the crab apple and Japanese cherry trees were in full bloom and the paths were lined with tulips, cowslips, and daffodils, the Chamberlains took the Kennedys walking on the downs around the estate. Accompanying them were his chancellor of the Exchequer, Oliver Stanley, and his wife; Viscount Lee, who had donated Chequers for the use of Britain's prime ministers; Conservative chief whip David Margesson; and the Chamberlains' daughter and son-in-law. Annie Chamberlain, Neville's wife, had a special interest in archeology. To Rose's delight, Annie led them to the ruins of a Druid altar, and, overlooking the estate, the remains of the ancient castle of Cymbeline, where Caractacus, the chieftain who led the British resistance to the Roman conquest of England, was reportedly born in the same year as Christ.

Rose was struck with Annie Chamberlain's beautiful features, and thought she must have been "exquisitely lovely when she was young." Neville told Rose that "a combination of Irish and English was hard to beat and she [Annie] is half Irish and half English." Rose admired Neville's devotion to his emotionally and physically fragile wife. Highly strung, and driven to push herself too hard, Annie had undergone several breakdowns in the past two decades, with intermittent periods of depression, psychosomatic symptoms, and exhaustion. In recent years, however, she had become a stolid and calm support for her husband at a harrowing time.

At dinner Rose sat next to Neville, who looked "worn and tired." Since Joe did not want Rose to discuss her political views with his British colleagues, she and the prime minister had usually discussed flowers and trees. She longed to talk with him about the international situation, but again on this occasion, she stuck to a conversation about the difference between Scottish and English bluebells. Chamberlain did, however, speak "about the immorality and the changes for which a war is responsible and cited the

On May 25, 1939, Joe Kennedy and Winston Churchill receive honorary degrees from the University of Bristol. (*JFK Library Foundation*)

increase in divorce and the lack of morality following the last war"—opinions Rose would have endorsed. After dinner Neville showed Joe and Rose the residence's collection of historic artifacts, including the death mask of Cromwell, Queen Elizabeth I's ring, Napoleon's pistols, and autographed letters of Napoleon and Cromwell.

Kennedy soon found himself embroiled in the increasingly incendiary showdown over the future of Palestine. On May 17, the British government published an explosive policy statement, the so-called MacDonald White Paper on Palestine, presided over by Malcolm MacDonald, the secretary of state for the colonies and dominion affairs. The document called for an "independent Palestine state," and reversed the Balfour Declaration of 1922, which had facilitated the eventual development of a Jewish state in Palestine. The White Paper reduced the Jewish right to purchase land, limited Jewish immigration to Palestine for five years, and decreed that Jewish immigration after that time would require the approval of Palestinian Arabs. Six days later, Parliament, despite Winston Churchill's bitter dissent, approved the White Paper, provoking massive worldwide outrage and outbursts of violence. In his memoir, Joe called the White Paper a disappointment.

Jack arrived in Palestine in May 1939 on a fact-finding mission to investigate the viability of the British MacDonald plan for solving conflicts between Jews and Arabs. (*JFK Library Foundation*)

Jack arrived in Palestine just as the White Paper was published. On his first night in Jerusalem, a bomb blew up on the grounds of the King David Hotel, where he was staying; on his final evening, thirteen bombs exploded in Jewish neighborhoods, set by Jews infuriated by the MacDonald declaration. Jack conferred extensively with high-level British civil servants and army officers. Using some provocative hot-button language to negatively characterize Jewish political intentions in the area that perhaps reflected the opinions of his British hosts, he wrote his father that the MacDonald plan was not workable, and that it was "useless to discuss which [side] has the 'fairer' claim." He continued by saying that the "fundamental objections . . . are important. On the Jewish side, there is the desire for complete domination, with Jerusalem as the capital of their new land of milk and honey, with the right to colonize in Trans-Jordan. The Arabs acknowledge and fear the 'superiority' of the Jews." According to Jack, who had not done the kind of thorough investigation that would include talking to Arab and Jewish leaders, the people in that area seemed to favor the Arabs, partly because "the Jews have had, at least in some of their leaders, an unfortunately arrogant, uncompromising attitude." Sadly, most of Jack's other letters to his father from that trip have been lost.

While Jack was in Palestine, Joe received a distressing telegram from Benjamin Cohen, whom he knew from his tenure at the Securities and Exchange Commission. According to Cohen, American Zionists were spreading the rumor that Joe was telling British officials (namely Malcolm MacDonald) to ignore American Jewish outrage about Britain's new Palestine policy because it would have no effect on American public opinion. Joe wrote Rabbi Solomon Goldman, head of the Zionist Organization of America, that he was "frightfully upset" about these misrepresentations. He cabled Cohen, "However I am getting used to this type of experience." In fact, Joe was not getting used to it at all. Such allegations would embitter him, triggering anti-Semitic outbursts after he left his ambassadorship. Joe was mollified when Dr. Chaim Weizmann, the leading spokesman for organized Zionism, visited him at the embassy and apologized for the attacks.

At the same time, Kennedy was persisting in his efforts to rescue Jewish refugees. That spring, many boatloads of desperate German Jews were seeking asylum at ports all over the world. The German government engaged in an exportation policy: "the cruelty" of which "was almost beyond belief," Joe declared in his memoir. "A favourite expedient of the Germans . . . was to load a vessel with Jewish refugees and send it to some country for which these refugees had neither visas nor exit permits." The refugees' plight burst into the headlines on May 27 when the Cuban government refused to honor its pledge to give entry permits to 937 Jewish refugees who had arrived in Havana's harbor aboard the *St. Louis*. By early June, after the Cuban government forced the *St. Louis* to leave its national waters, the ship sailed along the Florida coast, awaiting word of a safe harbor. The day before the king and queen were to enter the United States, President Roosevelt ignored a telegram sent to him on behalf of the *St. Louis* passengers. FDR did not believe he had the political muscle to challenge openly the popular tight immigration quotas.

As the ship sailed back to Europe, the State Department worked through back channels to make sure that the passengers did not have to return to Germany. On June 10, Kennedy wired Cordell Hull that he and Sir Herbert Emerson, the League of Nations high commissioner of refugees, were busy looking for temporary homes for the *St. Louis* passengers. Kennedy met with banker and philanthropist Paul Baerwald, a member of Roosevelt's Advisory Committee on Political Refugees. Baerwald, who was in London setting up a coordinating foundation to assist German Jews, found the

American ambassador to be "extremely amiable." Right after their meeting, Kennedy telephoned British home secretary Sir Samuel Hoare and told him that he had to see him that evening "'to support the recommendation' that the British accept several hundred passengers." Kennedy and Baerwald prevailed upon the British government to take in three hundred passengers. France, the Netherlands, and Belgium agreed to take approximately two hundred passengers each. Tragically, the passengers who did not end up in Britain would later be sent to concentration camps after the Nazis occupied France and the Low Countries, and the plight of the *St. Louis* would become a notorious example of America's failure to save European Jewry.

The noose was tightening. On May 22, Italy and Germany formalized their alliance with the treaty called the Pact of Steel. The next day, Hitler ordered his military leaders to begin preparing for a war with Poland. Following a familiar pattern, Goebbels made sure that Germany asserted that the Poles were abusing the German minority in Poland. Joe Jr. and Jack, on their intelligence-gathering trips across Europe, would be astonished by the creativity and effectiveness of the Nazi propaganda machine.

Their father, worn down by criticism at home and frustrated with FDR's circumvention of him during the preparations for the U.S. royal visit, reserved a seat on one of the first Pan-American transatlantic flights, planning to offer the president his resignation after the king and queen returned from the United States. FDR prevailed upon him to stay on until the fall so that the administration's foreign policy would not appear divided. Rose sailed to New York on May 28 with the excuse that she might be able to offer assistance to the king and queen, who were touring Canada at the time and were still ten days away from entering the United States.

President Roosevelt had hoped to welcome Britain's king and queen with congressional legislation authorizing material support for England if war broke out. He had pushed the House of Representatives to repeal the arms embargo provision of the Neutrality Act, which forbade him to provide arms to nations at war. Even though an April 1939 Gallup poll showed that 57 percent of the American people wanted the Neutrality Act to be changed to allow munitions to be sent to Britain and France, the strongly isolationist Congress thwarted the president's attempt to gain leverage for Britain in its attempts to block Axis aggression.

After a remarkably successful tour of Canada, King George and Queen Elizabeth crossed the border by train at Niagara Falls on June 7, becoming the first British monarchs to enter the United States. Two days later the royal couple arrived at Washington's Union Station to a rapturous reception, and were greeted by Franklin and Eleanor Roosevelt.

Rose, who had been in New York and then Hyannisport during the royal visit, captured the essence of the royal couple's American success: "Everyone unanimous in their praise of the king and queen. Her charm, her kindness, her understanding, her constant smile which puts everyone at their ease." She wrote in her diary, "Then, too, the unexpected incidents, the fact that they mingled with the crowd on different occasions, the fact that they spoke to the newspaper reporters on the train and saw the press at the White House, their willingness to fulfill the social engagements under sweltering heat and overcrowded programmes. Then, too, the king's slim, straight, almost boyish face and figure, his simplicity, unaffected charm, his readiness and even eagerness to cooperate."

Joe perceived the royal visit as an effective warning to the dictators about the potential power of the Anglo-American bond. Deliberately calling attention to his absence from Washington and implying that it was a premeditated policy choice and not the personal slight it actually was, Kennedy acted as the monarch's London public relations man, calling the welcoming handshake between the king and the president at Washington's Union Station "the most important handclasp of modern times." He added, with more hyperbole, that the king and queen had "made more friends for their country than any two people in history." Even as Britain and America moved demonstrably closer, Kennedy maintained his philosophical objection to American intervention in Anglo-European affairs, publicly worrying that the visit might encourage Britain's dependence on the United States and lead his country into war. "A lot of people tell me that Britain is relying on two things today: One is God and the other is the United States, and recently you don't seem to have been counting too much on the Deity," he told Associated Press correspondent James Reston.

Chamberlain, meanwhile, was acknowledging that, with or without America's help, Britain would soon be at war. He told Kennedy he believed Hitler had decided to take on Britain. When Kennedy asked when, he replied, "In August—probably just in time to spoil our vacations."

The king and queen's absence, along with unseasonably cool and rainy weather, made for an Ascot so dreary that it seemed emblematic of the disintegration of the tightly organized late-1930s social world. The London *Times* complained, "Yesterday it was a case of furs . . . of overcoats, of few silk hats and many gray ones . . . It was indeed a sad Ascot from the point of view of fashion . . . It is many years since so few new clothes have been seen. And yet there is evidence that many new clothes were ordered."

A week after Ascot, the Kennedys and members of the British cabinet waited at Waterloo Station to welcome the king and queen back to

London. According to Joe's diary, when the queen greeted him, she asked, "Are you satisfied?" He remembered replying, "I am, if you were. I have to say I knew you would be a tremendous hit."

The king and queen returned home comforted by Franklin Roosevelt's private and premature reassurance during their visit to his home at Hyde Park that America would come to London's aid if the city was bombarded by Germany. The next day at the monarchs' welcome-home luncheon at Guildhall, the Kennedys heard the newly confident king proclaim that the Empire stood as a powerful force protecting "peace and goodwill among mankind." Rose noted in her diary that the king spoke without stuttering. Joe told Halifax, "King George VI became a real king of the British Empire today at lunch." Halifax agreed.

The night of the royal return, the Kennedys hosted Eunice's "small" coming-out dance at 14 Prince's Gate. The British nobility showed up in force at what would be the Kennedys' last great hurrah in London. Jack, Joe Jr., and their parents looked on as Eunice, in a peach dress from the French designer Paquin, greeted Lady Astor, Baroness Ravensdale, the duke of Marlborough, and the duchess of Northumberland. Eunice was a reluctant debutante: "I hated those parties," she remembered. "They were terrible. I'd go into the ladies' room and wait for the dance to get over . . . You'd go hide there . . . Then you'd go back and maybe your card was filled for the next dance . . . then bam you'd go back to the ladies' room." Only a week before her own coming out, Eunice had attended Baroness Ravensdale's large ball for her niece Vivien Mosley. Vivien befriended Eunice, remembering her as "a terribly nice girl, actually, though shyer, much more reticent than Kick. Now Kick had established herself as a tremendous character . . . but Eunice was a different kettle of fish. She was awfully sweet, though, and pretty—very pretty."

The current countess of Sutherland, then Elizabeth Leveson-Gower, remembered that "Eunice was much more serious than Kick, not quite so with it. She was very nice—they were all very nice. Eunice wasn't classically good-looking, but she was very attractive because of her terrific energy and her good figure. She was most enjoyable to be around." Eunice did have plenty of spunk. With her lively intelligence and her witty parries, she was far more interesting than most of the British debutantes.

About 2:30 in the morning, Rose noted in her diary, everyone started "doing the 'big apple,' and everybody got very gay." The duke of Marlborough, who had made a request— unusual for a father—to be included in the evening's festivities, was one of the leaders of the "big apple." Rose was "quite surprised and a little shocked" because she had "never seen people reach that state." For Elizabeth Leveson-Gower, the dance was chaotic and enjoyably out of control: "Everyone formed a chain and ran around the house," falling on the floors.

URING THEIR EUROPEAN TRAVELS that spring and summer, Joe Jr. and Jack chronicled Europe's last months of peace. In Hungary on June 10, young Joe reflected on the perils of interventionism and critiqued the flip-flopping U.S. foreign policy. "Are we going to fight for the liberties of the people of the world when [it] is really none of our damned business but is up to the people in those countries themselves?" he asked in a memorandum to his father. "Are we going to guarantee liberty in every country [in] the world and if there then isn't that liberty, are we going to march in? Are we going to yell bloody murder when the Italians go into Ethiopia and Spain and the Germans in Czechoslovakia and then do nothing about it except to call the English cowards for not fighting? . . . Does it ever occur to people that there are happy people in Italy and Germany?" He believed that the United States needed to clarify its foreign policy "rather than the half-hearted mamby pamby policy skipping one way then to the other." If the United States was planning to stay out of European conflicts, he wondered, why did government officials continue to give speeches about the importance of liberties and freedom? If America was prepared to back up its statements with a clear position that German hegemony in Europe was a threat to U.S. interests, then he believed that his government should start giving more funds to countries that might soon have to serve as bulwarks against Nazi expansion.

Expressing a dismissal of the crisis among European Jews that was rare in his written opinions, Joe Jr. wondered, "Do we want to get frightfully aroused by the treatment of the Jews when Cath[olics] and others were murdered more cruelly in Russia and in Republican Spain and not a word of protest came? Do we want an increasing anti-Semitism in our country brought about by the production of forty thousand Jews and political undesirables in our country from Europe . . . ?" He was impressed with the Poles, who "have no nerves at all and are showing a marvelous display of courage in the face of overwhelming odds. They have no fear of Germany . . . their spirit is unbeatable." He recognized, however, that the Polish military equipment could not match the Reich's war machine.

A week later in Berlin, Joe witnessed little talk about war, he told his father. "Hitler is regarded by many people as a God," he wrote, and he believed that Hitler had the support of about 80 percent of the German people even though many of them disagreed with his policy against the Jews. German propagandists, he thought, were working to convince the diplomatic community that Britain would not intervene as Poland came under the influence of Moscow, and that Germany would win a war within several months.

In cheeky and penetrating letters to Lem Billings, Jack chronicled his own tour of the sites of European crisis. He spent time in Paris with a woman who claimed to have been the mistress of the Duke of Kent. To seduce Jack, she pulled out her cigarette case, on the inside of which was a racy engraving of Snow White surrounded by seven very excited dwarfs. Jack hardly needed this enticement. While in Paris, he observed to Lem how anxiously the French awaited a Nazi attack on Poland. In May in Warsaw, he visited with Ambassador Tony Biddle for a week and then sampled the fading domain of old-world Eastern European aristocracy as a guest of Polish aristocrats who lived on vast estates of 100,000 acres worked by ten thousand impoverished peasants. He also bedded a Romanian princess. In Lithuania, he posed as an angel for a religious panel being carved by the wife of an American diplomat. The panel with Jack's likeness would eventually be incorporated into an altar at the Vatican.

Moving on to Danzig, Jack noticed how Nazi symbols dominated the town, its citizens eager to exchange the "Heil Hitler" salute. He wrote Lem, "lst The question of Danzig and the corridor are inseparable. They [Germans] feel that both must be returned. If this is done then Poland is cut off completely from the sea . . . If they [the Poles] return just Danzig . . . they [the Germans] could thus control Polish trade, as by means of guns they could so dominate Gdynia . . . that they could scare all the Jew merchants into shooting their trade thru Danzig . . . Poland is determined not to give up Danzig . . . She will offer compromises but never give it up . . . Germany . . . will . . . try to put Poland in the position of being an aggressor—and then go to work. Poland has an army of 4,000,000 who are damn good—but poorly equipped . . . France can't help . . . and England's fleet will be of little assistance, so Poland will be alone. But they are tough here and . . . they will fight over Danzig as they regard it first as symbolic + 2nd as the keystone."

While the Danzig crisis had temporarily abated, the simmering Sino-Japanese war suddenly heated up. On June 14, four Chinese men suspected of murdering the Japanese manager of the Tientsin branch of the Federal Reserve Bank in northern China took refuge in the British concession there. The Japanese insisted that the British consul-general hand over the suspected murderers; they imposed a blockade on the British and French concessions when their demands were not met. When it became clear that the United States would not offer Britain naval support, Chamberlain had no choice but to enter negotiations with the Japanese.

Ambassador Kennedy's moods vacillated wildly that spring as events in Europe and the Far East presaged a catastrophic war at one moment and the possibility of a prolonged peaceful interlude the next. Walter Lippmann visited him in London on a day when Joe was discouraged, telling the journalist that Britain did not stand a chance against the Nazis and that the Japanese would attack the West. His on-the-record remarks were a major mistake. Spouting off to Lippmann would cost Joe dearly in his relationship with Winston Churchill, who was on the ascendant in the aftermath of the Munich pact.

On June 14, at art historian and broadcaster Kenneth Clark's dinner party in celebration of Royal Hunt Club Day at Ascot, Lippmann told Churchill that Joe thought war was inevitable and that Britain would be beaten. Diarist Harold Nicolson recorded Churchill's defiant and dramatic response. Sitting "hunched there, waving his whisky-and-soda to mark his periods, stubbing his cigar with the other hand, Churchill said, 'It may be true, it may well be true that this country will at the outset of this . . . almost inevitable war be exposed to dire peril and fierce ordeals. It may be true that steel and fire will rain down upon us day and night scattering death and destruction far and wide . . . Yet these trials and disasters . . . will but serve to steel the resolution of the British people and enhance our will to victory. No, the ambassador should not have spoken so, Mr. Lippmann; he should not have said that dreadful word. Yet supposing (as I do not for one moment suppose) that Mr. Kennedy were correct in his tragic utterance, then I for one would willingly lay down my life in combat, rather than, in fear of defeat, surrender to the menaces of these most sinister men.' "

Others, however, shared Kennedy's despair. "Why can we not be left alone? We are doing no harm. We care for fine and gentle things. We wish only to do good on earth," Harold Nicolson wrote to his wife, Vita Sackville-West. "Why is it that we are impotent to prevent something we know to be evil and terrible? I would willingly give my own life if I could stop this war."

After a dinner party for some of Kick's friends at Prince's Gate, the ambassador screened a film about World War I. With images flashing on the screen of British soldiers being slaughtered in trench warfare, he embarrassed Kick by declaring, "That is what you'll all be looking like in a month or two." Joe's children and their British friends were as divided as the British public about the moral necessity of going to war against the dictators.

Like many young British men, Billy Hartington and David Ormsby-Gore were imbued with a sense of honor and did not question their duty to fight. Jack refused to take sides as Kick's friends argued about the ambassador's anti-war sentiments.

On the last day of June, Jack and Eunice attended one of the great coming-out dances of the Season—the countess of Sutherland's party for her niece Elizabeth Leveson-Gower, who would one day herself assume that title. Elizabeth was seated next to Jack Kennedy at dinner and had trouble talking with him. "I was uncomfortable sitting next to him at the party because he was so intelligent and tended to dominate the conversation," she remembered. "He didn't make small talk. He wanted to talk about politics." Jack was particularly energized because Lord Halifax and Winston Churchill had just made major speeches challenging Hitler.

Lord Halifax, speaking about Britain's accelerated rearmament, had said, "We are creating a powerful weapon for the defence of our own liberty and that of other peoples. With every week that passes, the effort gains momentum . . . Behind all our military effort stands the British people, more united than ever before." Churchill addressed Hitler directly, flattering him as a leader, and gave him reason for pause: "Consider well before you take a plunge into the terrible unknown. Consider whether your life's work—which may even now be famous in the eyes of history—in raising Germany from frustration and defeat to a point where all the world is waiting for her actions, consider whether all this may not be irretrievably cast away."

At the end of June, Chips Channon deftly captured the international situation in his diary: "The whole outlook is appalling. Hitler is a bandit; we are all mad; and Russia is winking slyly—and waiting." Even with the prospect of a busy Season and Joe's persistent attempts to bargain for peace, the Kennedys faced the summer of 1939 with dread.

CHAPTER 14

The Glittering Twilight

A S SUMMER BEGAN, Rose confided in her diary that it was a "difficult time because the papers are full of war." The newspapers touted evacuation plans and lists of recommended wartime supplies for the home. Sensing how much she had to lose, Rose latched onto the motto of her outspoken friend Lady Simon, wife of the chancellor of the Exchequer, "Fear knocked at the door, Faith open[ed] it; there was no one without."

Engaging in healthy denial, Rose and Joe attended the two last grand English balls before the onslaught of war ripped apart the social fabric. On July 6, they went to the overcrowded dance for Rosalind Cubitt, the grand-daughter of King Edward VII's renowned mistress, Mrs. Keppel. Rosalind's daughter Camilla Shand may one day be the queen of England.

Joe and Rose's car joined an excruciatingly long line of traffic as one thousand guests turned off Kensington High Street into the gates of the floodlit Holland House, the red brick Jacobean mansion set in its own seventy-acre park—like a country estate inside the city. Holland House, which would be destroyed by the Luftwaffe in 1942, had been an important Whig center at the start of the nineteenth century, but this July night in 1939 it symbolized not only the ending of an era but the final loosening of the starchy royal and aristocratic mores of the early part of the twentieth century. Along with the queen of Spain and playwright Noël Coward, King George VI and Queen Elizabeth gave the night an especially glamorous frisson by attending the ball of a descendent of the late king's mistress—an egalitarian act unheard of during Queen Mary's days as consort.

The next day the duke and duchess of Marlborough gave their coming-out ball at Blenheim Palace for Lady Sarah Spencer Churchill, who had be-friended Eunice. "Having received every beauty treatment available," and advice from every possible member of her family, Eunice headed off for the palace in Oxfordshire, a "national monument," she thought, looking like a "giant sentinel guarding the peaceful countryside."

Jack also went to Blenheim which, he told Lem Billings, was "nearly as big as Versailles." Missing his sidekick, he wrote, "[I]t's really too bad you're not here as it's all darn good fun—never had a better time." Jack brought his new friend Tony Loughborough, who would become the sixth earl of Rosslyn and Baron Loughborough when his grandfather died two months later. Tony and Jack had fashioned themselves as the girl-catching team of "RossKennedy." Enjoying older women, they vied for the at-tentions of the glamorous duchess of Kent. Jack had recently savored the chance to spend time alone with the duchess when she drove down to Lord Dudley's country house with him.

Chips Channon wondered, with good reason, whether England would ever see the likes of that evening again: "I have seen much, traveled far and am accustomed to splendor, but there has never been anything like tonight. The palace was floodlit, and its grand baroque beauty could be seen for miles. The lakes were floodlit too and, better still, the famous terraces, they were blue and green and Tyroleans walked about singing . . . It was gay, young, brilliant, in short, perfection. . . . There were literally rivers of champagne."

"Slightly nervous, but very excited," Eunice proceeded to dinner, pass-ing "stolid butlers dressed in knee breeches and powered wigs," and en-tered the reception room, where she noted that "great battles are still being won in Brussels tapestry." Eunice dined with her young friends on a terrace overlooking the sinuous lake. One of the debutantes, Mollie Acland, re-membered seeing Winston Churchill and Anthony Eden standing together on the terrace, chatting and smoking. Did Jack Kennedy shadow his two role models that evening? Or was he too busy charming the ladies?

For Jack, who was "fascinated by English political society with its casual combination of wit, knowledge, and unconcern," Arthur Schlesinger, Jr., noted, these weekends at country houses were "history come alive" and "had a careless elegance he had not previously encountered." Jack, who had a strong lifelong affinity for British sensibilities and values, would later claim that *The Young Melbourne*, David Cecil's biography of Queen Victo-ria's prime minister, Lord Melbourne, published around the time Jack was at Blenheim, was one of his two favorite books. Jack was captivated by the Whig manner and the mixture of the rational and the urbane in Whig society. He was "enchanted by the Whig zest, versatility, and nonchalance; he liked the idea of a society where politics invigorated but did not monopolize life." Kick Kennedy's good friend David Cecil could have been describing Kennedy when he wrote of Melbourne, "[H]e was a skeptic in thought; in practice a hedonist." Jack saw in Melbourne a role model: a politician who could heroically serve his country while privately engaging in all manner of carnal fun. This Blenheim weekend, the Kennedys, like Lord Melbourne's aristocratic family, the Lambs, partied with abandon: "Good living gave them zest; wealth gave them opportunity; and they threw themselves into their pleasures with animal recklessness."

With an American orchestra providing the music for dancing to the "Big Apple," the "Lambeth Walk," and foxtrots, "round and round we glided," Eunice remembered, "in a ballroom of flowers; lilies, pink and white hydrangeas [which] took the place of the 20,000 valuable books— for the library was converted into a ballroom for this occasion. As dawn slowly lit the skies, the houseguests finished off the party with coffee and hotdogs!"

Chips Channon was taken with Jack and Tony. He invited them the following Tuesday for a luncheon at his home at 5 Belgrave Square in honor of the intelligent, twenty-year-old Princess Cecile, "the half-cross-eyed" younger sister of Kick's great friend Prince Frederick of Prussia. Chips knew he could count on Jack to liven up the luncheon for the princess and a "dark engaging damsel" friend of hers. After a "hilarious party," Chips took Jack and Tony to see the prime minister speak in Parliament.

The next night, at a dinner at society hostess Laura Corrigan's house, Chips sat next to Jack's mother and was not as taken with her: "She is an uninteresting little body, though pleasant and extraordinarily young looking to be the mother of nine. She has an unpleasant voice, and says little of interest." She did, however, have one saving grace: "She keeps a diary, and I always like people who keep diaries; they are not as others, at least not quite."

That uninteresting little body, decked out in an "ice blue satin gown, diamond tiara, ostrich feather fan, and long blue gloves," accompanied Eunice on July 12 for her presentation at Buckingham Palace. Rose received a rude shock when an usher informed her, "I'm very sorry, Madame, but you must have a pair of white gloves." Mrs. Alan Kirk, the wife of the American naval attaché, in a later oral history revealed, "Oh, there was great distress about that!" During the presentation, Rose was forced to wear a pair of ill-fitting spare white gloves furnished by the ushers.

Joe stood next to the German ambassador, who considered the whole court procedure to be a waste of time. When Rose asked his brusque wife if there was anything comparable to the court in Germany, the ambassadress said, "No they were too busy with other things."

Eunice, wearing an ivory tulle crinoline and ivory satin train by her favorite dressmaker, Paquin, was uncharacteristically childlike in writing her impressions of the event: "As I entered the Palace more excitement and joy seized me than ever before in my life." After her name was called, she started to walk toward the king and queen, wondering "if ever I would reach the throne thirty feet away; but somehow, I did. As I made my curtsy . . . I realized that at this moment I was the center of interest of the king and queen and all the pompous ceremony that England hold so sacred."

Joe and Rose actively promoted a refurbished image of Britain in the United States, arranging for royals and politicians to court the American press. The day after the court presentation, the couple held a luncheon for the prime minister to explain his strategy for handling the dictators to American reporters. A few days before, Joe and Rose had included Eunice at a dinner where Queen Mary met American newspapermen.

THAT SUMMER, as war jitters increased, some of the press and the populace showed increased interest in having Churchill, representing toughness, included in the cabinet. After meeting with Chamberlain on July 20, Joe eagerly sent FDR a report critical of Churchill. Chamberlain feared that extending the cabinet would simply make his "international policies the subject of continual football playing." He was unwilling to include Churchill "because he does not believe in the first place that he could deliver nearly one-tenth as much as people think he could; he has developed into a fine two-handed drinker and his judgment has never been proven to be good." He would also lead Britain into a war, Chamberlain thought. "If he was a lot of trouble outside the Government," he told Joe, "he was 20 times more trouble inside" when he served with him in the cabinet. Chamberlain wrote his sister Ida, "His [Winston's] are summer storms, violent but of short duration often followed by sunshine. But they make him uncommonly difficult to work with."

AS THE FINAL SEASON of peace wound down in July, the Kennedy family scattered across Europe for their summer holidays. Kick, Joe Jr., and Hugh Fraser took off for Spain, where Kick had her first taste of the devastation of war. Jack, his Harvard roommate Torbert (Torby)

Macdonald, and David Ormsby-Gore headed first to Paris, and later to Germany.

When David showed up at Prince's Gate to collect Jack for their European journey, Rose asked him what was in his trunk. Inside his valise was a pile of eighteen books, which left room for only a couple of pairs of trousers and shirts. Rose then insisted on inspecting the contents of Jack's suitcase. She was embarrassed because there was not a single book in his case. From then on, according to Ted, Rose would insist that all Kennedy children prove that there was an adequate number of books in their suitcase before they were allowed to leave on a trip.

The ambassador cautioned Jack and David to "bend over backwards to stay out of trouble" with Germans, who were "very tough and paid no attention to laws and rules, and, if anything happened, just to back away." After David returned home for his twenty-first–birthday celebrations, Jack and Torby encountered German hostility in Munich. Driving in a car with British license plates, they slowed down to look at a monument to a Nazi hero. They were heckled and attacked with stones and bricks by Nazi storm troopers. Torby remembered that Jack asked, "You know, how can we avoid having a world war if this is the way these people feel?"

Before he left for the south of France, Joe met with Chamberlain. According to Joe's memoir, Chamberlain believed that Hitler was "intelligent enough not to take that gamble" of starting a war with Britain, and, thus, "we are witnessing the greatest and most expensive dress rehearsal for a show that will never be produced." According to Joe, he paused and added, "At least that is my prayer."

Rose and Joe rented the grand château Domaine de Ranguin, sitting on the hilltop of Mougins and surrounded with a forest, five miles outside Cannes. The château had marvelous rose gardens and a plantation of olive trees, and faced south toward the sea. Joe needed a deep rest. On August 8, he wrote to Admiral Land, from the Maritime Commission, that he was "doing little work if any work. I am dictating this letter to a beautiful French girl, so if it does not make any sense blame it on the French."

Marlene Dietrich, her daughter, her husband, and her lover, novelist Erich Maria Remarque, were spending another August at the nearby Hôtel du Cap at Antibes. Joe swam at the Eden Roc bathing club with Dietrich and Norma Shearer, and watched as seven-year-old Teddy, egged on by his older siblings, mustered his courage and dove off the high point of Eden Roc into the sea below. The ambassador also went yachting with the duke of Windsor and accompanied Rose to Elsa Maxwell's parties.

But Joe was troubled, as he wrote FDR on August 9, by the "very strong anti-Semitic feeling" he noticed "on the part of caddies, waiters and residents" in the south of France. There was also "a general sense of wary waiting for almost anything to happen."

FDR sent him Arthur Krock's July 18 *New York Times* article suggesting that Joe wanted to resign, but that Roosevelt had prevailed upon him to stay on until the fall. The article also detailed how "[t]he young New Dealers have long ceased to approve of Mr. Kennedy." Hoping to drive a wedge between Kennedy and his U.S. booster, FDR told Joe that Krock "has never in his whole life said a really decent thing about any human being without qualifying it by some nasty dig at the end of the praise." The president called him a "social parasite . . . who in his heart is a cynic who has never felt warm affection for anybody. . . ." Disingenuously, FDR wrote Joe that he had "complete confidence" in him and that he was "doing a good job there."

Joe was not fooled by the president's letter. He wondered whether his knowledge and experience were being wasted in London. "After all, I recognize that in this day and age an ambassador may be hardly more than a glorified errand boy," he wrote FDR. In his memoir, Joe complained that he had received little guidance about foreign policy—"Practically nothing except administrative minutiae filtered back to me from the State Department." He had to glean changes in U.S. foreign policy by listening to the public comments of officials. The U.S. State Department did not keep him informed about the substance of conversations they were having with the British ambassador in Washington; sometimes he heard about them through the British Foreign Office. The telephone was only used for emergencies. Joe wrote, "The result from my standpoint was that a sense of disorder and a lack of coordination characterized our foreign policy and that in the machine created to make it effective the ambassador to the Court of St. James's was an inconsequential cog."

There was no malice underlying this, Joe wrote in his memoir, but it was a situation designed to get worse as the pressure mounted during crises. Partly, Joe had valid criticism about the way U.S. foreign policy was run at that time; partly, it was the result of deliberate presidential and State Department circumvention of him.

Joe's August 9 letter to the president suggests why he might have stayed on: "When I was a youngster, my father taught me two principles: gratitude and loyalty . . . he told me that I should never let any act of kindness go by without in some way returning it." His father also told him that "no matter how you may fail in ability you can make it up by being unfailingly loyal to your friends." He owed the president a "debt on both counts," he wrote, and he was trying to live up to these principles. Joe stayed loyal to FDR's mandate, as he saw it, of keeping the United States out of war. He did, however, vent his frustration in London's social circles about his circumvention by the president and the State Department. His behavior was impolitic at best. Word would, of course, get back to the nonconfrontational president, who would withdraw further behind a curtain of official denials.

On several occasions during the spring and summer, Kennedy sent dispatches expressing concern that Russia might turn toward Germany in frustration over the plodding negotiations with the British. The British government was not seriously concerned about a German-Soviet rapprochement, he reported. Chamberlain had told Kennedy in mid-July that he thought the "Russians have made up their minds not to make a deal with anybody and to watch them all tear themselves apart." The U.S. government knew about Russian-German negotiations, Kennedy later claimed in his memoir, but was derelict in not informing him. Had he been able to pass on this information to Halifax and Chamberlain, he believed, the British might have put an end to their stalling tactics. Given Chamberlain's antipathy toward Russia, Joe's conclusion is debatable.

O N AUGUST 12, Jack and Torby left Cannes for their second trip through Germany that summer. After spending time in Munich, Jack headed alone for Prague—where Rose noted in her diary, "we are told no one is allowed" to go—but only after his father pulled rank to get him there. "No trains were running, no planes flying, no frontier stations existed," U.S. Foreign Service officer George Kennan recalled. "Yet in the midst of this confusion we received a telegram from the embassy in London," saying that Kennedy had sent Jack on a fact-finding tour of Europe and "it was up to us to find a means of getting him across the border and through the German lines" so that he could include Prague in his agenda. "We were furious . . . His son had no official status and was, in our eyes, obviously an upstart and ignoramus."

Meanwhile, Joe Jr. dropped Kick off with the family in the South of France, stayed for a brief visit, and then headed for Austria and Germany, where he would gather first-hand intelligence for his father. As much as Kick enjoyed sunbathing on the Riviera, she desperately wanted to return to England for Billy Hartington's grand twenty-first–birthday celebrations at Chatsworth. Rose refused to let her go and Kick missed an extraordinary event: Over two days of brilliant weather, five thousand people attended a series of parties. "The atmosphere [of the party] had something of the Duchess of Richmond's ball before the Battle of Waterloo," Billy's younger brother Andrew recalled. "We sensed it was the closing of an age."

The *Boston Post*, in a story headlined "Kennedy Girl May Wed Peer," announced that Kick and Billy were secretly engaged. Both Joe Kennedy and the duke of Devonshire immediately dismissed the rumor. Although they liked Kick, Billy's parents were edgy about the relationship. Billy dared not ruin his birthday celebrations by confronting them with how strongly he felt about her. Kick, like her brother Jack, was wary of forming deep emotional attachments, and was not ready to make a commitment or cause her parents grief.

ONCE AGAIN Joe watched warily as Winston Churchill made a radio broadcast to the United States. On August 8, Churchill warned Americans of the serious danger ahead. "Holiday time, ladies and gentlemen!" he greeted them before launching into gloomy predictions. "Currently all across Europe there is the hush of suspense, and in many lands, it is the hush of fear. One can also hear the tramp of armies; the armies of Germany and Italy."

In a visit to Danzig, Joe Jr. astutely captured the dismal scene. "For myself," he wrote his father, "I don't see how the issue can be decided without war . . . The people there are at the boiling point . . . They can be worked up no higher. Now they go around singing that Germany is theirs today and tomorrow the whole world will be. Goebbels . . . and the Fuhrer [have] told them that . . . It is a question of waiting till the opportune moment comes and the Fuhrer will take over Danzig. They do not see why the great powers should fight over what is rightly a German city."

The first major hints of trouble occurred when the German press declared on August 16 that there would be no compromise over Danzig. Rose noted in her diary that day that "reports keep coming in that war is imminent and August 29 seems to be the date, as the harvest in Germany will have been reaped and all the reserves have been called." Three days later, intelligence reports suggesting Germany would soon attack Poland motivated Chamberlain to return to London after a vacation in the Scottish highlands during which he had "never enjoyed a carefree mind."

In the middle of August, a French and British military delegation was in Moscow trying to wrap up negotiations for an Anglo-Russian accord. But suddenly, on August 21, Russia and Germany revealed that they had agreed to a non-aggression pact. The next day Joe flew back to London and

Winston Churchill returned from his brief stay in Normandy. Appalled by the prospect of another war and unwilling to see Hitler's world-conquering agenda as Churchill could, Kennedy and Chamberlain would explore every possible avenue for peace.

On the twenty-third, Joe met with Chamberlain, who looked like a "broken man." The prime minister told Joe that he could not fly again [to Germany] "because that was good only once." Worried about the prospect of war, Mussolini had urged the British to push the Poles into general negotiations with Germany, even if they were not ready to discuss Danzig. "It is no use for me to urge the Poles to make concessions," he told Joe, "for that would only be interpreted as weakness on our part. . . . The Poles can't be saved. All that the English can do is wage a war of revenge that will mean the entire destruction of Europe." Joe asked if the pope could help, but Chamberlain shook his head. He requested that Joe urge FDR to tackle three diplomatic fronts: pressuring Poland's foreign minister, Jozef Beck, for concessions; strategizing about how to turn Japan and Spain, which were unnerved by the German-Russian pact, against the Axis; and influencing Italy to serve as a moderating influence on the Reich.

Ribbentrop went to Moscow and, in the early morning hours of August 24, formally signed the treaty with Russia. Ecstatic, Hitler told Ribbentrop that the agreement would "hit like a bombshell." The British Parliament—with members restless and irritable about shortening their summer break—was called into session for that day. Chamberlain, speaking calmly—in Harold Nicolson's words, "like a coroner summing up a case for murder"—told the Commons that Britain would honor its commitments this time. "We shall not be fighting for the political future of a far away city in a foreign land," he told them, "but rather for national honor and principles of just international relations, which underlay peace and security."

Chips Channon summed up the numb reaction in the city: "I suppose it is like getting married; the second time it is impossible to work up the same excitement. Certainly tonight London is quiet and almost indifferent to what might happen. There is a frightening calm."

Parliament passed the Emergency Powers Act, which gave the government enormous power over the mobilization of industries, personnel, and resources. On the streets of London, civil defense volunteers methodically sandbagged public structures and shielded illuminated street signs and lights. White lines were painted on the curbs and streets so people could make their way under blackout conditions.

Joe Kennedy issued an urgent press release advising American travelers to leave England: "We feel that it is our duty to warn those Americans now in England that, by remaining longer, they are running the risk of inconvenience and possibly danger." Kennedy worked feverishly to convince Dutch, Swedish, and Norwegian lines to shift their boats from other runs, dock them in British ports, and pick up travelers anxious to leave England. Despite his efforts, there was still not enough space aboard ships for everyone who was desperate to leave. All Americans staying in England were required to register with the American Consulate.

In Europe, panic ensued. Politicians, aristocrats, and debutantes scurried to escape their summer retreats. Rose quickly gathered her children—she dragged Kick and her friend Jane Kenyon-Slaney off the beach in their bathing suits—for a train ride to Paris. On the way, they watched trains bearing French troops headed toward Poland.

On the twenty-fourth, prompted by calls from Horace Wilson asking how FDR would respond to Hitler's illegal decision to place Albert Forster, the gauleiter of Danzig, in the position of chief of state, Joe called FDR and urged him to put pressure on the Poles to start negotiations.

"I don't care how it is done," Joe remembered saying, "so long as something is done and done quickly."

"All right," the president said, "something will be done tonight." But he was only giving lip service to his determined ambassador. FDR and his State Department advisors were not interested in becoming responsible for a "second Munich," according to European bureau chief Jay Pierrepont Moffat's diary. Roosevelt did appeal to Hitler and President Ignacy Mościcki of Poland to resolve their disputes short of war, suggesting a mediator from a South American country.

THE NEXT DAY, Joe waited restlessly for news about British ambassador Henderson's meeting with Hitler in Berlin. At 10 P.M., Joe and his private secretary Jack B. Kennedy hailed a taxi to 10 Downing Street. Murmuring, "The American ambassador," the large crowd thought his late-night presence might be significant. Horace Wilson provided Joe with Henderson's cables, which indicated that Hitler had made a "ridiculous" proposition: Hitler declared that, now that Russia would back him up with supplies, Poland would be carved up by Russia and Germany. The Fuhrer demanded that Britain urge Poland to make concessions to Germany. In return for Britain's help, Hitler would "limit armaments, go back to peaceful pursuits, and become an artist, which is what he wanted to be." In an aside, Kennedy wrote Hull that "he is now [an artist] but I would not care to say what kind."

Wilson invited Kennedy into the cabinet room where he was meeting with Chamberlain, Halifax, and Cadogan. When asked for his advice, Joe remembered that he told Chamberlain, "You must pass the hat before the corpse gets cold." The prime minister did not understand. "Propose a general settlement that will bring Germany economic benefits more important than the territorial annexation of Danzig," Kennedy explained. "Get the United States to say what they would be willing to do in the cause of international peace and prosperity. After all, the United States will be the largest beneficiary of such a move. To put in a billion or two now will be worth it, for if it works we will get it back and more." Kennedy still relied far too heavily on economics as a lever; while he understood that Hitler was a liar and a bully, he could not grasp the Fuhrer's obsession with the ideology of hatred. Blinded by his hopes for peace, Kennedy failed to imagine that Hitler had an entirely different and far more sinister agenda. As he left the Cabinet Room, he put his hand on Chamberlain's shoulder and said, "I still believe God is working with you."

Still struggling to overcome his sense of himself as an insignificant outsider, Joe was excited by his brush with decision making at a crucial hour. "When I left No. 10 I thought to myself that incident has probably been the most important thing that has ever happened to me," he wrote in his memoir. "Here I am an American ambassador called into discussion with the P.M. and the foreign secretary over probably the most important event in the history of the British Empire. I had been called in even before the Cabinet and had been trusted not only for my discretion but for my intelligence. It was a moving experience." FDR, however, would not be moved.

Enamored of drama and danger, Joe Jr. stayed in the German capital to soak up the final days of war preparations. On the day the German-Soviet agreement was reached, he met Debo Mitford's older sister, twenty-five-year-old Unity Valkyrie. He was appalled by her appearance—"She is not at all pretty, with very bad teeth and terribly fat, however with a certain fine Aryan look"—and her views. He informed her about the accord, which she thought would prevent war. He found her, understandably, to be in "a state of high nervous tension," and preoccupied with thoughts of Hitler. Unity told Joe that Hitler was not merely a genius; he was a man who had not made a mistake—in fact, many who "know him well consider him a God." She had once said that sitting next to Hitler was "like sitting beside the sun." Joe described her view thus: "The situation in England and the United States was due mainly to Jewish propaganda and the only way to clear it up was to throw them out. Of course, she felt sorry for them but you had to get rid of them."

Several days later, Hitler dismissed British ambassador Nevile Henderson, who had delivered a letter from Chamberlain reaffirming Britain's commitment to Poland, after a brief meeting, and then had a leisurely lunch with Unity. She must have pleaded that day with Hitler to make a deal with her country. According to her biographer David Pryce-Jones, Hitler reassured her that England would back down over Poland, that he would protect her, and that she could ignore those who told her to leave Germany.

Joe Jr. traveled to Hamburg and Munich, sending his father reports on German attitudes. Young Joe was stunned by the effective Nazi propaganda: Newsreels showed crying German women and children, who had been turned out of their houses by the Poles; newspapers were filled with accounts of planes being attacked and soldiers being tortured. Joe observed that even as anti-aircraft guns were mounted in Berlin, the populace seemed to be in denial about the likelihood of war. In Hamburg, with its better connections to the West, citizens were more aware of the danger, but still doubtful that war would result. The alliance with Russia had given the German people false hope. Joe Kennedy proudly passed his son's reports on to Sumner Welles.

Meanwhile, Jack was in Berlin on the day that the Nazi-Soviet nonaggression pact was signed. He witnessed people celebrating in the streets after the state-controlled radio broadcast news of the agreement. Jack bought a movie camera and projector and took movies of Berlin and its inhabitants in the last days before the onset of war. He then went to the American embassy in Berlin, picked up a top-secret note from the American chargé d'affaires, Captain Alan Kirk, and brought the letter to his father in London.

Deeply disturbed by the Soviet-German alliance, Joe scrambled to learn everything he could about it. He met on the twenty-fifth with Kadri Rizan, the Turkish chargé d'affaires in London, who told him that the pact had secret and horrifying provisions—Poland would be split between Hitler and Stalin; Germany would get parts of Yugoslavia, Bulgaria, and Greece; while Russia would be granted free rein against Japan, even though Japan was Germany's ally. Joe forwarded all of this intelligence on to Roosevelt, who chose not to pass this provocative information on to Japan.

THE LAST DAYS of August strained Chamberlain's and Kennedy's nerves almost to the breaking point. "I feel like a man driving a clumsy coach over a narrow crooked road along the face of a precipice," Chamberlain wrote to his sister Hilda, "there comes times when your heart seems to stop

still for minutes together until you somehow round the next corner. . . ."
The most gut-wrenching moment for the prime minister came on August
25, when word arrived that Hitler had sent for Nevile Henderson that afternoon. Chamberlain sat with his wife "in the drawing room, unable to
read, unable to talk, just sitting with folded hands & a gnawing pain in the
stomach."

Hitler had offered Henderson a carefully crafted deception: Even
though he found Poland's "provocations" to be intolerable, he claimed that
he had no desire to dominate the world. After the issues with Poland had
been resolved, he would offer to safeguard the British Empire in return for
colonial territories. However, that same afternoon, Hitler gave his military
the final go-ahead for an attack on Poland, though he canceled it five hours
later when Ribbentrop informed him about an Anglo-Polish alliance, highlighting Britain's readiness to fight, and Mussolini demurred about offering
military aid. Hitler was temporarily stunned, but ultimately undeterred.

About this time, CBS radio commentator H. V. Kaltenborn visited Kennedy at the embassy. As he entered the ambassador's office, he noticed that
Kennedy "was pacing the room in his shirtsleeves in a dramatic mood. He
raised his hand and said, 'You have come to me in one of the most important moments in history! We are engaged in a fight for time!'" Kennedy did
not know it yet, but peace could not be bought by time. Most everyone else
had already realized that there was no further room for negotiation.

ON SUNDAY, August 27, Chamberlain met with Swedish intermediary
Birger Dahlerus, who had talked with Hitler the previous day. Hitler
had demanded that both Danzig and the Polish Corridor be reunited with
Germany. As British cabinet deliberations ended that evening, Joe, spurred
by anxious calls from Sumner Welles, called Halifax and asked to see him.
Halifax said, "I'd love to see you but I am terribly tired and am going home
to bed for a few hours." Desperate for a progress report, Joe offered to
pick him up and take him home. He jumped in his Chrysler and was at the
back door of the cabinet offices within ten minutes. While he was waiting
for Halifax, amidst cheers from the crowd for the U.S.A., the famous black
cat of Downing Street, who had been spotted during the previous Czech
crisis, made an ominous appearance. As the two men entered Joe's car, the
crowd cheered them. Suddenly, while maneuvering his car safely through
the crowd, Joe's back bumper caught on the mudguard of a car at right
angles to him, and they were stuck. The crowd laughed along with Halifax
and Kennedy. While the police gathered eight to ten young men to help free

the car, people stuck their head through the window, saying, "Please don't let us go to war," and "You'll save us I know," and "I don't want to send my boy except to fight for Britain not for Poland," and so forth. As they drove away, Joe remembered Halifax saying, "Quite a sight, the great British public lifting the car of the American ambassador to safety."

On Monday the twenty-eighth, without consulting the cabinet, Halifax wired the Polish government and asked them to go into direct negotiations with Germany. Two hours later the Poles offered to do so. When Henderson went to the Reich Chancellery that evening, Hitler agreed to negotiate with Poland, but only if a Polish negotiator, with full powers to cede territory, arrived in Berlin within twenty-four hours; cynically, he explained to Henderson that the explosive situation merited fast action. In reality, this almost impossible stipulation was designed to lay the failure of negotiations at the door of the Poles, and to provide Britain a pretext for backing off their commitment to Poland. Meanwhile, Germany had introduced rationing, closed airports, and called up all reserves.

That evening Kennedy met again with Chamberlain, who claimed, as Kennedy cabled the State Department, to be "more worried about getting the Poles to be reasonable than the Germans," especially in light of Eden's and Churchill's efforts to buck up Polish resolve to hold firm. That day the Admiralty had taken over all British merchant shipping.

Joe suggested to Chamberlain that he put war regulations into place to "[g]ive the British people a little taste of what is to come. They might not be so anxious for the Poles to refuse to negotiate and so start a war."

When Goering opined to Hitler on August 29 that it was not necessary to "go for broke," Hitler told him, "In my life I've always gone for broke." On the thirtieth, according to Joe's memoir, Henderson had "belatedly but now almost hysterically" urged the Poles to begin negotiations with the German government. The next evening the Poles, who at this point completely mistrusted the British, sent an ambiguous note. Ribbentrop told Henderson that it was too late.

Despite the unbearable tension, Joe made time to write a letter to Henry Kittredge, the rector of St. Paul's prep school in Concord, New Hampshire. Joe had enrolled Bobby to start the fall term as soon as it was safe to send him home. Joe asked Kittredge to be patient with his son, who had bounced around from school to school in the past few years and would be living away from home for the first time. Of Bobby, he wrote, "I think he is reasonably smart, with a great lack of concentration, which has been a serious handicap to him so far. However, he is earnest and industrious and anxious to get along."

Joe had other reasons to be worried about his family and his staff. Throughout his ambassadorship, he had requested an air-raid shelter for Prince's Gate, but nothing had been done and there was no protection. The embassy, which housed the important Code Room, had a shelter that could accommodate 150 people. However, "it had no proper escape doors, and, should the upper floors collapse, the floor above the basement would not be able to sustain the weight and would fall in upon the occupants and bury them alive."

CHAPTER 15

The Party Is On

T DAWN ON FRIDAY, September 1, Hitler attacked Danzig, and then unleashed fifty-seven divisions, with heavy air support, across the border into Poland in a speedy and overwhelming invasion in what would become known as the first Nazi Blitzkrieg, or "lightning war." German propagandists insisted that Poland had invaded Germany and that the Reich was counterattacking against Poland's military installations. Joe had barely finished a late-night phone conversation with the president when the worst possible news started coming over the wires. "The news . . . came with a rush," he remembered, "like a torrent spewing from the wires—German troops had crossed the border; German planes were bombing Polish cities and killing civilians; the Germans were using poison gas." The American ambassador to Poland, Tony Biddle, awakened Roosevelt before 3 A.M. with the news, and a distraught Joe called soon thereafter. Roosevelt tried to comfort him. Kennedy then called Hull and told him, "It's all over. The party is on."

Joe was certain that England would declare war before the end of the day. He was wrong. Chamberlain and Halifax dithered, hoping that their feelers for peace might yet garner results. Still resisting a commitment to war, Chamberlain engaged in conciliating efforts on three separate fronts in the forty-eight hours following the invasion: holding secret communications with Goering through the Swedish intermediary Birger Dahlerus; reviewing Mussolini's proposal for a September 5 conference to revise parts of the Versailles Treaty that Germany had long found unfair; and considering French requests to delay the actual declaration of war until they could mobilize and evacuate their women and children from their major cities. Meanwhile, Britain sent Germany a warning, but not an ultimatum.

For Joe, September 2 was "a day of ominous waiting silence." Late that night the cabinet agreed that Sir Nevile Henderson would deliver Ribbentrop an ultimatum at 9 A.M. the next day: Unless Germany withdrew from Poland, Britain would be forced to declare war. Ribbentrop did not bother to show up. The head interpreter at the Foreign Office in Berlin accepted Henderson's missive. Early Sunday morning, Joe and Rose left their weekend residence, Wall Hall, the Hertfordshire abbey lent to the U.S. government by J. P. Morgan, and returned to London. It was a sunny, cloudless day. Rose went to mass at the Brompton Oratory, which was packed mostly with women, and Joe gathered the embassy staff to listen to Chamberlain's 11:15 A.M. radio speech to the nation. Listening to Chamberlain's bitter pronouncement that "all my long struggle to win peace has failed," Joe was on the verge of tears. He called the prime minister and told him that the speech was "terrifically moving . . . Well, Neville, I feel deeply our failure to save a world war." Chamberlain replied, "We did the best we could have done, but it looks like we have failed." "His voice still quivered, deeply moved after his broadcast," Joe recalled. Kennedy cabled Hull that Germany had not withdrawn from Poland, and "Great Britain is in consequence at war with Germany."

A few minutes later, the first prolonged air-raid alarm wailed throughout London. Chaos ensued. A group of people, including many American citizens, rushed into the entryway of the American embassy. Some of the embassy personnel were running around with "the canister and other vital parts of the gas mask dragging like old rags." Joe ordered the staff to guide the crowd across the street to the large and "reasonably good" basement under the shop of the dressmaker Molyneux. Rose arrived at the embassy in a car, and Joe told Joe Jr. and Jack to take her to the Molyneux basement. As they waited for bombs that did not fall that day, some of the Americans started to panic—Joe noticed "quite a few white faces amongst the men"—and they started demanding that the embassy find boats to get them home. It was a plaint Joe would hear often in the coming days.

Immediately after this incident, Joe's assistant military attaché would make plans for a proper air-raid shelter for the embassy, and the State Department begrudgingly authorized $10,000 for it.

Page Huidekoper stayed in the embassy. She read Neville Chamberlain's speech as it came across the ticker, but was immensely frustrated when, in the middle of the speech, the ticker suddenly jumped to reporting on a game of snooker in South Kent. She never saw the rest of the prime minister's talk to the nation. A young club man interrupted to tell her that several letters had arrived at the embassy. They included a formal announcement of the declaration of war, an official letter asking the United States to take over British interests in countries controlled by Germany, and a letter asking the United States to help get a mom-and-pop circus out of Czechoslovakia.

Joe consoled himself by thinking that the conflict would be short: "The war is definitely not going to have the long run they predict," he wrote in his diary with more wishfulness than evidence or prescience. "The women and children at home in *all* belligerent countries are going to have a terrific moral pressure on the men fighting." Yet while telephoning the president to read him Chamberlain's declaration of war, Joe briefly gave in to despair. His voice choked with emotion, he muttered what would become his often quoted and much scorned lament: "It's the end of the world . . . the end of everything." Given how fervently Joe had identified himself with the aversion of the very war that was now erupting across Europe, how exhausted he must have been after days of nonstop diplomacy and administrative work, air-raid warnings, and unremitting tension, his lapse into plaintive emotion is understandable, even expectable. It was unfortunate that Roosevelt, who hated to deal with powerful sentiments, was at the other end of the line. Soon thereafter, showing no compassion for Joe, FDR would ridicule him, mimicking his outburst to his cousin Joseph Alsop and most likely to other colleagues as well.

A FTER THE ALL-CLEAR SOUNDED on the afternoon of September 3, Joe and Rose went with Joe Jr., Jack, and Kick to listen to Chamberlain's speech. A famous photograph of the three oldest Kennedy children shows them walking hurriedly toward Parliament. While Joe and Kick look somber and preoccupied, Jack appears eager to witness history happening. They had just taken their places at 12:05 P.M. when another air-raid siren went off. They hustled to a shelter underneath Parliament. Returning, they heard Chamberlain's speech. Kennedy himself could have uttered the disarmingly honest words he spoke: "This is a sad day for all of us . . . Everything that I have worked for, everything that I had hoped for, everything that I have believed in during my public life has crashed into ruins." With Churchill's idealistic oratory, Joe was in less sympathy. "This is no war for domination or imperial aggrandizement or material gain; no war to shut any country out of its sunlight and means of progress," Churchill proclaimed. "It is a war . . . to establish . . . the rights of the individual, and it is a war to establish and revive the stature of man."

That evening, FDR told the American people in a Fireside Chat that while their nation would remain neutral in the new European war, he could not require every American to remain neutral in thought as well. His declaration of neutrality echoed that of Woodrow Wilson at the outbreak of what would be called the Great War, in 1914. Joe would compare the lead editorial in the *New York Times* from August 5, 1914 with that of September 4, 1939. They appeared identical to him. Joe did not want the United States to become entangled with a country that was mainly "fighting for her possessions and place in the sun just as she has in the past."

That afternoon in Munich, a well-dressed Englishwoman calmly drove to the Ministry of Information and handed a party leader a heavy envelope, then left. When the busy official finally opened the envelope, he found a signed portrait of Hitler, a Nazi party badge, and a suicide note. Several hours later the police discovered a young woman, shot through the temple but still alive, on a bench in the English Garden. She was, of course, the idealistic Unity Mitford, distraught that her native land and adopted homeland were at war. She would be repatriated back to England and live, brain-damaged, until 1948, the first British casualty of the war that would eventually claim the lives of over 450,000 British citizens.

At 14 Prince's Gate, there was domestic upset that first night Britain was formally at war. Teddy accidentally ripped the blackout curtain at the residence. Five minutes later, air-raid wardens called and ordered the family to block the light pouring through their window. The hall light was immediately shut off, and then Jean fell down the stairs and sprained her ankle.

Joe confided to a friend that his days as a diplomat had ended with the advent of war, adding, "Now I'm just running a business—an officer of a company." Nonetheless, Joe informed the State Department that he would remain in London even when bombing began, along with Chamberlain and the Foreign Office staff. He pointedly told State that "we have nothing [here] to protect ourselves except our umbrellas, and from all accounts they are not very safe."

On September 3, Neville Chamberlain officially invited Winston Churchill into a War Cabinet as the First Lord of the Admiralty, having made him wait forty-eight hours since he had first offered the position. Although Chamberlain complained at first about Churchill's tendency to be long-winded in his advice, "very rhetorical, very emotional, and, most of all, very reminiscent," the prime minister was able to assert his own authority with his new minister. Churchill curtailed his advice giving, and the two leaders worked together with surprising equanimity.

Halifax told Kennedy that the prelude to war reminded him of a dream in which he had been tried for murder and found guilty—and was relieved that the verdict was in. Now that he was not burdened with preventing war, he was invigorated, sending a squadron of planes to fly over Hamburg and other German cities to drop six million leaflets, telling the people that the British were fighting against Nazism and not against them, Kennedy informed Hull. The British bombed Germany carefully to avoid killing women and children, Joe correctly thought, in order not to turn American public opinion against Britain.

ON THE NIGHT OF SEPTEMBER 3, Joe had just retired when the phone rang at 2:30 in the morning. The British ship *Athenia*, its 1,347 passengers including 311 Americans, had been torpedoed two hundred miles off the northwest coast of Ireland. It was sinking. Within four hours the embassy staff, now on duty twenty-four hours a day, sent reports to Washington listing the American passengers and where they had boarded the ship.

Before dawn, Joe awakened Jack and told him to travel to Glasgow with Eddie Moore to assist American survivors, who had spent hours adrift in lifeboats before being ferried by British destroyers to bases in Scotland. The sinking of the *Athenia* was the war's first attack on British and American citizens and galvanized the press on both sides of the Atlantic. The German propaganda machine claimed that Winston Churchill had staged the whole event to gain American sympathy.

On the night of September 6, Jack, dubbed the "schoolboy diplomat" by the *Telegraph* and mistakenly described as eighteen years old, arrived in Glasgow to meet with the American survivors at the Beresford Hotel. Due to incomplete passenger manifests, it would take weeks to sort out the exact number of casualties and survivors. One hundred and twelve people, including twenty-eight Americans, had been killed. The London *Evening News* reported that Jack displayed a "boyish charm, and natural kindliness" as well as the "wisdom and sympathy of a man twice his age," as he continued to comfort the survivors in hotels and hospitals.

That afternoon, according to the *Telegraph*, Jack listened to "their polite but firm demands for some assurance of adequate protection when they sailed for home in a specially chartered freighter now on its way from New York." Unfortunately for them, FDR had recently decided that, to safeguard America's neutrality, naval convoys would not accompany refugee ships in the Atlantic. When Jack explained the president's position, a "storm of protest burst from the refugees," one American reporter cabled home. "I don't believe it," one woman yelled. As Jack tried to calm the crowd, a man from

New Jersey shouted, "Ninety destroyers have just been commissioned by the United States Navy and surely they can spare us a few. Six billion dollars of United States Navy and they won't do this for us?"

Jack told the survivors it would be preferable for them to return home on an American boat rather than a British ship "even if it was accompanied by the whole fleet." In response, many of the traumatized survivors began to yell, "You can't trust the German Navy! You can't trust the German government." They were right on both counts. After the war, at the Nuremburg trials, a German admiral testified that a German submarine commanded by an inexperienced officer had acted on its own initiative in shooting at the *Athenia*, mistaking the civilian ship for a British auxiliary cruiser.

Back in London, Jack explained to his father that the *Athenia* survivors were in a "terrible state of nerves," and that placing them on American ships for the seven-day journey to the United States without a convoy would "land them in New York in such a state that the publicity and criticism of the government would be unbelievable." Joe warned Hull that "a great deal of attention is being paid to these people and they are beginning to feel terribly important and they are having an awful lot to say, most of which the censor is not permitting to go through, particularly criticism of the government." Impatient with the pace of U.S. government assistance to the survivors, Joe went around the State Department. Officials were embarrassed when Kennedy was overheard by a reporter complaining to Max Truitt, the chairman of the Maritime Commission, "The governmental authorities at home seemed unbelievably slow in making facilities available and unconscionably bureaucratic in advancing funds to persons in need." Joe justified his actions to Hull—the American press was pressuring him to provide more boats. Meanwhile, Joe was paying out of his own pocket for 150 prompt telegrams daily to anxious relatives of Americans in England. To great relief at home, he would ensure that the American passengers were brought safely back to the United States on the American merchant ship *Orizaba* without a convoy.

Shortly after the *Athenia* survivors made it home, Joe was hurt when FDR circumvented him to contact Winston Churchill directly with reports that a bomb had been placed aboard the U.S. steamship *Iroquois*, which was carrying American citizens across the Atlantic. Joe was embarrassed at his own ignorance when Churchill called him, assuming he had been warned of this plot to bring America into the war. The bomb threat proved just that; a U.S. convoy met the *Iroquois* and escorted it uneventfully to New York. But amid the urgency of war news and planning, the American ambassador would be an often inessential figure.

IN A NOTE, Kick eloquently captured the wartime British capital, with its nightly blackouts: "It is an eerie experience walking through a darkened London. You literally feel your way, and with groping finger make sudden contact with a lamppost against which leans a steel helmeted figure with his gas mask slung at his side. You cross the road in obedience to little green crosses winking in the murk above your head . . . Gone are the gaily-lit hotels and nightclubs; now in their place are somber buildings surrounded by sandbags. It is a new London . . . now one hears tap, tap, tap, not of machine guns, but of umbrellas and canes as Londoners feel their way homeward, for it is a perilous task . . . more have been killed in the darkness than in battle—during the first month of the war." One night, Kick was awakened by the "piercing blasts" of an air-raid siren. "Offering my soul to the Lord," she ran downstairs amid family members "ordering one another about, and trying at the same time to put on gas masks." They raced across the road into an air-raid shelter, where the "ladies looked most unlovely with their creamed faces and their paper curled hair."

Jack sympathized with the plight of the three-quarter million children and teachers being evacuated from London. After watching the heartrending good-byes between parents and children at Euston Station, he wrote his friend Claiborne Pell, "The big men of Berlin and London sit and confidently give their orders, and it is these kids—so far as I can see—who are the first casualties." The ambassador wrote FDR a thoughtful report detailing the successful evacuation and outlining the possible long-term social and economic consequences of moving citizens out of crowded population centers—a vigorous decentralization and reorganization of the social structure.

Feeling gloomy about Britain's future, Joe went to the palace for tea on September 9. The king attempted to reassure him, an effort that left the monarch depressed—and enraged. Passionate about the British Empire's role as protector of smaller countries, the king was infuriated by Joe's point of view: "He looked at the war very much from the financial and material viewpoint," he wrote in his diary. "He wondered why we did not let Hitler have SE Europe, as it was no good to us from a monetary standpoint. He did not seem to realize that this country was part of Europe, that it was essential for us to act as policemen, & to uphold the rights of small nations & that the Balkan countries had a national spirit." King George went on to write Joe an angry letter—what his private secretary Alan Lascelles called "a stinker"—but both Chamberlain and Churchill cautioned him to send a more temperate upbraiding. "As I see it, the USA, France, and the British Empire," the king wrote, "are the three really free peoples in the World, and two of these great democracies are now fighting against all that we three countries hate and detest."

Understanding he had strayed into hazardous territory, Joe wrote a subtly apologetic response: "I was greatly touched by your gracious and friendly letter . . . May I reaffirm here my deep appreciation and affectionate esteem? . . . You were most considerate in explaining the British viewpoint . . . Of this you may rest assured, whatever strength or influence I possess will be used every hour of the day for the preservation of *'that life'* we all hold dear, and in which cause you and your gracious queen help to lead the world." The king, writing in his diary, recognized that his letter had unnerved Kennedy: "I was surprised as I had never seen him rattled before."

King George had much to worry about. On a personal level, as he had admitted to Joe, the advent of the war meant the troublesome return of the duke and duchess of Windsor to England. But the king was more seriously concerned that after Hitler took over Poland, he would tempt England and France with a peace offer, which the Chamberlain government might accept. Such a pact would cause the British people to throw the conservative government out of office. The king had even less faith in the capacity of the Liberal or Labor party heads to lead the country in wartime.

In the same letter, Joe informed the king that Roosevelt had just called a special session of Congress to consider repealing the Neutrality Act embargo on arms sales to belligerents to accomplish "what most Americans want—to help England and France economically, but not to send troops to Europe." (It would be considered on September 21.) When Kennedy told Roosevelt that British war minister Hore-Belisha believed Britain would not be able to pay for U.S. war assistance for long, FDR replied, "What you need to do is put some steel up their backbones." He wanted the British to appear tough enough to give Hitler pause. As the prime minister did not have the political capital to make another public move toward appeasement, Joe felt there was only one man who could, at this late date, salvage peace. That man was Franklin D. Roosevelt. He wrote FDR on September 11, telling him Britain was in an impossible position: "They know that if the war continues [for a long time] . . . it signifies entire social, financial, and economic breakdown and that after the war is over nothing will be saved. If the war were stopped, on the other hand, it would provide Herr Hitler with so much prestige that it is a question of how far he would be carried by it." That left the American president, Joe declared, to "play the role of savior of the world . . . there may be a situation where President Roosevelt himself may evolve world peace plans."

According to Kennedy biographer David Koskoff, FDR "himself was privately considering such efforts," but he resented Kennedy's suggestions—and particularly being informed what "the president should be thinking about." Roosevelt told Hull to set Kennedy straight, which Hull did that same afternoon. "This government . . . sees no opportunity nor occasion for any peace move to be introduced by the president of the United States," Hull cabled Kennedy. "The people of the United States would not support any move for peace initiated by this government that would consolidate or make possible a survival of a regime of force and aggression," namely Germany. The same day that Hull reproved Kennedy, Roosevelt wrote to Winston Churchill, as one naval administrator to another, inviting Churchill to keep in touch with him personally through sealed diplomatic pouches. Churchill obtained Chamberlain's approval to keep up backdoor communications. September 11 would mark a significant rupture in Kennedy's fragmenting relationships with Roosevelt and Churchill.

Kennedy would be given the humiliating task of delivering to Churchill, a man he saw as a danger to the United States, secret messages from FDR, which he was not allowed to read, and then sending Churchill's private replies home through diplomatic pouches. Was it reasonable to expect that he could gracefully handle being an errand boy for his disgruntled president? Bitter about this lack of respect and despondent about peace prospects, Joe began a downward spiral into resentment and despair, and his ambassadorship became more isolated and less effective.

Yet not everyone discarded his judgment, even when his pessimism was disturbing. Chips Channon noted in his diary, "I trust that . . . the jaunty American ambassador is wrong, for he prophesies the end of everything, and goes about saying that England is committing suicide. My reason tells me he is wrong, that everything is on our side, but my intuition warns me he may have something." Kennedy's behavior was unwise and undiplomatic. But three days after Kennedy's missive to Roosevelt, the British ambassador to Washington, Lord Lothian, asked Chamberlain to summon Kennedy and deny that the British government had any intention to negotiate with Germany. Chamberlain rebuffed Kennedy's dire but ultimately prophetic assessment that the war would cost Britain its empire and his calls for a realistic approach to Britain's dilemma. Their close bond had begun to fray.

IN MID-SEPTEMBER, Roosevelt's isolationist critics, including Charles Lindbergh, Idaho senator William Borah, and radio personality Father Charles Coughlin, tried to thwart FDR's plans for persuading Congress to aid Britain and France. Lindbergh warned the American people in a radio address that "we should never enter a war unless it is absolutely essential to the future welfare of our nation." Ambassador William Bullitt warned Roosevelt that if the Neutrality Act was not revised, France and England would be defeated easily. Several days later, Kennedy called Bullitt, who told him that if Congress stalled the neutrality legislation, he would go home and "stop at nothing. Bullitt wanted the Neutrality Act repealed: 'You've never seen me in a fight. I'll lay the opposition low. . . .' " In general, Kennedy thought Bullitt was talking like a "damn fool" and was "more rattle-brained than ever," as he wrote Rose. "His judgment is pathetic and I am afraid of his influence on FDR because they think alike on many things." But FDR had indeed come to rely more on Bullitt than on Kennedy.

On Sunday, September 17, Lord Beaverbrook phoned Kennedy with the distressing news that the Soviet Red Army had invaded the eastern regions of Poland, effectively undercutting any chance the Polish army had of stemming the German advance from the west. Kennedy responded to this sign of deepening catastrophe by hardening his belief that the United States should not become entangled in Europe's morass.

That same day, all eleven Kennedys gathered at Wall Hall for a final family get-together before all the children but Rosemary were sent home. Even with the prospect of physical danger and separation in wartime, the family exhibited its customary vigor and energy. A guest, Tom Egerton, recalled their "sheer exuberance, the happiness, the enjoyment in each other and the moment." But Kick was distraught. She begged to stay in England so she could join British civilian war efforts and be close to Billy, who had already been called up to his regiment. The ambassador would not allow Kick to put herself at risk, nor would he further encourage an affair that disturbed her devout mother. Kick was also angry because Rosemary would be allowed to live in the Hertfordshire countryside, studying to be a Montessori teacher, while she was forced to return home to get a college education.

Rose had carefully prepared her children to handle difficult times like the advent of war. In the family's memorial volume *Her Grace Above Gold*, Ted Kennedy described her influence on her children: "Her faith was her rock. It explains her sense of hope and optimism, her acceptance of tragedy and loss . . . She taught us early that the birds will still sing when the storm is over, that the rose must know the thorn, that the valley makes the mountain tall."

Joe had promised Page Huidekoper's father that he would send her home at the first sign of danger. He sent her back on the U.S.S. *Manhattan*, which passengers nicknamed "Gone With the Wind" due to British hostility toward Americans. The ship was also nicknamed the "U.S.S. *Diaper*" because so many British children were aboard—being sent to safety in America. The swimming pool was full of cots. Knowing how much Page wanted to stay at the embassy, Joe later wrote her a telegram saying, "I feel so mean to have sent you back."

The day after the family gathering, Joe Jr., who was starting Harvard Law School, boarded the British ship *Mauretania*, which sailed with an armed naval convoy. Jack, because of his work with the survivors of the *Athenia*, had missed the first two weeks of his senior year at Harvard. He flew home on the new Pan-American "flying boat" *Yankee Clipper*.

PAT, JEAN, and Teddy sailed home with their governess on the *United States*. The family came home on several ships so that they would not all be killed in a Nazi attack. Rose, Kick, Bobby, and Eunice made the journey home on the overcrowded S.S. *Washington*, in waters infested with Nazi submarines. "People are sleeping in the lounge, swimming pool, gymnasium, in fact everywhere thinkable, but it is all great fun," Eunice wrote her father on September 17. "Nobody has their bags, and Kick and I wear the same costume for breakfast, lunch and supper but then, so does everybody else." Bobby collected autographs from shipboard celebrities including actor Robert Montgomery and tennis stars Samuel Tilden and Don Budge. Two people had asked Bobby for *his* autograph, "so at present he is feeling very important," Eunice wrote. "It all seems like a beautiful dream," Kick wrote about her sojourn in London. "Thanks a lot Daddy for giving me one of the greatest experiences anyone could have had. I know it will have a great effect on everything I do from herein."

Jack carried home with him an affectionate letter from his father he delivered to "Rose darling." "My family gets smaller and smaller," Joe wrote. His wife was "still the most attractive woman in the world," he said, and "I will miss you terribly." But he did not want her to worry; he was relieved the family was safely ensconced in America. Joe told her that he considered his post in London to be "probably the most interesting and exciting in the world," and that it afforded him an opportunity to put the brakes on "this catastrophic chaos."

INCREASINGLY ISOLATED because of his conviction that Britain "would go down fighting," on September 30, Joe sent FDR several letters summing up his bleak views. He had conferred with naval and military experts from many countries, and none of them thought England had "a Chinaman's chance." With the "invention of the airplane and the increase in industrial powers in other countries" and "the decline in English ability and forcefulness . . . Britain has passed her peak as a world power some years ago and has been steadily on the decline," Joe wrote. "There are signs of decay, if not decadence, here, both in men and institutions . . . But for all Halifax's mystical, Christian character and Churchill's prophecies in respect to Germany, I can't imagine them adequately leading the people out of the valley of the shadow of death." Joe was also convinced that the nation faced bankruptcy. He was not alone in that prediction: Chancellor of the Exchequer John Simon thought Britain would run out of money after three years, and Montagu Norman, the governor of the Bank of England, gave his country two years of solvency.

Kennedy expressed to Roosevelt his fear that even if Germany were somehow defeated, it would fall to communism; FDR would respond that he believed that Germans would not tolerate "the Russian form of brutality for any length of time." Efforts at democratizing these countries had contributed to the new war, Kennedy averred. For Joe, although democracy was "the only kind of government I want to live under," he believed that "forcing democracy on the conquered nations" at the end of the First World War had "aligned democracy and the status quo," and led the forces of change to take on an anti-democratic nature. Eschewing British talk that the war against Germany was a crusade for democracy, Joe believed that Americans should curb their democratic sentimentality and protect "our own vital interests" in the Western Hemisphere.

TO ASSUAGE HIS LONELINESS, Joe relied on visits from Rosemary and missives from home. Rosemary was delighted when her father offered to invite her and several of her school friends to watch movies on the weekends at Wall Hall. Joe Jr., writing from Massachusetts, reported that "everyone at home is unanimous in wanting to stay out of the war," and bucked his father up with the news that his letter on the bombing of

Valencia would be published in the October issue of the *Atlantic Monthly*. Kick wrote to tell him she did not get into Sarah Lawrence College, but would attend Finch junior college. She watched her longtime suitor Peter Grace play polo and went to the theater with him, but found that he did not compare favorably to Billy. "That's the amazing thing when one's been away," Kick wrote her father; "one expects things to have changed & they haven't." She reported that Jack was going to date the beautiful Protestant heiress Frances Ann Cannon again. Jack would soon have his feelings hurt when Frances Ann introduced him to her fiancé, writer John Hersey.

O N SEPTEMBER 27, crushed by the Blitzkrieg, Poland surrendered to the Nazis. The next phase of the war, quiet and pernicious, began in October.

CHAPTER 16

"A Damned Disagreeable Life"

I AM TERRIBLY LONELY without the family," Joe wrote to Harvard classmate Robert Fisher, "because you can't have all those kids around for a year and then not have anybody in one fell swoop, so all these factors contribute to a damned disagreeable life, although an interesting one." As Britain responded to the declaration of war, Joe was initially told that he would not be able to call his family because the transatlantic telephone could only be used to relay important wartime messages, a prohibition that contributed to his growing depression. "I'm sick of everybody so I'm alone tonight by choice," he wrote Rose on October 2. "It's funny that nobody in the world can be very long without boring me to death. You are the only individual in the world I love more every day."

Concerned, Rose wrote back, "My darling: "I am wondering when I shall see you and what is happening! It is all so heartbreaking . . . Of course I am not complaining. I just hope and pray daily that you are taking care of yourself and are not too terribly lonely."

Joe exerted pressure on British Cable and Wireless and won permission to speak to his family for ten minutes every Sunday. Rose arranged for each of the children to have a minute with their father. In particular, seven-year-old Teddy missed Joe, worried about him, and tried to please him: "I hope not many-bombs drop near you," he wrote in one letter. In telling his father about a Halloween party, the boy wrote that he got dressed up as a ghost, but "didn't scare because you said not to scare because they may have a weak heart."

On October 7, Joe and Rose celebrated their twenty-fifth wedding anniversary with a seven-minute phone conversation. The king and queen and the president sent congratulations. "Your dear remembrance was the brightest spot in a day which Rose's presence here would have made perfect," Joe cabled the president. Addressing Rose with a tenderness that evidenced the marital bond between them in spite of their physical separation and the troubled history of their marriage, Joe wrote, "[T]o say they have been great years is an understatement. They've been the happy years that poets write about. I would like to live every day of them over again with you, but wouldn't want to live one more without you. . . . I love you devotedly. This job without you is comparable to a street cleaner's at home."

As for the war arising around them, Joe wrote Rose that he was "never giving up on the idea of *Peace* on which I work every day—and we will get it too." Churchill, however, believing that Kennedy's isolationism and freelance peace negotiations were undermining the war effort, tried to sway the ambassador's opinion by arguing that a German conquest of Britain would hand them the British navy and dominance over the United States. "If the Germans bomb us into subjection," Churchill told Kennedy, as he recorded in his memoir, "one of their terms will certainly be that we hand them over the fleet . . . If we hand it over, their superiority over you becomes overwhelming and then your troubles begin." Yet despite his reservations about Kennedy, Churchill kept him informed about British merchant marine and naval strategy, knowing that as onetime U.S. maritime commissioner, he would fully appreciate the challenge the nation faced. In the first months of the war, German U-boats sank twenty-three British merchant ships. Churchill armed merchant ships and fast liners, organized them into convoys, and ordered zealous night-and-day attacks on U-boats, thus managing to minimize further losses. The British public was shocked when on October 14 a German U-boat penetrated the British fleet anchored at Scapa Flow off the northeast coast of Scotland and sank the battleship *Royal Oak*, but a few days later, Churchill was able to reassure them that Britain had sunk one-third of the German submarine force. A British naval blockade, in which ships searched all vessels heading to Germany and removed any cargo that could supply the Reich, would become a key part of the British strategy to stop the war.

The British called this phase of the conflict the "Bore War"—a pun on the Boer War, which England fought in Africa at the turn of the century—because neither Britain nor France was actively engaging Germany in ground combat. Chamberlain saw this part of the conflict as vital, sustained as he was by two erroneous notions about Germany: first, that the British economic blockade would strangle the Reich into regime change, and second, that the Germans could be convinced that they could not win a war against the West. Thus, Chamberlain did not push British industry to make a rapid conversion to a wartime economy, and he tolerated the continued plodding pace of Britain's rearmament. "The picture of England girding herself for war," Joe wrote in his memoir, "trying to make up for lost time, yet fumbling," is the "story of these late months of 1939."

On October 5, Churchill read the American ambassador FDR's secret letter inviting the First Lord to initiate a personal correspondence. For the humiliated Kennedy it was, as he said in his memoir, "[a]nother instance of Roosevelt's conniving mind, which never indicates he knows how to handle any organization. It's a rotten way to treat his ambassador and I thinks shows him up to the other people. I am disgusted."

Churchill, during a radio broadcast reviewing the first month of the war, had invoked the American Civil War, inadvertently equating the South in the war with Nazism. Worried that he might have undermined British-American relations, he called Kennedy for help. Kennedy investigated, learned that the president was not bothered by the remark, and told him he was "lucky and [to] say nothing." Churchill has "energy and brains and no judgment," Joe wrote Rose. If he took over as prime minister, "England's march downhill will be speeded up." During a meeting between the two men, "He kept smiling when he talked of 'neutrality' and 'keeping the war away from U.S.A.' I can't help feeling he's not on the level," Joe wrote in his diary. "He is just an actor and a politician. He always impressed me that he'd blow up the American Embassy and say it was the Germans if it would get the U.S. in. Maybe I do him an injustice but I just don't trust him."

The British government felt likewise about Kennedy. The American section of the British Foreign Office had begun maintaining a file of "Kennediana"—including reports and secondhand gossip scribbled in Foreign Office documents (the minute books)—chronicling the ambassador's public and private comments. They tracked his statements on keeping America out of the war, on Britain's future, and on relations with Germany. Many of the reports attributed selfish motives to Kennedy, implying that he was seeking to preserve his wealth and advance his family and his own political career. British government circles and London's American press community spread rumors that Kennedy used his inside information—about upcoming government trade contracts, or political maneuvers that would affect trade—to profit in the stock market, rumors that Kennedy biographer David Koskoff could not confirm. Engaged as it was in a comprehensive campaign to bring America into the war on Britain's side, the British government was understandably threatened by Kennedy's bearish assessment of England's future prospects. The new British ambassador to the

United States, Philip Kerr, the eleventh marquis of Lothian, as a part of Lady Astor's inner circle had become friendly with Joe Kennedy. By the time he arrived in Washington, Ambassador Lothian had renounced his earlier support of appeasement, but he shared Kennedy's hope that Britain could negotiate peace with Hitler. On October 3, 1939, the Foreign Office sent a memo to Lothian in Washington asking if they should complain to Roosevelt about Kennedy's "defeatist" statements. Sir Berkeley Gage of the Foreign Office suggested that a complaint "might make him shut up, but in that case we shall neither know what he is thinking nor what he is telling the U.S. government." The British and American governments would, however, increasingly use Lothian to circumvent Kennedy.

AFTER WAR WAS DECLARED, Chamberlain's biggest fear was that Hitler would proffer a peace initiative that would galvanize both the "peace-at-any-price" advocates like Joe Kennedy, on the one hand, and the promoters of more aggressive war, who would insist on an all-out attack beyond what the prime minister thought Britain could mount. For once, Chamberlain read the Fuhrer correctly. In a speech to the Reichstag on October 6, Hitler offered the West what his biographer Ian Kershaw called an "olive branch cloaked in a mailed fist." Insisting on the division of Poland with the Soviet Union, the ceding of important colonial territories belonging to Britain and France, and a free hand in Eastern Europe, Hitler's peace proposal—in the apt characterization by the San Francisco Chronicle—amounted to the "simple proposition that a burglar should be confirmed in his loot and given complete amnesty, in return for which he offers a conditional promise to cease housebreaking." Six days later, Chamberlain spoke to the House of Commons and in an "icy and calm" tone rejected Hitler's proposal for a peace conference. Secretly, Hitler was already preparing a November attack on the West, an attack he would later postpone.

Back in the United States, Joe Jr. was settling in at Harvard Law School that fall, and Jack, who had been celebrated in cinema newsreels and newspaper accounts of the Athenia disaster, was thriving at Harvard. Jack concentrated on studying the various political systems then sweeping the world, including fascism and communism, and evaluating the role of idealism, realism, and rhetoric in twentieth-century European politics. In an anonymous October 9 Harvard Crimson editorial, "Peace In Our Time," he declared that Britain should allow Germany to keep Poland and that President Roosevelt should intervene to mediate a peace that granted colonial concessions and "a puppet Poland" to Hitler. At this point, Jack still embraced his father's view that appeasement of Hitler made the most sense, but as he worked on his senior thesis on British foreign policy, he would emerge with a more muscular outlook. Jack captured the American mood perfectly when he quipped to his father, "Everyone here is still ready to fight till the last Englishman."

His sister Kick, now at Finch College, longed for every scrap of news about Billy and her circle of friends in London. Nancy Astor stoked the young woman's yearning with a letter recounting a Cliveden house party that Billy and his brother Andrew had attended. "They bemoaned your absence," Lady Astor wrote. "They tried to be cheerful and succeeded in part, but it was very difficult."

In Washington, D.C., in October, press magnate Lord Beaverbrook visited FDR. The president spoke highly of Joe, knowing his comments would get back to the ambassador. "One's influence on this country is primarily dependent on how they think one stands with the president," Joe wrote FDR in thanking him for his support. But Beaverbrook gave Joe more ominous news—his impression that Roosevelt did want war.

AFTER SIX WEEKS of acrimonious congressional debate over the Neutrality Act, Roosevelt signed a revision into law on November 4. Congress had insisted that American arms could be sold to belligerents only on a cash-and-carry basis, meaning Britain could obtain the weapons or ships it needed but would not be extended credit. Heartened, Chamberlain wrote Roosevelt that this change in law was likely to have "a devastating effect on German morale."

Kennedy, meanwhile, remained dubious about Churchill's ambitions, even after his inspiring speech to the House of Commons in which he assessed the war's first month, declaring, "We have only to persevere to conquer" and leading many MPs to believe that "they have found their leader." When Kennedy met with Chamberlain and asked whether Churchill was after his job, the prime minister said he was not sure. "Winston has the art of the showman," he said. "I never could have that." During a cabinet meeting that day, Churchill had spoken poetically about the torpedoing of a Greek ship: "wind shrieking, waves so high." He sounded like a man making a speech to ten thousand people rather than to the nine cabinet ministers present.

By early November, Joe was feeling estranged from both Chamberlain's cautious chess game of war-waging—a static defense and an economic blockade—and Churchill's belligerence. Joe favored direct negotiations offering economic incentives and territorial concessions to Hitler in order to end the war quickly. He carefully monitored the relations between the two leaders. Joe had soon come to believe that Chamberlain "bitterly distrusts Churchill, and is well aware he is after his job."

On November 28, Kennedy had a reassuring dinner with General Sir William Ironside, chief of the Imperial General Staff, at Nancy and Waldorf Astor's home. In introducing Ironside to Joe, Nancy whispered to him that the tall and handsome general "looks like a battleship ready to be launched." Ironside was proud of the fact that he had moved 189,000 men, 29,000 motor vehicles, and 300,000 tons of equipment to France to shore up that nation's defenses. He told Joe that Britain had one and a half million men in training, and a force of 180,000 they could already call upon. If the Nazis attacked the east coast of England, he could greet them with 150,000 troops within twenty-four hours. However, Joe would not feel hopeful about England's chances until he saw evidence of parity in the air—and that would not happen until the next summer.

After attending the unusually small and modest ceremony opening Parliament, Joe had lunch with the king and queen. The king, already beleaguered by the incessant demands of the wartime monarchy, "did not look well, thin and drawn, and stuttered more than I had ever seen him," Joe noted in his diary. Before lunch, the king asked him if he had "taken to drink yet." Joe replied, "No, but the temptation was becoming greater every day." As Joe remembered their conversation, the queen agreed with him that the United States should not send its soldiers to Europe even though the British Empire was fighting for its survival. Joe stuck up for Lindbergh when the queen criticized him for a recent radio address in which he questioned the right of Canada to draw the United States into a war protecting England. The king was keen to know whether FDR would run for a third term. "All of England hopes so," he told Joe.

As the situation in London grew more straitened, Joe and the American embassy staff shouldered massive burdens. "Sleep was at a premium; the telephone rang at all hours with its insistent demands," he recalled in his memoir. "Almost every day brought its own incident." Major headaches arose from the long delays in examining American vessels stopped by the British naval blockade. Moreover, with all communications cut off between the Reich and England, the American embassy had to represent the interests of the 3,500 British subjects still in Germany at the beginning of the war. All inquiries from their friends and relatives had to be channeled through the American embassy.

In addition, Joe worked on forging British-American trade agreements that would relieve the stress on the wartime kingdom even as they maintained America's interests. Their nation's economic burdens led the British to attempt to conserve money for essential war needs. The British government tried to reduce by over 200 percent the fees they paid for using American films. Britain had been paying $35 million yearly to import American films, but wanted to reduce its annual payment to $5 million. Joe engaged in extensive and at times bitter bargaining with Oliver Stanley at the Board of Trade to forge an agreement at four times the original offer—Britain would now pay $20 million.

By the time Joe left London on November 29 for a visit to the United States, he had lost fifteen pounds. He could not wait to get to Palm Beach, where, he wrote, "then I would not have to be on guard. I could read detective stories and sleep and swim and sleep again." In December, when he would be evaluated at the Lahey Clinic in Boston, his condition would be assessed as "worse than I had anticipated," with a diagnosis of acute gastritis and colitis. The doctors would recommend hospitalization; he agreed instead to rest for two months. Joe asked Dr. Sara Jordan to write FDR—cynical biographers claim he paid her—to explain why he could not return to London in early January as the president had hoped. The president expressed his sympathies.

As Joe began his circuitous route home, the Russians invaded Finland. Britain and the United States would be heartened when the outnumbered Finns outfought the Russians. Churchill, Chamberlain, and Hitler all mistook the Finnish triumph as evidence that Stalin's purges had eviscerated the Russian army, leaving it incapable of playing a major role in the escalation of the war.

On December 6, Joe flew home to New York from Lisbon aboard the *Dixie Clipper*. Rose broke through the press lines to kiss him, and he told the awaiting reporters that he looked forward to the time when he could give up his public life and focus on his family. He declared that Britain was not counting on U.S. troops to come over and fight. Delighted to be home, Joe found that "even the lights of Times Square seemed to blaze more brilliantly as I thought of the blackness of London." He claimed to have no idea whether he would be a factor in the 1940 presidential election, but he immediately began investigating who might be lining up to seek the Democratic nomination if Roosevelt stood down.

Arriving at Washington's Union Station early on December 8, Kennedy gave a brief statement to the press saying he felt Roosevelt should seek a third term. America's problems were so great that "they should be handled by a man it won't take two years to educate." Meeting with Kennedy, FDR heartily denied he would be a candidate. "I can't. I'm tired. I can't take it," he told Joe. "What I need is one year's rest. That's what you need too. You may think you are resting, but the subconscious idea of war and its problems—bombings and all that—is going on in your brain all the time. I just won't go for a third term unless we are in war." At a press conference that afternoon, Kennedy observed that the exhausted president "didn't flash the way he used to."

When Kennedy met the next morning with the exhausted but genial president in his White House bedroom, FDR was eating breakfast in bed and making his own coffee in a bowl. Kennedy gave him what the president described as his "bearish" view on Britain's future; the ambassador also expressed concern about how the sale of British holdings of American securities in the United States, when necessary to help finance the war, would affect the American economy. However, he jollied FDR by showing him Churchill's impressive roster of submarine sinkings. Most important, he outlined his own plans, ones he had shown Churchill, for American ships to take over British shipping routes between nonbelligerent ports—such as bringing wheat from Australia to Canada—allowing British ships the shortest routes possible.

Churchill had asked Kennedy to seek Roosevelt's approval for a plan to mine Norwegian waterways to halt German ore shipments in the area. Kennedy took out paper and drew the coast of Norway on the top of a mahogany tallboy, showing FDR where the mines would go. With FDR's approval, he sent Churchill the pre-arranged code for agreement: "My wife cannot express an opinion but is much more friendly to the idea than I anticipated."

On December 10, at a celebration at Boston's Our Lady of Assumption Church, where Joe had been an altar boy, he spoke extemporaneously, reiterating the isolationist sentiments he had already expressed to Britain's leaders: "There's no place in the fight for us. It is going to be bad enough as it is." London's *Spectator*, while admitting that Britain had "perhaps been a little spoiled" by the solicitude of U.S. ambassadors, nevertheless lamented that "a man who knows all our anxieties, all our ordeals" found it necessary to voice publicly such vociferous isolationism. A tidal wave of criticism of Kennedy's position, in both the United States and Europe, soon followed.

Withdrawing temporarily from the maelstrom, Joe spent the Christmas holidays with his family in Palm Beach, recuperating by the swimming pool surrounded with journalists and political cronies. In the next months, the war he had so deplored would rain down on him.

1940

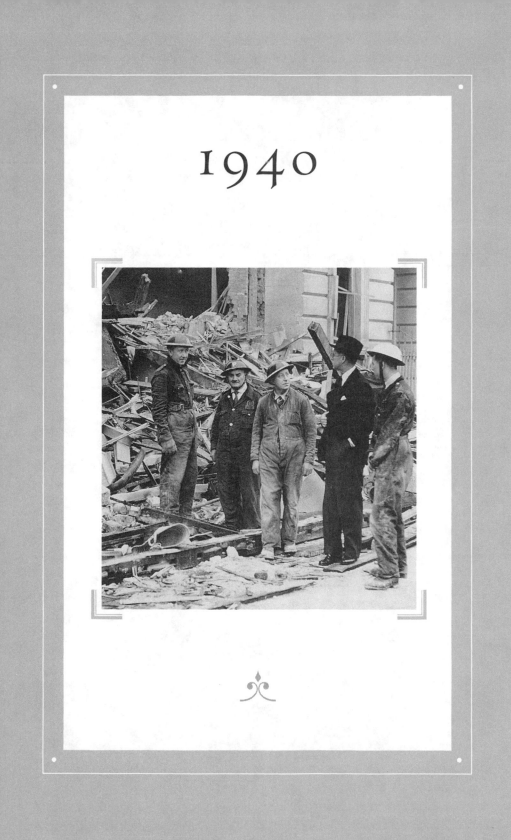

CHAPTER 17

Shutting Down the Pipeline

FOR JOE KENNEDY, 1939 had devolved into a ghastly year. The end of what W. H. Auden called "a low dishonest decade" and the advent of a new one offered scant promise of better things to the embattled U.S. ambassador, his dispersed family, his increasingly threatened nation, and the tottering British Empire. Nineteen-forty would bring Kennedy unparalleled anguish. It would shatter his reputation and permanently scar his psyche, even as, according to his own lights, he valiantly endeavored to safeguard America. As the Nazis overran Europe, Britain would be pushed to the edge of extinction and the United States caught between war and peace.

Having withdrawn to Florida, Joe recuperated from his damaging year in London and pondered his political future, consulting with friendly journalists as well as Lord Lothian, the gregarious British ambassador who shared his fading hopes for negotiating peace with Nazi Germany; Supreme Court Justice William Douglas; and Undersecretary of State Sumner Welles.

Suspicious that FDR was preparing the American people to enter the war once an opportune moment arose, Joe must have had mixed feelings about Roosevelt's annual message to Congress on January 3. The president gave a nod to those who wanted to keep America's boys out of the European war, but he also told the American people that it was becoming clearer that "the future world will be a shabby and dangerous place to live in—yes, even for Americans to live in—if it is ruled by force in the hands of a few." Joe remembered how FDR had told him during one of their consultations—a year previously—that he would start out "a bitter isolationist, then help with arms & money & then depending on the state of affairs get in," as he wrote in his diary. "I'm very leery."

Traveling to Washington, Kennedy championed his Allied shipping plan, saying that it would allow American ships to cover some British routes, free British shipping for crucial war efforts, and allow the United States to supply products unavailable in England. He warned Congress that British financial problems could bring down the American market, urging governmental oversight as the British liquidated their American investments to pay for the war. If the British jettisoned their gold stocks too abruptly, he said, it would shock the American economy. While Joe was in the capital, Rose returned from Palm Beach to the family home in Bronxville with Teddy, Pat, and Jean. A chauffeur drove Pat and Jean each school day to the Maplehurst Convent of the Sacred Heart on the edge of the Bronx, while Eunice, attending Manhattanville College of the Sacred Heart, her mother's alma mater, came home on weekends. Rose moved Bobby from the overly Protestant St. Paul's School in Concord, New Hampshire, to the Catholic Portsmouth Priory in Narragansett, Rhode Island.

Tensions were rising between Great Britain and the United States. Britain had refused to accept the Declaration of Panama, saying that unless all German shipping was kept out of the Western Hemisphere, it would not agree to honor the neutrality zones the American republics had drawn around it. In December, British warships had trapped the German pocket battleship *Admiral Graf Spee* in the harbor of Montevideo, Uruguay. The captain had destroyed his ship rather than surrender it. Joe was, of course, riveted by all matters maritime. In his memoir he quoted at length from Churchill's apologetic cable to Roosevelt about this incident, noting, however, that Churchill had ignored the legal implications of the British attack.

The Anglo-American relationship was further strained by Britain's strategy of forcibly escorting neutral and American ships into combat zones to examine their cargo, and by British censorship of American mail traveling through Bermuda and Gibraltar.

Churchill was intent on keeping America bound to Britain, recognizing that the war would soon escalate. More attuned to American sensitivities than Chamberlain ever was, Churchill secretly cabled Roosevelt that he had ordered the Admiralty to offer the United States special treatment: It would discontinue herding American ships into the combat zones for examination. Despite the frictions between the two countries, British ambassador Lothian cabled the British Foreign Office in February with a hopeful prognosis: "There is a rising feeling here that the U.S. is playing an unworthy role in one of the great dramas of history, and is in danger of losing her soul unless she shoulders her share of the burden."

In the early months of 1940, the "Phony War," as American newspapers had dubbed the "Bore War," was slowly turning real, and a wartime mentality began to pervade Britain. Starting in January, wartime deprivations included rationing of sugar and butter; meat would be added to the list two months later. During one of the coldest winters on record—the River Thames froze for the first time since 1888—tensions would ratchet up monthly as the spring neared, spring being a suitable season for invasions. In January the Nazis offered a chilling reminder of their air power, attacking twelve ships off the English coast and killing British citizens on board.

Early in January, rumors that Hitler would soon invade Western Europe gained veracity when a German military plane was forced down in Belgium. The British and the French moved troops to the Belgian border. Hitler did in fact intend to invade, in an attack code-named Operation Yellow, but bad weather and concerns about compromised intelligence forced him to postpone it.

All winter, the Allies watched nervously as Russia waged a vicious air and land war against the valiant Finns. Americans felt warmth and sympathy toward Finland because it was the only one of the World War I debtors to fully repay the United States government. According to Joe, Russia's bombing of the civilian population of Finland "shocked the American conscience." Roosevelt responded by placing a vague moral embargo—that is, a summons to American business to volunteer to suspend shipping—of all military supplies (including airplane parts) to the Soviet Union, but it was never rigorously enforced.

JOE MOVED THAT WINTER through a Washington rife with rumors and machinations around the fall's presidential election. Postmaster General James Farley, the Democratic Party chairman, had refused to wait for FDR to declare his intentions; he took a strong stand against a president's remaining in the White House beyond two terms. With Farley's entry into the Massachusetts presidential primary on February 10, several newspapers and commentators declared Kennedy should run as well. Despite his previously announced support of the president for another term if he wanted it, the *Boston Post* headline story of February 12—perhaps planted mischievously by the White House to flush out Kennedy's intentions—suggested that he might want to be a candidate after all. The next day during a White

House meeting, FDR, according to Joe's memoir, egged him on. "Why don't you run in Massachusetts, Joe," Roosevelt suggested. "You can easily win over Jim and he shouldn't have invaded your home state anyway." Joe did not take FDR's bait. The president enjoyed encouraging potential rivals to run, hoping they would cancel each other out while he moved stealthily toward his firm but unstated goal of reelection.

A master of self-promotion, Joe milked the headlines about his political ambitions. He announced that he would make a statement about his plans on the evening of January 13. That night, he took the high moral ground, declaring that his ambassadorship "involves matters so precious to the American people that no private consideration should permit my energies or interests to be diverted."

Up in Cambridge, Joe's oldest son, despite being tutored by his father's friend Judge John Burns, was hardly sailing through his first year of Harvard Law School. He would finish two hundredth out of his class of five hundred. Sharing a flat in the Bay Street Apartments near Harvard Yard with several roommates, two black servants, and a pet Florida alligator that lived in the bathtub, Joe Jr. threw parties, chased slightly older girls, and sang in barbershop quartets. Classmates recall that he was jealous of Jack's recent academic successes and his brother's "golden tongue" when speaking in public. Determined to outshine his talented younger brother, Joe enrolled in night classes for public speaking at Staley's School of the Spoken Word. He also made his political debut, announcing he would run for a seat as a Democratic convention delegate from Brookline, pledged to Farley. While this stance would likely irk Roosevelt, it would please his father, who believed in taking honorable, if unpopular, stands.

When another contender challenged the legitimacy of Joe Jr.'s candidacy (Joe was not a registered voter in the Brookline district), he successfully argued his case before the State Ballot Law Commission. After campaigning with typical Kennedy vigor in the Massachusetts primary, Joe barely won a half seat at the convention. Later in the year he would garner attention with a principled stand against the president that would rile FDR's friends and drive them to contact Joe in London.

THAT WINTER, President Roosevelt had to navigate a narrow channel between critics accusing him of preparing to intervene in the war in Europe and those who claimed he was not doing enough to foster chances for peace. Acting as his own secretary of state and without giving any warning to his foreign ambassadors, FDR announced on February 9 that he was sending the undersecretary of state, Sumner Welles, on a fact-finding tour of Paris, Rome, Berlin, and London. Roosevelt's main goal was to keep Mussolini from abandoning Italy's stance of neutrality and entering the Axis orbit.

The president's peremptory act alienated and embarrassed Hull, Kennedy, and Bullitt. Joe Kennedy liked Sumner Welles; he was the kind of patrician politician whose approval Joe sought. Welles was a tall, handsome, self-assured, yet reserved diplomat who spoke German and French fluently. The scion of a wealthy and prominent family, he was the namesake of his great-uncle Charles Sumner, the crusading abolitionist senator from Massachusetts. A Harvard graduate, Welles had married the heiress to a Massachusetts textile fortune. The Welles and Roosevelt families were so close, as the president would tell Chamberlain in a letter of introduction, that young Sumner was a page at FDR's wedding.

Although Joe deeply resented being circumvented by the president, he may have looked kindly on Welles's mission. The undersecretary of state was his friend, and Joe was grateful to him for arranging his appointment to the pope's coronation the previous winter. Now Welles would be examining the viability of peace negotiations, Joe's own hope for resolution of the war. In his memoir, Joe whitewashed any negative feelings he had about Roosevelt's effort to get another opinion about what was occurring in Europe: "Contrary to reports then current, I welcomed it. I felt it was worth trying anything to bring the war to an end." Not averse to making Bill Bullitt look bad, he claimed Bullitt "reacted strongly" against the announcement, considering the appointment a reflection "upon his own ability to interpret and communicate to Washington French sentiment at the highest government levels."

The relationship between Joe Kennedy and Bill Bullitt had become intensely competitive, thanks in part to FDR's penchant for pitting his ambassadors against each other. But now it was deteriorating under the strain of their rapidly diverging positions on the war. Right before Kennedy sailed back to Europe that February, tensions exploded when he dropped in on a meeting in Bullitt's State Department office, where the ambassador to France was giving an interview to Joseph Patterson, the editor-in-chief of the *New York Daily News*, and his reporter Doris Fleeson, both of whom were friendly to Joe. Bullitt gave Kennedy's enemy Harold Ickes his account of the dustup, but Joe did not record his version in his diary or memoir. Kennedy purportedly told the reporters that "Germany would win, that everything in France and England would go to hell, and that his one interest was in saving his money for his children." According to Ickes's account, when Kennedy deprecated the president in front of Patterson and Fleeson, they became uncomfortable and left the room. Bullitt told Kennedy that he was disloyal to disparage FDR in front of the press, a statement that triggered rage in Joe, for whom loyalty was an essential value. Kennedy stormed out, telling Bullitt "[h]e would say what he god-damned pleased before whom he god-damned pleased." Bullitt told him he should keep his mouth shut. Joe would not heed him; he was fed up with Bullitt's superior airs and what he saw as his bullish naïveté about the future course of the war. Whereas Kennedy had once looked up to Bullitt as an experienced diplomat and mentor, now he would trust his own diplomatic instincts instead.

Joe would aver that "the State Department was hunting for some basis on which to fashion a policy" for dealing with the European war and that the differences between his and Bullitt's outlook echoed the division of opinion in the State Department, favorably comparing his predictions with those of his rival. "I was certain that war on a furious scale would break out soon, most likely in early Spring," he wrote in his memoir. Bullitt, on the other hand, "thought that Germany would crumble within the next three months." While he recognized that Bullitt supported uncollateralized loans to the British and the French to allow them to purchase supplies in the United States, Joe thought his government should give Britain the necessary funds outright. Even if it managed to survive, Britain would be broke at the end of the war, Joe believed, and the American people deserved to understand the cost of helping their motherland.

While Joe continued to recuperate in the United States, Herschel Johnson, the chargé d'affaires, was running the London embassy. On the afternoon of February 7, a courier delivered a nasty surprise to Johnson: a top-secret message from G. M. Liddell of the British Secret Intelligence. According to Liddell, a spy, code-named the Doctor, had been sending Joe's dispatches to Washington to the German secret service. Joe was stunned. The case would remain a serious problem for both the ambassador and the president for the rest of the year. When news ultimately broke about the security breach, Joe would be suspected of betraying both England and the United States.

Joe hurried back to London. On February 24, he sailed for Genoa on the *Manhattan*. Before embarking, the press insisted that he comment on a recent Italian newspaper article citing him as a prime example of Roosevelt's fondness for filling diplomatic posts with "rich greengrocers whose sole qualification was that they had contributed heavily" to FDR's election campaigns. Taking a jab at the Italian foreign minister Galeazzo Ciano,

Mussolini's son-in-law, whom Joe had met the year before at the pope's coronation, Joe quipped that "at least I did not have to marry the boss's daughter to get my job."

Sailing through dangerous seas toward further perils abroad, Joe sought comfort, spending every night aboard ship with Clare Boothe Luce, whose "gay conversation," among other more intimate assets, was a "contrast to the grayness of sea and sky." Clare was on assignment from *Life* magazine to do commentary on the European situation. Her observations of battle-fronts in Italy, Belgium, the Netherlands, France, and England during the Nazi offensive would portray a world where men decided to die together because they could not find a way to live together and would be published in her book *Europe in the Spring* late that year.

In London the previous summer, Joe was her most frequent escort, taking her to the theater and to Ascot, and competing with Winston Churchill's son Randolph, among others, for her attention. Two weeks before they would sail together on the *Manhattan*, Clare sent Joe an intriguing telegram: "Please call me Waldorf [Astoria] between ten and one tomorrow . . . Important. Love, Clare." According to Clare's biographer Sylvia Morris, Joe and Clare began a brief, opportunistic affair at this time. When he got to London, Joe would write Rose and mention casually that Clare and a *Vogue* society editor happened to be on board his ship.

Joe would not go directly to London, however; he had diplomatic fact-finding to do in Italy first. During his tenure as ambassador, he had discovered that the Vatican had "vast sources of intelligence reaching almost every corner of the world." The pope had particularly good access to information about the conditions and attitudes in Germany, Austria, and Italy. For several years Joe had lobbied the president to appoint an official U.S. representative to the Vatican—an appointment he felt could foster peace and enhance intelligence gathering, as well as formalize the bond between the Vatican and America and its Catholics. He had been delighted, just before Christmas, when Roosevelt had created the position, appointing the former chairman of the United States Steel Corporation, Myron Taylor, as envoy.

After landing in Naples, Joe proceeded to Rome, where he learned from U.S. ambassador William Phillips that Mussolini was still leaning toward making a formal alliance with Hitler, even though the rest of the Italian government, including Ciano, favored the Allied cause. Joe remembered from their meeting that Taylor echoed his own feelings—criticizing FDR for cutting "right through the normal diplomatic procedures" to send Sumner Welles to Europe. Additionally, Roosevelt had insulted the French, Italian, and British ambassadors to the United States by not informing them of his plans. "I think the president wanted to make a stage play," Taylor asserted. "It's like Roosevelt though," Joe recalled himself saying. "That's hardly the way to build up an organization."

Joe's memoir arguably presents an often self-promoting version of events, but its chapter on Welles's visit is corroborated by other sources. Welles's grandson and biographer Benjamin Welles wrote that "Kennedy was a compulsive note-taker, and his records provide the only private account of Welles's activities and views on the final stage of his mission." After the war, James Landis, who edited Joe's diplomatic memoir, sent Sumner Welles the chapter on his visit to Europe. Welles wrote Landis that he had studied the document "very carefully" and "had no criticism of the essential facts." Although he had no corrections, he noted that quotations were approximations of what was actually said, given that there had been no stenographer present.

In Milan, Joe boarded a train to London. Learning that Sumner Welles was on board traveling to Paris for consultations with the French government, Joe joined him in his compartment and listened to his account of his consultations in Germany and Rome. For Welles, Mussolini was "ponderous, moving with an elephantine motion, his face falling in rolls of flesh." In their depressing meeting, Il Duce had suggested to Welles that Britain and France were underestimating Nazi military prowess, but that negotiations were still possible if the Allies granted concessions to Germany and Italy. Welles also met with Ciano, who opposed the war, and found him to be a surprisingly direct and intelligent man—one who could be a rare ally among the leaders of the fascist countries. Welles told Kennedy he had dangled before Ciano the prospect of greater trade with the United States and South America, trying to enlist the Italian foreign minister's cooperation in negotiating a durable peace. The undersecretary had also presented Mussolini with a letter from Roosevelt requesting a meeting between the two leaders, but events in April would ultimately thwart his plan.

Kennedy surprised Welles by telling him he had learned that German foreign minister Ribbentrop was going to meet with the pope to discuss peace prospects, counter the effects of Welles's visit, and showcase Germany as a peace-seeking nation. In Rome, Kennedy had met with his friend Count Enrico Galeazzi, a top Vatican administrator and financial consultant, who had astonished him with news of Ribbentrop's impeding visit. "The pope has no present hope of peace," Galeazzi told him, adding that he himself mistrusted "the whole business" of negotiating with Germany to end the war.

Welles arrived in Berlin on March 1 without fanfare. Hitler, fearing the German people might view his arrival as heralding peace, banned all publicity about the visit. In their meetings, Welles sought to convince the Nazi leaders that Mussolini was willing to throw his weight behind a negotiated peace plan. After a depressing meeting—one of the "most unpleasant of his life"—with Ribbentrop, who lied constantly, displaying a closed and "stupid mind," Welles met with Hitler, among others. All the Nazi leaders insisted that Britain wanted to destroy Germany and had rejected previous peace offers. Welles soon understood that Mussolini had less leverage with Hitler than Roosevelt had hoped. Although Welles didn't particularly like Hitler, he thought the Fuhrer was in "a mood to make a reasonable peace," or so Joe wrote Rose. Welles claimed in his memoir that in Berlin he concluded "it was tragically plain that all the decisions had already been made. The best that could be hoped for was delay." On the day of Welles's meeting with the Fuhrer, Hitler had given orders for the spring invasions of Norway and Denmark.

KENNEDY'S RETURN TO BRITAIN was not awaited with pleasure in government circles. At the end of February, Harold Nicolson went to the Foreign Office to see the chief diplomatic advisor, Sir Robert Vansittart. "He says that Kennedy has been spreading it abroad that we shall certainly be beaten," Nicolson reported, "and he will use his influence here to press for a negotiated peace." Vansittart despised anyone who might play into Hitler's hands in any way, and he accordingly denounced Kennedy, writing in the Foreign Office minute books that the American ambassador was "a foul specimen of double-crosser and defeatist. He thinks of nothing but his own pocket. I hope that the war will at least see the elimination of his type." Victor Perowne at the British Foreign Office desk noted warningly in the minute books that Kennedy "rightly or wrongly, is regarded as having achieved a very special position here" because of his intimacy with Chamberlain and other British leaders. "This belief, which is widespread, of course only enhances the importance of any views he may express and their effect."

In the Foreign Office minutes, one diplomat suggested that it would be useful if Kennedy would no longer be treated "like an honorary member of the Cabinet." A fellow colleague replied, "I should think it is a diminishing temptation." Sir Alexander Cadogan, permanent undersecretary for foreign affairs, sent out word to key political officials to shut down the pipeline of inside information Kennedy and his embassy associates had received as allies of Chamberlain.

When Joe arrived in Britain, reporters pressed him about U.S. isolationist attitudes: "If isolation means a desire to keep out of the war, I should say it is definitely stronger," he was quoted as saying. "It is not that Americans do not want to support the Allies or that they are selfish. . . . the American people understand the war less and less as they go along." Joe wrote Rose claiming he had actually said that "there were many phases of the war they didn't understand." But he was publicly perceived as making inaccurate claims about American wartime attitudes, and, as he wrote Rose, "they have been giving me a terrible hiding ever since." The British government believed Kennedy was confusing his own feelings with those of his fellow citizens. His comments were "not received graciously" by the British press, which "lashed out at me quite bitterly," Joe recalled. Harold Nicolson gave him a particularly nasty welcome in the *Spectator*, declaring that Kennedy will "be welcomed by the native or unhyphenated rich, who hope that he may bring with him a little raft of appeasement on which they can float for a year longer before they are finally submerged . . . He will be welcomed by the shiver-sisters of Mayfair and by the wobble-boys of Whitehall . . . the friends of Herr Ribbentrop . . . Lord Tavistock [a pacifist right-winger] and the disjecta membra of former pro-Nazi organizations . . . A solemn gladness will even crown the brows of M. Maisky, ambassador of the U.S.S.R. Few envoys, on returning to their posts, can have received a welcome of such embarrassing variety." Nicolson acknowledged that it is usually difficult for an ambassador to get below the surface of London politics and society, but that if Kennedy could, he would see that "Great Britain, although a difficult proposition, is also extremely tough."

German journalists sought to incite discord between Britain and the United States by reporting that Kennedy's relationship with the British government had frayed. Claiming that the British government had seen a confidential Kennedy dispatch to the State Department stating that Britain had "no chance of winning the war on Germany's Western Front," and that Kennedy blamed Chamberlain and his cabinet for "diplomatic blunders," the German reports indicated that he had lost the friendship of the British government. These German attacks did not go unanswered. Even Cordell Hull rushed to Kennedy's defense. "This is clearly intended to be a trouble-making story," Hull told the press. "It is wholly unsupported by any facts." Publicly, Kennedy called the German reports "the best fairy tale I have read since Snow White," but privately he noted that the reports had their intended effect in Britain, that "it soon became evident that a coolness had developed toward me in those circles, official and otherwise, whose use for America was to embroil her in a war."

Joe Jr. wrote from Harvard telling his father that the papers had carried the story of the "purported rift between you and the English government." By this time Kick, according to her biographer Lynne McTaggart, had become an "ardent proponent of intervention." She visited Harvard for the Hasty Pudding Club dance, but she ached to get back to London, see Billy, and participate in the war effort. Billy was stationed with the Coldstream Guards in southern England, and was squiring her friend Sally Norton around London on his days off. Sally had taken a job as a semi-skilled mechanic in a factory that made Royal Air Force planes. And Kick's friends were getting married: Debo Mitford and Andrew Cavendish, David Ormsby-Gore and Sissy Lloyd-Thomas, and Janie Kenyon-Slaney and Colonel Peter Lindsay. Kick was missing out on romance and its fulfillment, and on the sense of purpose war could bring.

"Kick is very keen to go over—and I wouldn't think that anti-American feeling would hurt her like it might us," Jack wrote his father, due to her being a girl—"especially as it would show that we hadn't merely left England when it got unpleasant."

Joe refused to let Kick visit Britain. The children should not come over, he wrote Rose. They would be shocked by how anti-American their British friends had become, and if the war got worse, "I am sure they will all hate us more." For Kick, in particular, Joe asserted that discussing the U.S. position on the war with her London friends would "undo all the pleasant memories she has." Their sons would have the same problem; as for Rose, if she returned, she would be "annoyed, but it wouldn't be so important" because she was used to being ostracized.

The day after his return to London, Joe met with Chamberlain and Halifax. He was reassured to find that Chamberlain was (at least outwardly) his "usual gracious self," welcoming him back with warmth. Neville told Joe that he had originally been disturbed about Welles's mission, fearing that its purpose was to "put over a peace plan"—one that would split the Allies and strengthen Hitler's hand. But Chamberlain had come to realize that Welles could explain to the American people the motivations of the warring European countries.

Whatever warmth Kennedy had felt from Chamberlain was dispelled by a distinct chilling in his relationship with Nancy Astor, who had been such a fervent friend. Visiting with the Astors on March 10, he detected a clear anti-American attitude and a *froideur* in Nancy. The evening featured animated speculation about when and where the war would be engaged.

The public announcement of Welles's mission led to a flood of unsubstantiated rumors that various diplomats from neutral nations would soon be offering peace proposals. Joe eagerly listened to the rumors and half-baked plans. He learned that Lord Tavistock claimed to have received tentative but reasonable peace proposals from the German government through his contacts in the German legation in Dublin. However, Tavistock, who believed Hitler was a misunderstood statesman, became a laughingstock when the German government officially denied the reports. In 2002 it would be revealed that the British intelligence agency MI5 had identified Tavistock as the likely leader of a Nazi puppet regime if Britain had been invaded.

Joe reviewed a naïve memorandum proposing unlikely terms for peace written by the duke of Buccleuch, a German sympathizer who was soon dismissed from the king's household. Meeting with the duke, Joe found his "appreciation of the forces that were gripping the world was too meager to rest anything upon it" —a charge some of Joe's critics would soon level at him.

CHAPTER 18

Missing the Bus

O N THE MORNING OF MARCH 11, Joe Kennedy and Sir Alexander Cadogan, the permanent undersecretary for foreign affairs, met Sumner Welles and Jay Pierrepont Moffat, the chief of the State Department's European Affairs department, at Heston airport in Hounslow, west of London, and whisked them into the capital city. Kennedy had arranged a packed four-day schedule of meetings for them. At lunch, Kennedy stressed to Welles that Britain would accept only a comprehensive peace agreement—one that would insure that there would be no more disputes over territory and that war would not flare up again in the near future. Welles asked him when Churchill might take over from Chamberlain. "Chamberlain is convinced that he can handle Churchill and he doesn't think Churchill is conspiring against him," Kennedy told him.

When Kennedy expressed his pique to Welles about not being invited to join the undersecretary at a tea with the king and queen—the first sign of royal frostiness toward the outspoken American ambassador—Welles arranged to have him included. Welles did not want the press speculating about a snub to Kennedy, suspecting a conflict between the two American diplomats, or suggesting that the British wanted to put one over on Welles. At tea, the king sat down in what he cheekily called the Ribbentrop chair—the same chair that the then-ambassador had occupied the day of his final meeting with the king after the invasion of Austria. Welles intrigued the royal couple by recounting how, during his meeting with the German foreign minister, Ribbentrop "sat with his hands on the table in front of him and his eyes closed, as if he were communing with the spirits. It was weird."

After the social call with the king and queen, Kennedy accompanied Welles and Moffat to 10 Downing Street for a meeting with Chamberlain in the poorly lit cabinet room at the back of the ground floor of the prime minister's residence. Chamberlain was relieved to learn that Welles had merely listened to Hitler and Mussolini without offering a peace proposal of his own. He was blunt in his skepticism about the usefulness of further negotiations. The relationship with Hitler lacked "confidence," he said. He vehemently declared it was impossible to make agreements with a Nazi regime that had completely betrayed his trust. Kennedy, who had a deep need for security, and who, thus, remained politically and psychically invested in the possibility of a negotiated peace, felt threatened by Chamberlain's attitude. Wouldn't it be acceptable, he asked, "if the Allies get a peace which they feel gets the right results in Poland and Czechoslovakia, and also gives security in Europe?" Chamberlain demurred. The issue went beyond just the resolution of Eastern European border disputes; the prime minister did not see a realistic way to achieve a phased and monitored disarmament and ensure enduring security in Europe without war.

The next day, Kennedy and Welles went to the Admiralty to visit Churchill. He was in a celebratory mood because the British cabinet had finally approved Operation Wilfred, his plan to take the war to the Germans by mining the Norwegian Leads—the narrow stretch of Norway's territorial waters lying between its outer string of islands and the mainland—and send troops to seize Narvik and other Norwegian ports, thus bottling up transport of the Swedish iron ore that supported the Nazi war machine.

Sitting by the fireplace in a big chair, smoking a cigar, Churchill was reading the afternoon newspaper with a highball at the ready when the two Americans arrived. According to Welles, "It was obvious that he had consumed a good many whiskeys before I arrived." For the next hour and fifty minutes, Churchill proceeded to deliver what Welles would tell Roosevelt was a "cascade of oratory, brilliant and always effective, interlarded with considerable wit." In Joe's more cynical account of the meeting, Churchill spoke as if "to thousands" of listeners, gesturing broadly, and characterizing the Nazis as "a monster born of hatred and fear." Disarming Germany and taking over its industrial plants would "cost us dear," Churchill acknowledged, "but we will, of course, win the war and that is the only hope for civilization." When Welles pointed out that war would lead to economic devastation, Churchill objected, saying, "That is taking the short view of it." Kennedy recalled interjecting, "The well that the water has been taken out of has become drier and drier" when it came to economics.

Kennedy was disturbed by the British approach to conducting the war,

as well as their dismissal of what he saw as its inevitably disastrous repercussions. The next day he would tell Welles, "There seems no real fire
anywhere, no genius, no sense of the shambles that are to come," and in
his memoirs Joe recalled that Welles agreed: "They talk about moral values
that must be restored . . . But they don't seem to realize that these moral
values will have a slim chance to survive a war of devastation."

After meeting with Churchill, Kennedy and Welles returned to 10
Downing Street, where Chamberlain and Halifax hoped that their second
encounter would be more fruitful. Chamberlain began by acknowledging
that although the Finnish situation had now changed, due to an impending peace agreement, he was not afraid that Russia would assist Germany.
The Finns were preparing to sign a peace treaty with Russia ceding about
10 percent of their territory, and 20 percent of their industrial capacity, to
the Soviet Union. The March 15 peace treaty would thwart Franco-British
preparations to send support to Finland in its struggle against German
plans for a peaceful occupation to secure northern Sweden's iron ore, and
hinder the Allies' plan to block German access to that crucial component
of war materials. Against Churchill's vociferous objections, Chamberlain
would temporarily scuttle the plans to stop the traffic of ore to Germany.

When Welles asked if a German pullout from Poland and parts of
Czechoslovakia, a phased disarmament monitored by an independent
body, and a pledge to hold plebiscites in Austria would convince the British
to consider negotiations, Chamberlain offered a ray of hope, saying that
he could not predict what the reaction of the British cabinet would be, and
that he was receptive to a miracle.

On their last night in London, Welles and Moffat joined Kennedy at a
stag dinner with Clement Attlee, Chamberlain, Churchill, and other prominent officials. Moffat wrote in his diary that toward the end of the evening
of all-male camaraderie, "under the cloak of horseplay" Joe was "able to
get across many unpalatable home truths regarding Anglo-American relations. It was superbly done. He made it clear . . . that taking our ships
into the combat area could not be done without risking a serious flare-
up." When Churchill spoke about the toughness of the British nation, Joe
quipped, "Well if you can show me one Englishman that's tougher than
you are, Winston, I'll eat my hat."

Joe went on to tell the group that, before returning from America to
London, he had said to Cordell Hull that if his ship was attacked during the
crossing, the United States should not use his death as an excuse to declare
war: "I thought this would give me some protection against Churchill's
placing a bomb on the ship!" Amidst the laughter, Churchill proclaimed,

jestingly, that he was certain that the United States would "come in later anyway."

After Welles left, Joe prepared to move from J. P. Morgan's Wall Hall, the estate he had borrowed for weekends in Hertfordshire, to a new home at St. Leonard's, which was a three-quarter-hour drive from the embassy at Grosvenor Square. Horace Dodge, the heir to the automobile fortune, had agreed to allow Kennedy to use the seventy-room estate for free. St. Leonard's would serve as a retreat in case London was bombed. "It is not an English type of house; it's the most modern thing you can imagine—rather big," Joe wrote Rose. With its spacious rooms, its formal and impersonal furnishings, and its unfinished outside terraces, the house would be a profoundly lonely residence for Joe, despite its sixteen-member staff. The main attraction was that the house stood on a wide sweep of ground overlooking its own private nine-hole golf course with a view of the Windsor Great Park and Windsor Forest two miles to the south. Two of Joe's favorite golf courses, Stoke Poges and Sunningdale, would be nearby.

Apart from helping to coordinate a visit like Welles's, "There is nothing to do except stagnate" at work, he wrote Rose. "I just never will be happy over here without you and the children." "Knowing myself as I do," he wrote, "when I've been home 6 months I'll want to get going again. Maybe old age and a bad stomach will change me. I don't know. I guess I'm a restless soul: Some people call it ambition. I guess I'm just *nuts!*" Such sentiments were as close to introspection as Joe ever managed.

After Welles's departure, Joe became increasingly aware of his diminished stature in England. "You would never believe the way public opinion in this country has turned anti-American and incidentally anti-US Ambassador Kennedy," he wrote to Rose on March 20. British aristocrats and social doyennes were claiming he had sent his frightened family home and that he had moved to the country because he was afraid he would be bombed in a German air raid: "All rotten stuff but all the favorite dinner parties of Mayfair go right to work hauling the U.S. Ambassador down." Joe had taken considerable risks in bluntly standing up for what he perceived as America's best interests, but his recent attempts lacked the finesse his tactful wife would have counseled had she been on the scene. Dogged by the social opprobrium he felt had besieged him since his upbringing in Brahmin Boston, Joe felt once again like an aggrieved outsider. During this trying period he wished Rose could be at his side: "3 months with you all the time [back in the United States] makes me miss you all the more," he wrote her.

Rose suggested a diplomatic way to diminish British fears about being abandoned by America: "Joe dear . . . it would be a wonderful feat if you could put over the idea that altho you are against America's entering the war—still you are encouraging help to England in some way. {Most Americans would be sympathetic,} and it would endear you to the hearts of the British." Joe missed her entreaty to be more tactful, replying in dismissive practical terms, "It's easy enough to say we should do something, but the real difficulty is—what?"

Once again, Joe turned to his daughter Rosemary for comfort. Dining with her right after his return from America, he noticed that she had gotten "a little fatter but her disposition is still great," as he wrote his wife. After lunching with her at Claridges, he told Rose, "I really don't have any trouble with her when she is alone. She is not 100% of course, but no real difficulty." Rosemary wrote him from school, telling him, "Mother says I am such a comfort to you. Never . to leave you . Well Daddy . I feel honour because you chose me to stay." She added a poignant postscript: "P.S. I am so fond of you. And. Love you very much. Sorry . to think that I am fat you . think—"

As Kennedy essayed to convince Churchill and the U.S. Maritime Commission to begin negotiations on his plan to have American ships take over some British shipping routes in the Pacific—and thus free up British ships for the war effort—Sumner Welles paid a return visit to Italy, making one last effort to move Mussolini into the Allies' camp. Then, on March 18, Hitler and Mussolini met in Il Duce's private coach at the railway station on the Italian side of the Brenner Pass. Alerting Mussolini that he was about to strike the West, Hitler convinced the Italian leader, who admired nothing more than force and power, to join the Axis. Mussolini asked, however, for several months to prepare to enter into a public military alliance.

Upon Welles's return to Washington, Roosevelt publicly admitted that there was "scant immediate prospect for the establishment of any just, stable, and lasting peace in Europe."

JACK SPENT THE WINTER OF 1940 writing his senior honors thesis, "Appeasement at Munich," which explored the reasons behind Britain's sluggish shift from disarmament to a rearmament policy in the 1930s. Conversations with British ambassador Lord Lothian in Palm Beach, and again in Washington, "started me out on the job," Jack later wrote Lothian. James Seymour, his father's press secretary, provided crucial assistance, sending Jack a wide range of British political pamphlets and books he could not obtain at Harvard. Scotland Yard and MI5 were closely monitoring the U.S. embassy and its ambassador after having discovered that classified documents were being leaked from the embassy to the enemy. The Ministry of Information intercepted Jack's cable "Rush Pacifist Literature" to Seymour and thought, because it was signed simply "Kennedy," that it was a missive from the ambassador. The treacherous Joe Kennedy was "Becoming a Pacifist!" wrote one of the alarmed officers at the American desk in the British Foreign Office. The Foreign Office would continue to malign him until he left his ambassadorship.

By the middle of March, Jack had completed his 150-page study of why, as he put it, at the time of Munich, "England was so poorly prepared for war." Using parliamentary speeches, newspaper editorials, and political pamphlets, he tracked how its belief that collective world security would be overseen by the League of Nations, its concerns about the financial burdens of rearmament, its lingering fear about another war, and the unwillingness of politicians to stand up against popular pacifism all prevented Britain from arming itself in the early to mid-1930s. These factors all converged, Jack concluded, to make appeasement at Munich a necessary strategic choice, buying Britain time to build military parity with Germany. He held the last two prime ministers, Baldwin and Chamberlain, responsible for the nation's lethargic response, but instead of blaming only these two leaders, Jack focused on what he saw as an inherent weakness in the nature of democracies. According to Jack's thesis, free nations could not match totalitarian countries in their ability to make people sacrifice in order to mobilize effectively and quickly for war.

Echoing his father's position, Jack minimized the moral dilemma of Munich, stressing instead the need for the democracies to maintain an unsparingly realistic appraisal of their geopolitical dangers and opportunities. Countries facing foreign threats could be adequately protected, he posited, only if their leaders eschewed denial or belligerent counterattack as a response to peril.

The thesis represented "more work than I have ever done in my life," he wrote his father. Joe Jr., obsessive and punctual like his mother, wrote his father detailing Jack's last-minute machinations to complete the work: "Jack rushed madly around the last week with his thesis and finally with the aid of five stenographers the last day got it in under the wire. I read it before he had finished it up and it seemed to represent a lot of work but did not prove anything." Historians often cite his letter as evidence of his jealousy of his brother. Most chroniclers, however, omit Joe Jr.'s final, more encouraging observation: "However he said he shaped it up the last few days and he seemed to have some good ideas so it ought to be very good."

The committee of professors reading the thesis critiqued Jack's sloppy spelling and prose, but they concluded that his thesis presented an impressive intellectual dissection of a complicated question. They gave him thesis grades between magna cum laude and cum laude plus, grades that would help him graduate cum laude from Harvard in June. In early April, Joe Jr. wrote his father that Arthur Krock had read Jack's thesis and declared it to be excellent. In fact, Krock had found it "amateurish in many respects," as he later recalled in an oral history at the Kennedy Library, but agreed to edit it for potential publication. He thought it could be shaped into an interesting book, and he wanted to please Joe. To be marketable, Jack's work would have to expend more effort showing how democracies could defend themselves.

Jack celebrated his success by taking a spring vacation in Florida, where, as he wrote his father, there were "three girls to every man—I did better than usual . . . finished up the week in a blaze of glory." Back at Harvard, Jack wrote his father that Krock had suggested that his thesis be prepared for a publisher with the new title *Why England Slept*, which would echo Churchill's incendiary book of 1938, *While England Slept*, which examined the failure of Britain to play a strong peace-keeping role in the 1920s and 1930s while Germany was engaging in a military buildup. Jack sent the thesis to his father for approval, asking whether he thought it was worth publishing, and whether it could be published while his father was ambassador and Chamberlain was still in office. Jack was beginning to find his own voice, but his powerful father's opinion still mattered to him. Although Jack focused in his book on the need for a country's armaments to equal its commitments, he still supported his father by defending the Munich agreement. Meanwhile, Joe Jr. had become one of the leaders of the Harvard Committee Against Military Intervention, and was moving toward a strident isolationism that surpassed what his father espoused.

IN THE AFTERMATH of the French failure to help defend Finland, the government of Prime Minister Edouard Daladier fell on March 19. Forming a new government was Paul Reynaud, who had long argued, like Churchill, for faster rearmament and a tougher line on Germany. A week later, on March 28, Reynaud came to London for the convening of the Anglo-French Supreme War Council of French and British cabinet officials. The council approved a modified version of Churchill's plan to mine the Norwegian Leads.

The next day Germany's Foreign Office released its soon-to-be-infamous

German White Paper, based on diplomatic documents that had been captured from the Polish Foreign Office after Warsaw had fallen to the Nazis. The Germans claimed that the documents showed that Poland had been pushed into war with Germany by the Allied powers, that Roosevelt was less neutral than he pretended to be, and that he planned to enter the war at a later point.

According to the White Paper, William Bullitt had meddled in French government affairs and told the French "that they were practically certain of our [American] support once they went in." Bullitt rescued Roosevelt by releasing a letter from former prime minister Daladier, now the French war minister, denying that Bullitt had said that the United States would enter the war. Both Roosevelt and Hull dismissed the reports as propaganda. Joe, however, did not spare his rival ambassador in his memoir. According to Kennedy, Welles quoted a European diplomat saying that Bullitt was "an unbalanced war monger" and that he and Ribbentrop were the "two most dangerous men in Europe to the cause of world peace."

Also included in the White Paper were Kennedy's conversations with the Polish ambassador to London in the summer of 1939, in which he boasted of Roosevelt's respect for Joe Jr.'s opinions about the European situation and said that his two sons would be lecturing audiences at home about the European crisis. He was also depicted pressuring the British government to aid Poland with cash. For once, Kennedy did not get the worst of the publicity—that distinction was reserved for Bullitt. "I wasn't at all disturbed by the German White Paper," Joe wrote Rose, because the documents offered a reasonable account of his conversations and he had said nothing that was anti-American.

As spring commenced, London was again plagued with alarming rumors about German air attacks or a ground invasion of the West, but Chamberlain was skeptical. "We continue to receive the most positive information from the most reliable sources of the imminence of the great offensive," Chamberlain wrote to his sister Ida on March 30, "accompanied by hair-raising & blood-curdling developments arising out of new secret weapons of unheard of power." The British prime minister had a hard time believing that Hitler, given uncertain morale and insufficient supplies at home, would risk everything on an invasion of Britain, and did not imagine that the Fuhrer would pit his small navy against the intimidating British fleet.

Joe recognized not only Britain's anger at America but also its restiveness toward their own government's passive approach to the war, in the face of what appeared to be a growing threat. "Nobody has the slightest idea what is going through the minds of the General Staff in Berlin," Joe wrote Rose in an April 5 letter. In England "there is still a feeling that America should stop talking about the mistakes the Allies are making." People were wondering why the Allies "don't turn loose on the Germans and settle up once and for all," he wrote Rose. The Twilight War, as Chamberlain had dubbed it, offered less relief than apprehension.

In the wake of Mussolini and Hitler's recent meeting, Kennedy believed it remained crucial to try to align Italy with the Allied cause. Worried about Italy's dangerous flirtation with the Nazi regime, he dispatched Eddie Moore and his wife, Mary, to Rome to gather the latest intelligence about Ribbentrop's meetings with the pope and with Mussolini, and to see what Moore could learn about Hitler's private tête-à-tête with Mussolini at the Brenner Pass. Moore reported to Kennedy that when Pope Pius XII met with Ribbentrop on March 11, Ribbentrop spoke of the Reich's imminent invasion of Western Europe and chastised the pope for siding with the Allies. But, to Kennedy's relief, Moore told him that the meeting ended abruptly after the pope read Ribbentrop a list of German atrocities against the Jews. Moore could not sleuth out whether Hitler had won over Mussolini. (Unbeknown to Welles, Mussolini had committed to join Hitler in the war after Germany had conquered France.)

By the time Moore got to Paris, he was laid low at the Ritz Hotel with a bad case of the flu. Joe reported to Rose that he had gone to Paris on April 1 to bring Eddie home. Joe did not tell her that he had spent a few days closeted in a hotel room at the Ritz with Clare Boothe Luce, who noted decorously in her diary one day that Joe had been "in bedroom all morning." Joe found Clare to be not only beautiful and brilliant, but also passionate and bold. The two shared a desire to play a pivotal role in geopolitical events, and they loved discussing politics and big ideas. A skillful seductress, Clare loved conquering powerful men, and, at least temporarily, Joe fit the bill. Joe and Clare were both in sexless marriages, and their brief affair was expedient for both of them.

After his family left Britain, Joe had no doubt consoled himself with many of the showgirls and secretaries he favored. In London, he had begun what would become a ten-year affair with Daye Eliot, a dancer in Fifi Ferry's Les Girls troupe out of Le Touquet in France. Joe had a soft heart for people, and especially women, in trouble. Even before they had become romantically involved, he had paid for a gynecological operation Daye needed. He would later arrange for her to meet Cardinal Spellman and convert to Catholicism.

Back in London, Churchill was in "seventh heaven," as Joe said, because

Chamberlain had appointed him chairman of the Military Coordination Committee, which formulated war strategy. The prime minister, addressing a Conservative Central Council meeting on April 4, made an utterance that would shortly return to haunt him. Speaking of Hitler's failure to launch an attack on the West, he said that "one thing is certain: he missed the bus." Chamberlain was unaware that German intelligence had known of British plans to mine the Norwegian harbors—though not the exact date—for weeks, and that the German troops, concealed in empty ore freighters, had left for Norway the previous day. The Americans had received this intelligence on April 3, when Alexander Kirk, the American chargé in Berlin, had reported that large numbers of German troops were concentrated at Stettin, the largest port in Poland, on the Baltic Sea. It is not clear why the Americans did not share this information with the British. Unbeknown to Chamberlain, the bus had indeed departed without him.

On April 8, Operation Wilfred finally began. The British began mining the coastal waters around Narvik in order to force German transport ships into international waters where the Royal Navy could attack them. Kennedy was immediately informed, but the cautious British government did not reveal that they were also sending troops to take over the Norwegian ports. They did not want a U.S. embassy leak to reveal their plans to the enemy.

But the Nazis trumped the British effort. At dawn the next day, April 9, Germany stunned the Allies by invading Norway and Denmark. Within hours, King Christian X of Denmark and the Danish Parliament, aware that their army was no match for the advancing German troops, ordered their forces to surrender. The Nazis occupied Copenhagen within days.

Kennedy met that afternoon with Halifax at the Foreign Office, and was told that Churchill was delighted at this turn of events because Hitler had made a key strategic mistake by taking on the British navy. Two days later in the House of Commons, Joe listened to Churchill give what he allowed was an "oratorical feat of the first magnitude" that "breathed confidence at every pore," with rhetoric suggesting the First Lord of the Admiralty had complete mastery of the situation, even though the Nazis had already seized Norway's key ports and overrun Oslo. Yet as historian Graham Stewart aptly noted, "Far from missing the bus, Hitler was driving it, right past the British waiting at the bus stop." Within days of making his comment about missing the bus, Chamberlain would be branded as being out of touch with the realities of the war.

The Royal Navy sank three German cruisers and ten destroyers. The Germans, however, had the advantage of having cracked British cryptography to the extent that they could interpret about 30 percent of the British naval signals. British and French troops landed in Norway on April 15. Initially they expelled the Germans from their positions, but eventually they had to retreat in the face of devastating attacks by the Luftwaffe on both the soldiers and their supply ships.

As the discouraging news trickled slowly into London during the second half of April, it began to dawn upon Joe that the British were losing. "The Norwegian invasion by Hitler," he wrote Rose, "was a staggering blow to the British." Joe did not share Churchill's optimism that Hitler had over-reached. Already alarmed at the extent of Nazi air power, he realized that Hitler had maintained supremacy in Norway through control of the air from German bases in Denmark. Joe also worried that a German victory in Scandinavia would have a "devastating effect" on the neutral Balkan States, Holland, and Belgium, and especially on Mussolini—pushing them all into the Axis orbit.

Nonetheless, in the face of all these discouraging developments, Joe did not waver in his commitment to keep America out of an entanglement in Europe. "We may have to fight Hitler at some later date over South America," he wrote Rose, "but we had better do it in our own back yard where we will be effective and not weaken ourselves by trying to carry on a fight over here." Meanwhile, on the last day of April, the war crept closer to England when a German plane crashed in the British town Clacton-on-Sea, killing two people on the ground, the first civilian wartime casualties.

Churchill had to take responsibility for the failure of the Norwegian campaign, which had relied heavily on the navy. "The situation in Norway which some people are already characterizing as the second Gallipoli," Kennedy cabled FDR, "has caused Mr. Churchill's sun to set very rapidly." Kennedy was not unhappy to see Churchill diminished, but his worst fears about the capability of Britain's government seemed to be coming true. "England lacks efficient leadership from top to bottom," he wrote FDR, "and unless there is a terrific change, and quickly, things will be as serious as one can imagine."

At the end of April, Roosevelt appealed to Mussolini to help end the war in Europe. Mussolini did not reply. As the Norwegians succumbed to Hitler, Roosevelt yielded to despair about Britain's chances of winning the war. Nonetheless, he bucked up Joe, wiring him on May 3, "These are bad days for all of us who remember always that when real world forces come into conflict, the final result is never as dark as we mortals guess it in very difficult days." During the coming months, Joe would receive very little additional encouragement from the president.

CHAPTER 19

"Tumbled to Bits
in a Moment"

THE ENGLISH BLUNDERED," Joe Jr. wrote his father, joining the chorus of criticism about the Norwegian debacle. Instead of "impressing upon everyone the difficulty of their maneuvers," he perceptively concluded, the British government made a mistake in "impressing upon people that Hitler made a strategic blunder and giving the impression that their fleet was doing a lot of damage." Churchill had demonstrated once again, as he had at the World War I battle of Gallipoli, an imperfect grasp of strategy, but the British public would reward him nonetheless for his tough stance against the Nazis and his prescient warnings about their intentions, blaming Chamberlain instead for the fiasco.

On May 7, the prime minister faced his critics in the "inquest on Norway" in the House of Commons. Historian Andrew Roberts, reading the Hansard report of the merciless two-day parliamentary debate, concluded that it was so theatrical that it sounded "like the script of a West End play." As Chamberlain entered the House of Commons, he was greeted with loud cheers from his supporters and equally vocal insults from the opposition: "Have you missed the bus?" some called out. Ambassador Kennedy felt that in Chamberlain's opening speech, his friend had left "no impression that he had a mastery of the facts." But Joe still believed the prime minister had the votes in Parliament to forestall a plunge from power; he could not anticipate how swiftly the moral tone of the debate would turn against him. Complaints came from Chamberlain's own party. Senior Conservative MP Leo Amery declared that "we must get into the government men who can match our enemies in fighting spirit, in daring, in resolution, and in thirst for victory." Facing Chamberlain directly in the crowded confines of the house, Amery ended his devastating speech by repeating the words Oliver Cromwell had uttered in dissolving the Long Parliament that had sat through two English civil wars and ordered King Charles I's execution in 1649: "You have sat too long here for any good you have been doing. Depart, I say, and let us have done with you. In the name of God, go." Churchill later wrote: "These were terrible words coming from a friend and colleague," especially one from Birmingham, Chamberlain's hometown. Former prime minister David Lloyd George, who had led Britain to victory in World War I, exuding two decades of venom for his successor, brutally insisted that Chamberlain should resign, thus offering the British people an example of the sacrifice he had demanded from them.

The next evening, Joe sat between the Russian and Belgian ambassadors in the gallery for the closing debate before the Commons would vote on what was unofficially a motion of confidence in the government. Historian William Manchester would liken the debate to a "runaway jury . . . moved by forces deep within the House of Commons" that wanted decisive leadership for the critical hour at hand. In defending himself, Chamberlain made what turned out to be a crucial error, appealing in personal terms for support to his allies in Parliament ("I say to my friends in the House, *and I have friends in the House*"). Even though Chamberlain's reference to his friends was a "conventional parliamentary expression for party colleagues rather than a cynical call upon personal friendship," according to Chamberlain biographer Bob Self, the opposition was outraged. "The issue before the House," Joe recalled in his memoir, "went beyond any concept of friendship: upon its resolution might rest the fate of England itself." According to Joe, Churchill's speech, defending a government about which he was ambivalent, was not "the ablest of his performances." Churchill took responsibility for the naval disaster at Trondheim, but covered himself by revealing that the battle plan had been the unanimous decision of the Chiefs of Staff. Churchill "saw in the distance the mantle being lowered on his shoulders," Joe thought, and "he took pains, despite an occasional loss of temper, not to encourage too much enmity from any quarter."

The vote of confidence gave Chamberlain a meager majority, stunning Kennedy, the other diplomats in the gallery, and the riotous members of Parliament. Damningly, forty-four Conservative members—including Anthony Eden and Duff Cooper—voted against him, and to his shock, his former booster Lady Astor was one of sixty Conservative members who abstained. As Chamberlain departed the chamber, the downtrodden prime minister's opponents shouted, "Go in the name of God, go." Seriously shaken, Chamberlain told Churchill that he doubted he would be able to continue as prime minister. When the Labor Party refused to serve in a National Coalition government headed by Chamberlain, the prime minister knew his leadership was doomed. Kennedy called FDR that night and briefed him on the parliamentary drama. The president interrupted him to say he had just heard that Germany had delivered an ultimatum to Holland. Kennedy immediately called Churchill with the news, and then reached John Cudahy, the U.S. ambassador to Belgium, in Brussels at 2 A.M. Cudahy was not sure whether the Dutch had actually received an ultimatum, but he reassured Kennedy that he did not expect an attack the next day.

King George, the prime minister, and the majority of the Conservative MPs wanted Lord Halifax to replace Chamberlain. But the day after the vote, Halifax told Chamberlain that a prime minister could not succeed if he was neither in charge of the war—which Churchill, due to his character and experience, would undoubtedly continue to supervise—nor a member of the House of Commons. In any case, the thought of taking power in wartime had left him with a terrible stomachache. He knew that Churchill would be a more effective wartime chief and believed that, from a seat within the cabinet, he could better manage him and, as Halifax's biographer Andrew Roberts described it, "dissuade Churchill from disastrous over-reactions."

Back in America, Rose prepared to move the family to Cape Cod for the summer and did her part for the cause of the Western democracies, attending New York City's glamorous Allied Ball with the French ambassador and other dignitaries. Kick brought a date, but Rose was unable to find an escort for Eunice, who was otherwise preoccupied with tennis tournaments and swimming matches. At one tennis match, Eunice dressed in the white shorts she wore at Cannes, which were "very respectable," she wrote her father, but the nuns insisted she go back to the gym and dress in a "girl's skirt and shorts which must have had a size 64 waist," but "both proceeded to fall off in the middle of the match." Eunice masked her humiliation, writing to her father, "Such is life!" Rose, however, told Joe that "her bloomers loosened & to the snorts & laughter of the team—she had to be ushered off the field again & tighten up the borrowed attire. Her legs are so long that her stockings . . . do not reach to her shorts & the gap is now the subject of concern and comedy at the games." Not a reassuring incident for a gawky young woman unable to score a date for a ball.

Eunice took Teddy to the circus and caused a commotion by buying a big lizard that jumped out of its container. "You would have thought I had let a lion out of his cage," Eunice wrote her father. "Everyone started to shriek, one lady shrieked out, 'My heart, my heart,' and I was running like mad trying to catch him which I finally did."

On May 9, Kick, Jack, and some of his Harvard friends traveled to Maryland for the Maryland Hunt Club's steeplechase race. Jack, who was still pining for his former girlfriend Frances Ann Cannon, took Kick's friend Charlotte McDonnell as his date, while Kick, who longed to be in England with Billy, partied with a young man named Johnny (Zeke) Coleman, who was infatuated with her. For the Hunt Club ball, Jack dressed in white tie and tails and the girls wore their finest gowns in an evening glamorous enough to remind them of London's social whirl, now lost to wartime blackouts and deprivations.

ON MAY 10, Cordell Hull awakened Joe at 6 A.M. to tell him the horrifying news that Holland and Belgium were under attack and that Luxemburg, with an army of four hundred infantrymen, was being invaded. Hitler had begun a massive and brilliantly planned assault on the West. Joe rang up the Admiralty, whose staff he found "singularly uninformed." The American embassy's naval attaché, Captain Alan Kirk, met with Joe, noting that the U.S. ambassador was "tearing his hair."

As the sun came up that May morning, the Luftwaffe had flown in over the tulip fields from the North Sea, surprising the Dutch air force and annihilating its bases and airports. In a stunning wartime innovation, three thousand Nazi troops parachuted into Holland, invading the country from the inside out. Within five days Holland would surrender, and Queen Wilhelmina would flee into exile in England. That morning, Ambassador Cudahy told Joe that Brussels had been bombed at 5:30, and then reached Halifax, who informed him that the British were moving by air, land, and sea to engage the German armies. British troops landed in Iceland to protect that strategic area, and also crossed the border from France into Belgium, but did not have the military intelligence to know where to link up with Belgian troops; in the months before the Nazi onslaught began, the Dutch and Belgian governments, fearing Nazi reprisals, had refused to discuss strategy with the British government.

As the German air force diverted attention over Holland and Belgium,

Hitler ingeniously sent his panzers, tanks, armored cars, and motorcycles, along with elite infantrymen, stealthily through the dense Ardennes Forest in the Low Countries bordering eastern France. The Germans appeared just to the north of the French army's famous Maginot Line, which consisted of a string of five hundred buildings and forts protecting France from Germany. Before noon that first day, the Germans crossed rivers into France, encircling all the French defenders near Belgium from the south.

R EACTING TO THE DEVASTATING NEWS, Chamberlain considered remaining in office, but his cabinet colleagues convinced him that Britain needed a national government that included the Labor and Liberal parties, whose leaders were not willing to serve under him. As evening fell on May 10, sixty-five-year-old Winston Churchill realized his lifelong dream: At Buckingham Palace, King George VI formally asked him to take over the government. The king, concerned about Churchill's reputation as a volatile and impetuous adventurer and his penchant for imperious and patronizing male behavior (which irritated the queen), and remembering Churchill's support of the duke of Windsor during the abdication crisis, reluctantly initiated Britain's most crucial prime ministership, as well as what would eventually become an extraordinary wartime partnership that exemplified British courage and resolve.

But at this juncture, there was plenty of doubt to go around. As he left the palace Churchill told his driver, "I hope it is not too late." Tearing up, he continued, "I am very much afraid that it is. We can only do our best." The next day the king, who had been bitterly opposed to Churchill's assumption of power, wrote in his diary, "I cannot yet think of Winston as P.M."

Joe called the new prime minister to offer congratulations and teasingly told him that he was partly responsible for Churchill's new job. Referring to his code message the previous December informing Churchill about Roosevelt's approval of mining the Norwegian Leads, Joe told him, "[H]ence Norway, hence Prime Minister." It is unlikely that Churchill relished the remark, reminding him as it did of his dubious role in the failed naval campaign; nor would such a jest be appreciated by a man who believed he was "walking with destiny." Churchill's first act as prime minister was to write his predecessor asking him to stay on as the head of the Conservative Party and saying, "How grateful I am to you for promising to stand by me & to aid the country at this extremely grievous and formidable moment . . . To a very large extent I am in your hands—& I feel no fear of that."

At a time when his world had "tumbled to bits in a moment," as Chamberlain wrote his sisters, he was touched by Churchill's gesture. When Joe Kennedy met with the former prime minister on May 16, he thought that he looked "ghastly," and that he was "definitely a heartbroken and physically broken man." Two days later, trying to buck up his friend, Joe requested that Chamberlain send him an inscribed photo that he could hang on his wall to remind him "constantly of a man who worked with all his capacity to keep peace in the world . . . and with whom I am most happy to have been associated with in the 2 most eventful years of my life."

The great newspaper editor and writer A. G. Gardiner summed up the new prime minister's theatrical persona: Churchill was, he wrote, "always imbued with a profound sense of playing the leading part in a great drama" during which "it is always the hour of fate and the crack of doom." This was his hour. On May 13, three days after taking office, Churchill appeared in Parliament for the first time as prime minister. That same day, the Germans smashed open a sixty-mile breach in France's Maginot Line. Asking the Commons to approve a resolution of confidence in the new national government he had formed, Churchill gave a speech that would bring his audience to its feet. Paraphrasing Italian military leader Giuseppe Garibaldi's famous remarks ("I offer neither pay, nor quarters, nor food, I offer only hunger, thirst, forced marches, battles and death"), Churchill declared, "I have nothing to offer but blood, toil, tears, and sweat. We have before us an ordeal of the most grievous kind . . . You ask, what is our policy? . . . it is to wage war, by sea, by land and air, with all our might . . . against a monstrous tyranny, never surpassed in the dark, lamentable catalogue of human crime . . . You ask, what is our aim? . . . It is victory, victory at all costs, victory in spite of all terror, victory, however long and hard the road may be; for without victory, there is no survival."

According to historian William Manchester, Churchill's Manichean language reflected his moral outlook. He believed in "absolute virtue and absolute malevolence, in blinding light and impenetrable darkness . . . in the forces of good against the forces of evil." Such a moral vision would recast Joe Kennedy's pragmatic accommodationism as ignoble.

In a conversation with Kennedy at the Foreign Office, Lord Halifax told the American ambassador that Britain would need every airplane the United States could muster. He urged Kennedy to support Churchill in an appeal to FDR for military aid. Kennedy was willing to help by asking for any military equipment the United States could spare without damaging its own defensive capacity. Late on the night of May 14, he was summoned for a midnight meeting at the Admiralty with Churchill and the publisher and former minister of information Lord Beaverbrook, who had just been offered the crucial job of minister of aircraft production. When he arrived, Joe noticed that Admiralty House was completely blacked out and surrounded with a large detail of soldiers.

To Joe, Churchill looked "ill-conditioned." Joe worried, as always, that Winston had been drinking too many Scotch highballs—not realizing that Churchill watered down his drinks. The American ambassador was concerned, as he noted in his diary on May 15, that "the affairs of Great Britain might be in the hands of the most dynamic individual in Great Britain but certainly not in the hands of the best judgment in Great Britain." Finding Churchill and his staff to be uncharacteristically gloomy, Joe sensed that "a very definite shadow of defeat was hanging over them all." But defiant as always, Churchill announced that within a month there would be "bombs and murder and everything terrible happening to England, but it would still not deter them." Kennedy, in response, deepened his commitment to help provide Britain whatever military and financial aid America could reasonably offer. "You know our strength," he told Churchill. "If we wanted to help all we can, what could we do?" Churchill told him that he would ask for more airplanes and for older destroyers.

That night it became clear that the long battle for Mussolini's loyalty to the Allies was nearing an unfortunate end. Kennedy showed Churchill and Beaverbrook a worrisome telegram he had just received from Ambassador Phillips in Rome, relaying foreign minister Ciano's admission that Mussolini, impressed with Hitler's triumphs in Holland and Belgium, was ready to enter the war on the side of the Germans. Adding Italy's submarines to the German fleet would multiply British losses. "We all have to put on a good front," Churchill exhorted Joe. Kennedy told him that he had "no trouble putting on a front," but he "couldn't help my inner thoughts based on the facts."

As he was pressed once more to make a case to Roosevelt and the State Department for massive aid to the Allies, Joe spoke bluntly about America's position. "It isn't fair to ask us to hold the bag for a war that the Allies expect to lose," he recalled saying. "Right now our navy is in the Pacific, our army is not up to requirements and we haven't enough airplanes for our own use." Churchill remained insistent about aid and resolute in his determination to fight on at any cost. England, he said, would "never give up as long as I am in power even though England is burned to the ground." If necessary, the British would take their fleet to Canada and "fight on." Such tenacity gave Joe pause. "I think this is something we should follow up," he cabled Hull and Roosevelt at 2:00 that morning.

The next day he would send to FDR Churchill's message indicating that the Allies had only a slight chance of winning once Italy entered the war. "He needs help badly is the reason [sic] for the message to you," Kennedy told the president.

Churchill was frantically seeking out every option that would help to save Britain. On Wednesday, May 15, before going to Paris to buck up French prime minister Paul Reynaud's resolve to fight, Churchill, calling himself "Former Naval Person," reinitiated his correspondence with the American president. "The small countries are simply smashed up, one by one, like matchwood. We must expect . . . that Mussolini will hurry in to share the loot of civilization. . . . If necessary, we shall continue the war alone, and we are not afraid of that," he told FDR, but "the voice and force of the United States may count for nothing if they are withheld too long." Churchill directly asked Roosevelt for several hundred aircraft, anti-aircraft guns, steel, submarines, the loan of forty to fifty old destroyers, an American squadron in Irish ports that would underline to the Germans the fact of Irish neutrality, and a strong American naval presence in the Pacific to contain the Japanese. Roosevelt would eventually devise an ingenious way of circumventing the Neutrality Act in order to provide Britain with the warplanes it desperately needed. He would secretly arrange to have the planes flown to the Canadian border, hauled across, and then flown to Newfoundland, where they could be brought to England aboard ships.

On May 16, FDR went before the Congress and in a galvanizing speech, called on the country to produce the unimaginable number of fifty thousand warplanes during the next year (twenty-five times the number built in 1939). Saying that the nation would need "a toughness of moral and physical fiber" to defend itself in the face of a burgeoning European war, the president exhibited a newly forthright seriousness of intent about American rearmament. Asking for a budget of $1.2 billion for national defense and announcing plans to expand the armed forces, Roosevelt received one of the longest standing ovations Congress had ever given him.

"Everyone is unanimous in thinking that Roosevelt made a marvelous speech," Joe Jr. wrote his father. "Some wonder what we are going to do with 50,000 planes, and suspect that it is Roosevelt's intention to get the country into war immediately after the election, whereas to others it is a natural defensive reaction." Joe Jr. continued to serve as his father's political scout at home. "Overnight the people turned strongly sympathetic to the allies, and now many people are saying that they would just as soon go to war . . . there is a kind of feeling here that we are bound to be in the war, like a mysterious force which is ever bringing the country closer." Young Joe also told his father "how panicky" people were becoming about the possibility that America might be invaded. "Some of them have asked for muskets for protection against parachute troopers and you would think the war was in their backyard." The work of gearing up the nation's defenses for war was the kind of effort the ambassador was cut out for, young Joe opined, and might make an excellent excuse for bringing his father back home.

The American president was still curtailed by American public opinion—a recent poll had shown that only 7.7 percent of the public favored immediate entry into the war, while a mere 19 percent favored going in if the Allies appeared headed to defeat. At this forlorn moment, Kennedy joined Churchill in pinning his hopes on FDR. Predicting that France would soon fall to Hitler, he looked to Roosevelt for a miracle. "The President might start considering, assuming that the French do not stiffen up, what he can do to save an Allied debacle," the ambassasor cabled FDR on May 16.

At midnight on May 16, Kennedy received a cable from Roosevelt stating that destroyers could not be made available without an act of Congress, and that the timing was not right for such an appeal. In any case, the ships would take seven precious weeks to be prepared for service. FDR told Kennedy to express hope to Churchill that he could find a way to circumvent Congress. Early the following morning, upon his return from Paris, where he had agreed to send the desperate French more British planes, Churchill telephoned Kennedy, who relayed the contents of the president's cable and agreed to meet with the prime minister at the Admiralty. Churchill told him he was pleased that the president had not mentioned asking England to pay for American supplies. He was also heartened by FDR's speech to Congress. Roosevelt, worried that the prime minister had been discouraged by his cable, called Kennedy that evening, asking him to reassure Churchill that he wanted to help him as much as possible.

But Churchill took no chances; he maintained the pressure on FDR. Writing Roosevelt on May 20, he intimated that if the United States left Britain to a dismal fate, Churchill's hypothetical successors, "who in utter despair and helplessness might well have to accommodate themselves to the German will," could offer Germany the British fleet in last-ditch peace negotiations.

Still, Britain was not giving up. Going on the counterattack, in mid-May, British bombers struck German industrial targets in the Ruhr, and several days later hit oil refineries and railways in German cities, killing thirty-four German civilians in the attacks. Germany, meanwhile, was closing in on the English Channel. On May 17, the Nazis entered Brussels, and the next day they took over Antwerp, Belgium's main port. On May 19, Churchill addressed the British people in his first radio broadcast as prime minister, telling them that "it would be foolish to deny the gravity of the hour. It would be still more foolish to lose heart or courage."

Within days German troops progressed in a wide semicircle, moving behind the Allied troops and reaching the northern French coast, within easy reach of the three channel ports, Calais, Boulogne, and Dunkirk, where they hemmed in the British Expeditionary Force. As Joe said, "Each day brought new disasters."

CHAPTER 20

Narrow Escapes

ON SATURDAY, May 18, Joe Kennedy was spending the weekend with Clare Boothe Luce at St. Leonard's when he was interrupted by an urgent call from Herschel Johnson, the embassy counselor. Speaking with caution over the open phone line, Johnson told Kennedy that a British intelligence agent had visited him and revealed alarming news: British intelligence reports suggested that one of the embassy's code clerks was giving out confidential information to sources close to the Nazis.

Shaken, Kennedy asked Johnson to brief him out at St. Leonard's the next day. That Sunday, before visiting Kennedy, Johnson called on Sir Alexander Cadogan at the Foreign Office. Cadogan conferred with legal consultants, who determined that there would be no legal impediment to searching the home of a U.S. embassy employee.

The news that there appeared to be a spy in the American embassy could not have come at a more perilous time for Kennedy and the British war effort, and the incident would contribute to Joe's increasing pessimism about Britain's chances of surviving the war. With the fall of the Low Countries and the invasion of France heightening fears of a Nazi invasion of England, the British people realized they were fighting for their lives. The public had been ordered to put up air-raid shelters, "even if it means spoiling the lobelias," according to *New Yorker* correspondent Mollie Panter-Downes, "and to have their respirators fitted as speedily as possible with new filters to handle smoke gases." At the same time, British intelligence services were alarmed about the possibility of fifth-column agents subverting or overthrowing the government. In response to the escalating danger from within and without, Britain was becoming, for all practical purposes, a dictatorship. Parliament had just passed additional provisions of the 1939 Emergency Powers Bill that gave the government power to "require persons to place themselves, their services, and their property" at the disposal of the state. The right of individuals to habeas corpus was suspended.

Just days after Joe was informed of the investigation into a possible mole on his staff, the British cabinet ordered widespread detentions of Nazi sympathizers and British Fascist Union members—especially those who believed in a negotiated peace with Germany, a position that was now seen as treacherous. "Various foreign-inspired organizations," Panter-Downs wrote, "which had counted on the well-known British combination of warm heart and wooden head to leave them pretty for the duration, woke up to find themselves in Brixton prison."

One of the first to be targeted for arrest was British Union of Fascists leader Sir Oswald Mosley. He and his wife, the former Diana Mitford, were put under surveillance. While tracking possible foreign agents and exploring a way to justify detaining Mosley, MI5 (Military Intelligence) had concluded that a fifth columnist was operating within the U.S. embassy. It is possible to reconstruct the sequence of events around the investigation from State Department documents, declassified for this book, consisting of U.S. embassy staff reports on the situation.

That Sunday at St. Leonard's, Johnson gave Kennedy an extraordinary account of Scotland Yard's probe into Tyler Kent, a handsome and reserved twenty-nine-year-old code clerk at the embassy. The son of a career diplomat, and from a prominent Virginia family, Kent was a multilingual Princeton graduate. He did not believe he had been employed at a level commensurate with his abilities either in his previous position as a clerk under William Bullitt in the Moscow embassy or in his current job translating cables at the U.S. embassy. Kent had first come to the attention of MI5 because of his connection with members of the right-wing organization the Right Club. MI5 believed this group was conducting pro-German activities under the guise of disseminating anti-Semitic tracts. Its leader was Captain Archibald Maule Ramsay, a prominent Conservative member of Parliament. Johnson told Kennedy that Scotland Yard had put Kent under surveillance the previous October when a Swede known to be a Gestapo agent had visited Kent's rooms, leaving with a heavy manila envelope. Kennedy was appalled at Kent's behavior and deeply worried about the consequences it might have for him and his country.

On Monday morning, May 20, Franklin C. Gowen, the second secretary of the embassy, accompanied MI5 captain Maxwell Knight and several detectives on a raid on Kent's rooms in a private boarding house at 47 Gloucester Place in London. Gowen had been instructed on how to thwart any objections Kent might make—based on his diplomatic immunity—to having his room searched. The detectives smashed through Kent's door, discovering Kent and his mistress, a married woman named Irene Danischewsky, clad in pajamas. After telling the couple to dress, they sent Danischewsky home. Kent denied having any materials related to the American embassy, but detectives found several suitcases filled with what turned out to be 1,929 embassy documents. In addition, Kent had photographic plates of two cables Kennedy had sent containing messages from Churchill to Roosevelt. Kent was brought to the U.S. embassy.

Joe Kennedy sat grimly in his office as officials from MI5 opened the suitcases in front of him. Inside he saw copies of telegrams sent between the embassy and the State Department, as well as copies of letters and telegrams to other embassies in Europe. Kent's cache of material could not have been more explosive. The papers included correspondence between Roosevelt and Churchill, revealing that Roosevelt was privately trying to help Churchill even as he publicly proclaimed his support for America's neutrality.

Kennedy was furious and not a little scared. In the wrong hands, these materials could derail American aid to the Allies, cost Roosevelt a third term, and destroy Britain's chances to survive the war, not to mention torpedo his ambassadorship. The unnerved ambassador, Captain Knight, and Herschel Johnson interviewed Kent for fifteen acrimonious minutes, trying to ascertain his motives and what he had done with the documents.

"This is quite a serious situation that you have got your country involved in," Kennedy told Kent. "From the kind of family you come from—one would not expect you to let us down."

"In what way?" Kent asked.

"You don't think you have? What do you think you were doing with our codes and telegrams?" Joe asked.

"It was only for my own information," Kent replied.

"Why did you have to have them?" Kennedy pressed.

"Because I thought them very interesting," Kent countered.

In a 1944 interview with the *Washington Daily News*, Kennedy would claim that during his interrogation, Kent "played up and down the scale of an intense anti-Semitic feeling, showed no remorse except in respect to his parents and told me to 'just forget about him.'" The recently declassified State Department transcript of the interview supports Kent's later assertions that he did not act in this manner. However, as Bryan Clough, who wrote a book on the Kent-Wolkoff affair, reveals, the official file could have been doctored—which would not be surprising given the eagerness of the British and American governments to keep the whole affair secret. It is also possible either that in his later conversation Kennedy conflated the sentiments of the anti-Semitic pamphlets found in Kent's rooms with his responses during the interview, or that he lied to the reporter to enhance his image as a man who would not tolerate prejudice against the Jews.

Knight told Kent that Scotland Yard knew he had been associated with a White Russian woman, Anna Wolkoff, whom detectives believed to be a pro-German propagandist and a conduit to Germany. Wolkoff, a lively and engaging woman, worked in a fashionable dress shop but spent a lot of time socializing at the Russian Tea Room, a gathering place for White Russians in South Kensington. The restaurant was owned by her parents, who were a former admiral in the czar's navy and a former maid of honor to the czarina. Kent had met Wolkoff there; she had introduced him to Danischewsky, his Russian mistress. Both Irene and her husband were under surveillance by MI5 as possible Russian spies. MI5 investigators would soon determine that Kent allowed Wolkoff to take several documents out of his flat so that she could have them photographed.

When Knight showed Kent a locked leather-bound volume they had found in his room, Kent remained nonchalant. Captain Ramsay had given it to him for safekeeping, he said, but he had no idea of its contents. Knight broke it open. The volume contained a list of Right Club members. Although Kent belonged to the group, it turned out he had joined only weeks before his arrest.

"Don't you think it strange that a Member of Parliament should come to you, a minor official in an embassy, and give you a locked book to take care of for him?" Knight demanded.

"I don't know," Kent replied.

Kent went on to tell Kennedy and the others that he had invited Wolkoff and Ramsay to his rooms and showed them some of the stolen documents, allowing Wolkoff to make copies of some of the Roosevelt-Churchill correspondence. He later claimed that he had shown the documents to Ramsay hoping he would pass them on to politicians who could act against Roosevelt. It remained for the MI5 to determine the extent of Kent's connections with many fifth columnists they had rounded up several days after his arrest. A Mrs. Nicholson, who was arrested with Anna Wolkoff and Captain Ramsay, had a rough pencil copy of Churchill's May 16 message to Roosevelt. She had copied this from Wolkoff, who had gotten the telegram from Kent. It was not clear whether Kent was a spy or simply a disgruntled American isolationist.

Ever since Kent arrived at the embassy the previous October, he had, at Kennedy's behest, been making copies of embassy documents, which included the Roosevelt-Churchill correspondence, telegrams between the embassy and the State Department, and letters and telegrams to other embassies. These were to be collected in the ambassador's personal files (Joe wanted the papers as references for the memoir he intended to write, and to protect himself, if necessary, against Roosevelt). Investigators would later learn that as Kent translated messages into the State Department Gray code (surprisingly, the lowest grade code used by the State Department), he became obsessed with the idea that Roosevelt was "secretly and unconstitutionally plotting with Churchill" to sneak the United States into a Jewish-inspired war. He was gathering evidence to present to the U.S. Congress, the isolationist America First Committee, and the press in order to derail Roosevelt's campaign for a third term. He had been particularly incensed by FDR's encouraging May 16 response to Churchill's request for older American destroyers. Kent's prompt detention provided Roosevelt, Kennedy, and Churchill with a narrow escape from disastrous revelations leaking out to the press and the public.

MI5 had originally planned to deport Kent, but on that Monday morning as he was being taken into custody, a speedy secret cable arrived from Washington approving the removal of his diplomatic immunity. "The interrogation . . . was not too deftly conducted, but it produced enough to warrant his further detention," Joe wrote in his memoir. Two days later, the State Department fired Kent, and on May 23, he was given a dismissal notice backdated to May 20. The British government issued a deportation order on the twenty-third so that he could be brought to the United States, but the president wanted him tried secretly. That could only happen in England, a country already committed to the security exigencies of war.

Roosevelt wanted to make sure that no document Kent had copied could be used against him, and that the public would not learn about his secret correspondence with Churchill. Joe Kennedy had been handed an opportunity to destroy his presidential rival and further advance the isolationist cause. If he allowed Kent to be deported, the whole affair would become public during a sensational trial. But however tempted the frustrated American ambassador might have been, Joe was not prepared to be that disloyal to his boss or to his country. Nor did he want to destroy his own political future. Joe would not profit from newspaper stories about his disloyalty nor from suggestions that he had harbored a spy.

As relieved as he was that a security leak at the embassy had been stopped, Joe was deeply perturbed that Scotland Yard had monitored him and the embassy for months, and, after uncovering Kent, had given him no indication that their secret codes were being compromised and top-secret cables were being copied and passed on. This breach of security could not have come at a worse point. The arrest "threw our entire communication into confusion," Joe wrote in his memoir. "Our existing codes were no longer safe, and their violability imperiled the secrecy of diplomatic communications throughout all of Europe." At a time when the embassy needed to transmit to the president and the State Department a flood of information about the German advance through France toward the British Channel, embassy officials now had to improvise. However, there were more invulnerable codes available in the U.S. diplomatic services, including the M-138 military cipher, a higher-grade cryptography. Starting in mid-1941, these more secure codes would be used for Roosevelt-Churchill communications.

Working to limit the damage, Joe got the chief censor in the British Home Office to assure him that no news of Kent's thefts would appear in the English press. News did seep out in America, but the June 1 *New York Times* article was so vague as not to incite further coverage, mentioning only that Kent had been detained and that the charges were not being revealed. In a telegram declasssified for this book, Kennedy cabled Hull that the restrictions on British newspapers were necessary "since this case stinks to heaven." He sent his secretary Eddie Moore back to the United States with his daughter Rosemary, promising Hull that Moore was bringing with him "a fairly complete story" of the situation with Kent. In Brixton prison, Tyler Kent would undergo further interrogation to determine the extent of his activities and connections. Kent would be charged, under the Official Secrets Act, with obtaining documents that could aid the enemy.

The arrest of the American Tyler Kent was only a small event in MI5's accelerating crackdown on British subjects considered to be security risks. Early on the evening of May 23, three days after Kent was detained, Sir Oswald Mosley was arrested. The Mitfords and many other families found themselves pitted against each other in the new wartime state, in a nation where the public searched the skies for Nazi parachute troops at dawn and dusk. Nancy Mitford gave detectives in the intelligence services evidence against her sister, and a month after Oswald Mosley was arrested, Diana was imprisoned along with her husband. Unity Mitford, in the aftermath of her suicide attempt as the war with Germany began, had arrived back in England in January. Her return to her family home by ambulance received lurid press coverage. Despite public calls for her incarceration, Unity, who was severely brain damaged, was allowed to remain with her parents.

THE SAME DAY that Tyler Kent was hauled off to Brixton prison, Joe wrote letters to Rose and Jack. He could not reveal in a letter his shock and distress over Kent's perfidy. Rose had planned to fly to England on May 10, visit Joe, and bring Rosemary home, but Hitler's blitzkrieg through Europe made the grueling five-day journey to London via Brazil, West Africa, and Lisbon seem impossibly hazardous. The leg from Lisbon to London would have been on the inaugural British Airways flight between the two cities, which could easily have been shot down by the Nazis. Rose already feared flying in inclement weather; flying through a war zone was more than she could face. At a time when pessimism was on the rise in England, as measured by Mass Observation—the first-hand reports of a nationwide panel of spectators—Joe succumbed to gloom: "The English will fight to the end," he wrote Rose, "but I don't think they can stand up to the bombing indefinitely." Joe thought the British would have to submit to Hitler's peace terms, giving up the British navy to Germany. America would find itself "in a terrible mess." Thus, he wrote, the "great adventure" of his ambassadorship was "near the finish."

Overwhelmed with the work of war and reeling from the arrest of Kent, Joe could not attend the ceremony in which Rosemary received her school degree at Belmont House in Hertfordshire. Instead, he sent her a telegram expressing his love and pride. Rose remained in Massachusetts, waiting for Rosemary and the Moores, who finally left England on May 26. Flying from Lisbon on the Pan Am *Clipper*, they were forced to make an unscheduled landing in Bermuda due to a storm. Rosemary was completely unnerved when British agents boarded the plane and seized the mail, some of which came from Germany. Rose was equally unsettled when she learned that her vulnerable daughter had undergone this trauma. When Rosemary arrived home, in order to hide her disability, reporters were fed the line that she had stayed in England "to continue her art studies."

"Heartbroken," he said, that Rose could not join him in Britain, Joe was buoyed by his efforts at helping Jack turn his thesis into a book. Joe carefully digested Jack's *Appeasement at Munich*, sent the manuscript to numerous expert readers in the world of politics and economics, and integrated their responses into an extraordinarily thoughtful letter to Jack that demonstrates the older man's commitment to producing excellent work, which Jack himself would absorb, and his ability to marshal facts to support a nuanced argument. Although Jack had done a "swell job," and had worked hard, Joe felt he needed to alter the emphasis of his work. Several readers felt that Jack had put too much blame on the British public for the events at Munich, and that he had been too eager to absolve Chamberlain and the previous prime minister, Stanley Baldwin, of responsibility. Joe was no longer protecting his good friend Chamberlain from criticism; in fact he was encouraging Jack to take an even more critical stance. The leaders "were caught at Munich. They had to shut up because they couldn't put up," Joe wrote, meaning that they did not have the military power to stand up for what they thought was fair. There were, he averred, multiple reasons for the government's failure to rearm: its belief that encouraging steady economic growth during a depression would ultimately be better for the national defense than a colossal expenditure on rearmament; its underestimation of the Nazi danger; its fear of jeopardizing its own political positions; and the leaders' underestimation of the willingness of the people to support rearmament.

Germany had "got the jump" on the Allies in rearmament, Joe wrote, by establishing the manufacturing foundation for a "large-scale output" of war materiel (for instance, using an automobile plant to produce engines for planes—a substitution that could not be easily perceived by other countries' intelligence gathering). The major political parties comprising the British National government had been in power from 1931 until 1940, and should have used their mandate to "arouse their countrymen to the dangers with which Britain obviously was confronted." Joe suggested that Jack reread his thesis and carefully examine those points where, in placing blame on the public, he was giving "an appearance of trying to do a complete whitewash of the leaders." He pointed out that a "leader is supposed to look after the national welfare, and to educate people when, in his opinion, they are off base. It may not be good politics, but it is something that is vastly more important—good patriotism."

Joe contrasted the failure of British leaders to insist on arming England with Roosevelt's vigorous stand, despite great resistance, to arm the United States. He agreed with the president's conviction that America must rearm quickly. Most important was Joe's suggestion for a relevant and winning new conclusion for the book—a focus on how America could profit, before it was too late, from Britain's experience. Jack incorporated some of his father's comments verbatim into the book's conclusion: "Democracy in America, like democracy in England, has been asleep at the switch. . . . Any person will wake up when the house is burning down. What we want is a kind of government that will wake up when the fire starts, or, better yet, one that will not permit a fire to start at all. We should profit by the lesson of England and make our democracy work. Any system of government will work when everything goes well. It's the system that functions in the pinches that survives."

E VEN AS JOE was encouraging his son to wake up America to the need to defend its borders from fascist aggression, his country continued to resist further involvement in European affairs. The students at Finch College, where Kick was studying art and design, took a vote about whether the United States should join the war against the Nazis. "I and one other girl were the only two yeses," Kick defiantly wrote her anti-interventionist father. "At the moment it looks like the Germans will be in England before you receive this letter. In fact from the reports here they are just about taking over Claridges now. I still keep telling everyone 'the British lose the battles, but they win the wars.'" Kick had received dispirited letters from Billy, who was on the Maginot Line in France with his regiment. "Daddy, I must know what has happened to them all. Is Billy all right?" She was worried about David Ormsby-Gore, the Astor boys, and Hugh Fraser as well.

Billy was one of 240,000 British troops, and 100,000 French soldiers, who were encircled and entrapped by Hitler's sweep along the northern coast of France—a crucial battle that would culminate at the French port of Dunkirk near the Belgian border. On May 24, as the Allies attempted to fight off the Nazis' conquest of Belgium, Kennedy cabled Hull, saying, "I do not underestimate the courage or guts of the people [the Allies], but . . . it is going to take more than guts to hold off the systematic air attacks of the Germans coupled with their terrific superiority in numbers." But Hitler did not take advantage of his numerical edge. Believing that the retreating British Expeditionary Force could be annihilated by the Luftwaffe, he ordered his tanks to halt so that his troops could rest and replenish their supplies. This two-day break allowed the British and French troops to consolidate their defenses and to prepare for evacuation to England.

After receiving an urgent cable from Hull, Kennedy asked Churchill whether there were plans to ship British gold supplies to Canada. Churchill rebuffed him, saying that such a move might lead the country to feel that the government had panicked. Churchill was not interested in Kennedy's suggestion (or a similar one from the British Foreign Office) to consider sending the British fleet, securities, and royal family to safety in Canada. "I was learning rapidly that one can become unpopular by offering advice that people don't want to hear," Joe said in his memoir. "My contacts with the Churchill cabinet were certainly far less friendly than with the old government. Yet my first duty was to the United States and I had to tell them that they could not count on us for anything but supplies. And the worse the situation became, the harder it was to tell them."

The evacuation began on May 27—a discouraging day when no one knew how many men could actually be rescued. The next day King Leopold of Belgium, against the advice of his government, ordered his country to stop fighting. Joe, who shared the king's sentiments that the battle for Belgium had been lost, later defended the king as "a human being who could not stand useless sacrifice." He cabled home his impressions: "It could not be worse. Only a miracle can save the British expeditionary force from being wiped out." Kennedy told Hull that there was a row in Churchill's cabinet between those wanting a settlement with Germany ("numbers who realize that the physical destruction of men and property in England will not be a proper offset to a loss of pride") and the "do-or-die" group that would fight to the death.

That same night, in the aftermath of the Belgian surrender, in what historian John Lukacs argues was the turning point of the entire war, Churchill convinced cabinet ministers that Britain must fight Hitler until absolute victory or defeat. Ironically, Chamberlain immeasurably helped Churchill win the debate by switching his allegiance from Halifax's proposal for negotiations to Churchill's position that Britain should "avoid being dragged down the slippery slope with France," which was on the verge of succumbing to the Nazis.

On May 30, when Joe went to Buckingham Palace to deliver personal letters of support from President and Mrs. Roosevelt to the royal couple, King George confirmed to him that over eighty thousand members of the British Expeditionary Force had been rescued by Operation Dynamo in the triumphant evacuation at Dunkirk over the past four days. The king was confounded by the conduct of the French. "They seem to be thoroughly muddled," he told Joe, who replied that he, too, had been surprised by the rapidity of their collapse. As for British war efforts, they were both heartened by the rapid pace of air production under Lord Beaverbrook, whom the king, nevertheless, found to be "a very peculiar man." Joe agreed, but called him "a great hustler."

The next day Halifax updated Joe with the news that approximately 144,000 soldiers had been evacuated from Dunkirk—including Billy Hartington. Over the past two days, four hundred small craft had responded to a call from the Ministry of Shipping and had played a crucial role ferrying soldiers from the beaches to the waiting ships. "The Mosquito Armada," as Churchill called the eight hundred boats that came to the aid of the BEF, would eventually help save 330,000 men. According to Joe's memoir, cloudy weather and "soft sand which muffled the explosion of the German bombs" helped mute the power of the Luftwaffe.

But "[w]ars are not won by evacuations," Churchill told Parliament. In an oration that mobilized the British people and inspired the world, he declared, "We shall go on to the end . . . We shall fight on the beaches, we shall fight on the landing grounds, we shall fight in the hills; we shall never surrender . . . until in God's good time, the New World with all its power and might, steps forward to the rescue and the liberation of the Old." This last line, not often quoted, elucidates how passionately and persistently Churchill counted on American involvement.

T HE FINAL BATTLE for France began on June 5 with a German attack on the Weygand line, a group of forty infantry divisions spread out in a defense along the Somme River to the Maginot Line. Italy would soon join the war on Germany's side. That same day, Joe met with a broken-hearted Chamberlain. The former prime minister told him that he thought the French "will quit and quit soon." The only solace Joe took from that meeting was Chamberlain's offer to read Jack's book when it came out. Although Joe might feel awkward having his friend read a book that criticized the former prime minister's decisions, he would tolerate that discomfort to further Jack's career.

British impatience with American inaction was escalating. U.S. protests about German aggression sounded to the British like "a note sent over by neighbors complaining of the way a homicidal lunatic is carrying on in someone's garden," Mollie Panter-Downs told Americans, "when it's obvious that a band of men with good stout ropes would be understood by the killer better than any amount of elegant phraseology." Acutely aware of these increasingly anti-American sentiments, Joe tried to convince Hull to let him release a statement clarifying that the lack of American aid was due to a paucity of equipment—not an absence of resolve to help. "Many people in high places were saying that all they got from the United States was conversation," he wrote Hull. Joe worried that "if things went badly the British would be looking for someone to blame." And he knew that someone might be Joe himself.

Earlier in his ambassadorship Kennedy represented Anglo-American solidarity, but now he was a symbol of American intransigence and stinginess. Churchill struggled privately with his own pessimism and doubts;

he did not need them reinforced by the American ambassador. Kennedy's relations with the entire British government were increasingly chilly, but at times he took Churchill's lack of availability as a personal affront. On June 11, when Churchill changed and then cancelled Kennedy's first meeting with him in three weeks, Joe was offended. He was increasingly jealous of the thorough briefings Bill Bullitt received from the French government. Joe complained about his treatment to Lord Beaverbrook, who told him that Randolph Churchill, who considered Joe to be a potential traitor, had poisoned his father against him. Halifax later tried to mollify Joe by explaining that Churchill operated differently than Chamberlain had. Churchill sequestered himself with his military chiefs. Even Halifax was able to see him only every four to five days.

Yet for at least a short time at this critical juncture, Joe Kennedy would remain useful to the leaders of France, Britain, and the United States. However much Churchill and Roosevelt distrusted him, they needed to keep him a party to their complex dance of negotiations, lest he use his considerable political influence to undermine their efforts by advocating for an agenda that would, in his belief, better protect America. When Churchill rescheduled the meeting he had previously cancelled with Joe, he was particularly gracious to him. Reacting to Italy's entrance in the war, Joe recalled, Churchill called Mussolini "a jackal and a betrayer of all things good and fair." By contrast, for Churchill, Hitler was a gentleman. "The American people will want to come in when they see well-known places in England bombed," Churchill warned Joe. "We'll hold out until after your election and then I'll expect you'll come in." Joe retorted, "You sure picked a nice time to be prime minister," and Churchill told him that he wouldn't have been given the position "if there was any meat left on the bone." Churchill was, however, optimistic that the French would not be defeated by the Axis because a "good new general had entered the picture"—Charles de Gaulle.

Roosevelt, meanwhile, was taking further steps to aid Britain and France more openly and aggressively. He was already authorizing "surplus" arms to be sent to Britain, and the same evening that Kennedy met with Churchill, in a commencement speech at the University of Virginia, he presented his case for aiding Britain and France. If the Axis dictators dominated the world, the American people would be encircled by fascism, "lodged in prison, handcuffed, hungry, and fed through the bars from day to day by the contemptuous, unpitying masters of other countries." As the president spoke, Italy was attacking France; Roosevelt told his audience that "the hand that held the dagger has struck it into the back of its neighbor." He ended his speech with a rousing proclamation: "We will extend the opponents of force the material resources of this nation," and will go "full speed ahead" to arm the United States. Churchill cabled Roosevelt that his speech had given the Allies "strong encouragement in a dark but not unhopeful hour." He implored FDR again to supply Britain with its older destroyers and pleaded for aid to France, to encourage its dire battle with the advancing German army, as did French prime minister Paul Reynaud. But it was too late. After the Germans crossed the Seine below Paris, the French government declared Paris to be an open city and fled to Tours on June 11; two days later it withdrew to Bordeaux. Roosevelt sent a message to Reynaud on June 13, with a copy to Kennedy, urging France to keep fighting and promising that America would accelerate its attempts to furnish her with war materials.

Churchill summoned Joe to Admiralty House at 9:30 on the evening of June 13. When Joe arrived, Winston was sitting down to dinner with Clementine and two of his daughters. Because he was about to dive into a substantial entrée, to be followed by jellied chicken, fish, and strawberries, Winston asked Joe to read aloud the president's message to Reynaud. Visibly excited, he took the cable from Joe and read it three or four times, concluding, as Joe wrote in his diary, that it meant that "America assumes a responsibility if the French continued to fight." Joe agreed that this seemed to be a commitment.

Churchill discussed the cable with his cabinet; they agreed that it appeared likely that the United States was about to join the Allied cause. Desperate to buck up the French, Churchill insisted that Joe, whom he had summoned back to the Admiralty at 11 P.M., call FDR immediately, in front of him, to push the president to publish his cable to Reynaud. According to the account in Joe's memoir, Churchill heard the president tell Joe that it could not be printed because Hull thought it would suggest too strong a commitment. Later, former president Herbert Hoover, who knew of this encounter through Joe, related a different story. He said that while Churchill listened, Joe persuaded FDR over the phone to withdraw the message, believing that it implied a much stronger commitment than America was ready to make at that time. According to Hoover's account, Kennedy told him that "Churchill hated him from then on."

Churchill then tried to convince Joe to write a cable to FDR in his presence, saying that Roosevelt's message to Reynaud needed to be published in order to give the French courage to fight on. Joe demurred, telling the prime minister that he needed to send the cable in code. Back at the embassy, he did indeed write Roosevelt, but after acknowledging how a pro-French public statement from the president would hearten "these poor people . . . I nevertheless see in the message a great danger . . . The danger of publication of your note to Reynaud," Joe cabled Roosevelt, "is that Churchill sees . . . an absolute commitment of the United States that if France fights on the United States will be in the war."

FDR, waiting impatiently for messages that had not yet arrived and worried that France might assume he had pledged America to their cause, woke Joe up at 4:30 in the morning, insisting that he tell Churchill that the president's message to Reynaud was not intended to be a commitment and should not be published. Later that morning, Joe called Churchill and delivered the upsetting news. He passed on FDR's promise that the United States would harbor the French navy if it sailed away from the Nazis.

For his part, Reynaud cabled Roosevelt a second time. If America would not enter the war, he wrote, "[t]hen you will see France go under like a drowning man and disappear, after having cast a last look toward the land of liberty from which she awaited salvation."

Even after witnessing the collapse of the French defenses, the world was still stunned when, on June 14, German troops entered Paris, without incident, and marched down the Champs Elysées. The French men and women who watched wept openly. Two million Parisians had fled the capital, but William Bullitt decided to remain. Two days later, in Boulogne, Prime Minister Reynaud resigned rather than ask Germany for an armistice. Within a week, the eighty-four-year-old First World War hero Marshal Philippe Pétain, who had officially replaced Albert Lebrun as president (although Lebrun never resigned), had signed an armistice with Germany, giving the Nazis control over the north and west of France—including Paris. With France crushed, Joe Kennedy and the British populace braced themselves for the German invasion. The ultimate battle was upon them.

CHAPTER 21

"Waiting for the Curtain
to Go Up"

After six miserable weeks watching the Nazis conquer Europe, Joe was particularly lonely on June 20 and 21, when his family gathered without him for Jack's graduation festivities at Harvard. Tracking the fall of France for the State Department and frantically trying to arrange for Americans trapped in England to return home on specially commissioned ocean liners, Joe could not leave his job to return to the United States. Two years before, he had avoided Joe Jr.'s Harvard commencement out of pique at the university for denying him an honorary degree, but this time he wanted to be there.

Eight-year-old Teddy wrote to his father that Jean and Teddy stayed "down in cap-card [Cape Cod]" with Joe, while "Mother has gone to jacks graduoin." Rose, Bobby, Eunice, Kick, and Rosemary attended Class Day in Harvard Yard, and a day later sat in the Harvard quadrangle as Jack received his degree. "He is really very handsome in his cap and gown," Rose wrote to Joe, "as he had a tan which made him look healthy and he has got a wonderful smile." Joe sent Jack a telegram saluting his intelligence and commending him for being "a swell guy."

Gathering afterward in Hyannisport for their summer vacation, the Kennedy children competed in sailing races and went swimming despite remarkably chilly, fall-like weather. Rosemary spent a few days with the family before Rose took her to a camp in Massachusetts, where Rosemary would teach arts and crafts for the rest of the summer. Rose then arranged for her to teach at St. Gertrude's School of Arts and Crafts in Washington, D.C. Kick, still frustrated she could not return to England, did volunteer work with the Red Cross and planned a fundraiser for the Allied Relief Fund, which assisted British seamen disabled in the war.

All the children wrote letters of encouragement to their father, who braced himself for a Nazi invasion of England. "We are like the fellow sitting in the theater," Joe replied to Bobby, "waiting for the curtain to go up." Bobby, who had spent several days in bed with boils on his knee, revealed that Pat had a tall new boyfriend about whom the children had made up a song, "6 feet 7, Straight from Heaven." Twelve-year-old Jean reported that Pat had spent most of her vacation stumbling and falling in the unseasonably cool ocean and that Eunice had returned from a tennis tournament in Cleveland buoyed—finally—by a press report saying that she was beautiful. Eunice also tried to buck up her beleaguered father: "The chief topic of conversation during the trip [to Cleveland] was your brains and what a wonderful job you are doing."

A S FRANCE WAS FALLING, Winston Churchill was agonizing about Britain's fate. Nonetheless, he knew he needed to rally his country-men or else, he told Joe, "The people of England would tear me to pieces." On June 18, in a rousing House of Commons oration now recognized as one of the greatest speeches of the twentieth century, Churchill proclaimed Britain's determination to fight on to victory:

> I expect that the Battle of Britain is about to begin. Upon this battle depends the survival of Christian civilization. . . . The whole fury and might of the enemy must very soon be turned on us. Hitler knows that he will have to break us in this Island or lose the war. If we can stand up to him, all Europe may be free and the life of the world may move forward into broad, sunlit uplands. . . . Let us therefore brace ourselves to our duties, and so bear ourselves that, if the British Empire and its Commonwealth last for a thousand years, men will still say, "This was their finest hour."

When word came that France had surrendered, "London was as quiet as a village," *New Yorker* correspondent Molly Panter-Downes wrote. "You could have heard a pin drop in the curious, watchful hush." With the col-lapse of the French, Winston told Joe that Britain was like a house in which the girders had fallen while the building was being built; but it was, he said, a home that he would put into shape even without the girders. Incredibly, France was now Britain's enemy. On June 22, the French signed an agreement handing over their airfields, weapons, munitions, and industrial centers to the Nazis for use against England. Hitler humiliated the French by insisting their representatives sign the armistice at Compiegne, in the same railway car in which the Germans had surrendered at the end of the First World War.

The next evening, Kennedy appealed to America for support for Britain. Speaking to the American people on an NBC Red Cross broadcast from London, he implored them: "We cannot give too much, or give too soon." Americans would offer homes for British children, and provide money and clothing for war victims, and donate blood for British soldiers. Rose would write him that "everyone seemed to think the speech was excellent and the newspaper commentator at 6 spoke very favorably of you." In an expression of his personal support for England, later that summer, Joe would arrange for British royalties from Jack's book *Why England Slept* to be given to the severely damaged town of Coventry, and would personally arrange for Hollywood to fund London relief organizations aiding civilians who had lost their homes in the bombing.

Churchill castigated the French government for capitulating to the Germans but called Joe that evening to reassure him, "Everything looks good to me tonight." Relentless in his expression of optimism, Churchill was accelerating his campaign to convince the American Congress and president that Britain was confident and prepared, and thus worth saving.

Joe, projecting his own feelings onto his fellow Americans, told Chamberlain that "everyone in the United States says we shall be beaten by the end of the month." But the French government did manage to send its fleet to safety in North Africa, easing some of Kennedy's (and Roosevelt's and Churchill's) fears that the French ships would augment a Nazi invasion force.

The British cabinet soon ordered the French fleet to sail to designated ports for internment. French ships already at British ports and at Alexandria in Egypt were easily demobilized, but the Vichy government refused to turn over the ships at Mers-el-Kebir near Oran, Algeria. Britain attacked the French fleet, killing 1,250 French seamen and destroying several of the ships. Seven escaped. On July 5, the French Vichy government severed all relations with Britain.

At this dark hour, Joe Kennedy was heartened by Lord Beaverbrook's extraordinary success producing the fighter planes that would defend Britain. Beaverbrook's confidence about Britain's chances of repelling a German air attack was "the only solid basis I could find for optimism," Joe said, but it was enough to buoy him about the Allies' chances for survival.

Joe felt more sanguine about his own standing as well. In early August, when he went to see the London opening of Clare Boothe Luce's play *Margin for Error*, the audience gave him a round of applause. He believed, erroneously, now that some of his war predictions (including the fall of France) had come to pass, that British government officials had taken a kinder view of him. But he did not fool himself that his standing was secure.

"While people at home [America] were becoming definitely alarmed as they felt the hot breath of a military regime on their necks," Joe declared in his memoir, "people in England had an interlude of cool calm. Their spirit was admirable and their mood a little gayer." In the United States, notwithstanding Britain's peril, a late June Gallup poll indicated that 64 percent of Americans preferred to stay out of the war and did not want the United States to help Britain. British ambassador Lord Lothian was deeply concerned that Americans' defeatism and wariness of entanglement would prevent Roosevelt from providing essential aid to England. But Roosevelt's own pessimism about Britain's chances had begun to lift. He was newly impressed by Britain's resolve in attacking the French fleet and by its rapid expansion of the Royal Air Force and its radar defenses.

Churchill, having rallied his countrymen, in late June renewed his efforts to enlist Roosevelt's help. The president would bypass Kennedy and conduct negotiations on a deal to give Britain destroyers through Lord Lothian at the British embassy in Washington, but Kennedy would play a role counseling Churchill on how to handle Roosevelt. Winston pestered Joe to get answers from Washington about the president's political readiness to give Britain the older destroyers he had requested. "We have got to get those," Joe remembered Winston telling him, "because if we don't we will all go down the drain together." Joe cautioned him that he was being too insistent; Roosevelt was not someone who could be rushed. The president had to make a tough decision. Should he give fifty to sixty old destroyers to a country that might soon be conquered by the Nazis, or keep them for defense of the Americas?

Meanwhile, Churchill received intelligence suggesting that Hitler would attack England in mid-July. In fact, the Battle of Britain began on July 10, when 120 Nazi planes struck British convoys in the English Channel. As the month went on, England suffered significant losses at sea: More than 200,000 tons of British shipping were destroyed and half of its destroyers sunk. "Germany's fast motor boats, submarines and dive-bombers, are seriously handicapping the progress of imports and exports," Joe wrote to his oldest son. He worried that Britain would face serious shortages of food and supplies that winter.

THOUGH KENNEDY was becoming more hopeful that Britain could withstand an Axis attack, he and his embassy were sending Roosevelt mixed signals about England's ability to beat back the Nazi aggression. Kennedy's still-frequent dubiousness about British chances had been echoed by the naval attaché, Alan Kirk, but the military attaché was optimistic that Britain could successfully resist an invasion. FDR understandably wanted to obtain an independent estimate of Britain's chances. William Stephenson, the intrepid chief of British espionage in the United States, had been handpicked by Churchill, his mission to help draw America into the war by coordinating British propaganda efforts within the United States; he recommended to FDR that he entrust this crucial assessment to Roosevelt's Columbia Law School classmate, William "Wild Bill" Donovan, a prominent Republican. A winner of the Congressional Medal of Honor for his exploits in World War I, he had been a candidate for the governorship of New York. Donovan, Stephenson privately believed, would serve British interests by making an accurate assessment of their current wartime strengths and weaknesses. Roosevelt agreed. When Cordell Hull cabled Kennedy to inform him of Donovan's mission and asked him to smooth Wild Bill's way in London, Kennedy reacted harshly; the undertaking was, he said, the "height of nonsense." The American ambassador was threatened that another ambitious, self-made Irish-American was being sent over to duplicate his embassy's current efforts.

Donovan would not be the only Roosevelt operative to encroach on Kennedy's turf. In the aftermath of the arrest of Tyler Kent, Roosevelt was increasingly worried that saboteurs were plotting operations in America; he asked Edgar Mowrer, the London correspondent for the Chicago *Daily News*, to study ways of identifying fifth columnists. Kennedy protested that his assistant Harvey Klemmer was already studying the issue and defiantly told Hull he would inform the British government that Mowrer was not entitled to see secret files. If he kept getting "Mowrers and Colonel Donovans over here," he asserted, "this organization is not going to function effectively." Joe called Sumner Welles and asked him to tell Roosevelt directly about his strong reservations. Typically, the president tossed the squabble back to his underlings, remarking only that "[s]omebody's nose seems to be out of joint."

With Kennedy resentfully trailing along, Donovan received unprecedented access to London social, political, military, and business circles. The Astors invited him to dine with the king and queen. The king met with Donovan and showed him a copy of Hitler's July 16 order to prepare for

LEFT: During the family Christmas vacation in St. Moritz, dashing and reckless Joe Jr. broke his arm while skiing but sloughed it off, and was photographed skating with Megan Taylor, the attractive world champion figure skater. (*Photofest*)

RIGHT: December 1938. Billy Hartington and Kick Kennedy dine at the fashionable Café de Paris, where Cole Porter showcased his new songs. Despite their parents' reservations about a British Protestant scion dating an American Catholic, Billy and Kick were growing closer. (*JFK Library Foundation*)

Joe and Rose are escorted by the pope's personal friend Count Enrico Galleazzi (at right) during the ceremonies for Pope Pius XII's coronation. Being named as the official U.S. representative at the coronation meant a great deal to Ambassador Kennedy; this was one of FDR's few genuine kindnesses to him. (*Corbis*)

May 5, 1939. Joe and Rose flew in moth orchids from Paris and Virginia ham from America for their dinner party saluting King George VI and Queen Elizabeth at the U.S. embassy. The royal couple was leaving the next day on their North American tour. Security was tight because recent IRA bombings had made Scotland Yard nervous about an Irish-American ambassador entertaining the king and queen. (*Photofest*)

June 22, 1939. Joe Kennedy joined the king and queen on the dais for their triumphant homecoming luncheon at Guildhall following their wildly successful North American tour. When the king spoke confidently without stuttering, Joe told Lord Halifax that "King George VI became the real king of the British Empire today at lunch." (*JFK Library Foundation*)

June 22, 1939. Jack shares an intimate moment with his sister Eunice in the dressing room as they prepare for her coming-out party. (*Peter Hunter/Nederlands Fotomuseum*)

LEFT: June 22, 1939. Jack charms a beautiful young British woman on a grand staircase at Eunice's party. (*Peter Hunter/Nederlands Fotomuseum*)

RIGHT: Rose watches as Eunice undergoes the final preparations for her presentation to the king and queen at Buckingham Palace. (*Cleveland Public Library Special Collections*)

Rosemary thrived in the Hertfordshire countryside, where she was studying to be a Montessori teacher. (*JFK Library Foundation*)

This unpublished photograph shows Rosemary at her loveliest.
(*JFK Library Foundation*)

September 3, 1939. An iconic photo of the three oldest Kennedy children walking to Parliament to hear Neville Chamberlain declare war on Germany. They had just experienced their first air raid, but had no idea how much suffering the war would bring them: death, serious injury, and widowhood. (*JFK Library Foundation*)

September 3, 1939. This photograph of Joe and Rose walking to Parliament is less well known. Rose looks as if she has had a premonition of the tragedies that would befall her family. (*JFK Library Foundation*)

ABOVE: Joe Kennedy inspects
bombing damage during the Blitz.
(*JFK Library Foundation*)

RIGHT: October 1940. Joe Kennedy
stands outside 10 Downing Street
with his rival Winston Churchill.
Joe was leaving his ambassadorship to return home. (*Wide World
Photos*)

This is the only known photograph of Joe Kennedy and
his friend Neville Chamberlain together. (*UPI*)

the invasion of Britain, thus showcasing Britain's extraordinary ability to intercept and decode top-secret German war directives. Churchill, his cabinet ministers, and Colonel Stewart Menzies, who was secretly in charge of the covert British intelligence service MI6, gave Roosevelt's emissary highly classified intelligence. Donovan inspected RAF fighter stations and was impressed by British radar installations.

A politically astute Donovan turned down Lady Diana Cooper's invitation to dine with Winston Churchill so that he could keep a dinner invitation with Joe Kennedy, whose cooperation he sought in advocating Britain's strength. "I am happy to tell you that Winston was in his most engaging and invigorating form," Lady Diana later wrote Donovan. "I hope you had a hideous evening with Joe."

In order to elicit more American support, British government officials were presenting American representatives with the rosiest possible perspective on Britain's capability to turn back the Axis. "This, from Great Britain's viewpoint," Kennedy cabled the State Department on July 31, "is a war being conducted with their eyes only on one place and that is the United States." Donovan would return from his eighteen-day trip to Britain full of optimism that Britain could win the air war and repel an invasion. From Washington, intelligence chief Stephenson cabled London with the cheering news that "Donovan . . . has strongly urged our case re destroyers and is doing much to combat defeatist attitude in Washington."

Roosevelt meanwhile had become the first president ever nominated for a third term, at the Democratic convention in Chicago. Two weeks later, on July 30, the British made the official decision—still kept secret from the public—to prosecute Tyler Kent for violations of the Official Secrets Act. Although the investigators had needed time to determine whether Kent had accomplices, in particular MP Captain Ramsay, the authorities had likely waited until Roosevelt had been safely nominated. The secret trial would not be held until late in the fall—just before the American Election Day. News of Kent's indictment could still be leaked to the press, but Kennedy and Roosevelt seemed primed to escape the case's repercussions at a pivotal moment.

AS BRITAIN PUBLICLY WELCOMED DONOVAN, Hitler made an intentionally vague "peace" offer designed to lay the responsibility for a widened war at the feet of the British. In a July 19 speech before the Reichstag at the Kroll Opera House in Berlin, Hitler tried to reach the British people over the head of Churchill, appealing "once more to reason and common sense in Britain." Warning that a continuing war would lead to the ruin of the British Empire, he offered, instead, to govern the world alongside Britain and the United States. Railing against Churchill, Hitler declared that "seldom have any countries in the world been ruled with a lesser degree of wisdom, morality and culture than those which are at the moment exposed to the ragings of certain democratic statesmen." But Hitler had misjudged Churchill's ever more spellbinding hold over Britain. The British government took one hour to refuse Hitler's offer.

Joe worried that Britain's increasing ability to obtain American assistance would incite Hitler to launch a devastating blitz on England before the United States could effectively provide aid. On the other hand, Joe correctly assumed that if the Luftwaffe did not quickly destroy the RAF, Britain would be safe from a land invasion. In letters home, he explained to fourteen-year-old Bobby and to Jack why he thought Hitler would need to conquer Britain quickly: first, because Britain would soon receive American support; and second, because economic conditions in the countries the Nazis conquered could cause rebellion ("millions of people . . . may find it difficult to eat this winter and when people are starving, there is no limit to what they will do"). To Jack, he added that Hitler "has had his own radio tell his own people that England was weak and demoralized and practically a push-over any time he wanted to invade it" and now needed to look strong. On July 23, he wrote Bobby that the British were expecting Hitler "to bomb the whole place out this week."

O N THE LAST DAY OF JULY, Churchill intensely entreated Roosevelt once again to provide destroyers to Britain, saying that "with great respect, I must tell you that in the long history of the world this is the thing to do now." Bolstering the nation's naval defenses was a matter of safeguarding British trade and food, he said. The Germans could launch U-boat and dive bomber attacks on British supply ships from anywhere along the entire coast of France. To butter up the American ambassador, Churchill added, "I . . . now send this through Kennedy, who is a grand help to us and the common cause."

Two days earlier, reacting to the often intense conflict between British and American political agendas, Clare Boothe Luce had cabled Joe: "Confucius say man who gets to be American ambassador should make up mind first whether he looks best in pine or mahogany." Buoyed by Churchill's praise of him, Joe told her he "didn't need to order a coffin yet . . . but would continue wearing a helmet."

When the president called Joe Kennedy on August 1, he sensed that

FDR wanted to "soft-soap" him lest he precipitously quit his London post before the election. Kennedy had remained in London while Bill Bullitt had quit France, William Phillips had left Italy, and the ambassadors to the Low Countries and Scandinavia had returned home. In the phone call, FDR told Joe that the subcommittee of the Democratic Committee wanted him to come home to run the Democratic campaign that fall, but the State Department felt he was too valuable in England. Joe was not taken in. The "president telling me that the State Department wants to do something different from what he wishes," he sardonically told Clare Boothe Luce, "is something new in my life." He told FDR, "I am not doing a damn thing here that amounts to anything, and my services, if they are needed, could be used to much better advantage if I were home."

"That's where you are all wrong," FDR rejoined. "I get constant reports of how valuable you are to them over there and that it helps the morale of the British to have you there and they would feel they were being let down if you were to leave." He also inveigled Joe to stay by asserting that his presence in London provided comfort to Americans who were complaining that their country was not doing enough to aid Britain. Joe responded that he would assess the situation over the next month and then see what his plans would be. "I am not fooling myself," he wrote Rose, "and I haven't the slightest doubt that they would turn around and throw me in the ash can." Joe wanted to stay in Britain until England suffered through a significant bombing campaign. He did not want to leave in a manner that would reflect poorly on his family or compromise his prestige or influence after his ambassadorship. But he did not want to take himself out of FDR's election calculus by agreeing to stay.

Joe was discouraged on yet another front. On July 29, after several months of experiencing increasingly bad stomach pain, Neville Chamberlain had undergone an abdominal operation. The doctors discovered he had terminal cancer of the bowel but, in the protocol of the era, told Chamberlain and his highly strung wife that the operation had been a success. Joe visited Chamberlain in a nursing home shortly after his operation and ferreted out the truth from the physicians. "I think my poor old friend is finished," he wrote Rose on August 2.

As a distraction from his dismay about Donovan's visit and Chamberlain's impending death, Joe was encouraging Joe Jr. in his budding political career and Jack's efforts at journalism or teaching. At the Democratic convention in Chicago in mid-July, young Joe was a member of the Massachusetts delegation, pledged to Postmaster James Farley. After FDR's operatives whipped up a "draft Roosevelt" movement and Roosevelt announced that he would consider a third term—as if accepting a call to duty—Farley refused to fold. Roosevelt's men put enormous pressure on Joe Jr. to switch his vote, reminding him how much FDR had done for his father, urging him not to damage his father's career, and telling him that a vote for Roosevelt was a wise move for an ambitious young man. When Joe Jr. did not budge, Roosevelt's friends called the ambassador in London, asking him to help change his son's mind. Joe refused. "I didn't want you to be in a position," he wrote his son on July 23, "where any decisions you made must be dependent on how they affect me, because it isn't fair to you . . . I think the incident will stand you in good stead. After all people do appreciate a straightforward opinion, and that includes those you oppose." He also recognized that his son's defiance might redound against him with Roosevelt, but he placed a higher priority on Joe Jr.'s development than on appeasing FDR, with whom he already had so many more important political conflicts. Jack was discomforted by his brother's rebellious stance. He would always be more nuanced and supple than his father or brother in dealing with people. A pragmatist and a conciliator, he would often avoid taking stands that would alienate others.

Jack was celebrating his own startling success with the publication of *Why England Slept*. The 3,500 copies of Wilfred Funk's first edition sold out within days of publication in late July, and the book would eventually sell eighty thousand copies in the United States and Britain. Joe was thrilled with the astonishing success of his son's book and sent copies to Churchill, Chamberlain, and his political associates on both sides of the Atlantic. He reminded Jack that what was important for Jack's future was not its bestseller status but its quality: "So, whether you make a cent out of it or not," he wrote his son, "it will do you an amazing amount of good, particularly if it gets a good standing. You would be surprised how a book that really makes sense with the high-class people stands you in good stead for years to come."

Joe had no little hand in fostering the book's prospects. Not only had he asked Arthur Krock to edit it, but he had persuaded Henry Luce, the politically conservative founder of *Life* and *Time* magazines and Clare's husband, to write the introduction. Luce told Americans, whom he said were now "thoroughly aroused and awake," that they needed to read this remarkable book, combining "a breadth of understanding with the truest instincts of patriotism," as an act of "national preparedness." Americans felt newly vulnerable after the fall of France, and were receptive to Jack's exhortation for them to avoid England's mistakes and summon the will to mount a strong national defense.

Critics almost uniformly praised the book as fresh, penetrating, and opportune. The *London Times Literary Supplement* suggested that this "young man's book" contained "much wisdom for older men." However, Jack's former mentor Harold Laski concluded that the book should not have been published because it was superficial, immature, and poorly organized, and said so to the author's father. "Thinking is a hard business," he wrote Joe, "and you have to pay the price of admission to it." Jack knew that the book's success had more to do with perfect timing than great writing, and owed no little of its attention to his family's celebrity and connections, but he relished the laudatory letters from Cordell Hull, British ambassador Lothian, and even Franklin Roosevelt, who told him that it presented "a great argument for acting and speaking from a position of strength at all times." Jack valued FDR's words not only because they were praise from a president, but because he saw Roosevelt as someone who had met the challenge he himself constantly faced: surmounting bodily weakness.

DURING THE SUMMER IN 1940, Joe Kennedy was publicly derided as a coward by British government officials, American newspaper reporters in London, and the city's social arbiters, because in their view he had deliberately removed himself from the line of fire. Since the fall of France, Joe had spent many evenings and workdays at St. Leonard's, his home in Windsor Great Park. One upper-crust jibe, "I thought my daffodils were yellow until I met Joe Kennedy," epitomizes the hostility directed toward him. At the end of July, Joe decided to spend the workweek in London at Prince's Gate, inhabiting only one bedroom and a study and leaving the rest of the house closed because, as he wrote Jean, there were "so many things going on." Had he recognized that he needed to be closer to the diplomatic action or was he tired of being mocked, or both?

On August 2, Roosevelt acknowledged to his cabinet that "the survival of the British Isles under German attack might very possibly depend on getting those destroyers." The president was ready to act, but first he needed certain assurances from Churchill that would mollify Wendell Willkie, the Republican presidential candidate, and the U.S. Congress. On August 13, FDR asked Kennedy to present Churchill with his conditions for sending destroyers to Britain in exchange for ninety-nine-year leases to British naval and air bases in Newfoundland, Bermuda, and Canada. Kennedy was amazed that Churchill, after weeks of waiting, delayed the afternoon meeting with him "on which he said the fate of civilization might well depend." But, wearied by managing the war, Churchill's 3:30 P.M. nap was crucial to his own fate.

FDR also wanted a guarantee that if Britain were conquered, the British fleet would sail to other parts of the Empire to continue the fight against Germany. Kennedy reminded the prime minister that America might have to take responsibility for the safety of the Western Hemisphere and the president had just asked Congress for $5 billion to build a navy to protect that side of the world. Roosevelt had to convince everyone at home that these destroyers would never end up in German hands. Although Churchill was willing to give private guarantees, he would not utter anything publicly that would "give people the idea we are in muddy waters." This was acceptable to the Americans.

The next evening when Churchill summoned Joe to receive his formal written acceptance of the destroyers-for-bases deal, he continued his ritual of offering the American ambassador a Scotch and soda—which Joe saw as irksome, because he never remembered that Joe had sworn off drinking and smoking for the duration of the war. "My God, you make me feel as if I should go round in sack cloth and ashes," Churchill replied. The prime minister, who had fleetingly proposed a union of Britain and France in mid-June, now impulsively told Joe that a union between Britain and America might be necessary to safeguard civilization.

For Kennedy, the survival of Britain and the safety of America depended on whether or not Hitler had the air strength he claimed. Joe was encouraged when General Charles de Gaulle—in Joe's opinion, a practical man with a shrewd understanding of the military situation—told him that the RAF would not be defeated by the Nazi air force, and that the momentum of the British people's morale would carry them to victory over the superior German forces. By mid-August, when British optimism reached a zenith, Beaverbrook gave Joe further reason for hope: "If we can last through the next few days, I think we will go through for some time." But the Battle of Britain was just beginning.

CHAPTER 22

"There's Hell to Pay
Here Tonight"

JOE KENNEDY and Britain's military establishment had been waiting all summer for England's moment of reckoning with Hitler's Luftwaffe—those massive attacks that would determine whether the Germans could decimate the RAF, invade Britain, and conquer the last major democracy in Europe. At the end of July, Lord Halifax wrote British ambassador Lothian in Washington, D.C., with word of Kennedy's prognostications about the coming German air attack: Joe believed that Hitler would wear down the British people's morale with a heavy air bombardment before crossing the English Channel and invading Britain. The assault the Germans code-named "The Day of the Eagle" finally began on August 13. The Nazis were confident that their victory would be swift and inevitable. "The defense of Southern England will last four days," Field Marshal Hermann Goering told his staff, "and the Royal Air Force four weeks." He added, "We can guarantee invasion for the Fuhrer within a month." But British air chief marshal Hugh Dowding had learned from the disasters that had befallen European air forces, and bought time by dispersing his fighter planes so that they could not be wiped out in one big attack.

On the first day of the air campaign, the Nazis lost twice as many planes as the British did. The Luftwaffe naïvely thought they could finish off the RAF on August 18 with a massive air attack that demolished British airplanes on the ground, destroyed RAF bases, and killed pilots in the air. Instead, the war started to turn in Britain's favor. Seventy-one Nazi planes were shot down, while the British lost only twenty-seven planes. The British government had an additional reason for optimism: They had cracked the German air force's Enigma code messages, and were thus able to ascertain the Nazis planned no invasion until at least the middle of September.

Joe Kennedy was relieved by the plucky British pilots' success in the skies, but he must have listened with decidedly mixed feelings to Churchill's exuberant, almost triumphant House of Commons speech on August 20 celebrating RAF pilots and Anglo-American cooperation, in which he famously declared, "Never in the field of human conflict has so much been owed by so many to so few." Joe clung, despite mounting evidence to the contrary, to his belief that superior German air power would subjugate Britain. At times Joe could chomp down on an idea and then have difficulty letting go of it or adapting it, even when a sophisticated analysis of new evidence might warrant doing so. Even as his fear overwhelmed his powers of observation, he did continue his support for aid to Britain. But he still had reservations about pouring key resources into a country that was likely to be defeated.

Churchill rattled Joe in announcing the destroyer-for-bases deal, soon to be completed with the United States, by saying that the two countries would be ineluctably joined together over the next couple of years: "No one can stop it. Like the Mississippi, it just keeps rolling along. Let it roll. Let it roll on full flood, inexorable, irresistible, benignant, to broader lands and better days." To Joe, an inexorable flood of aid to Britain threatened to become a tide that would sweep across the Atlantic and carry America into a war that would drown its own hopes for better days. He would do his best to channel and slow down Churchill's efforts to entangle America in the war. When the prime minister called him to discuss his speech, Joe peevishly told him that people were too concerned about the air raids to pay much attention to the destroyer story.

Churchill invited Kennedy to a dinner with top British political and military leaders at 10 Downing Street in honor of an American armed services mission FDR had sent to Britain to review Britain's military situation, headed by Admiral Robert Ghormley, who was assistant chief of Naval Operations and director of the navy's War Plans Division. The generals and admirals were officially described by the British and American governments as Kennedy's new naval and military attachés. Joe was once again displeased by the presence of these interlopers. According to the diary of his journalist friend George Bilainkin, Kennedy and his staff called the embassy offices of these generals and advisors the "Snoopers' room."

Compounding Joe's displeasure was the fact that British circles learned about the formation of this intelligence operation before he had been informed by his own government. Joe pointedly told the State Department that this absence of communication was improper: "Not to tell me, is poor treatment of me, and is bad organization." Churchill, aware that Roosevelt had slighted Kennedy, seated Joe at his right hand at dinner. In front of Joe, he asked Cadogan, the permanent undersecretary of state for foreign affairs, to send the American ambassador copies of his recent telegrams to FDR. Churchill had told Roosevelt that he did not want public attention given to the bases the British had given up in the deal because, Joe recalled in his memoir, "people would say that the British were giving much more than they were getting and would say there was no market for the American destroyers and therefore they had no value." Eventually a compromise would be reached whereby the Newfoundland bases would be leased "out of friendship," and the Caribbean bases would be leased in exchange for the destroyers. Roosevelt could boost his election chances by claiming he had pulled off a shrewd deal, and Churchill could save face. Both agreements would be made without Kennedy's assistance, which left the ambassador resentful and further estranged from the center of U.S. and British diplomacy.

Brimming with optimism at dinner that night because of a three-day lapse in the German bombing, Churchill told Joe that Britain "is very much like a big animal fighting a small animal; the little animal keeps biting at the large one, but is being crushed, but if the big one stops for a minute, the little one goes on with renewed vigor, and this it what is happening with the Air Force fight." Joe knew that Churchill was always endeavoring to put the best face on the war for him, and through him, for the American audience, and he continued to treat Churchill's optimistic pronouncements with skepticism.

But Churchill also made clear what he expected from the United States: The war, he said, "is going to be a battle of industry and what we want from America is that it shall be a manufacturing depot," he told Joe. "Of course, we will pay as long as we can and after that you will have to give us the money." Joe instantly recognized the serious intent behind Churchill's presumptuous remark: Britain, believing it was fighting on America's behalf, had no compunctions about making America pay to finish the war. Joe believed that there should be no loans until the British had run out of money, disdained their sense of entitlement, and resented their manipulations: "The British have a cheap way of taking Americans into camp," he wrote in his diary, referring to the evening as "a good dinner with important company."

A few days later, when Joe read a front-page *Daily Herald* story revealing that Roosevelt's clandestine envoy, Admiral Ghormley, had met with the prime minister and the king, he was apoplectic. American newspaper reporters in London had learned about the secret mission from the British War Office. Joe rightly pointed out to Cordell Hull that isolationist American reporters would interpret this news as evidence that Roosevelt was secretly conducting negotiations to bring America into the war. "The least, it seems to me, that can be done for the American ambassador in London is to let him . . . run his own job . . . I either want to run this job or get out."

It was the first time Kennedy had directly threatened to resign. He soon complained bitterly to Roosevelt that while British ambassador Lord Lothian had been kept informed every step of the way about the destroyers-for-bases deal, he had been sidelined. The information he did receive came mainly from the cables to FDR that Churchill shared. Kennedy was fed up: "I have been fairly active in any enterprise which I have taken up for the last twenty-five years. Frankly and honestly I do not enjoy being a dummy." If the situation in England were not so desperate, he suggested, he would have quit his post immediately.

After Kennedy's many maverick public statements and efforts at rogue diplomacy, the wily president had long since cast aside any trust he once had in him. FDR was annoyed that Kennedy would bother him with complaints at such a critical hour, but, aware that Kennedy still possessed political pull in the United States and had the ear of those dubious about any kind of assistance to Britain, the president tried to soothe him, offering a dissembling reason for freezing him out. "There is no thought of embarrassing you," FDR told him, "and only a practical necessity for personal conversations makes it easier to handle details here." But, even though such maneuvers are part and parcel of politics and diplomacy, the president was more than inconsiderate keeping Kennedy so much in the dark. In fact, Roosevelt was well aware of Kennedy's sensitivity to exclusion. FDR's biographer Conrad Black acknowledges that Roosevelt was "sadistic" in his treatment of his prominent ambassador. One of the reasons that he distanced himself from Kennedy was that the president was struggling with his own private pessimism about the situation in Europe. Eleanor Roosevelt found her husband to be "gloom personified." He told her how terrible a world presided over by Nazis would be and imagined himself and his wife as "the first Americans sent before the firing squad." He could ill afford to expose himself to Joe Kennedy's pessimism.

CHURCHILL KEPT THE PRESSURE ON HITLER, announcing to the Commons on September 5 the completion of the deal for fifty older American destroyers and trumpeting Britain's impending increase of strength at sea. Focusing on the growing involvement of the United States, he acknowledged that Hitler would not like the transference of destroyers "and I have no doubt that he will pay the United States out, if he ever gets the chance. That is why I am very glad that the army, air, and naval frontiers of the United States have been advanced along a wide arc into the Atlantic Ocean, and that this will enable them to take danger by the throat while it is still hundreds of miles away from their homeland." Such a statement was intended not only to irk Hitler but to drive home his point to Americans that their aid to Britain was in their interest as well.

The next day, Joe Kennedy's fifty-second birthday, air-raid sirens seemed to wail every couple of hours. He celebrated by going horseback riding during one air-raid warning, "riding through the fields and looking up in the sky . . . for air raiders and bombs." He noted in his diary that Churchill called with birthday greetings. The prime minister, always monitoring Roosevelt's reaction to his every move, mostly wanted to know whether the president was pleased with his speech. Joe reassured him, according to his diary, "he certainly should be." Churchill prodded Joe to remind Roosevelt that Britain was expecting the rifles, flying boats, and torpedo motor boats that had been included in the deal. Whatever antagonism had existed between him and Joe, Churchill still needed Kennedy as an ally who could intercede with Roosevelt on Britain's behalf. Joe did not grasp this. Churchill "knows quite well that I have no standing at the moment" with Roosevelt, he wrote in his diary. "Why he bothers to count on me is a mystery."

That day Joe also received from Rose a phonograph record, entitled *Voices*, on which each of his children recorded a birthday greeting for him. Joe wrote Jack how much he had enjoyed hearing his voice on the record, but acknowledged that it had "made me plenty homesick." To his dismay, Joe had already missed the family's annual Labor Day gathering, with its touch football games and lively dinner conversations, at Cape Cod. The *New York Times* reported that, in the Labor Day weekend sailing competition of the Hyannisport yacht club, the Kennedy children had garnered twelve trophies, including silver trays, cups, and clocks. When Joe saw a *Life* magazine picture of his kids sailing on Cape Cod, he was freshly reminded of all he was missing at home.

As summer turned to fall, the three eldest Kennedy children took a respite from politics and war. Joe Jr. had wangled an invitation from his father's friend William Randolph Hearst to spend several weeks that summer fishing and hunting with his friend Tom Killefer at Hearst's "Wyntoon" ranch on the McCloud River in California, near Shasta National Forest.

After serving as a delegate to the Democratic National Convention in July 1940, Joe Jr. took the rest of the summer off, relaxing in California before returning to Harvard Law School. (*JFK Library Foundation*)

He spent the rest of the summer with Tom at the Killefer family home in Hermosa Beach, California. They swam, surfed, and chased girls. In September, he entered his second year of Harvard Law School. Three weeks after his return, Joe registered for the draft.

Jack had planned to start Yale Law School, but his doctors suggested that he take a year off because his health was fragile. Instead, he decided to audit business classes at Stanford University amid the mild and dry climate of Palo Alto, California. He thrived in Palo Alto's low-key and playful atmosphere and found himself a typically bright and beautiful heiress, Harriet Price, to date. Kick essayed to block out her worries about Billy's welfare and that of her British friends by spending the month of September with several friends at the Flying Cloud Ranch near Butte, Montana, before returning to Finch College.

While Rose supervised her children's summer vacations and their return to school, the war was not far from her mind. She busied herself raising funds through charitable committees to pay for American ambulances to be sent to Britain to transport injured victims of the Blitz. On September 2, Joe formally presented the first American ambulance to the mayor of Windsor, saying he was proud to present the gift at a town that had shown Rose and him so much hospitality.

The first Nazi attack on London was an accident. Some of the hundred Luftwaffe bombers aiming for military targets on the outskirts of London drifted off course and bombed the center of the city. Several Londoners were killed. England's capital city was outraged, and Winston Churchill ordered quick retaliation. The next night, British bombers flew over Berlin and dropped leaflets asserting the British were not fighting the German people, but the German government, but they, too, missed their bombing targets. Nonetheless, the German people's feeling of invulnerability had been shattered. Luftwaffe head Hermann Goering had convinced the German populace that the British air force would never be able to reach

On September 2, 1940, Joe Kennedy presents an American ambulance to the mayor of Windsor. Through U.S. charities, Rose had raised the money for an ambulance to transport injured victims of the Blitz. (*Fox Photos*)

Berlin. Several days later, a follow-up raid was more successful, and some German civilians were killed. Hitler was furious; he saw the bombing of Berlin as a disgrace. On September 4, in a speech at the Sportzpalast in Berlin, he threatened massive retaliation: "The people of England are curious," Hitler declared tauntingly. "They ask, 'Why in the world don't you come?' We're coming, don't worry, we're coming." He sputtered, "We will raze their cities to the ground."

Hitler ordered a full-scale attack on British cities. He hoped that constant bombardment would break the morale of the British people and force them to insist that Churchill begin peace negotiations. It was a disastrous mistake. Hitler had taken Churchill's bait. Halting the assault on the weakened RAF airfields and support installations would allow the RAF to regroup at a crucial moment. On September 7, Field Marshal Goering ordered the bombing of London. At 4:00 that afternoon, virtually unopposed, a huge wave of Luftwaffe bombers followed the Thames Estuary up to London, decimated the East End slums, and set the docks and warehouses ablaze with smoke so intense that it obliterated the late-afternoon sun. The sympathetic American broadcaster Edward R. Murrow, whose "This is London" radio broadcasts brought the sounds of German bombs directly into millions of American homes, remarked that evening that "the fires up river had turned the moon blood-red." Kennedy cabled Hull a one-sentence summary: "There's hell to pay here tonight." Hell, indeed. This was the first of fifty-seven straight days of bombing known as the Blitz, when an average of two hundred planes would attack London nightly. Three hundred thousand people would lose their homes in the first six weeks of the Blitz. Approximately eighty-five hundred would die.

According to Joe, betting on "just when the invasion would come became an indoor sport." Top government officials regularly conveyed the impression that the Germans were coming "within the next 72 hours." Most British thought that an invasion would have to take place before the second half of September, when the weather in the British Channel becomes stormy and foggy. When some incoming intelligence was misinterpreted, officials relayed the code word "Cromwell"—meaning imminent invasion—to all British forces. At the first sign of a surface attack on British shores, church bells were to ring out all over England. The alert stayed in place for twelve days. Kennedy took comfort in Lord Beaverbrook's repeated avowal that there would be no invasion because the Germans had failed to establish supremacy in the air. The Nazis had gathered a large group of ships and barges along the French coast, Joe wrote Bobby on September 11, and there was evidence that the Germans were magnetic-mining all the harbors in order to trap British ships. But, Joe noted, Hitler "has never lacked an element of surprise, and his preparations for invasion seem so obvious that one hesitates to believe that this is his method."

On Sunday, September 22, the American president himself precipitated an invasion scare. While Kennedy was relaxing at Windsor, he received word from the British War Office that Roosevelt had told them that he had heard from sources in Berlin that an invasion was to start that afternoon at 3 P.M. It was a false alarm. Kennedy, of course, had not been informed by State Department sources of the intelligence FDR had received. The embassy's naval attaché Captain Kirk could only conclude that Roosevelt's warning was the result of a misinterpretation of a report Kennedy had sent to Washington saying that the Japanese contemplated entering Indochina at 3:00 that afternoon.

MORE THAN THREE HUNDRED PEOPLE were killed in London, a city of 8.2 million people, in the first day and night of bombing. Kennedy claimed to his friend George Bilainkin that, nonetheless, he slept on the second floor of Prince's Gate. Several days later, Churchill addressed the nation on radio, speaking defiantly of "a people who will not flinch or weary of the struggle—hard and protracted though it will be." But some demoralized and terrified citizens started leaving the capital city, "the wealthy in cars," Tim Clayton and Phil Craig wrote, "the poor on foot, pushing prams and barrows, loaded with what little they had saved from the wreckage of their homes."

A Home Intelligence report indicated that "[w]hen the siren goes, people run madly for shelter with white faces." At night, many Londoners slept in improvised beds without privacy in the basements of warehouses and in the underground subway stations. A quarter of the population slept in domestic shelters, while 60 percent remained in their homes. Residents of the East End of London—so many of whom had been bombed out of their homes—were in enormous distress. Joe was moved by their suffering. "It is really terrible to think about, and all those poor women and children and homeless people down in the East end of London all seeing their places destroyed," he wrote to Teddy. "I hope when you grow up you will dedicate your life to trying to work out plans to make people happy instead of making them miserable, as war does today . . . I know you will be glad to hear that all these little English boys your age are standing up to this bombing in great shape."

There was further daytime bombing on the ninth and eleventh of September, and air attacks came every night. In the early morning of the tenth, a bomb that had landed inside the grounds of Buckingham Palace the night before blew out the windows of the king's study and demolished the swimming pool.

The next day, Joe Kennedy was nearly killed when a delayed time bomb exploded fifty yards from his car, tossing it up on the sidewalk in the Mayfair section of London. He was not hurt. This was not Joe's first brush with death; twenty years earlier, he had been hurled to the ground by an anarchist's bomb that killed thirty-eight people in a Wall Street attack on J. P. Morgan and Company. Joe kept a stiff upper lip for his family and did not mention this near miss in any of his letters. Fatalistically, he wrote Rose, "I don't think anything is going to happen to me, and for that reason it doesn't worry me the slightest bit." To Jack, he displayed a steely persona: "Haven't the slightest touch of nervousness. But I can see evidences of some people beginning to break down." MP Harold Nicolson was more forthright about the psychic toll of the bombardments, writing in his diary that "underneath, the fibers of one's nerve resistance must be sapped."

During the initial thrust of the Blitz, the Germans dropped, by Joe's estimate, ten bombs within two hundred yards of the U.S. embassy. They were aiming at a nearby power station. Joe donned a steel helmet and watched from the roof of the Chancery as the Nazi bombs started massive conflagrations. "You could see the dome of St. Paul's," he wrote Rose, "silhouetted against a blazing inferno that the Germans kept adding to" by dropping more bombs. The Natural History Museum was nearly gutted. "When they drop these big bombs," he wrote home, "for three or four hours and you see fires starting in a complete circle all around, Cape Cod seems like an awfully good place."

Yet, as one Mayfair housewife described it, "an extraordinary mood of exaltation sweetened the air of London . . . The combined sense of danger and unity was exhilarating." People held rounds of parties, even while London was becoming a ghostly city, full of rubble, its surviving buildings covered in gray dust. Joe was so busy that he forgot to shave for several days, almost leaving for a dinner party with scraggly whiskers on his face.

Spotters, situated on the U.S. embassy roof, alerted the staff about impending raids. The embassy staff was able to work only three hours a day because they spent most of their time huddled in air-raid shelters. Over the course of ten days, the constant bombing and the anti-aircraft barrages made sleep impossible. A group of female embassy employees asked to be relocated to a safer place. After the embassy garage was bombed, Joe arranged with Lord Derby for the staff to stay, rent free, at the eighteen-room Coworth Park in Sunnydale. To keep their spirits up, Joe and embassy staff members played golf on courses where the military had dug "bit holes"(pits filled with baulks of timber along with a variety of other pieces of old machinery and scrap) in the middle of the fairways to protect against possible Nazi parachutists and gliders landing.

After several days of horrific bombing attacks, Joe sat down to write his family reassuring letters and thereby comfort himself. Worried that Rose was "frightfully nervous" reading about the attacks, he wrote to her, "The chances of anything happening to someone is one in a million." Even as Joe sought to reassure Rose, he did not spare her or his family the terrible details of what residents of London endured. On September 11, the Nazis bombed the West End of London, where, as he wrote Eunice, "they are dropping them all 'round 14 Prince's Gate." A bomb hit the barracks facing Rotten Row and another dropped in the bridle path facing the house. Herschel Johnson, the counselor of the embassy, was almost killed when the house next to his was totally demolished.

Relieved that his children were safe in the United States, Joe wrote Eunice, "I can't tell you what my state of mind would have been if any of you had been over here. I think I should have gone mad." He was, however, miffed at Teddy and Bobby for being poor correspondents and neglecting their embattled father, urging them to develop the discipline of writing every week. He praised Jean, who was "one of my best little correspondents," and asked her to "get that fat little brother of yours to write a little more frequently." He tried to engage Teddy by conveying a vivid portrait of what the boy might have faced in London. "I am sure, of course, you wouldn't be scared," he wrote Teddy, "but if you heard all these guns firing every night and the bombs bursting you might get a little fidgety. I am sure you would have liked to be with me and seen the fires the German bombers started in London."

In the absence of his family, Joe had taken Jack's friend Tony Loughborough, the sixth Earl of Rosslyn, under his wing as something of a surrogate son. Tony would stay over at St. Leonard's whenever he could, playing golf with Joe and his aides. The duchess of Kent, whom Jack fancied, had come out to dinner one Sunday night and told Joe that she was reading Jack's book and was impressed that he had written such a remarkable work at his young age. Provocatively, Joe had replied to the duchess, "My sons were very precocious!" He wrote Jack, titillating him, "She can take that any way she likes. I think you are very strong there."

The Air Ministry decided to camouflage St. Leonard's, Joe wrote Jean, because it was painted such a bright color. But there was no safety anywhere. One evening, Joe told her, he was outside the house watching searchlights and anti-aircraft fire when he heard a bomb coming and "dove into the bushes." It landed with "a dull thud" 250 yards from the house.

While the Luftwaffe was bombing England, Hitler sent, via Sweden, a peace initiative, proposing that Britain retain its empire and maritime strength while Germany possessed economic control of Europe. The British government rejected the offer immediately. The Nazis then launched an immense air attack, in a desperate attempt to pave the way for an invasion before it was too late, with 700 fighters and 230 bombers targeting London and five other major cities. Although two thousand British citizens, mostly in London, were killed in the attacks, militarily the air offensive was a failure. Fifty-six Nazi planes were destroyed, while the RAF lost only twenty-eight. Making a mistake so grievous that it would eventually cost them the war, German intelligence overestimated by more than 100 percent the number of British planes lost in the Battle of Britain that summer (770 estimated, versus 330 actual losses). Lord Beaverbrook's aircraft factories had produced over seven hundred new fighters since the first of July—far more than the Germans had calculated. Meanwhile, in America, Congress served notice that the U.S. government had to prepare seriously for the prospects of war. They passed the Selective Training and Service Act on September 16, making sixteen million men eligible for military service.

In mid-September, Hitler, thwarted by the growing difficulty of subjugating Britain and the more aggressive posture of the United States, postponed his planned invasion of England, code-named Sea Lion, and turned his focus to the east. He was determined to find a way to distract the United States from its commitment to Britain. One means of doing that would be to turn on his ally Stalin and conquer the Soviet Union. Then, he believed, America would be forced to focus on the Far East to contain the unchecked threat of an increasingly powerful Japan. He began developing plans to accomplish what Napoleon could not: invade and subjugate the European east.

Unaware of Hitler's decision as well as the extent of the RAF's success and increased resources, Joe Kennedy remained pessimistic about Britain's survival. Still under the spell of Lindbergh's wildly inaccurate assessment of the strength of the Luftwaffe, he believed that Hitler had not yet inflicted one-twentieth or one-thirtieth of German air power on England. Joe did not know what Hitler was waiting for.

Joe also felt the State Department had ignored the American embassy in its finest hour. After he and his staff had suffered nine sleepless nights of bombardment, he was furious that no one in the State Department (much less the president) had called to express concern. Joe telephoned Sumner

Welles and vented his anger, complaining that "no one in the State Department had any idea of what we were going through and seemed to care less." He had a point. FDR was complaining to his friend Breckenridge Long, the assistant secretary of state, that Kennedy was overreacting to surviving a few bombings, labeling him "a trouble-maker and as a person entirely out of hand and out of sympathy." When FDR finally called to perfunctorily express support, Joe was downright sarcastic with him.

Kennedy was becoming increasingly worried about Churchill's judgment—especially after he launched Britain's first war offensive, which Joe saw as ill-fated from the start. On September 23, when a squadron of battleships, carriers, and destroyers, in a mission dubbed Operation Menace, tried to land Charles de Gaulle's Free French forces in the port of Dakar, the capital of Senegal in French West Africa, the Vichy-controlled government there repulsed the attackers with surprisingly heavy firepower. To Joe, this effort was another Norway debacle, and an example of how easily air power could dominate a conflict. The British navy had once again been ineffective in operations near enemy air bases.

In a September 27 cable to Washington, Kennedy said the Dakar fiasco was "a bitter pill for the entire cabinet and the entire country. . . . This is the first real break in the Prime Minister's popularity and there is a general feeling that they have a Generalissimo and not a Prime Minister." Kennedy had long been a man literally and figuratively under fire; his exhaustion and demoralization led him to lose perspective on the progress of the war. "I cannot impress upon you strongly enough my complete lack of confidence in the entire conduct of this war," he told the State Department. Despite the British government's public pronouncements that it did not want the United States to enter the war—because America would no longer safely provide supplies as a technical noncombatant—Joe believed the British were "hoping and praying" for an incident that would bring the nation in. That day brought further reason for discouragement: Japan joined Italy and Germany in a formal Axis coalition.

Joe was convinced that his morose assessment of Britain's war capacities reflected reality; he had previously written Hull to express his concern that, given the tight censorship in the press, the American public had little idea about the extent of Britain's plight. American correspondents were painting a picture of a plucky Britain fighting off the Nazi menace. Joe believed Americans should know that if they entered the war, they would be taking up "a struggle that looks rather hopeful on the surface but is definitely bad underneath." The Luftwaffe's nightly bombing raids were doing significant damage to Britain's ability to fight, Kennedy averred, and "production is definitely falling, regardless of what reports you might be getting." On September 11, he had cabled Hull with his reservations about U.S. involvement in the war: "And for the United States to come in and sign a blank check . . . is a responsibility that only God should shoulder unless the American public knows what the real conditions of this battle are."

The end of September brought Joe more psychic and physical peril. German bombers destroyed several cottages neighboring St. Leonard's. On September 24, the *New York Times* reported that while Kennedy and an embassy colleague were inspecting burnt-out shells on his Windsor property, his colleague found one shell marked with the ambassador's initials, JPK. "That one had your name on it," he told Joe. "Initials don't count," Kennedy reportedly said. Kennedy biographer David Koskoff doubts this story because the ambassador did not recount it in later years (and it was expunged from a later draft of his diplomatic memoir), but Koskoff did note that "military suspicion has it that if a soldier be missed by a shell with his initials on it, he is safe for the duration of the conflict."

Maybe that unsuccessful shell did indeed save Joe, because a few days later a Messerchmitt 109 was shot down over his house at Windsor, crashing onto the property and missing the house "by inches." Bobby wrote his father: "We read in the paper [the *New York Times*] this morning that a plane crashed very near you and that it came so close that you could see the fuzz on his face and count the buttons on his coat." Joe gave his own account to Clare Boothe Luce: "I could see the pilot's face, his head lolling over to one side . . . head straight for the ground. I imagine it will take a long time to get the drone of German motors out of my ears after I get back."

The American ambassador was suffering profound battle fatigue. After six years of government service, two and a half years of an embattled and dispiriting pre-war and wartime ambassadorship, and a month of a war raining directly down on him, Joe yearned to go home. "If you ride horseback with German aeroplanes overhead, shoot a golf game with a battle going on," he wrote Rose, "and eat all your meals and do all you[r] sleeping under the strain of the present situation, that, it seems to me should entitle you to a rest for a while." But as much as he wanted to go home, he remained convinced he must "see this through." He didn't want "to do anything that will harm the British" and undermine their crucial relations with America. But Joe also recognized the redemptive value of being perceived as a survivor of wartime fire. He would not leave his post, he told Rose, until there had been "enough concentrated bombing on all of us in London so that nobody in America could think I had left before I had seen a big part of the show."

CHAPTER 23

"Telling the World
of Our Hopes"

I N EARLY OCTOBER 1940, Churchill wrote FDR, "The gent"—
Hitler—"has taken off his clothes and put on his bathing suit but the
water is getting colder and there is an autumn nip in the air. We are
maintaining utmost vigilance." Meeting with Lord Beaverbrook, Joe
learned that Roosevelt had approached the air minister to ascertain how
many planes and pilots Britain had left after its battles with the Luftwaffe.
FDR obviously did not want any record of his extracurricular intelligence-
gathering, and he clearly did not trust his ambassador to serve as his lieu-
tenant in any matter of vital interest to him. The incident convinced Joe
that he no longer had a viable role in Britain. Beaverbrook and Churchill,
learning of his intention to resign and fearing that his departure might suggest a diminishment of British-American cooperation, encouraged him to
keep at his post until after the November U.S. presidential election.

But Joe, amid the pounding of Nazi bombs, had had his fill of circumvention and calumny. He would later calculate that he had been through
244 bombing raids—enough to merit a return home with honor. The *New
York Times* referred to him as "our most bombed diplomat," and Arthur
Krock gave Kennedy cover in an October 8 article in which the columnist
echoed the *Times*'s description, saying he had earned the "unenviable so-
briquet of 'our most bombed ambassador'" and portraying him as gallant
amid "real and protracted peril." On October 11, Kennedy paid a farewell
visit to the king and queen, telling them that he was going home "to be
of such assistance as I could without our getting into the war." He was
heartened when the queen told him, "But we don't want you to get into the
war," and by her declaration that the British people thought very highly of

him. "Of course, that doesn't include Mayfair," Joe interjected, referring to the high-society denizens of Mayfair who had taken to critiquing him as an anti-British coward. "Who would pay attention to them," the queen replied. "Their opinions don't amount to anything and they make no contribution to the life of England."

Along with his farewell calls on his fellow ambassadors, Joe met with Lord Halifax, who confessed that he was not certain whether a U.S. declaration of war at this time would confer any real advantage on Britain. In final meetings with Labor leaders Ernest Bevin and Herbert Morrison, Joe listened intently as they expounded on their view that, as he put it in his memoir, "the old order was gone forever and that some of Democracy would prevail saturated with National Socialism but stopping short of Totalitarianism" in Britain because of the economic and social consequences of a devastating war. Within the month, Joe would do mortal damage to his career by expounding on these ideas in an off-the-cuff interview about the state of democracy in the world.

In mid-October, the Blitzkrieg of London was at its most murderous. Over 250,000 people had lost their homes, and on October 10, St. Paul's Cathedral had been bombed. On October 15, four hundred German planes attacked London and killed 435 civilians, destroyed a building fifty yards from the U.S. embassy, and dropped a bomb that lay buried and unexploded fifty feet from the embassy's door. Two days later, Kennedy met with Churchill for his most crucial parting meeting. He asked if Churchill would stick with an earlier pronouncement that he did not want the United States in the war. Churchill said he would, then added, "Of course, as soon as they want to come in, I do want them to come in." Churchill did not give Kennedy the kind of statement he could use back in America in a crusade to keep the United States out of the war.

Kennedy may have thought he was resigning, but that October, Roosevelt told the press on several occasions that his ambassador was staying put. Syndicated columnists Joseph Alsop and Robert Kinter reported on October 7 that the president wanted Kennedy to stay in London, where FDR felt he could do less harm to his election chances. That day Rose talked with Kennedy colleague John Burns and then wrote Joe that "the Pres does not want you to come before the election due to your explosive—defeatist, point of view, as you might so easily throw a bomb which would explode sufficiently to upset his chances." Rose was ready to fight to bring her husband home. "I wanted to go to the W.H. [White House] as a wife, say I am worried about your health," she wrote with unusually spunky humor, "think you have done enough—guarantee to chloroform you until after the election." She told Joe that, contrary to last spring, when Americans worried that their ambassador "could not take" the stress of bombardment, now they (her polling sample included clients at Elizabeth Arden and Saks) felt he had done enough.

Arthur Krock responded to Alsop and Kinter's column by saying that although Kennedy has been "gloomy" in his assessment of the war, he "has been right." Krock stated his belief that efforts to keep Kennedy in London were based on the fallacious assumption that he was "temperamentally unable to resist speaking what is in his mind, regardless of the consequences," which of course Joe sometimes was. Krock also pointed out that, except for Ambassador Alexander Weddell in Spain, Kennedy was the last ambassador left in Europe.

On October 16, Joe sent a cablegram to FDR and the State Department insisting that he be allowed to come home. Roosevelt, aware of rumors that publisher Henry Luce had lined up Kennedy to endorse Republican presidential candidate Wendell L. Willkie, instructed Hull to keep him in London. Willkie, the charming, progressive, and intellectual businessman whose unlikely candidacy had sprung, in Alice Roosevelt Longworth's words, from "the grass roots of a thousand country clubs," had been attacking Roosevelt as a warmonger and a proponent of big government, and was catching up to him in the polls—so much so that an alarmed Roosevelt felt a need to go on the campaign trail and on the offensive. The last thing the president needed was an angry Joe Kennedy campaigning against him.

Kennedy would not stay put. He telephoned Sumner Welles and informed him he would come home whether or not he was officially allowed to. Upping the ante, Kennedy told Welles that he had sent a memorandum with his frank views on the war and U.S. foreign policy to his aide Eddie Moore in New York, and had asked Moore to release it just before the election if he was not allowed to return. The president had too many secrets to protect and too close an election fight; he could not call Kennedy's bluff. He gave his ambassador official permission to return.

ON OCTOBER 19, during his final weekend in England, Joe saw Neville Chamberlain for the last time. The former prime minister, suffering from stomach cancer and unable to work or visit friends, told him that he wanted to die; he had witnessed how miserably his father had lived for eight years after suffering a stroke. "I don't want to be a burden," he said. "So perhaps God in his mercy will take me soon." As the two men recounted the events of the last year, Joe reminded him of the irony that it was Churchill's strategic failure in Norway that had cost Chamberlain his prime ministership. Chamberlain smiled sadly. When they spoke about Britain's slow preparation for war, Chamberlain acknowledged that leaders have to try to stay ahead of public opinion, declaring, "A democracy will not wake up until the danger is imminent." As they parted, Chamberlain reached out with both hands and clasped Joe's hand, saying, "This is good-bye, we will never see each other again."

Before Joe left London, Chamberlain wrote him a farewell letter—which Kennedy would proudly show the president—saying there were "few cases in our history in which the two men occupying our respective positions were so closely in touch with one another as you and I." He had always spoken frankly to Joe, he wrote, "because I found in you an understanding about what I was trying to do and an integrity of character which particularly appealed to me. And you never betrayed my confidence or failed to give me your encouragement in times of difficulty or your sympathy in my disappointments." If only Roosevelt and Churchill had felt the same way about Joe.

Joe wrote back immediately, saying that he had only ever met two men who had dedicated their lives selflessly for the good of humanity: the present pope and Chamberlain. Any service Joe had given to Chamberlain marked the "real worth while epoch in my career." Joe went on to express the commitment he believed would animate his return to America, to assure that "the world will yet see that your struggle was never in vain. My job from now on is telling the world of our hopes." They dreamed of finding ways to buy time that would allow their countries to build a powerful military arsenal that would deter further fascist aggression. Joe hoped that he could help America's young men stay safe—even as they built up America's defenses.

That Monday, journalist George Bilainkin went to the U.S. embassy to say good-bye to his friend, noting in his diary that Kennedy looked "mentally exhausted; physically tired, lacks interest." The next day, Kennedy addressed the senior members of the diplomatic services and the clerical staff; according to Bilainkin, "several men and women, as they filed out of the study . . . were in tears." Shaking hands with him for the last time, staff members paid "tribute," Bilainkin wrote, "to one whom I know to be an exceptionally hard task-master." As Kennedy descended the steps of the embassy for the last time, photographers besieged him. Walking alone down Grosvenor Square, "the [his] steps seemed shorter and shorter," Bilainkin thought, and he "looked just an ordinary man."

In a final interview, Kennedy said that Londoners had surprised him with their grit and determination: "I did not know London would take it," he declared, "I did not think any city could take it. I am bowed in reverence." Joe Kennedy left the country on the night of October 22 on a flight to Portugal, where he boarded the transatlantic clipper for New York.

That same day, in a secret proceeding at Old Bailey, London's central criminal court, U.S. embassy code clerk Tyler Kent went on trial. In addition to being charged under the Official Secrets Act with obtaining documents that could aid the enemy, Kent was accused under the Larceny Act of stealing documents that were the property of Ambassador Kennedy.

After four days of prosecution testimony, Kent, the only defense witness, testified that he had fulfilled a higher duty to the people of his country, who wanted to stay out of Britain's war; it was, he said, an allegiance greater than the one he owed to the ambassador he worked for. Two days after Roosevelt was safely reelected, the jury found Kent guilty of five charges under the Official Secrets Act and one charge under the Larceny Act. He was sentenced to seven years' imprisonment and was jailed on the Isle of Wight. At the end of the war he would be released and deported to the United States, where in spite of his public pro-fascist views the FBI would regularly investigate him on suspicion of being a Soviet sympathizer.

AT 2:30 P.M. ON SUNDAY, OCTOBER 27, a crowd of over two thousand at LaGuardia Field (as the airport was then known) in New York watched as a Pan Am clipper landed in the bay. Joe walked briskly down the gangway carrying an emblem of the Blitz—an air-raid siren that would later be used to summon the Kennedy children to meals at Hyannisport. Maritime commissioner Max Truitt immediately handed him a personal invitation from the president to spend the night at the White House. Roosevelt was determined to debrief and defuse his ambassador before anyone else got to him. Following FDR's orders, Joe batted away questions from the large contingent of journalists waiting to capture one of the biggest political stories of the year—the homecoming of a man who could play a pivotal role in the imminent presidential election. Rose, Eunice, Kick, Pat, and Jean, all decked out in fur coats, greeted him in the terminal building, distracting the reporters by spontaneously rushing into Joe's arms. "Tears of joy flowed freely, and the ambassador wiped his own eyes . . . ," the *Boston Post* reported. "Mrs. Kennedy's youthful face was buried in her husband's shoulder, and her tall daughters alternatively wept and thumped their dad on the back."

Joe escorted Rose and a few friends into a private room at the terminal to discuss face to face whether his grievances were reason to abandon the president. Henry and Clare Luce were expecting him at their Manhattan apartment to urge him to support Willkie, but Joe could not bring himself to refuse a presidential invitation. Earlier he called the president, who said, "Ah, Joe. It is good to hear your voice." FDR, with House majority leader Sam Rayburn and his protégé Lyndon Johnson looking on, told Joe, "Please come to the White House tonight for a little family dinner." Grinning, Roosevelt added, "I'm dying to talk to you," as he drew his finger across his throat.

The president flew Joe and Rose to Washington on an official plane. On the flight, Rose reminded her aggrieved husband of the honor FDR had bestowed upon him in making him the first Catholic ambassador to the Court of St. James's. Rose did not want her husband to ruin her own first dinner at the White House—much less her family's political future. She played on Joe's sense of loyalty and his concern for his family's reputation: "You would write yourself down as an ingrate in the view of many people if you resign now." An abrupt resignation followed immediately by an endorsement of Willkie would not stand him in good stead with his own party or his country, Rose thought.

After his presidential dinner and just before the election, after Joe had already publicly announced his choice for president, he would learn from Supreme Court Justice Frank Murphy that the entire evening at the White House had been scripted by Roosevelt. FDR had met with Supreme Court Justices Murphy, Felix Frankfurter, and William Douglas and his advisor Harry Hopkins to plot how to manipulate Kennedy into making a speech that would win over the Catholic vote for the president and defuse isolationist anger and mistrust of FDR.

Joe greeted the president briefly in his study before they were joined by Rose and South Carolina senator James Byrnes and his wife, whom Roosevelt had added to the evening as buffers. Rose observed FDR sitting at his desk "shaking a cocktail shaker and reaching over for a few lumps of ice with his powerful hands." The president would need fortification for the drama ahead. During a typically meager Sunday-night Roosevelt dinner of scrambled eggs, sausages, and toast, Byrnes, "acting as though a wonderful idea had just struck him," according to Joe, told him that he could make an enormous difference in the election if he would make a radio address on behalf of the president. Throughout dinner, Byrnes persisted in selling the idea. Joe watched as "the president worked hard on Rose, whom I suspect he had come down [to the White House] because of her great influence on me." FDR softened Rose up by charming her with reminiscences about her father and offering hints about fostering Joe's political future, saying she was "not to let this fellow think he is going to get away from me and loaf."

When dinner was over, "Joe did most of the talking," Rose remembered. "The President looked rather pale, rather ashen, and I always noticed the nervous habit he had of nervously snapping his eyes." "Since it doesn't seem possible for me to see the President alone," Joe announced, "I guess I'll just have to say [it] in front of everybody." Pulling no punches, using his most colorful language, Joe told the president how sore he was about having been circumvented by the State Department, left out of the destroyer-for-bases negotiations, and kept in the dark about the military missions to London. "All these things were conducive to harming my influence in England," he said, explaining how he had to tell the British "your country is going to find me most unfriendly toward the whole situation" if they didn't keep him informed. "So I smashed my way through," Joe concluded, "with no thanks to the American government."

Masterfully, FDR denied everything. He was disgusted with the career men at the State Department, he told Joe—they always did everything wrong. He was indignant about their mistreatment of his friend. He promised that, after the election, heads would roll. Joe may have been moved by the president's fervor, but he was unpersuaded of his sincerity. "Somebody is lying very seriously," he would write in his diary that night, "and I suspect the president." Rose, realizing that the confrontation might soon burn all the Kennedy family's carefully constructed bridges with the presidential family, diplomatically chimed in that it was difficult for both of them to maintain "the right perspective on a situation that was 3,000 miles away." Then Roosevelt, in a final burst of manipulativeness, made it personal, a matter of family—and family ambition. "I stand in awe of your relationship with your children," he told Joe. "For a man as busy as you are, it is a rare achievement. And I for one will do all I can to help you if your boys should ever run for political office." After hinting that he would find Joe a suitable government position after his ambassadorship and declaring that he would support his sons' political ambitions, FDR asked Joe to deliver the pre-election speech.

Joe, satisfied that the president had at least listened to his complaints, and believing that a third term for FDR might be best for the country and for his own family's future, agreed to make the speech—on his own terms. "But I will pay for it myself, show it to nobody in advance and say what I wish," he told the president. He would ensure he would not be publicly seen with the president until then, thus expertly building suspense among

Willkie supporters, Roosevelt loyalists, and British Foreign Office officials anxious to see Roosevelt reelected.

Even as Joe returned to New York to write his speech in seclusion at the Waldorf-Astoria, Clare Boothe Luce was determined to maneuver him into supporting Willkie. But Joe refused to take Clare's calls. In exasperation, she wrote him a letter directly playing not only on his patriotism but on whatever romantic feelings he had for her:

> Please remember that the rift that the election of F.D.R. will drive through my heart is the same rift your speech in support of a third term is going to drive through mine tomorrow . . . I know good guys and great guys and patriots when I see them. Our friend Willkie is all three. And I've *always* believed you were all three. Well, these are the good old days now. At least they are until you speak tomorrow.
>
> Love, Clare

> Holy God, the thing I can't bear is everyone telling me . . . "See what we had told you about Kennedy [that he could be bought off by Roosevelt] is true!"

Would Kennedy betray his president, or would he turn the tide for FDR? Joe answered that question the night of October 29 in a thoughtful and compelling speech, paid for by his wife and children, and broadcast over 114 stations of the Columbia Broadcast System. Earlier that day, Mussolini had invaded Greece. "Even the most staid isolationist is now alive to the danger facing any nation in the modern world," Kennedy told the American public. "The realization that oceans alone are not adequate barriers against revolutionary forces which now threaten civilization has not come too late. We are rearming . . . It is our guarantee of peace."

He went on to warn Americans, "Unfortunately, it is true that a democracy such as ours is difficult to rally when it is neither desperate nor frightened." Indulging himself with a plug for Jack's *Why England Slept*, Kennedy mentioned Britain's failure to apprehend the peril of Germany's military buildup, defended the Munich Pact as "but an armistice" allowing time to recoup from that tragic failure of apprehension, and emphasized the need for American military strength, which would remove the danger of that "miserable thing that does nothing but destroy—war" from American shores. "If, as some of my critics say, I am 'steeped in gloom,'" why would anyone be cheery when a "large part of the productive capacity of the world is devoted to the cause of killing?"

Addressing one of the election's central issues, Kennedy strongly disputed Willkie's allegation that FDR was trying to entangle the United States in Europe's war: "Such a charge is false." If the United States declared war, it would have to stop shipping the crucial war materials that were keeping Britain afloat, an effort that was vital to American interests, because "England's valiant fight is giving us time to prepare." Britain had paid a high price for war, not only in blood, toil, tears, and sweat but in freedom, Kennedy went on to say. Describing how Britain had enacted the Emergency Powers Act, giving it near-dictatorial power over people and property, he urged that "Congress should pause a long, long time before declaring war . . . Democracy—our freedoms—all become jeopardized."

Making a compelling case for FDR's reelection, he opined, "Events move so quickly—the man of experience is our man of the hour . . . It is later than you think . . . We do not have time to train a green hand." Franklin Roosevelt would be the best candidate to ensure a bright future for "our children and your children," who "are more important that anything in the world." Then, in what would become the speech's most famous and portentous statement, he declared, "After all, I have a great stake in this country. My wife and I have given nine hostages to fortune. . . . The kind of America that they and their children will inherit is of grave concern to us all." Rose Kennedy then spoke as well, at the urging of Betsy Cushing Roosevelt, the president's daughter-in-law, reiterating that Roosevelt would not send her sons or theirs to war.

Joe's muscular speech was widely lauded, except among Willkie's disappointed supporters. *Life* magazine called it "the most effective vote-getting speech of the campaign." Roosevelt wired Joe that it was a great address, and one of the president's friends likened it to "hitting a grand slam home run in the 9th inning." Lem Billings wrote Jack, "Listened to your pappy's speech tonight. It was the clearest and most sensible one I've heard in the whole campaign. I was a Willkie worker, but I could never argue too effectively with Big J.P." Jack cabled his father: "Proud to have sponsored you. Thanks for the plug. Love, Jack." That same day, he had received a low number in the draft lottery, virtually guaranteeing that he would be summoned for an army physical that he knew he would fail.

The Kennedys had never before wielded such great public and potent political influence. On Halloween eve, the president arrived at an election rally at Boston Garden with Honey Fitz and Joe Jr. at his side. Roosevelt declared unequivocally that American "boys are not going to be sent into any foreign wars," promised the British government that they could purchase billions of dollars' worth of armaments from the United States, and, campaigning hard for the Irish-Catholic votes, declared that he was delighted to "welcome back to the shores of America that Boston boy, beloved by all of Boston and a lot of other places, my ambassador to the Court of St. James's, Joe Kennedy." Kick wrote her father that "the Pres really went to town for you tonight in Boston amidst terrific cheers from the crowd 'that Boston boy etc' . . . It's great to be famous." She signed her note "Goodnight from your 4th hostage." In the November 5 election, Roosevelt beat Willkie by a relatively slim margin of the popular vote, but he handily won the electoral college, taking thirty-eight states to ten for Willkie. The Kennedys had been kingmakers. Joe believed that he and his family stood poised for success on the national level, but he was wrong.

THE DAY AFTER THE ELECTION, Joe went to the White House, congratulated the president, and offered him his resignation. If there was a chance for peace in Europe or an indication that the U.S. position there was in jeopardy, he promised he would return to England with minimal notice. FDR told him to take a long vacation, but said that he wanted to keep him on officially until he could find a suitable replacement. FDR hinted that he was considering other government jobs for him.

On November 9, Joe learned "with great sorrow" of Neville Chamberlain's death. "I had hard work to keep from crying," he recorded in his diary. "He was noble. He was kind and fair and brave." Although Joe did not yet know it, with Chamberlain's death he had no more friends in high places.

The day of Chamberlain's death was significant for another reason. That afternoon, through his own careless words and undiplomatic if misconstrued honesty, Kennedy would ruin his own reputation and political future. All he had sought for his family and himself, and all the good reputation he managed to create in spite of the stresses and misadventures of his ambassadorship, he destroyed through one imprudent if revealing newspaper interview. Joe and his family would spend the next twenty years making amends not so much for the events of the Kennedy ambassadorship as for what he said as it ended.

Joe was in Boston for a checkup at the Lahey Clinic. In his suite at the Ritz-Carlton, dressed casually, his suspenders hanging down, and eating apple pie, he was giving an informal background interview to two reporters from the *St. Louis Post-Dispatch*. Louis Lyons of the *Boston Globe*, who had been asked to do a soft Sunday feature on the ambassador, joined the other two reporters. Joe had made clear to the reporters from St. Louis that the interview was off the record, but—disastrously—he failed to do so with Lyons, who printed his wide-ranging and provocative comments without clarifying whether those comments were on the record and without adequately contextualizing them.

Lyons quoted Kennedy as saying, "Democracy is finished in England. It may be here." When the reporters asked what he meant, he replied, "Well, I don't know. If we get into a war, a bureaucracy would take over right off. Everything we hold dear would be gone." Kennedy was referring to the authoritarian measures he had observed being imposed in Britain, which he agreed that democracies needed to utilize to survive the severe challenges of war, even if they threatened their national freedoms. He did not provide the philosophical basis for these concerns, which he had discussed with Labor MPs and others, and his words were misconstrued.

They led to an avalanche of international criticism. "We can forgive wrongheadedness, but not bad faith," George Murray wrote in the London *Daily Mail*, "How little you know us . . . Plainly you know nothing of the fierce championship of freedom." Joe's remark that the queen "had more brains than the cabinet" was a mortal blow to his relations with the British government. The British *News Chronicle* noted that Kennedy's interview "had created a great deal of anger from MPs of all parties." Lyons damaged him further with the Roosevelt family, and with the Jewish leaders whom Joe had courted, when he quoted Kennedy as declaring that Eleanor Roosevelt was a lovely, helpful, and sympathetic woman, but "she bothered us more in our jobs in Washington to take care of the poor little nobodies who hadn't any influence than all the rest of the people down there together. She was always sending me a note to have some little Susie Glotz to tea at the embassy." "Susie Glotz" came across as an anti-Semitic reference. Many of Kennedy's most inflammatory comments were published in an abbreviated and distorted form in other magazine articles and books.

Lyons, who had given Kennedy favorable press coverage during the 1936 election, undermined the ambassador by publishing these remarks without clarifying the extent to which they were offered only as a background briefing, and by not probing Kennedy further to elaborate upon and justify his thoughts. But Kennedy laid himself open for such a disaster by speaking so provocatively. Reporters in England had protected him, and he had become careless. Joe was unfairly treated, but he also appears to have been unconsciously sabotaging himself. Having worked so hard to raise his standing during his three years in London and then offering timely and powerful support for the president and the Democratic Party, he cast himself out of the house of power just as its doors finally opened to him;

he became the pariah he still secretly believed himself to be. Only days after he had been widely praised for his speech, and he and his family had been celebrated by the president in Boston, he had become once again, partly through his own recklessness, a reviled and misunderstood figure. It was a stunning and tragic conclusion to his ambassadorship and it would be a cautionary tale for all of his children. Devastated, Joe may have remembered Boake Carter's prophetic words: "[Y]ou're going to be hurt as you were never hurt in your life."

In an impromptu speech at a luncheon at Warner Brothers in Burbank, California, Joe compounded the controversy, warning Hollywood motion picture magnates that because the Jews were in peril worldwide, movie producers should take care not to make films that would alienate the Reich and make the Nazis rain down even greater wrath. According to a report that actor Douglas Fairbanks, Jr. sent to FDR, Kennedy, who was still ambassador, had caused considerable confusion about the administration's policy by proposing that the United States could "reconcile itself to whomever wins the war and adjust our trade and lives accordingly." Roosevelt had struggled mightily to win the election, and knew he would have to use considerable guile and expend enormous effort to guide the country toward an increasingly robust support of the Allies and a greater recognition of America's moral agency across the world. The last thing he needed was Kennedy muddying his policy waters or leading an appeasement faction.

Kennedy then made a brief post-Thanksgiving visit to Roosevelt in Hyde Park to explain his *Boston Globe* interview. Eleanor Roosevelt related her version of the volatile encounter to writer Gore Vidal during his unsuccessful 1960 campaign for a Hudson Valley congressional seat. Eleanor had picked Joe up at the train station in Rhinecliff and brought him to see FDR in his small office in the estate's main house. All the accumulated tensions between the two men exploded in a ten-minute scrap. Eleanor had left the house to run errands, but she was summoned home by an aide, arriving just as Joe was exiting FDR's office. She "had never seen Franklin so white in the face," Vidal remembered her as saying. Franklin commanded Eleanor, "I never want to see that son of a bitch again as long as I live. Take his resignation and get him out of here." But even after Joe submitted his resignation on the first day of December—after a meeting with Roosevelt—the president and Kennedy continued their sabotage of each other.

On December 29, FDR addressed the nation in what would be an important speech that defined once and for all America's policy toward the European war, declaring, "Never before since Jamestown and Plymouth

Rock has our American civilization been in such danger as now . . . We must be the great arsenal of democracy." Roosevelt decried high-level American appeasers whom he said were busy spreading defeatism, aiding the enemy's agendas, and clamoring for a negotiated peace with a "gang of outlaws [that] surrounds your community and on threat of extortion makes you pay tribute to save your own skins. . . ."

Joe listened on the radio from Palm Beach, peeved at what he saw as a clear reference to himself. He was right. In a cabinet meeting several days before, Roosevelt had mentioned Kennedy by name as one of the American appeasers who could make trouble for his increasingly activist policy of aid and armament. Kennedy's formal resignation would not be announced until February 1941, when Republican politician John Winant, head of the International Labor Office in Geneva, Switzerland, was named to replace him, but already Joe was persona non grata in both Washington and London.

But Joe's loss of power did confer one advantage on his family. It came at a time when his children, tutored by war, chastened by their father's mistakes, and bolstered by their acceptance amongst Britain's political aristocracy, had begun to establish their own independent identities. It is possible that they would never have blossomed as they did if, like Franklin Roosevelt's children, they had been overshadowed by an unquestionably powerful man. Joe's ruin was not only instructive for his children but, like the fall of a giant tree, it cleared a space in the sky that allowed the sun to shine on the saplings. In *The Fruitful Bough*, a privately printed book of essays about his father, Robert Kennedy countered the myth of Joe's complete domination of the family, portraying him in a fashion that was probably more true after his ambassadorship than before or during it: "He did not visualize himself as a sun around which satellites would circle, or in the role of puppet master. He wanted us, not himself as focal points."

When in November 1940, Joe Jr. wrote to his father to announce his tentative decision to join the Navy Air Corps rather than the Naval Reserve, he told him that he did so because there was "a chance for some individuality." Although historians often suggest that Joe, unlike Jack, did not seek to distinguish himself from his father, he became a far more ardent isolationist than the ambassador ever was, opposing all U.S. military aid to Britain because he believed it would lead America into war. According to Rose's grandniece Kerry McCarthy, Joe and Joe Jr. would debate the issue so vigorously at dinnertime that others at the table wondered whether they would ever get to eat.

Jack, meanwhile, moved in a different direction to foster his own identity. His brother Joe Jr. wrote their father with what would become a sad prophecy fulfilled: "As far as the family is concerned, it seems that Jack is perfectly capable to do everything, if by chance anything happened to me. Also everyone seems pretty well grown up, thus I should think from that end, it would be OK."

Over the course of 1940, as America tensed for war and criticism of former ambassador Kennedy grew even more fierce, Jack sensed his father's despair and assumed the mantle of family leadership. He wrote his father a long memorandum suggesting ways he could combat his critics and set the record straight. He suggested that Joe could present himself as a heroic figure, one who eschewed political advantage to propound what he believed was best for his country over the long term. In a remarkable psychological moment, the son was now mentoring his father.

In the memo, Jack proposed that his father had more in common with Winston Churchill than was commonly thought: Both men exhibited a courageous and determined insistence on telling their fellow countrymen the hard truths—truths that would not win them political popularity, but ones that might save their countries. He suggested his father could say, "I am gloomy and I have been gloomy since September 1938 . . . let me note that Winston Churchill was considered distinctly unpleasant to have around during the years 1935 to 1939. It was felt that he was a gloom monger. In the days of the Blitzkrieg the optimist does not always do his country the best service. It is only by facing reality that we can hope to meet it successfully." Joe Kennedy, his son believed, was a profile in courage.

Joe must have been heartened by his son's advice and praise, and he would act on it the next year. He had indeed brought a passion and realism to his pursuit of peace, and creativity and courage to his efforts to protect his beloved country. Yet unlike Churchill, he had failed to grasp the absolute evil of Hitler's regime until it was too late, and he had not taken a clear moral stand about Hitler's rape of Europe. Like Chamberlain, he will be forever tainted by this failure of imagination and moral vision.

As an epitaph for this period of his life, Joe could share in the qualified praise a forty-eight-year-old private soldier bestowed upon Chamberlain in a letter in the fall of 1940:

"It is easy to be wise after the event and you will be criticized for generations, but your sincerity has been transparent, and I . . . have admired your efforts—particularly your efforts for peace, so heartrendingly unsuccessful."

"The Crowns of Suffering"

*"It would take a great dramatic novelist . . . to mix the rhythm of
earthy selfishness and higher loyalties that explained the motiva-
tion of Joseph Patrick Kennedy."*

PUBLISHER HENRY LUCE

PERCHED on a closed toilet seat in the bathroom of the family
quarters of the White House, Joe Kennedy watched the wheel-
chair-bound president, who was clad in gray pajamas, shave. It
was January 16, 1941, less than two months after FDR had sworn
to Eleanor that he never wanted to see Joe again. But for what he believed
to be the sake of the country, FDR was manipulating Kennedy one more
time. Joe had accepted an invitation from New York congressman Hamilton Fish to testify at the Lend Lease Congressional hearings that week,
and he would also be making an NBC radio address to the nation two days
hence. He was not surprised that Roosevelt had summoned him for a tête-
à-tête, but he was still vulnerable to the president's disarming power. FDR
staged their talk in a manner that would appear intimate, but that would
discomfit and deny the dignity of his aggrieved ambassador.

From atop the toilet, Joe expressed his indignation about the job the
president's "hatchet men" continued to perform on him in the press, and
most painful of all, the president's allusions to him as a defeatist appeaser
in his recent Arsenal of Democracy speech. FDR sidestepped the issue by
claiming that he knew all too well what it was like to be mistreated by the
newspapers. Joe reiterated that he was for all aid to Britain short of war,
but said he did have reservations about the authority vested in the president under the terms of the Lend Lease bill, saying, "It would leave a bad
taste in the mouths of people because of the request for vast power." FDR
mollified him a bit by saying he would consider an amendment keeping
Congress informed of how he used his power, but that the exigencies of

aid and rearmament required him to have the authority the legislation gave him. Mentioning alarmist Republican claims that under the bill's terms he could give the navy away, FDR said, "I could stand on my head under this Bill but I don't propose to do it."

Joe went on to tell him that the country was not sure that the president wanted to keep America out of the war. FDR replied adamantly, "I've said it 150 times at least. For the last seven years I have been going to get them into every war that has taken place in Europe and I haven't done it yet." Kennedy was not convinced by his assertion, "I have no intentions of going to war."

After ninety minutes, FDR finally dangled the possibility of sending Kennedy to Eire as a special emissary, handling troublesome negotiations with the British, who wanted to obtain naval and air bases on the Irish coast. He told Joe that his friend Sumner Welles "insisted [Joe] was the only one who could straighten it out."

As usual, the president's stratagem worked. In his radio address and in his testimony at the congressional hearings, Kennedy disappointed America First isolationists who had counted on his support and equivocated about the value of Lend Lease. During his radio speech, he defended his own record rather than rallying the president's opponents: "The saddest feature of recent months is the growth of intolerance . . . Many Americans, including myself, have been subjected to deliberate smear campaigns merely because we differed from an articulate minority. . . . A favorite device of an aggressive minority is to call any American, questioning the likelihood of a British victory, an 'Apostle of Gloom'—a defeatist." Americans, he thought, expected an ambassador to report "the bright side and the dark side—the good things and the bad things—the strength and the weakness," which Joe felt he had done. "I never thought it was my function to report pleasant stories that were not true." Acknowledging that he had publicly tallied the obstacles to Britain's victory, he denied reports that he had predicted England would be vanquished. He saluted the British people with whom he had endured the Blitz: "The morale of the British nation defies description. It is as fine a display of human courage as has ever been witnessed."

Kennedy also asserted that he had been caricatured as an appeaser who trusted the dictators' promises and sought to make deals with fascist leaders against the wishes of the British people. "The words of the tyrants have been shown to be worthless," he said, adding, "but if I am called an appeaser because I oppose the entrance of this country into the present war, I cheerfully plead guilty." He supported giving "the utmost aid to

England" so that the American people could secure for themselves "the most precious commodity we need—time—time to rearm. People who say that we will be drawn into the war no matter what we do, they are 'the real defeatists.'"

Fifteen-year-old Bobby listened to his father's speech at his prep school, Portsmouth Priory, where he had been tormented by classmates who attacked his father as a defeatist. He wrote his mother that the speech was "wonderful. I think it was the best speech he ever made. I thought he really cleared himself from what people have been saying about him." However, he also revealed to Rose that he had received "another one of those Post cards telling me like the last one how awful we Catholics are."

FREE OF THE CONSTRAINTS of the ambassadorship, Joe Kennedy took a belated yet firm moral stand against Hitler. On May 24, four months after formally relinquishing his post, he addressed the graduating class at Oglethorpe University, and vehemently decried fascism: "The American people have a deep seated antagonism for the forces of evil which the totalitarian states espouse. They repudiate their philosophy, their silly racism and their nightmare of world domination . . . National socialism lays claim to the whole life of man, to his thoughts, loyalties and devotion no less than his money, labor and his very life. . . . This new paganism proclaims its own beatitudes, which are not those you read in your prayer book. It says 'Woe unto the weak, woe unto the sick. The strong shall possess the earth.'"

Kennedy went on to provide a brilliant summation of the anti-interventionist philosophy in words that reverberate decades later: "Let us not forget the American destiny; let us not be deluded by any claim that self-interest should make us guardians of the peace of the rest of the world. I have the fullest conviction that few countries of the earth by and large want our kind of democracy. Most of them have neither the training nor the tradition for it—not even a proper understanding of it. Democracy cannot be imposed by force or otherwise."

From the time since he first sailed to London to his return three years later, Joe Kennedy had evolved from an embrace of a rigid isolationist stance toward an espousal of a nuanced and moderate interventionism. Two days after Joe's Oglethorpe speech, FDR declared an "unlimited national emergency" and invoked special powers that would allow him to respond to any outside threat. In his Fireside Chat the next night, he told the American people that Hitler was bent on world domination and might soon attack people in the Western Hemisphere. Kennedy, speaking at the Notre Dame commencement ceremonies shortly afterward, surprised his critics by setting aside his concerns about the dangers to democracy of wartime authoritarian acts, declaring that complete loyalty to the president's cause was the only correct response.

By the end of 1941, war would come to America. The next four years would bring to violent resolution the conflicts that had so consumed Joe Kennedy in London and the world at large. The result, for both Western democracy and the people whose lives and motives converged in pre-war London, would be victory and loss.

Franklin Roosevelt spent all of 1941 preparing the American people for entering the war against the Axis powers. In his visionary Four Freedoms speech, delivered in January 1941, he had declared that the United States was called upon to defend basic human rights throughout the world. That March he signed into law the Lend Lease Bill, giving aid to Britain and edging America closer to military involvement. When Roosevelt and Churchill met for the first time as heads of their respective governments on August 14, 1941, at Argentia Bay off Newfoundland, they issued the Atlantic Charter, a joint declaration laying out the common principles underlying their national policies as they fought the war against fascism. The two leaders would meet for twelve more conferences to plan Allied strategy for victory, redraw the map of postwar Europe, and prepare for the disarmament of Germany. When Winston Churchill heard about the attack on Pearl Harbor on December 7, 1941, he said, with great relief, "We are all in the same boat now." Roosevelt worked with Churchill to give priority to defeating Nazi Germany's military power, which appeared even more threatening than Japanese imperial might.

As for Joe Kennedy, on Pearl Harbor Day, he cabled Roosevelt: "Name the Battle Post, I'm Yours to Command." The president never responded; his secretary Steve Early sent a generic thank-you note. Over the course of the war, FDR would never offer Kennedy a position commensurate with his status, experience, or considerable skills in business and finance. Kennedy turned down the president's unappealing offers of two wartime jobs that would have put him in a nonpublic and subordinate role, one in shipbuilding and the other as the assistant to the War Transport administrator. Rose must have felt betrayed. The president had told her he would find Joe a suitable job.

Roosevelt guided the Allies through the war, but he wore himself out. By the time he died of a cerebral hemorrhage on April 12, 1945, he had firmly established the United States' status as an international superpower and its moral leadership role on the world stage. Joe Kennedy told a reporter that Roosevelt had "dedicated his life that the grave injuries to states and inhabitants should be rectified." Joe later told a friend that, despite all their conflicts, "I would never have done anything to hurt him."

A S HE HAD FEARED, World War II and its aftermath did indeed make Joe Kennedy's children hostages to fortune. His failure in London and his unfair reputation as a coward would motivate his sons to prove their bravery in the war.

Jack Kennedy volunteered for the U.S. Army in the spring of 1941, but was rejected mainly because of his back problems. That September his father, working through one of his former naval attachés at the embassy, arranged for him to be accepted into the U.S. Navy. After war was declared, Jack was sent to the South Pacific, where in August 1943, his boat, the USS *PT–109*, was cut in half by a Japanese destroyer. Although he reinjured his back, Jack courageously led his crew to safety—an act for which he received the Navy and Marine Corps medal for heroism. His escape from near-death deepened his preoccupation with the nature of courage, a subject he had so often debated with his London friends, including his future confidant as president, David Ormsby-Gore.

Joe Jr. felt he had lost status in the family. In September 1943, right after Jack's heroic PT boat incident, Joe arrived in England. He joined the U.S. Navy's VB–110 squadron in Devon, flying in operations with the RAF, and fell in love with Pat Wilson, the beautiful, Protestant wife of a British army officer stationed abroad, and the mother of three children. Joe flew enough missions to be eligible to return home, but he volunteered to stay on with his squadron. Hoping to boost his family's honor and enhance his own prestige, he volunteered for a top-secret and extremely dangerous mission: He would fly a PB4Y Liberator bomber carrying 2,200 pounds of explosives, parachute out, and detonate the plane over the German defenses on the Belgian coast. On August 13, 1944, his plane exploded in midair over the English Channel and he died.

Joe Kennedy was inconsolable; he found it unbearable even to talk about the death of his son. Joe would tell a friend that for a guy who worked so hard to keep out of war, he definitely had "the crowns of suffering" on his soul. He had lost most of his prestige and his eldest son, whose political ascendance, Joe had hoped, would help rebuild his family's reputation. In April 1945, a new destroyer named the *Joseph P. Kennedy, Jr.* in his honor was launched. In the memorial volume *As We Remember Joe*,

Jack provided an epitaph for his brother that was celebratory and insightful: "He had great physical courage and stamina, a complete confidence in himself which never faltered, and he did everything with great verve and gusto, and though these very qualities were in the end his undoing, yet they made his life a wonderful one to live."

Joe Kennedy's grief was pervasive and enduring; it darkened his hopes for the world. After the war's end, he bumped into Winston Churchill at the Hialeah racetrack in Florida, in January 1946. Churchill told him, "You had a terrible time during the war; your losses were very great. I felt so sad for you . . . The world seems to be in frightful condition." Kennedy asked him, "After all, what did we accomplish with this war?" Joe saw an empowered Soviet Union in the east, economic ruin in Europe, and that efforts to secure prosperity for the earth's people may have contributed to war instead of insuring the peace. "Well, at least we have our lives," Churchill replied. "Not all of us," Kennedy answered bitterly.

Joe's tenure in London led indirectly to another terrible loss for the family, postwar. Before Pearl Harbor, Kick had completed her studies at Finch College for Women in New York and taken a job in Washington, D.C., as an assistant to Frank Waldrop, the executive editor of the *Times Herald*. That October, learning that Billy Hartington had become engaged to her friend Sally Norton, she wrote her father, "I am so anxious to go back that I can hardly sit still." She made it to England in July 1943 with the Red Cross, volunteering with American military personnel, and reunited with Billy. In May 1944, after months of fruitless negotiations with Catholic and Anglican religious figures, Kick married Billy without the sanction of her church—or for that matter, the blessing of Rose, who was distraught about the condition of her daughter's soul. Anticipating their future roles as duke and duchess of Devonshire, Kick and Billy envisioned making his ancestral home, Chatsworth, the center of political and cultural power it had been in the Whig era. But Billy was killed on September 10, 1944, in Belgium.

Over the next four years Kick, known as Lady Hartington, remained close to her in-laws the Devonshires, becoming a prominent social hostess in postwar London. She considered but declined marriage to Richard Wood, the Protestant son of Joe Kennedy's friend Lord Halifax. She then fell wildly in love with the rakish, divorced, Irish Protestant Lord Peter Fitzwilliam. On May 14, 1948, while they were flying to Paris to seek Joe Kennedy's support for their marriage, their plane crashed into a mountain. A half hour after he heard they had died, Joe wrote of his daughter, "No one who ever knew her didn't feel that life was much better that minute."

After the war ended, Joe Kennedy worked only briefly in government service, as a member of two Hoover Commissions reorganizing government and on an intelligence oversight committee for President Eisenhower. In 1945, Kennedy headed a commission to develop a State Department of Commerce in Massachusetts, but otherwise he focused on philanthropic efforts and on his business interests, investing in real estate, most notably the Chicago Merchandise Mart, which he bought in 1945, and in the Texas oil and gas industry, as well as buying a part interest in Miami's Hialeah racetrack and backing a Broadway comedy. Mostly he kept a public silence about political and foreign policy issues.

For the next fifteen years, Joe's primary enterprise would be his behind-the-scenes efforts to restore his family dynasty to the place of prominence he and Rose had envisioned during the London years. He helped his children advance, his son Bobby said, "by doing what, for a strong figure, is probably the most difficult thing to do—to submerge his own personality." He demanded that all his children aim for excellence—"strive for it, perhaps not achieve it, but continuously strive for it," as he said. "After you have done the best you can," he would say, "the hell with it." Over the years, his summons to high standards would inspire and motivate his children. But along with his self-consciousness about maintaining norms of social behavior, his desire that his children excel contributed to his disastrous decision about handling Rosemary's mental and behavioral problems. She had thrived under careful supervision in England, but in the fall of 1940 while teaching at St. Gertrude's School of Arts and Crafts in Washington, D.C., she began having increasingly frequent, violent mood swings. Some nights she would wander the streets of Washington, D.C., after midnight by herself. Rose was anxious that her beautiful daughter might be kidnapped or might become pregnant.

Without consulting Rose, Joe authorized a prefrontal leucotomy, a Nobel Prize–winning surgical technique that was supposed to subdue aggression by cutting the connections to the prefrontal cortex. Joe was crushed when the operation failed. Rosemary was incapacitated and could not take care of herself. He concealed her condition, telling family members and friends that she was teaching in the Midwest. Rose did not immediately learn the truth. In the 1980s, in an interview with Doris Kearns Goodwin, she expressed bitterness about Joe's unilateral decision, but she rationalized that Rosemary was receiving wonderful care. Rosemary lived at a residential institution, St. Coletta's School for Exceptional Children in Jefferson, Wisconsin, from 1949 until her death in 2005.

Rosemary's tragedy led Joe Kennedy and his family to embrace efforts to raise public awareness and assistance for the mentally retarded—efforts that other family members saw as evidence of Joe's lifelong concern about vital social issues. In *The Fruitful Bough*, a tribute to his father, Bobby Kennedy declared, "Beneath it all he has tried to engender a social conscience. There were wrongs which needed attention. There were people who were poor and who needed help; mentally ill who needed assistance." In January 1942, Joe Kennedy had been made a Knight of Malta by the pope in recognition of his quiet, long-term contributions to Catholic and mental health charities. Joe and Rose would become important philanthropists in the decades following the war, setting up a Catholic convalescent home for children and making large grants to Catholic hospitals, schools, and charities through the Joseph P. Kennedy, Jr. Foundation, which they founded in 1946.

Eunice would be the first of Joe's children to make a career of social concerns, transferring in 1942 from Manhattanville College to Stanford University, where she received a degree in sociology. After a career as a social worker, she took over the direction of the Joseph P. Kennedy, Jr. Foundation and its mission toward increasing public knowledge about mental retardation and its causes and prevention, and improving society's capacity to help people with intellectual disabilities. She developed her work with the physically and mentally handicapped into the Special Olympics, a sports effort for mentally challenged children and adults, which became an international organization.

Her sister Patricia was inspired by her father's success in the movie business, graduating from Rosemont College and moving to Hollywood with plans to become a movie producer and director. "Pat is the one with the head for business," Joe said. "She could really run this town if she put her mind to it." As a woman in Hollywood, she found her ambitions thwarted and was limited to helping to produce patriotic and religious shows like singer Kate Smith's radio program and Father Patrick Peyton's "Family Rosary Crusade."

Her younger sister Jean shared Pat's affinity for business, attending Manhattanville College (where she befriended Bobby's future wife Ethel Skakel and Ted's future wife, Virginia Joan Bennett) and going on to work for the Christophers organization, a Catholic group whose mission is to encourage people to use their God-given talents to make a positive difference in the world, and later working as an executive at the Merchandise Mart.

IN 1946, the Kennedy family took the political stage for the first time since Joe's ill-starred ambassadorship. Jack, who had originally considered a career as a journalist but had become the Kennedys' political heir apparent with the death of his brother, ran successfully for the U.S. House of Representatives from a heavily Democratic district in and around Boston. Bobby, after finishing his military service as a seaman on the U.S.S. *Joseph P. Kennedy, Jr.*, came into the campaign full time. Rose was a gifted and tireless campaigner. Using her annual Fourth of July London embassy reception as a model, she fashioned a new and extraordinarily effective political strategy: campaign teas and receptions particularly tailored to women voters. Jack's sisters pushed doorbells and did staff work, and fourteen-year-old Teddy pitched in, too. Joe financed the campaign, and garnered the support of his political allies and press contacts.

In the eight years since Joe had assumed his ambassadorship, the world had been transformed by war, nuclear weapons, and the emergence of the Soviet Union as a global power, but one issue of contention remained constant in that time—and into our own: the role of the United States in preserving democracy and enforcing peace. In a politically calculated stance that also came authentically to the young veteran, and one that separated him from his wary father, Jack Kennedy presented himself as an unequivocal internationalist. His model was less Joe Kennedy than Winston Churchill. Communist Russia was for Jack and Bobby and their generation what Nazi Germany had been for Churchill: an evil state whose expansion must be thwarted. Combining a Churchillian activism with their father's passionate aversion to the Soviet Union, both young Kennedys advocated a strong anti-communist policy. As a congressman, although generally supporting President Harry S. Truman's foreign policies, Jack criticized what he considered the administration's weak stand against the Communist Chinese. Bobby, ideologically closer to his father at this stage than Jack ever would be, not only shared Joe's vigorous anti-communist views but, early in his career, also exhibited his tendency toward black-and-white thinking about political issues. He honed his legal skills while serving as Joe McCarthy's assistant counsel for the Senate Permanent Subcommittee on Investigations, which hounded communist sympathizers.

In 1952, the Kennedys reemerged onto the main stage of American life when they helped Jack defeat incumbent Republican Henry Cabot Lodge, Jr., for the U.S. Senate. Bobby served as campaign manager as Jack won in 1952 and again in 1958. During his first term in the Senate, during a period when he was recuperating from life-threatening back surgery, Jack wrote a book about senators who risked their careers by taking unpopular political stands. While the book's protagonists were all senators, he also found inspiration closer to home, in his father the ambassador. He had witnessed his father, Neville Chamberlain, and Winston Churchill, all in different ways, struggle with the conflict between acceding to political expediency and paying the lonely price for moral courage. Jack saw his father exhibit a stubborn bravery when he withstood severe criticism on both sides of the Atlantic for his noninterventionist stance and what he believed was his realistic commentary on Britain's obstacles to victory. He watched Churchill withstand contempt when he tried to warn his country about the Nazi danger. The resulting book, *Profiles in Courage*, won the Pulitzer Prize in 1957.

Did Jack harbor strong resentment against a controlling, demanding political albatross of a father, as some biographers have claimed? Jack Kennedy's speechwriter and alter ego Ted Sorensen says he never saw any evidence of that. According to Sorenson, Kennedy valued his father's loyalty, and the two willful men loved each other forthrightly. Kennedy biographer James MacGregor Burns concluded that while Jack "had to placate his father, he was quite independent" from him. Like any son of a powerful father, Jack must have struggled at times to define his own identity, but he realized that Joe wanted him to be an independent thinker. Even though Jack recognized that Joe Kennedy was more conservative and noninterventionist than he could ever be, he appreciated his father's help on tactical political matters, including public relations, and his willingness to utilize political connections to help him advance. Biographer Robert Dallek points out that Joe helped arrange Jack's appointment to the House Education and Labor Committee early in his congressional career. Eunice Kennedy recalled that during Jack's first campaign "there was many a night when he'd come over to see Daddy after a speech, he'd be feeling rather down," until his father helped him focus on his strengths and on what he could do to improve himself.

As Kennedy campaigned for the presidency, his model was once again not Joe but Winston Churchill, a leader whom he would later proclaim the first Honorary Citizen of the United States. Sorensen says Kennedy drew on Churchill for "his courage, bold pronouncements, and his brilliant oratory." Jack kept in mind Churchill's pithy warning about the importance of negotiation: "Better to jaw, jaw than to war, war." But it would be Joe Kennedy's reputation as a failed ambassador and his role in appeasement that would hover over Jack's run for the presidency and his time in the White House. During the televised presidential debates, Republican candidate Richard Nixon attempted to tar Kennedy as an appeaser after Jack said that there was no need to defend the islands of Quemoy and Matsu from Communist China. Nixon enumerated Chamberlain's accommodations to Hitler in 1938 and 1939 and tried to link Kennedy directly to his father's support for appeasement. Kennedy counterattacked by labeling the Republican vice president as "soft" on Cuba.

On the campaign trail, Kennedy publicly compared himself to Churchill and emphasized that America must remain strong militarily, while equating Nixon's all-is-well stance with 1930s prime minister Stanley Baldwin's unwillingness to tell the British hard truths. Kennedy won the election by a slim margin. During the campaign, making light of assertions that he was buying the presidency for his son, Joe Kennedy had written Jack, "Don't buy a single vote more than necessary. I'll be damned if I'm going to pay for a landslide."

Joe Kennedy would not get to long enjoy his son's ascent to the White House. In late 1961 he suffered a stroke that left him disabled and mute. He could not play an active role in his son's presidency, but his strong and uncompromising character, his commitment to public service, and the lessons of his ambassadorship would influence Jack's words and actions. As president, Jack Kennedy inspired the nation with the standards of excellence he had absorbed from his parents. Two of the greatest lines from his rousing inauguration address on January 20, 1961 germinated during his time in London. As Jack wrote his book *Why England Slept*, he first comprehended that there are times of crisis in democracies when individuals must subsume their personal needs for the good of the state.

According to Ted Sorensen, Rose Kennedy stressed throughout her children's lives one of her favorite phrases: "To whom much is given, much is asked," and Jack Kennedy came to see public service "as both an obligation and a joy." On inauguration day, Kennedy would challenge the world to the kind of engagement with public life that his parents had inculcated in him: "And so, my fellow Americans: ask not what your country can do for you—ask what you can do for your country. My fellow citizens of the world: ask not what America will do for you, but what together we can do for the freedom of man." His study of Chamberlain's capitulation to Hitler at Munich was evident in lines from the speech that spoke of the necessity of a nation to act from a position of strength: "For only when our arms are sufficient beyond doubt can we be certain beyond doubt that they will never be employed."

Notwithstanding his eloquence, Washington's military establishment worried that a young, untested president would appease America's foes as his father had attempted to just twenty years earlier. Kennedy was under intense pressure to respond militarily to international crises. Theodore Sorensen acknowledges that Jack's overlearning the lessons of his father's failed ambassadorship played an indirect role in his decision to accede to the April 1961 Bay of Pigs invasion by Cuban exiles in a catastrophic attempt to overthrow Castro.

In June 1961 in Vienna, Kennedy met with his chief international adversary, Soviet leader Nikita Khrushchev, but the encounter did not ease tensions. Barbara Leaming, in her book *Jack Kennedy: The Education of a President*, claims that Vienna was Kennedy's Munich—an encounter in which his adversary had sized him up as weak and had overwhelmed him. But Khrushchev's son later revealed that the Soviet leader found Kennedy to be very articulate and that the two "both gave as good as they got." In Khrushchev's memoir he called Kennedy "a real statesman." And when Khrushchev threatened to sign a treaty with East Germany that would have given it control over Western access routes to Berlin, Kennedy was resolute. According to Sorensen, Kennedy "always believed you had to warn and alert the people. Jack would say it was easier back in the days when you could see the enemy from the walls." Addressing the American people upon his return to the United States, Kennedy took care not to suggest that any progress had been made toward peace. The Soviets did not sign the treaty; instead they built a wall dividing East from West Berlin. Kennedy responded by convincing Congress to increase defense spending to counter the hardening of what Churchill had labeled the "iron curtain" dividing the Soviet sphere of influence from democratic Europe.

But Kennedy was also willing to acknowledge the limits of U.S. hegemony. On November 16, 1961, Jack gave a visionary speech which echoed his father's May 1941 anti-interventionist comments. Jack said, "We must face the fact that the United States is neither omnipotent nor omniscient . . . that we cannot right every wrong or reverse every adversity, and that therefore there cannot be an American solution to every world problem."

His father's reputation as an appeaser also entered the debate over Kennedy's choices during the Cuban Missile Crisis, when the Soviet Union challenged the American president by building offensive ballistic missile sites on Cuban soil. Air Force chief of staff Curtis Le May, who favored a direct military strike on Cuba, decried Kennedy's blockade plan in front of the other joint chiefs as being "almost as bad as the appeasement at Munich," a comment that had to rankle the president. Bobby Kennedy, serving as his brother's attorney general and most trusted advisor, played a crucial role in helping his brother take his first truly courageous presidential action. During this crisis Jack consulted with the close friend and advisor he had met first as a Harvard undergraduate in Britain, David Ormsby-

Gore, whom British prime minister Harold Macmillan had appointed as the British ambassador to the United States.

Ignoring the hawkish counsel of his military advisors, Kennedy refused to order a military strike. In an action akin to his father's maverick diplomatic efforts in London, he engaged in secret backdoor negotiations with the Russians to end the conflict, while making it look as if he had stared down the Soviets and forced them to blink. The Kennedy White House, ever aware of the power of historical allusion, put out the word that they had avoided another Munich.

IN THE LAST YEAR of his tragically truncated presidency, Jack Kennedy finally began to resolve the conflict between selfish motives and lofty aims that had been bequeathed to him by his father. Kennedy's bold and visionary steps in June 1963 evidenced his maturation into a morally courageous head of state poised to lead the American people toward greater justice at home and a more sustainable peace abroad. His great "Peace Speech," at American University on June 10, 1963, sought to take the first step in ending the Cold War by calling for the de-escalation of the international culture of fear and crisis, and by reversing the demonization of the Soviet people: "We all inhabit this small planet," Kennedy declaimed. "We all breathe the same air. We all cherish our children's future. And we are all mortal." These were remarkable visionary words for a man who had been steeped in the anti-communism of his father and of Winston Churchill. His speech led to the Nuclear Test Ban Treaty barring atmospheric testing of nuclear weapons.

Kennedy also actively sought greater peace and justice at home. Even though he had come late to an appreciation of the civil rights movement burgeoning across America in the 1950s and early 1960s, in the latter half of his presidency he went as far as to antagonize the American South, thereby risking his reelection, by federalizing the Mississippi National Guard—a move that allowed the first black student, James Meredith, to enroll at the University of Mississippi—and by championing a federal civil rights bill that would outlaw segregation in public places. Bobby, who had earlier authorized the wiretapping of Martin Luther King, Jr., had by now evolved into the moral center of the Kennedy administration, and he guided the president toward his principled stand on combating racial discrimination by enforcing the Supreme Court decisions desegregating Southern schools and public facilities. In his televised address announcing his introduction of civil rights legislation into Congress, Kennedy told Americans, "We are confronted primarily with a moral issue. It is as old as the scriptures and is as clear as the American Constitution." His moral stand ultimately led him to travel to Dallas, Texas, to try to repair the damage to his reputation in the South, where right-wing agitators like General Edwin Walker crusaded against Kennedy's "defeatist" foreign policy and his "socialistic" domestic agenda. John Kennedy was assassinated there on November 22, 1963. Joe Kennedy would have been pleased that Jack wanted his epitaph to be "He kept the peace."

Some say Kennedy's murder marked the end of an optimism and sense of promise America has never recaptured. Certainly, for the Kennedy family, it was a crushing tragedy. Rose Kennedy did not believe that time heals all wounds. She believed that the mind, in order to maintain its sanity, covers the wounds with scar tissue. For her, the pain lessened, but it never went away.

After his brother's death, Bobby Kennedy endured his own dark night of the soul, from which he emerged as a man possessed of his father's advocacy of moral courage and willingness to withstand withering criticism while expressing unpopular positions. But he grew capable of greater moral sensitivity than his father. Elected in November 1964 as U.S. senator from New York, he heeded his parents' call to bring social conscience to government. In 1966, Bobby championed the cause of the anti-apartheid movement, delivering, during a visit to South Africa, a widely hailed speech: "Few men are willing to brave the disapproval of their fellows, the censure of their colleagues, and the wrath of their society. Moral courage is a rarer commodity than bravery in battle or great intelligence. Yet it is the one essential, vital quality for those who seek to change a world which yields most painfully to change."

Responding to President Lyndon B. Johnson's escalating prosecution of the Vietnam War, Bobby entered the 1968 presidential race as an advocate for negotiating an early end to the war, as well as a proponent of racial and economic justice. In Cleveland, the day after civil rights pioneer Martin Luther King, Jr., was assassinated in April 1968, Bobby gave his greatest speech ("The Mindless Menace of Violence"), calling on his countrymen to respond to tragedy by deepening their commitment to humanity:

> But we can perhaps remember—even if only for a time—that those who live with us are our brothers, that they share with us the same short movement of life, that they seek—as we do—nothing but the chance to live out their lives in purpose and happiness, winning what satisfaction and fulfillment they can. . . . Surely we can learn,

at least, to look at those around us as fellow men and surely we can begin to work a little harder to bind up the wounds among us and to become in our hearts brothers and countrymen once again.

On June 6, 1968, minutes after winning the crucial California primary, Bobby Kennedy was assassinated. In eulogizing his brother, Ted Kennedy asked that he "be remembered simply as a good and decent man, who saw wrong and tried to right it, saw suffering and tried to heal it, saw war and tried to stop it."

Joe Kennedy lived long enough to endure the deaths of both Jack and Bobby, although he could not speak of his grief. Historians will long debate how much Joe's model of relentless ambition in the pursuit of superlative accomplishment contributed to his family's tragedies. After eight years of near total silence, he died on November 18, 1969.

Rose Kennedy lived for another twenty-five years. She had devoted much of the second half of her life to securing public support for the Joseph P. Kennedy, Jr. Foundation's goals and to helping her sons win elective office. In 1952, Pope Pius XII had made Rose a papal countess in recognition of her "exemplary motherhood and many charitable works." At the time of her death from complications of pneumonia at the age of 104 on January 22, 1995, she was the longest-lived presidential relative in history. At her funeral, her youngest son eulogized her as "a rare and wondrous person, a shining example of faith that sustained her through even the hardest sorrow . . . She was the most beautiful rose of all."

Edward M. Kennedy was elected a senator from Massachusetts when he was thirty years old and has become one of the longest-serving members in that body in history. His mother's empathy for the underdog, readily seen in the family's philanthropic efforts, made a strong impression on her youngest son. Ted told me that, in addition to his father's career, Joe Kennedy's September 11, 1940 letter to him, written during the Blitz, had a profound effect on him and led him to public service: "I hope when you grow up you will dedicate your life to trying to work out plans to make people happy," Joe wrote him, "instead of making them miserable, as war does today." Ted fulfilled his father and mother's wish by devoting his senate career to advocating effectively for the rights and needs of the poor and the disadvantaged. *Time* magazine saluted him as one of America's top ten senators, stating, "[H]e had amassed a titanic record of legislation affecting the lives of virtually every man, woman and child in the country." His parents, who had suffered from prejudice against their ethnic group, would have been particularly proud about his strong advocacy for immigrants.

Ted made a bid for the presidency in 1980 when he launched an insurgent campaign against Democratic president Jimmy Carter. He took up his father's mandate that the family remain a dynastic power, but was unable to articulate effectively why he wanted to run. His father's failed ambassadorship still casts its shadow. When I asked Senator Kennedy what he most admired about his father as ambassador in London, he replied, "No matter how busy he was, my father always took time to come home and read me stories." As a senator, Kennedy is well acquainted with the responsibilities of ambassadors, but he would not comment on the official side of his father's London life.

Perhaps in part because he remains influenced by his father, Ted Kennedy has taken a strong stand against hasty interventionism. Kennedy has said that the best vote he had ever cast in the Senate was his vote against giving President George W. Bush the authority to use force against Iraq.

The Kennedy daughters have also maintained the kind of significant public roles their parents encouraged. Like her mother, Eunice became an ambassador's wife. Her husband, Sargent Shriver, whom she married in 1953, served as the U.S. ambassador to France from 1968 to 1970. Two years later, she campaigned alongside Shriver when he was George McGovern's 1972 vice presidential running mate. Eunice is the only living woman whose portrait appears on a U.S. coin, the 1995 commemorative Special Olympics silver dollar, and she has been awarded both the Presidential Medal of Freedom and the Legion of Honor.

Highly sophisticated, Pat Kennedy traveled widely throughout her life. In her youth she accepted press assignments to write about her travels. She married actor Peter Lawford in 1954. Pat worked with the John F. Kennedy Library and Museum and the National Center on Addiction. In 1966 she moved to New York City, where she raised four children and devoted herself to charity auctions and fundraisers for the arts.

Joe Kennedy's youngest daughter, Jean, would become the second Ambassador Kennedy. She served as President Bill Clinton's ambassador to the Republic of Ireland from 1993 to 1998 and was instrumental in helping to bring about the Good Friday accord in the Irish peace process. Jean was a key conduit of the intentions of Sinn Fein, the political wing of the Irish Republican Army, and helped to push the British to take the process seriously. The accord was signed by the British and Irish governments on April 10, 1998, and provided that the constitutional future of Northern Ireland would be decided by a majority vote of its citizens and that all political parties would adhere to peaceful and democratic methods. Jean founded the Very Special Arts educational program, which continues to serve people with disabilities, and has served on the Board of the Carnegie Endowment for International Peace. She married Stephen E. Smith, who managed the Kennedy family's businesses. Their daughter Amanda Smith edited *Hostage to Fortune: The Letters of Joseph P. Kennedy.*

More than seventy years after Joseph P. Kennedy first presented his diplomatic credentials to King George VI, his ambassadorship offers up a cautionary tale—that a commitment to public service and peace can be undermined by headlong ambition, intemperate behavior, realism unleavened by optimism, and courage unsupported by an articulated moral vision. Joe and Rose Kennedy's sons, as well as some of their grandchildren, also failed to entirely master the art of pursuing lofty goals unimpeded by impolitic behavior. But, less encumbered by Joe Kennedy's sense of being an outsider, they have learned from his mistakes and transcended them.

We might all remember Bobby Kennedy's call to action in his June 1966 University of Cape Town speech: "Each time a man stands up for an ideal, or acts to improve the lot of others, or strikes out against injustice, he sends forth a tiny ripple of hope . . . those ripples build a current which can sweep down the mightiest walls of oppression and resistance."

Source Notes

ABBREVIATIONS

ARCHIVES/PAPER COLLECTIONS

JFKL: John F. Kennedy Library Foundation.

FDRL: Franklin Roosevelt Library.

JPKP: Joseph P. Kennedy papers (open only by permission), JFKL.

REFKP: Rose Kennedy papers open to public, JFKL.

JFKP: John Fitzgerald Kennedy papers, JFKL.

DM: Joseph Kennedy's unpublished diplomatic memoir in Series 8.3, Boxes 147 and 148, in JPKP, JFKL.

FO PRO: Foreign Office Files, Public Record Office, Kew, England.

JPK Diary: Joseph Kennedy Diary in Series 8.1, Appointments and Diary, Box 110, Diary 1938, 1938, 1940–16 folders in JPKP, JFKL.

REFK Diary: Rose Kennedy Diary in Series 1, Boxes 2 and 3, in REFKP at JFKL.

KK Diary: Kathleen Kennedy Diary in Series 7.9, Box, 128, in REFKP at JFKL.

SD: State Department Files in the National Archives [noted as NA].

FRUS: Foreign Relations of the United States.

PERSONS

CBL: Clare Boothe Luce.

CH: Cordell Hull.

EMK: Edward Moore Kennedy.

EK: Eunice Kennedy.

FDR: Franklin Delano Roosevelt.

JFK: John Fitzgerald Kennedy.

JK: Jean Kennedy.

JPK: Joseph Patrick Kennedy.

JPK Jr: Joseph Patrick Kennedy, Jr.

LB: Lem Billings.

NC: Neville Chamberlain.

PK: Patricia Kennedy.

REFK: Rose Kennedy.

RFK: Robert Francis Kennedy.
RK: Rosemary Kennedy.
WC: Winston Churchill.

PERIODICALS

LT: *London Times.*
NYT: *New York Times.*
DT: *Daily Telegraph,* London.

BOOKS

AK: Arthur Krock, *Memoirs: Sixty Years on the Firing Line.*
AS: Arthur Schlesinger, *Robert Kennedy and His Times.*
BL: Barbara Leaming, *Jack Kennedy: The Education of a Statesman.*
CB: Conrad Black, *Franklin Delano Roosevelt: Champion of Freedom.*
CC: James Robert Rhodes, *Chips: The Diaries of Sir Henry Channon.*
CH: Charles Higham, *Rose: The Life and Times of Rose Kennedy.*
DK: David Koskoff, *Joseph P. Kennedy: A Life and Times.*
DKG: Doris Kearns Goodwin, *The Fitzgeralds and the Kennedys.*
KC: Edward Klein, *The Kennedy Curse.*
FB: Kennedy Family Memoir, *The Fruitful Bough.*
FF: Richard Whalen, *The Founding Father.*
GB: George Bilainkin, *Diary of a Diplomatic Correspondent.*
GP: Geoffrey Perret, *Jack: A Life Like No Other.*
GS: Winston Churchill, *The Gathering Storm, Volume 1.*
HF: Andrew Roberts, *'The Holy Fox.'*
HN: Nigel Nicolson (Ed.), *Harold Nicolson, Diaries and Letters, 1930–1939.*
HTF: Amanda Smith, *Hostage to Fortune.*
IK: Ian Kershaw, *Hitler: 1939–1945 Nemesis.*
KAD: Peter Collier and David Horowitz, *The Kennedys: An American Drama.*
KAW: Edward Renehan, Jr., *The Kennedys at War.*
KF: Keith Feiling, *The Life of Neville Chamberlain.*
KK: Lynne McTaggart, *Kathleen Kennedy: Her Life and Times.*
KR: Michael Beschloss, *Kennedy & Roosevelt: The Uneasy Alliance.*
LL: Laurence Leamer, *The Kennedy Women.*
LP: Hank Searls, *The Lost Prince.*
LSOP: Angela Lambert, *1939: The Last Season of Peace.*
MG: Martin Gilbert, *Churchill: A Life.*
NCDL: Robert Self (Ed.), *The Neville Chamberlain Diary Letters, Volume 4.*
NGI: Winston S. Churchill (Ed.), *Never Give In! The Best of Winston Churchill's Speeches.*
NH: Nigel Hamilton, *JPK, Restless Youth.*
NM: Norman Moss, *19 Weeks.*
RAS: Peter Collier and David Horowitz, *The Roosevelts: An American Saga.*
RB: Roger Bjerk, *Kennedy at the Court of St. James's,* doctoral dissertation.
RD: Ralph deBedts, *Ambassador Joseph Kennedy 1938–1940: An Anatomy of Appeasement.*
RK: Robert Kee, *1939: In the Shadow of the War.*
RS: Robert Self, *Neville Chamberlain, A Biography.*
TTR: Rose Kennedy, *Times to Remember.*
WM: William Manchester, *The Last Lion.*

INTRODUCTION

xvii "the never-ending responsibilities." Interview with Robert Holmes Tuttle, June 1, 2006.

xix "ultimately widely . . . history of the United States." CB, p. 439.

xix "an old town clerk . . . of a municipal drainpipe." Dominique Enright, *The Wicked Wit of Winston Churchill*, p. 61.

xxi "It is not . . . *think* you are." Ralph Martin, *Seeds of Destruction*, p. xxi.

xxi "The president's . . . suggested itself to me." DM 1, p.3.

xxiii "He was our greatest fan . . . standards reachable." Kennedy Family, *Her Grace Above Gold*, p. 34.

xxiii Affair with Daye Eliot. Interview with Doris Lilly in David Heymann, *RFK*, p. 12.

xxvi "Is it appeasement . . . for appeasement." JPK, "An American Foreign Policy for Americans," UVA Law School Forum, December 12, 1950, 6: JPKP. HTF, p. 521.

PROLOGUE

2–3 "What would you . . . Court of St. James's." James Roosevelt, *My Parents*, p. 208.

3 "It certainly . . . wheelchair." Ibid., pp. 208–209.

3–4 Giving up Gloria Swanson and Missy LeHand. RAS, p. 291.

4 "Would you mind . . . not right for the job, Joe." KAD, p. 81.

4 "a great joke, the greatest joke in the world." HTF, p. 223.

5 "Well, I'm not going to . . . only one—I'll accept." AK, p. 333.

5 "in which . . . parallel in my experience." FB, p. 112.

5 "a complete surprise for Kennedy." KC, p. 98.

6 "very dangerous . . . I will fire him." Henry Morgenthau, Jr., Diary, December 8, 1937, Henry Morgenthau Papers, FDRL.

6 "it gave me a feeling of real pleasure." KR, p. 158.

6 "the Kennedy family has royal blood antedating the king's." KC, p. 99.

6 "the highest compliment Roosevelt could pay to Great Britain." KR, p. 158.

6 "senseless war . . . the vanquished." DKG interview with REFK, DKG, p. 272.

7 "Don't go buying . . . some money." KAD, p. 82.

7 "I want to say . . . you want done." JPK telegram to FDR, January 13, 1938. PSF 37 /Kennedy, FDRL. Also in HTF, pp. 235–236.

8 "[T]he job of Ambassador . . . hurt in your life." NH, p. 213.

CHAPTER 1

11 "suffocated . . . strangers by the thousand." JPK Diary, February 23, 1938.

11 "I'm just a babe . . . lion's mouth." *NYT*, February 24, 1938.

13 "In those days . . . Valentino." CH, p. 170.

13 "distinguished citizen . . . His Majesty the King." FDR to King George VI, January 1, 1938; and CH to JPK, January 17, 1938. SD 123.

13–14 "rough-hewn . . . do nuances." Author interview with Page Huidekoper, April 5, 2007.

14 "warm, kindly, considerate." FB, p. 88.

14 "Include the U.S. out." Author interview with Page Huidekoper, April 5, 2007.

16 "My uncle . . . worth the candle." Andrew Barrow, *Gossip*, p. 92.

16 "forebode ill . . . Czechoslovakia." DM, 1, p. 8.

16 "The president had given . . . on my own." HTF, p. 225.

16–17 "Be careful about one thing . . . could not be doubted." Ibid.

18 "This had been a good week for Dictators . . . his scalp." MG, p. 588.

18   "To tell you the truth . . . floundering." DM, 1, pp. 11–12.
18   "Locke, Milton . . . Lloyd George." CH, *Memoirs,* as quoted in CB, p. 337.
18   "slumped shoulders and downcast eyes." DKG, *No Ordinary Time*, p. 30.
18–19 "I have no misgivings . . . on a boat." JPK to William Gonzales, January 10, 1937, as cited in HTF, p. 235.
19   "sense of social . . . foreign policy." DM, 1, pp. 5–6.
19   "Friend after friend . . . difficult to resist them." DM, 1, p. 7.
19   "a gesture of independence . . . own traditions." DM, 1, p. 6.
19–20 "This race . . . real benefit." DM, 1, p. 8.
20   "a bantering postscript . . . couple of weeks' holiday." DM, 1, p. 7.

CHAPTER 2

21   uncharacteristically nervous. *NYT*, March 2, 1938.
21   "terrified . . . chew gum upon his arrival." Author interview with Page Huidekoper Wilson, April 5, 2007.
22   Condition of Prince's Gate from State Department files, quoted in CH, pp. 172–173.
23   "I have a beautiful . . . in my life." JPK letter to James Roosevelt, March 3, 1938: /James Roosevelt/Box 40, FDRL.
24   "Joseph Kennedy . . . 'Who's Who.' " JPK scrapbooks, Series 8.9 Clippings, Scrapbooks and Magazines, 1934–1944, Box 206, Scrapbooks, 1938, "Kennedy's nomination as ambassador to Great Britain," JPKP.
24   "watched me daily . . . a cad, sir!' " DM, 2, p. 2.
24   "I'll ring for the porter . . . surroundings." Rabbi Stephen Wise letter to FDR, March 4, 1938. PSF: Diplomatic: Great Britain: Kennedy: 1938–June 1939, FDRL.
24   "plainly horrified . . . sprang on him." JPK Diary. March 3, 1938.
25   "tall, spare, and aesthetic-looking man." DM, 2, p. 3.
25   "must not get in a mess counting on us to bail them out." JPK letter to Arthur Krock, March 21, 1938: JPKP/ "Political letters of JPK." Also in HTF, pp. 246–247.
25   "JK is going to be very helpful . . . broken." Rabbi Stephen Wise letter to FDR, March 4, 1938. PSF: Diplomatic: Great Britain: Kennedy: 1938–June 1939, FDRL.
26   "Politics . . . of reason." Chamberlain letter to Sir John Simon as quoted in MG, p. 157, and RB, p. 37.
26   "In manner . . . individual oar." Sir Arthur Salter quoted in Robert Rhodes James, *Churchill: A Study in Failure*, pp. 356–357.
26   "I talked to him quite plainly . . . well." JPK Diary, March 4, 1938.
26   "You can't expect me . . . next season." *NYT*, March 5, 1938.
26   "the triumph . . . to date." JPK Diary, March 5, 1938.
27   "I couldn't have done . . . best answer." Joseph P. Kennedy to James Landis, March 22, 1938, in James Landis Papers, Library of Congress, Office Files, Box 24. Also cited in RB, p. 33.
27   "filled . . . golfing triumph." JPK Diary, March 6, 1938.
27   "I am much happier . . . hole in nine." Joe McCarthy, *The Remarkable Kennedys*, p. 55, and DK, p. 122.
27   "Dubious about the hole in one." FF, p. 210.
27   "It's a quarter past . . . footmen." KR, p. 160.
27   "almost boyish looking . . . (without a beard)." KAW, p. 28. Reference cited in this book is incorrect.
27–28 "The show . . . loving 'the king.' " JPK Diary, March 8, 1938.
28   "by no means . . . here." Ibid.
28   JPK's indiscretion. FF, p. 211.
28   "less important . . . trousers." DK, p. 122.
28   "It is both unfair . . . that was to come." DM, 2, p. 8.

28   "In my mind . . . immediate future." JPK Diary, March 9, 1938.
29   "had been headed for a fall . . . a fallacy." DM, 2, p. 9.
29   "Nobody . . . wants it." JPK letter to FDR: FDRL/PSF 37/Kennedy.
29   "stay prosperous . . . economic stand." Ibid.
30   "She said that . . . socializing with adults." LL, p. 237.
30   "seemed fascinated . . . diplomatic scene." TTR, p. 217.
30   "Hurry that boat up . . . all of you." Telegram, JPK to RFK, March 12, 1938, Series 3.5, Family Correspondence, File 1991–1994, Box 55, "Joseph P. Kennedy, letters to family members," JPKP.
30   "I talked to Mr. Kennedy . . . nine children." CC, p. 150.
30–31 Chamberlain luncheon. GS, pp. 243–244, and HF, p. 91.
31   "I hope England . . . don't spoil it." Michael Bloch, *Ribbentrop*, p. 187.
31   "the last time I saw Herr von Ribbentrop . . . before he was hanged." GS, pp. 243–244.
31   "There is not . . . no time for marriage." David Pryce-Jones, *Unity Mitford*, p. 197.
31   "the entire population . . . dastardly outrage." Correspondence between Unity Mitford and Winston Churchill, Churchill Archives. CHAR 2/328. Reproduced with permission of Curtis Brown Ltd, London, on behalf of The Estate of Winston Churchill. Copyright Winston S. Churchill.
32   "The gravity . . . ward off the danger." NGI, pp. 159–162.
32   "some of the leading men . . . let the public know." JPK Diary, March 15, 1938.
32   "as vivacious . . . as wise as a dowager." Gail Cameron, *Rose: A Biography of Rose Fitzgerald Kennedy*, p. 115. Also in LL, p. 241.

CHAPTER 3

33–34 Joe Jr. and Jack in the U.S. NH, pp. 203–222; KAW, pp. 20–22.
35   "I want to see the dredger, Daddy." New York City's *Evening Journal*, March 18, 1938.
35   "Now I have got . . . just grand." LL, p. 240.
35   KATHLEEN, AGED 18, IS IN LOVE. KK, pp. 24–25.
35   "remarkable . . . Kennedys." Newspaper clipping, in Series 8.9, Box 207, Loose News Clippings, 1938, JPKP.
35   "The U.S.A.'s Nine-Child Envoy . . . His Country." KAD, p. 83.
35–36 "There are . . . outstripping the Quints." *Life*, April 11, 1938, p. 17.
36   George Buchanan's threats. SD 123 and CH, p. 175.
37   "like birds of paradise . . . in tweeds." LL, p. 242.
37–38 "He particularly hated . . . to the United States." David Heymann, *RFK*, p. 25.
38   "I was never . . . very rare." Author interview with the dowager duchess of Devonshire, March 21, 2005.
38   "did not have an intellectual bone in her body." Author interview with Page Huidekoper Wilson, April 5, 2007.
38   "happy, natural smile." TTR, p. 220.
39   "little make-up . . . lipstick." REFK Diary, March 25, 1938.
39   "suggestions for your consideration." SD 123. Also cited in HTF, pp. 243–244.
39   "so representative . . . America." LT, March 19, 1938.
39   "that it was difficult . . . the British." JPK to Arthur Krock, March 21, 1938: JPKP/ "Political letters of JPK," JFKL. Also HTF, pp. 246–247.
39–40 "we should . . . the other." DM 3, pp. 9–12.
40   "fell flat." JPK Diary, March 18, 1938.
40   Letters to Walter Lippmann . . . Senators Wheeler, Byrnes, Harrison, Pittman. KR, p. 165.
40–41 "The march of events . . . general interest." JPK to Arthur Krock, March 21, 1938 and March 28, 1938: JPKP/ "Political letters of JPK," JFKL. Also in HTF, pp. 246–249.

41   "the fundamental basis . . . Belgium." *LT*, March 25, 1938.

41   "masterpiece . . . Opposition." JPK letter to Arthur Krock, March 28, 1938: JPKP/ "Political Letters of JPK," JFKL. Also in HTF, pp. 247–249.

41   "After a boa . . . civilization." NGI, p. 165.

41   "[s]he sat . . . groomed." REFK Diary, March 29, 1938.

41   "one to rule the roost." JPK Diary, March 29, 1938.

42   "there was a fearsome . . . do." Author interview with the dowager duchess of Devonshire, March 21, 2005.

42   "How many toes . . . shoes and count." CH, pp. 174–175, and KC, p. 102. Neither author documents the exact source for this anecdote.

42   "Well, you see . . . *O weh ist mir!*" JPK letter to Lady Astor, May 10, 1938: Series 8.2.1 Correspondent File, London 1938–1940, Box 101A. "Astor, Viscountess Nancy," JPKF.

43   "scared to death . . . of them." KK letter to LB, April 29, 1938. DKG, p. 541.

43   "kindred soul . . . intelligence." REFK quoted in DKG, p. 542.

43   "very chummy . . . mad freshmen." KK letter to LB, April 29, 1938, DKG, p. 541.

43   "quite envied . . . last three youngsters." REFK Diary, March 30, 1938.

43   "She is great . . . marvelous." TTR, p. 245.

43   "Well, I am . . . lot of children." Article on REFK, *Boston Globe*, May 13, 2007.

43   "her husband . . . for lunch." JPK Diary, April 4, 1938.

43   Unity Mitford in Hyde Park. *Daily Mail*, April 11, 1938.

44   "driven . . . home." *NYT*, April 11, 1938.

44   "one of the most . . . East Boston." TTR, p. 221.

44–45   "When they remember . . . charming me." DM, 5, pp. 6B–6C.

45   "If you want him . . . victory." DM, 5, pp. 6C–6D.

45   "There was something . . . feel afraid." REFK Diary, April 9, 1938.

45   "believing that tragedy . . . happy families." Article on REFK, *Boston Globe*, May 13, 2007.

CHAPTER 4

47   "Your story . . . quite bad." JPK telegram to Drew Pearson, May 3, 1938: JPKP/ "Pearson, Drew and Allen." Also in HTF, p. 255.

47   "Certainly not . . . selected riff-raff." JPK Diary, May 5, 1938.

48   "clean-cut, humorous, and intelligent." Dorothy Hermann, *Anne Morrow Lindbergh: A Gift for Life*, p. 199.

49   "Society had been dominated . . . family silver." LSOP, p. 56.

49   "the most utterly . . . imaginable." TTR, p. 225.

49   "My train . . . very quickly." KK Diary, May 11, 1938.

50   "glamorous beyond belief." TTR, p. 225.

50   "more fun . . . with no partners." KK Diary, May 13, 1938.

50   "All the mothers say . . . night club afterwards." REFK Diary, May 1, 1939.

51   "in which everyone . . . a *Lambeth Walk*." Sally Bedell Smith, *Reflected Glory: The Life of Pamela Churchill Harriman*, p. 43.

51   "He acts . . . enchanting smile." REFK Diary, May 17, 1938.

51   "won the libidinous interest of the American ambassador." Sylvia Morris, *Rage For Fame*, p. 318.

52   "made all the preparations . . . too great." KF, p. 354.

52   "He is a very old man . . . rest of his days." Andrew Barrow, *Gossip*, p. 94.

52   "We seem to be living . . . of hand." JPK to James Roosevelt, May 31, 1938: FDRL/ James Roosevelt/Box 40. Also quoted in HTF, pp. 258–259.

52   "Joe Kennedy was . . . over Czechoslovakia." Harold L. Ickes, *The Secret Diaries of Harold L. Ickes*, 11, p. 405.

52–53   "everyone had decorations . . . gloves for all." KK Diary, May 23, 1938.

53   "carnival atmosphere . . . for Ascot." REFK Diary, June 1, 1938.
53   "forced to leave . . . crooning." KK Diary, June 1, 1938.
53   "quite a sweat . . . London." KK Diary, June 2, 1938.
54   "Our brawl went . . . wonderbar." KK to LB, April 29, 1938, DKG, p. 544.
54–55 Kennedy and von Dirksen meetings. *Documents of German Foreign Policy, 1918–1945, I*, pp. 713–718; Koskoff, pp.136–138; KAD, p. 87; CH, pp. 184–185.
55   "complete poppycock." HTF, p. 232.
55   "some muddling of the verifiable facts." Ibid.
55–56 totalitarian propaganda . . . throughout South America. SD 123. NA and CH, p. 180.
56   Werner Gudenberg's arrest. William Breuer, *Hitler's Unknown War*, as quoted in CH, pp. 180–181.
56   "The Duke of Kent . . . on her head." KK Diary, June 22, 1938.
56   "romantic spot . . . the bridge." KK Diary, June 24, 1938.
56   "The debs, too . . . best bidder." LSOP, p. 116.
57   "black homespun coat . . . satisfaction." REFK Diary, June 14, 1938.
57   "Well, if that's not just like Hollywood." TTR, p. 231.
57   "was a heart-warming . . . royal family was." TTR, p. 233.
57   "flicking cherry stones across the table." KK Diary, June 19, 1938.

CHAPTER 5

59   "beguiling . . . Rooseveltian personality." *Washington Post*, March 1938.
60   "No one can lightly . . . the United States." DM, 9, p. 3.
60   "I enlisted . . . President Roosevelt." DM, 9, pp. 5–9.
60   "Mr. Roosevelt . . . succeeded." DM, 9, p. 3–4.
60   "did not . . . objectives or techniques." DM, 9, pp. 5–6.
60   "castle or the outhouse." Nancy Clinch, *The Kennedy Neurosis*, p. 20.
61   "action . . . I think." DM, 9, p. 4.
61   "holding court . . . Baptist Hospital." JFK to LB, June 15, 1938, in NH, p. 227.
61   His gastric problems . . . Jack was allergic. *Time*, October 6, 1958, as mentioned in Perret, *Jack*, p. 69.
61   He would be damned . . . *his* "honors." KAW, p. 50.
61   "It was a terrible blow . . . never be admitted." Interview with Rose Kennedy in DKG, pp. 534–535.
61   "Can you imagine . . . degree from Harvard?" Harold L. Ickes, *The Secret Diaries of Harold L. Ickes*, as quoted in FF, p. 229.
62   "Kennedy's 1940 Ambitions . . . White House." KR, p. 171.
62   "The statement . . . answer it." JPK to Malcolm Bingay, July 22, 1938: American Newspapers, 7–9/'38. JPKP.
62   "president's real concern . . . recovery program." FF, p. 230.
62–63 "It was a true . . . something had happened." DM, 9, p. 9.
63   "Far too much time . . . affairs." DM, 9, p. 8.
64   "a little too impulsive . . . much about." Arthur Krock Oral History, JFKL.
65   "racial . . . concern us both." LT, July 5, 1938.
65   "the most roseate . . . to help." Chamberlain diary as quoted in KR, p. 174.
66   "Who would . . . such a noose? GS, p. 249.
66   "We are proud . . . honor our race." Maier, *The Kennedys: America's Emerald Kings*, p. 121.
66   "My parents . . . should come." Maier, p. 120. Also *NYT*, July 8, 1938.
66   "quite necessary . . . God and country." Hugh Fraser Oral History, JFKL. Also quoted in KAW, pp. 60–61.
66–67 "very generous . . . become them." Interview with the dowager duchess of Devonshire, March 21, 2005.

68   "Popular Girl Number One." KK, p. 43. Other information on Joe Jr. in LP, pp. 115–
        123, and BL, p. 50.
68   "a tattoo of a snake winding up her leg." and other descriptions of the Londonderrys.
        Anne de Courcy, *Society's Queen.*
68–69 "never drew . . . to bed." Interview with Jane Ormsby-Gore, May 29, 2006.
69   Jack Kennedy, David Ormsby-Gore, Hugh Fraser, and their political development are
        covered in BL.
69   "sent down . . . the group." Interview with the dowager duchess of Devonshire, March
        21, 2005.
69   "took things . . . of things." And cautioning Jack. Interview with Pamela, Lady Har-
        lech, May 28, 2006.
70   "it was a formal . . . each other." Interview with Ted Kennedy, June 12, 2007.
70   100,000 refugees. CB, p. 488.
70   "two kinds . . . could not enter." Commonly repeated phrase, quoted in Holocaust sec-
        tion of the Imperial War Museum.
71   "Certain nations . . . ahead of us." JPK Speech, July 12, 1938. Series 8.4, Box 155, JPKP.
71   "This morning . . . with the English." JPK to State Department, July 20, 1938: "1938,
        July to Dept.," JPKP. Also HTF, pp. 267–268.
72   "rather smart . . . the same." REFK Diary, July 18, 1938.
72   Rose recalled . . . that afternoon. As recounted in DKG, p. 545.
72   "very hot day . . . bowed." KK Diary, July 18, 1938.
72   "was a charmer . . . could imagine." Interview with the dowager duchess of Devon-
        shire, March 21, 2005.
72   "a fairly formed . . . serious politician." Interview with Lady Anne Tree, May 30,
        2006.
73   "is wildly in love . . . watch it, Kick." DKG, p. 543.
73–74 "I'm here . . . at the races." LL, p. 261.
74   "Peter Grace . . . the Devonshires." KK Diary, July 25, 1938.
75   "She is very sharp . . . papal shadow." The duke of Devonshire to Lady Astor, Septem-
        ber 12, 1938, KAW, p. 57.

CHAPTER 6

76   "azure blue, clear, deep sea." REFK Diary, July 25, 1938.
76–77 "her hair . . . about make-up" and sour milk. REFK Diary, July 26–27, 1938.
76   "Blue Mediterranean . . . golf." DM, 12, p. 1.
76–77 "His broad smile . . . generous to a fault." EMK on JPK, FB, p. 204.
77   "The greater . . . support he gave." RFK on JPK, FB, p. 211.
77   "Why did I . . . out of touch." Article on REFK, *Boston Globe*, May 13, 2007.
77   "acute grammarian . . . joyous and upbeat." Interview with Ted Kennedy, June 12,
        2007.
77   Jack confided . . . he had had an affair with Dietrich. Edward Renehan's interview with
        Claiborne Pell, KAW, p. 61.
77–78 "As usual . . . losing." REFK Diary, August 13, 1938.
78   "his father . . . on the spot." REFK Diary, August 21, 1938.
78   "over the fact . . . women's culottes." KK Diary, August 14, 1938.
78   "my love in French, German, and English." KK Diary, August 30, 1938.
79   "is still . . . ring around him." JPK to CH, August 30, 1938: JPKP/ 1938 July to Dept
        JPK. Also in HTF, pp. 269–270.
79   "the United States . . . think right." Halifax letter to Lindsay, September 2, 1938, as
        quoted in DK, 145.
79–80 "I should like . . . blood for." KR, p. 174.

80   "In certain parts . . . small ones." *The Evening Standard*, September 2, 1938.

80   "keep cool . . . rest of 1938." *Time*, September 12, 1938.

80   "I manage . . . everybody was disturbed." September 3, 1938, SD 123/110, Joseph P. Kennedy, in RD, p. 82.

80–81 "As you know . . . will understand." FDR to JPK, September 7, 1938: JPKP/ "Roosevelt, Franklin D." and HTF, p. 273.

81   "The young man . . . hard." John Morton Blum, ed., *From the Morgenthau Diaries: Years of Crisis, 1928–1938*, p. 518.

81   "flitting around like a hummingbird in flight." KR, p. 167.

82   "arranged it on top . . . as fountains." REFK Diary, September 2–5, 1938.

82   "terrifically expensive . . . exclusive design." REFK Diary, September 6, 1938.

82   "instead of indulging . . . half-century." JPK Diary, September 6, 1938.

83   Chamberlain's reasons for not threatening Hitler, RS, p. 309.

83   "racking . . . Halifax's breath away." KF, p. 357.

84   "How can he tell . . . themselves?" JPK Diary, September 8, 1938.

84   "My own observation . . . failed to see." JPK to CH, September 10, 1938: JPKP/ "1938, Sept. to Dept." Also in HTF, p. 274.

84   "be more specific . . . circumstances." CH to JPK, FRUS 1938, I, pp. 568–569. Also in DK, p. 147.

85   "[Kennedy] wondered . . . intervention." Halifax letter to Lindsay, September 10, 1938, as quoted in DK, p. 149.

85   "this miserable pygmy . . . Jew Devil." DKG, p. 552.

85   "grave . . . buildings bombed." David Pryce-Jones, *Unity Mitford*, pp. 211–212.

86   Joe called Roosevelt and asked him to move two cruisers. *The Diplomatic Diaries of Oliver Harvie.*

86   "I go sometimes only to read the newspapers." Lindbergh, *The Wartime Journals*, p. 79.

86   "There was a new glint . . . wonders in Germany." RD, p. 87.

87   Jack listening at Hyannisport. BL, p. 63.

87   "shrill . . . possibility." DM, 14, p. 2.

87   "to keep . . . prospective victims." KR, pp. 177–178.

88   "If the German Chancellor . . . peace of the world." JPK to CH, September 14, 1938: JPKP/ "1938 Sept. to Dept." Also in HTF, pp. 275–276.

88   "Everyone ready . . . moral support." REFK Diary, September 15, 1938.

88–89 "astounded . . . by half." Shirer, *The Rise and Fall of the Third Reich*, p. 383.

89   Chamberlain's previous flight. NC to Hilda, February 24, 1923, quoted in RS, p. 312.

89   "We should . . . any better." *The Complete Idiot's Guide to Germany*, p. 195.

89   "thoroughly convinced . . . hard look." DM, 14, p. 14.

89   "solve the problem . . . the better." DM, 14, pp. 14–15.

89–90 The prime minister skillfully cornering Hitler. RS, p. 312.

90   "very favorably impressed . . . my aim." NC to Ida, September 19, 1938, NCDL, p. 348.

90   "I am the most popular man in Germany." Ibid, p. 349.

90   "As usual . . . actual event." Graham Stewart, *Burying Caesar*, p. 300.

90   "We seem to be . . . adverse terms." MG, p. 595.

90   "the commonest . . . ever seen." RS, p. 312.

90   "In spite . . . his word." NC to Ida, September 19, 1938, NCDL, p. 348.

CHAPTER 7

91   "The telephone still rings . . . U.S.A." REFK Diary, September 18, 1938.

91   "[t]he whole plan . . . inevitable." JPK to CH, September 19, 1938: JPKP "1938, Sept. to Dept." Also in HTF, pp. 278–279.

91   "the British . . . not inevitable." JPK to CH, September 21, 1938: JPKP "1938, Sept. to
        Dept." Also in HTF, pp. 279–280.
92   "while Kennedy . . . the White House." HTF, p. 281.
92   "He was rosy . . . England's one." REFK Diary, September 21, 1938.
92   "The English . . . 'lion's den.'" Lindbergh Diary, September 21, 1938, in *The Wartime
        Journals of Charles A. Lindbergh*. New York: Harcourt Brace Jovanovich, 1970.
92   "For the first time . . . protect themselves." DM, 15, p. 5.
93   "the most terrible . . . of a State." WM, p. 338.
93   "The belief . . . fatal delusion." Christopher Sykes, *Nancy: The Life of Lady Astor*,
        p. 194.
93   "few days . . . United States." DM, 15, p. 1.
93   "You are . . . from me." WM, p. 344.
93–94   "shouting and shrieking . . . holy will." William L. Shirer, *Berlin Diary*, p. 118.
94   "did not applaud . . . like animals." CB, p. 474.
94   "All over London . . . protection services." DM, 15, p. 11.
94   "listening to the radio for news flashes." KK Diary, September 16, 1938.
94–95   "All you can hear . . . sick of it." KK to LB, September 23, 1938, JFKL, BL, p. 67.
95   "I will smash the Czechs." Christopher Sykes, *Nancy: The Life of Lady Astor*, p. 197.
95   Suggestions from FDR for Chamberlain. DM, 16, p. 5.
95   "How horrible . . . is irresistible." *LT*, September 27, 1938.
96   "Today individual . . . depressed." REFK Diary, September 27, 1938.
96   "very blue . . . God only knows." DKG, p. 558.
96   "who wants . . . the ice cream." REFK Diary, September 29, 1938.
96   "I hear that the war is very bad." JK to her parents, Sept. 29, 1938, JPKP. Also in HTF,
        pp. 289–290.
96   "I want you . . . proud of you." DK, p. 154.
96–97   "the solemn House . . . had ever known." CC, p. 170.
97   100 million people. CB, p. 475.
97   "We were all . . . approaching." HN, pp. 369–371.
97   "his whole face . . . triumphant." HN, pp. 370–371.
97   "That is not all . . . will be." GS, p. 284.
97   "like the biggest . . . heard." *Daily Mail*, September 29, 1938.
97   "We stood . . . enthusiasm." CC, p. 171.
97   "I never was so thrilled in my life." JPK, Diary, September 28, 1938.
97   "[N]ever again . . . dramatic speech." JPK to CH, September 28, 1938: JPKP "1938,
        Sept. to Dept." Also in HTF, pp. 288–289.
97   "I congratulate . . . lucky." HN, 1930–1939, p. 371.
98   "Well boys, the war is off." DM, 16, p. 16.
98   "the news came . . . such happiness." KK Diary, September 28–October 3, 1938.
98   "[I]t may be . . . once again." JPK Diary, September 28, 1938.
98   Nicolson was gloomy. HN, p. 371.
98   "GOOD MAN." DM, 16, p. 16.
98   "I fully share . . . justice and law." KR, p. 177.
98   "I had a feeling . . . kept it." FF, p. 244.
98   Stripping Czechoslovakia of its resources. RD, p. 96.
98–99   "[T]hat scrap . . . whatsoever." Bloch, *Ribbentrop*, p. 214.
99   "our enemies are small worms." IK, pp. 122–123.
99   "We all feel . . . question." REFK Diary, September 30, 1938.
99   "Kennedy . . . conference . . ." Lindbergh, *The Wartime Journals*, p. 79.
99   "He was kind . . . support." JPK Diary, October 6, 1938.
99   "this is . . . our time." KF, p. 376.
99   "it is . . . at stake." *LT*, September 26, 1938.
100   "The Prime Minister . . . mailed fist." WM, p. 364.
100   "sat quietly . . . criticism and blame." DM, 17, p. 2.

100   "that we have . . . olden time." MG, p. 600.

101   "singularly unimpressive." DM, 17, p. 1.

101   "fascinating . . . to follow." REFK Diary, October 5, 1938.

101   "quiet . . . way." REFK Diary, October 6, 1938.

101   Chamberlain close to a nervous breakdown. RS, p. 329.

102   "The stations . . . consult together." Martin Gilbert, *Churchill and America*, p. 169.

102   "virtuous idealism . . . peace that follows." DM, 20, p. 5.

CHAPTER 8

103   "I was sick . . . phone occasionally." REFK Diary, October 7, 1938.

103   Joe ordering gas masks. REFK Diary, October 3, 1938.

104   Luncheon with Baroness Ravensdale. REFK Diary, October 12, 1938.

104   "At times . . . his position." and Cudahy visit. REFK Diary, October 16, 1938.

105   "I think . . . many pitfalls." DM, 17, p. 1.

106   "He was forced . . . should not raise." DM, 18, p. 2.

105–106   "It has . . . like it or not." *New York Post*, October 20, 1938.

106–107   "one minute . . . out of." JPK to T. J. White, November 12, 1938: JPKP/Series 8.2.1, Correspondent File, London, 1938–1940, Box 109 "J1938." "White, Thomas Justin." Also in HTF, pp. 299–300.

107   "make a friend . . . understanding." *NYT,* October 21, 1938.

107   "Peace by fear . . . threat of war." CB, p. 484.

107   "Amateur . . . policy of their own." Walter Lippmann, "The Ambassador Speaking," "Today and Tomorrow" column, October 22, 1938. HTF, p. 301.

107   "It must . . . hair of the dog." KR, p. 178.

108   "hardly prepared . . . this onslaught." KR, p. 178, and DM, Chapter 18, p. 5.

108   "I am so . . . two weeks." KR, p. 179.

108   "It is unbelievable . . . free country." Trafalgar Day Speech files, Series 8.4, Box 155, JPKP.

108   "75% of the attacks . . . their advantage." JPK to T. J. White, November 12, 1938: JPKP/Series 8.2.1, Correspondent File, London, 1938–1940, Box 109 "J 1938." "White, Thomas Justin." Also in HTF, pp. 299–300.

109   "The belief . . . done before." HTF, p. 233.

109   "was appalled . . . in the embassy." Author interview with Page Huidekoper Wilson, April 5, 2007.

109   "Steyne . . . bow to Britain's monarch." GB, p. 145.

109   "I haven't been in the same place since." FF, p. 389

109   "natural Jewish . . . U.S. to stomach." JPK, Jr., "Answer to Lippmann Editorial Against Dad," November 14, 1938, HTF, p. 301.

109–110   "While . . . anti-fascist." FF, p. 249.

110   "the imponderables of the human spirit," and Wheeler-Bennett relationship. BL, p. 74.

110   "is looking better . . . little difficulty." Dr. Sara Jordan to JPK, October 25, 1938: JPKP/Series 8.2.1, Correspondent File, London, 1938–1940, Box 109 "J 1938," as quoted in HTF, p. 298.

110   "I worry . . . very soon." JPK to Dr. Sara Jordan, November 4, 1938: Ibid.

110   "a series of hideous . . . Jewish community." DM, 19, p. 5.

111   "[T]his last drive . . . could be gained." JPK to Charles Lindbergh, November 12, 1938: JPKP/ "Charles A. Lindbergh," JPKP. Also in HTF, pp. 300–301.

111   "most terrible . . . say a lot more." The *Star* newspaper of December 16, 1938, pasted in REFK Diary, December 16, 1938.

111   "should not . . . my share of it." DM, 18, p. 4.

111–112   "I myself . . . not in contemplation." FDR Press Conference #500, FDRL. 94% of Americans disapproved. CB, pp. 491–492.

112   "If the president . . . best I can." JPK to CH, October 28, 1938: JPKP/ "1938, Oct. to
       Dept." Also in HTF, p. 297.
112   "diamond tiara . . . launching that style." REFK Diary, November 15, 1938.
112–113 "You, Freddy . . . a political alliance." KR, p. 187.
113   "ease the public conscience." NCDL, p. 345.
113   "rather fat . . . with nice dimples." KK Diary, November 15, 1938.
114   "no attempt . . . broadest details." DM 18, p. 7.
114   "one . . . ills of the world." DM 18, p. 11.

                          CHAPTER 9

115   "how deeply grateful . . . in Alaska." Jewish Letters to JPK in Series 8.5, Box 163, Jew-
       ish problem, JPKP.
116   "If political . . . supplied." DM 19, p. 14.
116   "problem of financing . . . in spirit." DM 19, p. 8.
116   "that it looked . . . any solution." JPK to CH, November 18, 1938: JPKP/ "1938, Nov.
       to Dept." Also in HTF, pp. 302–303.
116   "countries . . . volunteered." REFK Diary, November 13, 1938.
116   Ceding British Guiana to the United States. Interview with Chamberlain's biographer
       Bob Self, Roosevelt MSS OF48A/41, FDRL; and Welles to FDR, January 11, 1939,
       Roosevelt OF48/2.
116   "I was both disturbed . . . situation." DM, 19, p. 5.
116–117 "talked . . . British Commonwealth." NYT, November 15, 1938.
117   "Among the extensive . . . of bird-watching." HTF, pp. 232–233.
117   "[i]f any contribution . . . from me." JPK to CH, November 18, 1938: JPKP/ "1938,
       Nov. to Dept." Also in HTF, pp. 302–303.
117   "What Mr. Kennedy . . . the moment." NYT, November 27, 1938.
117–118 "For months . . . tape and details." TTR, p. 243.
118   "was active . . . Jews escape." TTR, p. 243.
118   Jewish children emigrating. 123 JPK, SD. CH, p. 193.
118   "favoritism . . . department in my life." Letters to and from JPK, "K 1938" folder, in
       Ambassadorial Correspondence files, 8.2.1, JPKP.
118   Letters to and from Arthur Goldsmith. In "Letters to and from Eddie Moore," Series
       8.2.3, Eddie Moore Files, Box 134, JPKP.
119   "a political trick timed to soften a blow." DM, 19, p. 7.
119   "whether . . . cold cash." JPK Jr., "November 21," November 21, 1938: JPKP/ "JPK Jr.
       Mss-England." Also in HTF, p. 303.
119   "All Billy's relatives . . . an eyeful." KK Diary, November 23, 1938.
119   "rather frightening . . . dirty looks." KK Diary, December 9, 1938.
120   "going wild . . . inspiring ceremony." REFK Diary, December 4, 1938.
120   "is hipped . . . wholesale murder." JPK Jr., "Visit to Plymouth," December 6, 1938:
       JPKP/ "JPK Jr. Mss-England." Also in HTF, pp. 304–305.
120   "he was . . . difficulties of the present." LT, December 7, 1938.
120   "I don't know . . . outlook now." JPK to Charles Lindbergh, December 8, 1938: JPKP/
       "Charles A. Lindbergh." Also in HTF, p. 305.
121   "If I believed . . . rational manner." DM, 20, p. 13.
121   "firm up . . . to terms." Ibid.
121   "Dad claims . . . days." December 6, 1938: JPKP/ "JPK Jr. Mss-England." Also in HTF,
       pp. 304–305.
121   "I hope . . . the other night." RFK to JPK, December 11, 1938. Series 3.5, Family Cor-
       respondence File 1910–1994, Box 55, REFKP.
121   "I am going home . . . thinking about America." NYT, December 16, 1938, p. 13.

122   "a weak . . . Nazi ideals." DM, 20, p. 15.

122   "nothing. . . . second-war." DK, p. 182.

122   "I am . . . for peace." *NYT*, December 16, 1938.

122   "ringed . . . have to die." DM, 20, p. 16.

122   "had seemed . . . Hyannis Port." HTF, p. 224.

123   Walter Winchell's scoop. FF, p. 257.

124   "sleighs . . . the sleighs." REFK Diary, December 24, 1938.

124–125 "We had . . . been here." Family letters to JPK, December 26–27, 1938. Series 11, Family Correspondence 1938, Box 2, REFKP.

125   "a riot . . . stories about him." REFK to JPK, n.d., December 1938, Series 11, Family Correspondence 1938, Box 2, REFKP.

125   "Look . . . doesn't it?" and his accident. LP, p. 125.

125   "ASSOCIATED PRESS . . . JOE." HTF, p. 306.

125   "all the interesting . . . conferred upon Joe." FF, p. 258.

126   "It's pretty funny . . . that signifies." JFK to REFK and JPK, n.d. (fall 1938), Series 3.5, Family Correspondence. Box 56, "JFK '34–'39," JPKP.

126   New Year's Eve. REFK Diary, December 31, 1938.

126   "It has . . . will be worse." HN, p. 384.

CHAPTER 10

129   "Few years . . . 1939." RK, p. 17.

129   "There comes . . . of earth." RK, p. 24.

130   "People feel . . . was denied." KK to JPK, February 3, 1939. Series 1.1, Box 2, Family Correspondence 1939, JPKP.

130   "The weather . . . over the place." PK to JPK, January 25, 1939. Series 1.1, Box 2, Family Correspondence 1939, JPKP.

130   "it is rainy . . . darling." REFK to JPK, n.d., February 1939. Series 1.1, Box 2, Family Correspondence 1939, JPKP.

130   "Mother runs . . . in Christies." KK to JPK, January 25, 1939. Series 1.1, Box 2, Family Correspondence 1939, JPKP.

130   "Joe is teaching . . . extreme anguish." KK to JPK, January 17, 1939 and January 25, 1939. Series 1.1, Box 2, Family Correspondence 1939, JPKP.

130   "Mother left . . . cup of tea." KK to JPK, February 3, 1939. Series 1.1, Box 2, Family Correspondence 1939, JPKP.

130–131 Kick's winter social schedule. KK Diary, January 13–February 24, 1939.

131   "very nice, but enormous." KK Diary, February 9, 1939.

131   ("What about Unity I ask myself.") KK Diary, February 17, 1939.

131   "goes out . . . for mail." REFK to JPK, n.d., February 1939. Series 1.1, Box 2, Family Correspondence 1939, JPKP.

131   "inquired . . . rather pessimistic." JPK, Jr. to JPK, January 25, 1939. Series 1.1, Box 2, Family Correspondence 1939, JPKP.

132   "It is . . . with America." RK, pp. 95–98.

132   "the nervous strain . . . appalling." Lindsay to Welles, FRUS, 1939, I, pp. 18–20.

132   Herschel Johnson's report. FRUS, 1939, I, pp. 3–7.

132   "I never say . . . make trouble." DM, 21, pp. 12–13.

133   "totally unable . . . policy at all." NC to Hilda Chamberlain, February 19, 1939, NCDL, p. 383.

133   "to complete . . . international body." CB, pp. 504–505.

133   "The fog . . . wanderlust." TTR, p. 243.

133   "thrilling day . . . love Rosa." REFK to JPK, February 18, 1939. Series 1.1, Box 2, Family Correspondence 1939, JPKP.

133–134 "Sorry . . . Regards. Joe." LP, p. 130.
134   "damage . . . absolute helplessness." JPK Jr. to JPK, February 15, 1939: JPKP/ "Spain."
         Also in HTF, pp. 311–312.
134   "Hundreds of people . . . in no time." JPK Jr. to JPK, February 16, 1939: JPKP/ "Spain."
         Also in HTF, p. 314.
135   "Thank you . . . sees me." RK to JPK, two letters: February 27, 1939, and February ??,
         n.d. Series 1.1, Box 2, Family Correspondence 1939, JPKP.
136   "impractical . . . to disbelieve it." JPK to CH, FRUS, 1939, I, pp. 15–17.
136   "These men . . . lose their Empire." *Ciano's Diary*, pp. 9–10.
136   "vociferous . . . have been crushed." DM, 22, p. 8.
136–137 "are behaving . . . brutal realities." NC to Hilda Chamberlain, February 19, 1939,
         NCDL, p. 384.
137   "giving the Arabs . . . Charlie McCarthy" and reports of meetings. DK, p. 188.
137   "Why hadn't they . . . this before?" DK, p. 181.

                              CHAPTER 11

138   "glorified office boy" and Jack's debut. GP, p. 72.
138   "Been working . . . mightily attractive." JFK to LB, March 1939, NH, p. 255.
138   Lem Billings's same-sex attractions. David Pitts (*Jack and Lem*) states unequivocally
         that Lem Billings was gay. Sally Bedell Smith (*Grace and Power*) states that he was
         probably gay, Ralph Martin (*Seeds of Destruction*) suggests it. In *Joseph P. Kennedy*,
         Ted Schwarz concluded that he was gay and that Jack and Lem had had an affair in
         prep school.
139   "only human being . . . never obeyed me." Hans Jansen, *The Silent Pope*, quoted in
         www.piusxiiintel.
139   He lobbied . . . the president directly. DK, p. 189.
140   "overwhelming . . . universal appeal." *New York Herald Tribune*, March 14, 1939.
140   "awe-inspiring . . . God." JPK Diary, March 15, 1939.
140   "Everyone . . . worthy peace." JPK, Jr. to JPK, March 8, 1939. HTF, p. 315.
140   "the beauty . . . forgotten experience." DM, 23, p. 6.
141   Offer of papal dukedom and Order of Pius XI. GP, p. 72.
141   "talked to her . . . intimately." JPK Diary, March 13, 1939.
141   "seemed pleased . . . about the crucifix." TTR, p. 244.
141   "I told my sister . . . any." *NYT*, March 14, 1939.
141   "I hope you . . . end of that." AK, p. 127.
141–142 "Pacelli . . . knight you." JFK to LB, March 23, 1939, NH, p. 257.
142   "most saintly . . . this is the man." JPK to Moffat, March 17, 1939, as quoted in DK,
         p. 189.
142   "A more pompous ass . . . fleet of airplanes." JPK to Cordell Hull, March 17, 1939:
         JPKP/ "1938, Mar. to Dept." Also in HTF, pp. 321–322.
142   "I will go down as the greatest German in history." IK, p. 155.
142   "The House of Commons . . . map of Europe." RK, p. 142.
142   "most flagrant . . . in modern time." *DT*, 3/17.
143   "I have . . . that was said?" DM, 24, p. 1.
143   "Is this . . . lost its fibre." KF, p. 400.
143   "as Joe . . . go from here?'" NCDL, p. 394.
143–144 "affectionate birthday . . . only to deepen." JPK to Neville Chamberlain, March 18,
         1939: Series 8.2.1, Correspondent File, London, 1938–1940 Box 104 JPKP/ "Cham-
         berlain, Neville." Also in HTF, p. 322.
144   "I didn't see . . . selfish reasons," JPK Diary, March 18, 1939, JFKL.
144   Hitler might bomb London during presidential visit. JPKP: Notes, 3/17/1939. Series
         8.1, Appointments and Diary, 1938–1951, Box 100, 1939, February Folder, JPKP.

144 "Rose looked . . . smiled sweetly." JPK Diary, March 21, 1939.

145 State banquet compared to the Brussels Ball. NCDL, p. 395.

145 "Everyone thinks . . . though Dad does." JFK to LB, March 23, 1939, in NH, p. 257.

145 "crimson . . . he speaks." JPK Diary, March 21, 1939.

145 "scarlet waistcoat . . . largest ever seen." Anne de Courcy, 1939, The Last Season, pp. 54–58.

145 "Poland . . . Southeastern Europe." JPK to Hull, March 24, 1939. FRUS, 1939, I, p. 99.

146 "an unusual move . . . Franco-Russian pact." CH, p. 199.

146 "it probably means war." DM, 24, p. 15.

146 "In the event . . . their power." KF, p. 403.

147 "I'll brew them a devil's potion." IK, p. 178.

147 "He . . . loses the right to life." IK, p. 178.

CHAPTER 12

148 "The entrance . . . in their cars." LP, p. 140.

148 "The city . . . for joy." JPK Jr. to JPK, March 28, 1939, HTF, p. 323.

149 Potential articles in magazines. HTF, pp. 330–331.

149 "Turn those . . . girls to college." Author interview with Page Huidekoper Wilson, April 5, 2007.

149 Bobby Kennedy's diplomatic debut. "All the temples . . . English children." New York Herald article pasted in REFK Diary, April 1, 1939, and in RFK Youth file in David Heymann papers, Dept. of Special Collections, SUNY Library, Stony Brook, New York.

149 "looked very worn . . . in view." REFK Diary, April 4, 1939.

150 "him and the Offer . . . like George Steele." JFK to LB, March 23, 1939, NG, p. 258.

150 "Offie . . . wipe his arse." David Pitts, Jack and Lem, p. 73.

150 "listening to telegrams . . . throw him out." Orville Bullitt (Ed.), For the President: Personal and Secret, p. 273.

151 "Everyone stunned . . . the weekends." REFK Diary, April 7, 1939.

151 "Winston . . . resisting rash suggestions." NCDL, pp. 403–407.

151 "seemed . . . the moon." RK, p. 177.

151 "If this continues . . . a new map." DM, 26, p. 6.

151 "He has failed . . . talked like one." JPK to CH, April 17, 1939: FRUS, 1939, I, pp. 139–140.

151–152 "friendly intermediary . . . years to come." RK, pp. 178–180.

152 "If we had . . . so enormous." RK, p. 182.

152 "Unbridled . . . desperate alarm." RK, pp. 186–187.

152–153 "lovely and charming . . . served her right." JPK Diary, April 14, 1939.

153 Princess Beatrice story. JPK Diary, April 14–15, 1939.

153–154 "the man . . . down my neck." JPK Diary, April 14–16, 1939.

154 "interest in tightening her defenses." NYT, April 17, 1939.

154 "Nancy Astor . . . devoted to her family." REFK Diary, April 23, 1939.

154–155 "There is no one . . . central Europe." Anne De Courcy, 1939, The Last Season, p. 81.

155 Kennedy reports to Hull on Hitler's economy. DK, p. 194.

155 "talking . . . queen of the May." JPK dispatch to FDR and Hull, April 20, 1939: JPKP/ "1939. Apr. to Dept." Also in HTF, p. 330.

155 "war was not . . . without hope." LT, April 22, 1939.

156 "People . . . comparatively safe." KK to LB, April 30, 1939, DKG, p. 584.

156 "Last night . . . out of this one." LB to KK, April 12, 1939, DKG, p. 584.

156 "Without Russia . . . fellow-countrymen." RK, p. 200.

157   JPK and Davies's opinions. DK, p. 204, and DM, 25, pp. 3–4.
157   "I gather . . . paw gingerly." CC, p. 199.
157   "I can't . . . the latter view." NCDL, June 10, 1939, p. 420.
158   "unfortunate comment." Welles to JPK, May 4, 1939, SD 123, "Kennedy, Joseph P." /199.
158   "Each man . . . constructive." Joe's meeting with Wohltat and Mooney and press headlines. Seymour Hersh, *The Dark Side of Camelot*, pp. 68–69.
158   Mooney's opinion that MI5 had put Kennedy under surveillance. John Costello, *Ten Days That Saved The West*, p. 140. Christopher Anderson's history of the MI5, not yet published as this book goes to print, will reveal the contents of the secret intelligence archives and whether or not Kennedy was under surveillance.

CHAPTER 13

159   "Everyone was rather nervous . . . too extreme." REFK Diary, May 4, 1939.
160   "very elegant . . . as usual," JPK Diary, May 4, 1939.
160   "beautiful satin gown . . . a little weep." REFK Diary, May 4, 1939.
160   "Hitler unsmiling . . . her hero." LSOP, p. 77.
161   "[e]ndless successions . . . at its approximate peak." Jessica Mitford, *Hons and Rebels*, p. 78.
161   "In this way. . . . gas-mask mood." LSOP, p. 9.
161   "he had seen . . . for Kathleen." REFK Diary, May 4, 1939.
162   "pink frock . . . blue turquoise." REFK Diary, May 9, 1939.
162   Visit to Chequers. REFK Diary, May 13, 1939.
162–163 "exquisitely lovely . . . last war." REFK Diary, May 13, 1939.
164–165 "useless to discuss . . . uncompromising attitude." JFK letter to JPK, n.d., Series 5.1, "Letters from JFK 39–42," JFKP.
165   "frightfully upset." JPK letter to Rabbi Solomon Goldman, June 2, 1939, HTF, pp. 336–337.
165   "However . . . type of experience." JPK telegram to Benjamin Cohen, May 16, 1939, HTF, p. 336.
165   "the cruelty . . . exit permits." DM, 29, p. 6.
165–166 JPK and *St. Louis* passengers. Robert N. Rosen, *Saving the Jews*, pp. 99–103.
166   JPK's plans to fly home after royal visit. FF, p. 266.
167   "Everyone unanimous . . . eagerness to cooperate." REFK Diary, June 11, 1938.
167   "the most important handclasp . . . in history." LT, June 10, 1939.
167   "A lot of people . . . on the Deity." FF, p. 267.
167   "In August . . . spoil our vacations." JPK to CH, June 9, 1939: JPKP/ "1939 June to Dept." Also in HTF, pp. 337–338.
167   "Yesterday . . . clothes were ordered." As quoted in RK, p. 208. Also in LSOP, p. 118.
168   "Are you satisfied . . . a tremendous hit." JPK Diary, June 22, 1939.
168   "King George VI . . . at lunch." JPK Diary, June 23, 1939.
168   "I hated those parties . . . ladies' room." Eunice Kennedy as interviewed by Laurence Leamer. LL, p. 278.
168   "a terribly nice girl . . . very pretty." LSOP, p. 137.
168   "Eunice was . . . be around." Interview with the countess of Sutherland, March 19, 2005.
168–169 "doing the 'big apple' . . . reach that state." REFK Diary, June 22, 1939.
169   "Everyone . . . around the house." Interview with the countess of Sutherland, March 19, 2005.
169   "Are we going to fight . . . as a God." JPK, Jr. Travel Essays as quoted in HTF, pp. 338–343.

170   Jack's European tour and story of cigarette case. NH, p. 261.
170   Jack in panel in Vatican. GP, p. 74.
170   "lst The question of Danzig . . . the keystone." JFK to LB, n.d. (May 1939). NH,
      pp. 262–263.
171   "hunched there . . . most sinister men." RD, pp. 141–142.
171   "Why can we . . . this war." Nigel Nicolson (Ed.), *The War Years, 1939–1945*, Vol. II
      of *Harold Nicolson, Diaries and Letters*, p. 152.
171   "That is what . . . month or two." BL, p. 83
172   "I was uncomfortable . . . about politics." Interview with the countess of Sutherland,
      March 19, 2005.
172   "We are creating . . . more united than ever before." and polls as quoted in LSOP,
      pp. 130–131.
172   "Consider well . . . cast away." RK, p. 260.
172   "The whole outlook . . . waiting." CC, June 29, 1939, p. 203.

CHAPTER 14

173   "difficult time . . . no one without." REFK Diary, July 3, 1939.
174   "Having . . . peaceful countryside." Eunice Kennedy, "A Weekend at Blenheim Palace,"
      n.d. (June 1939), HTF, p. 344.
174   "nearly . . . better time." JFK to Lem Billings, July 17, 1939. NH, p. 268.
174   "RossKennedy" and focus on the duchess of Kent. Tony Rosslyn to JFK, November 18,
      1940, JFKL and BL, pp. 87–88.
174   "I have seen much . . . rivers of champagne." CC, pp. 204–205.
174   "Slightly nervous . . . Brussels tapestry." EK, "A Weekend at Blenheim Palace," n.d.
      (June 1939), HTF, p. 344.
174–175 "fascinated . . . monopolize life." AS, p. 83.
175   "[H]e was a skeptic . . . animal recklessness." David Cecil as quoted in Lance Morrow,
      The Best Year of Their Lives, pp. 98–99.
175   "round and round . . . hotdogs!" EK, "A Weekend in Blenheim Palace," n.d. (June
      1939), HTF, p. 344.
175   "the half-cross-eyed . . . not quite." CC, p. 205.
175   "ice blue . . . distress about that!" LL, pp. 279–280.
176   "No . . . other things." REFK Diary, July 12, 1939.
176   "As I entered . . . hold so sacred." EKS Recollections, JFKL cited in LL, p. 280.
176   "international policies . . . trouble inside." JPK to FDR: July 20, 1939/ PSF 37/ "Ken-
      nedy," FDRL.
176   "His are summer storms . . . work with." NC to his sister Ida, August 5, 1939, NCDL,
      p. 438.
177   David Ormsby-Gore's suitcase. Author interviews with Victoria Lloyd, June 2, 2006,
      and Ted Kennedy, June 12, 2007.
177   "bend over backwards . . . people feel?" KAW, p. 99.
177   "intelligent enough . . . my prayer." DM, 31, pp. 9–10.
177   "doing little if any work . . . the French." JPK to Admiral Land, cited in DK, p. 144.
177–178 "very strong . . . to happen." JPK to FDR, August 9, 1939: FDRL/PSF. 37/ "Ken-
      nedy."
178   "[t]he young New Dealers . . . job there." FDR to JPK, July 22, 1939: JPKP/ "Roo-
      sevelt, Franklin D."
178   "After all . . . errand boy." JPK to FDR, August 9, 1939: FDRL/PSF.37/ "Kennedy."
178   "Practically nothing . . . cog." DM, 22, p. 7.
178   "When I was . . . on both counts." JPK to FDR, August 9, 1939: FDRL/PSF. 37/ "Ken-
      nedy."
179   "Russians . . . tear themselves apart." DM, 31, p. 7.

179   "we are told . . . allowed." REFK Diary, August 12, 1938.
179   "No trains . . . upstart and ignoramus." George F. Kennan, *Memoirs, 1925–1950*, p. 91.
180   "The atmosphere . . . of an age." Andrew Devonshire, *Accidents of Fortune*, p. 26.
180   "Holiday time . . . of Germany and Italy." MG, p. 618.
180   "For myself . . . a German city." DM, 32, p. 5.
180   "reports . . . have been called." REFK Diary, August 16, 1939.
180   "never enjoyed a carefree mind." NC to Ida, August 19, 1939, NCDL, p. 440.
181   "a broken man . . . of Europe." DM, 33, pp. 2–3.
181   "hit like a bombshell." IK, p. 211.
181   "like a coroner . . . for murder." Nicolson Diary, August 24, 1939, as quoted in RS, p. 375.
181   "We shall . . . security." RS, p. 375.
181   "I suppose . . . frightening calm." CC, August 24, 1939, p. 209.
181–182 "We feel . . . possibly danger." HTF, p. 360.
182   "I don't care . . . done tonight." DM, 33, p. 5.
182   "ridiculous . . . what kind." JPK to Sumner Welles, August 25, 1939, cited in HTF, p. 361.
183   "You must pass . . . with you." DM, 33, p. 8.
183   "When I left . . . moving experience." JPK Diary, August 24, 1939.
183   "She is . . . a God." JPK Jr., "Unity Mitford," August 21, 1939: JPKP/ "JPK Jr. Mss-Germany." Also HTF, pp. 355–356.
183   "like sitting beside the sun." IK, p. 13.
183   "The situation . . . rid of them." JPK Jr., "Unity Mitford," August 21, 1939: JPKP/ "JPK Jr. Mss-Germany." Also HTF, pp. 355–356.
184   Jack was in Berlin witnessing celebrations and taking movies. David Pitts, *Jack and Lem*, p. 74.
184   Meeting with Rizan and FDR not passing news to Japan. SD 123 as cited in CH, pp. 205–206.
184–185 "I feel . . . pain in the stomach." NC to his sister Hilda, August 27, 1939, NCDL, pp. 440–441.
185   "was pacing . . . for time." DK, p. 206.
185–186 "I'd love . . . to safety." JPK Diary, August 27, 1939.
186   "more worried . . . the Germans." JPK dispatch, August 30, 1949, Roosevelt MSS PSF 21.
186   "[g]ive the British . . . start a war." DK, p. 208.
186   "go for broke . . . for broke." IK, p. 230.
186   "belatedly . . . hysterically." DM, 33, p. 2.
186   "I think . . . anxious to get along." JPK to Henry Kitteridge, August 30, 1939: JPKP/ "K–1939."
187   "it had . . . bury them alive." CH, p. 209.

CHAPTER 15

188   "The news . . . poison gas." DM, 33, p. 16.
188   "It's all over. The party is on." Cordell Hull, *Memoirs*, I, p. 672.
189   "a day . . . silence." DM, 33, p. 18.
189   "all my long . . . has failed." RS, p. 381.
189   "His voice still quivered, deeply moved after his broadcast." JPK Diary, September 3, 1939.
189   "Great Britain . . . with Germany." JPK to CH, September 3, 1939: JPKP/ "1939, Sept. 1–15. To Dept." Also in HTF, p. 367.

189   "the canister . . . old rags." Series 8.5, Box 165, U.S. Embassy (London) Air Raid Pre-
      cautions 1939. Memorandum on Plans for Air Raid Precautions, JPKP.
189   "quite a few white faces amongst the men." JPK Diary, September 3, 1939.
189–190 Game of snooker coming over ticker and letters to embassy. Interview with Page
      Huidekoper Wilson, April 5, 2007.
190   "The war . . . men fighting." JPK Diary, September 3, 1939.
190   "It's . . . of everything." KR, p. 190.
190   "This is . . . the stature of man." DM, 34, p. 3.
191   "fighting . . . in the past." JPK to FDR, September 30, 1939: FDRL/PSF 37/ "Ken-
      nedy." Also in HTF, p. 385.
191   "Now I'm just . . . officer of a company." FF, p. 274.
191   "we have nothing . . . not very safe." SD 123 as quoted in CH, p. 208.
191   "very rhetorical . . . very reminiscent." RS, p. 387.
191–192 Halifax dream and leaflets over Germany. JPK to CH, September, 4, 1939: JPKP/
      "1939, Sept. 1–15, To Dept." Also in HTF, pp. 368–369.
192   "boyish charm . . . twice his age." London Evening News, September 7, 1939.
192   "their polite . . . New York." DT, September 8, 1939.
192–193 "storm . . . this for us?" London Evening News, September 7, 1939.
193   "even if . . . German government." NH, p. 284.
193   "terrible state . . . the government." JPK to CH, September, 8, 1939: JPKP/ "1939,
      Sept. 1–15, To Dept." Also in HTF, pp. 370–371.
193   "The governmental . . . persons in need." DM, 34, p. 8.
193   Joe paying for telegrams. FF, pp. 273–274.
194   "It is . . . paper curled hair." HTF, p. 371.
194   "The big men . . . the first casualties." JFK to Claiborne Pell, September 19, 1939, cited
      in KAW, p. 114.
194   "He looked . . . national spirit." The king's diary, September 9, 1939, as quoted in
      Robert Rhodes James, A Spirit Undaunted, p. 173.
195   "As I see it . . . detest." King George VI to JPK, September 12, 1939, as quoted in HTF,
      p. 376.
195   "I was greatly touched . . . troops to Europe." JPK to King George VI, September 14,
      1939. JPKP. Also in HTF, pp. 376–377.
195   "What . . . steel up their backbones." DM, 35, p. 6.
195–196 "They know . . . peace plans." JPK to CH and FDR, September 11, 1939: JPKP/
      "1939, Sept. 1–15. To Dept." Also in HTF, pp. 374–376.
196   "himself . . . the president should be thinking about." DK, p. 212.
196   "This government . . . and aggression." CH to JPK, September 11, 1939, CH Papers,
      Library of Congress.
196   "I trust . . . may have something." CC, p. 225.
197   "we should never . . . our nation." A. Scott Berg, Lindbergh, pp. 395–396.
197   "stop at nothing . . . lay the opposition low." DM, 35, p. 8.
197   "damn fool . . . more rattle-brained than ever." JPK to REFK, September 18, 1939,
      HTF, p. 380.
197   "His judgment . . . on many things." AS, p. 29. Also KAW, p. 119.
197   "sheer exuberance . . . the moment." Interview with Tom Egerton, quoted in LL, p. 287.
197–198 "Her faith . . . makes the mountain tall." Her Grace Above Gold, p. 39.
198   "I feel so mean to have sent you back." Interview with Page Huidekoper Wilson, April
      5, 2007.
198   "People are sleeping . . . herein." TTR, p. 256.
198–199 "Rose darling . . . catastrophic chaos." JPK to REFK, HTF, pp. 379–380.
199   "would go down . . . shadow of death." JPK to FDR, September 30, 1939: FDRL/ PSF
      37/ "Kennedy."
199   "the Russian . . . length of time." FDR to JPK, quoted in FF, p. 277.

199   "the only kind . . . vital interests." JPK to FDR, September 30, 1939: FDRL/ PSF 37/
        "Kennedy."
199   "everyone . . . out of the war." JPK Jr. to JPK, September 27, 1939. HTF, pp. 381–
        382.
200   "That's the amazing . . . they haven't." TTR, p. 256.

                                     CHAPTER 16

201   "I am terribly . . . interesting one." JPK to Robert Fisher, October 23, 1939, quoted in
        HTF, p. 396.
201   "I'm sick of everybody . . . every day." JPK to REFK, October 2, 1939, quoted in HTF,
        p. 391–392.
201   "My darling . . . terribly lonely." LL, p. 294.
201   "I hope . . . weak heart." EMK to JPK, and EM, n.d., Series 3.5, Family Correspon-
        dence File 1910–1999, Box 56, "JFK 1940–Spring 1943," REFKP.
202   "Your dear . . . made perfect." JPK to FDR, telegram, October 9, 1939, HTF, p. 393.
202   "[T]o say . . . will get it too." JPK to REFK, October 2, 1939, HTF, pp. 391–392.
202   "If the Germans . . . your troubles begin." DM, 36, p. 2.
203   "The picture . . . months of 1939." DM, 37, p. 6.
203   "[a]nother instance . . . disgusted." JPK Diary, October 5, 1939.
203   "lucky and [to] say nothing." JPK Diary, October 4, 1939.
203   "energy . . . speeded up." JPK to REFK, October 2, 1939, HTF, p. 391.
203   "He kept . . . trust him." JPK Diary, October 5, 1939.
203–204 Foreign Office files and Sir Berkeley Gage's comments on Kennedy. FO 371/2287,
        PRO.
204   Chamberlain's biggest fear. RS, pp. 398–400.
204   "olive branch cloaked in a mailed fist." IK, p. 265.
204   "simple proposition . . . cease housebreaking." RK, p. 326.
204   "icy and calm." RS, p. 401.
204   "a puppet Poland" Harvard Crimson, October 9, 1939.
205   "Everyone . . . last Englishman." JFK to JPK, n.d. JFKPP, Box 4B, Correspondence
        1933–1950, folder on Gene Schoor's biography of Kennedy.
205   "They bemoaned . . . very difficult." Nancy Astor to KK, n.d., University of Reading
        Archives.
205   "One's influence . . . president." JPK letter to FDR, September 30, 1939, PPO, FDRL.
205   "a devastating effect on German morale." NC to FDR, November 8, 1939, FDRL: PSF
        32/303.
205   "We have . . . found their leader." MG, p. 627.
205   "Winston . . . waves so high." JPK Diary, October 4, 1939.
206   "bitterly distrusts . . . after his job." JPK Diary, November 8, 1939.
206   "looks like a battleship ready to be launched." DM, 36, p. 14.
206   "did not look . . . every day." JPK Diary, November 28, 1939.
206   "All of England hopes so." DM, 37, p. 16.
206   "Sleep . . . insistent demands." DM, 37, p. 13.
206   "Almost every day . . . own incident." Ibid.
207   Film negotiations. DM, 36, p. 10.
207   "then . . . I had anticipated." DM, 37, p. 28.
207   Diagnosis of acute gastritis and colitis. LL, p. 298.
207   "even the lights . . . of London." DM, 37, p. 4.
207   "they should . . . years to educate." NYT, December 9, 1939.
208   "I can't . . . we are in war." JPK Diary, December 10, 1939.
208   "didn't flash the way he used to." DM, 38, p. 6.

208   "My wife . . . than I anticipated." JPK to Winston Churchill, Radiogram, December 9, 1939, JPKP.

208   "There's no place . . . enough as it is." DM, 37, p. 10.

208   "perhaps . . . all our ordeals." *New York Herald Tribune*, December 16, 1939, and DK, p. 232.

CHAPTER 17

211   "the future . . . hands of a few." CB, p. 542.211

211–212   "a bitter isolationist . . . leery." JPK Diary, March 28, 1940.

212–213   "There is . . . of the burden." FO 371, Box 24238, PRO. Also in NM, p. 83.

213   "shocked the American conscience." DM, 39, p. 2.

214   "Why don't . . . home state anyway." DM, 39, p. 10.

214   "involves matters . . . to be diverted." *LT*, February 14, 1940. DK, p. 237.

214   "golden tongue" and Joe Jr. at law school. LP, pp. 146–156.

215   "Contrary . . . highest government levels." DM, 39, p. 12.

215–216   "Germany would win . . . god-damned pleased." Harold L. Ickes, *The Secret Diaries of Harold L. Ickes*, March 19, 1940.

216   "the State Department . . . a policy." DM, 39, p. 10.

216   "I was certain . . . early Spring." Ibid.

216   "thought that . . . three months." DM, 39, p. 11.

216–217   "rich greengrocers . . . get my job." DM, 39, pp. 17–18.

217   "gay conversation . . . sea and sky." DM, 40, p. 1.

217   "Please call . . . Love, Clare," Telegram from CBL to JPK, Feb. 9, 1940. Series 8.2.1, Box 110, L, 1940, JPKP.

217   Joe's affair with Clare Boothe Luce. Conversation with Sylvia Morris, February 2007.

217   "vast sources . . . the world." DM, 39, p. 1.

217–218   "right through . . . an organization." DM, 40, pp. 2–3.

218   "Kennedy . . . essential facts." Benjamin Welles, *Sumner Welles, FDR's Global Strategist*, pp. 250–251.

218   "ponderous . . . rolls of flesh." Sumner Welles to FDR as quoted in Benjamin Welles, *Sumner Welles, FDR's Global Strategist*, p. 247.

218   "The pope . . . whole business." DM, 40, p. 3.

219   "most unpleasant . . . stupid mind." Benjamin Welles, *Sumner Welles: FDR's Global Strategist*, p. 248.

219   "a mood to make a reasonable peace." HTF, p. 409.

219   "it was tragically plain . . . was delay." Sumner Welles, *The Time for Decision*, p. 105.

219   "He says . . . negotiated peace." Harold Nicolson diary, February 29, 1940. Nigel Nicolson (Ed.), *The War Years, 1939–1945*, Vol. II of *The Diaries and Letters of Harold Nicolson*, p. 60.

219   "a foul specimen . . . of his type." Vansittart comments, January 22, 1940, FO371/24251/A605/605/45.

219   "rightly or wrongly . . . their effect." Perowne comment on January 29, 1940. FO371/24248/A825.

219   "like an honorary . . . diminishing temptation." FO 371/24251/5862/ F168.

220   "If isolation . . . as they go along." *LT*, March 8, 1940.

220   "there were . . . understand." JPK to REFK, March 14, 1940. HTF, p. 409.

220   "they have . . . ever since." Ibid.

220   "not received . . . bitterly." DM, 40, pp. 6–7.

220   "be welcomed . . . extremely tough." *The Spectator*, "People and Things" by Harold Nicolson, March 8, 1940. Also cited in DK, p. 240.

220   "no chance . . . unsupported by any facts." *NYT*, March 17, 1940.
220   "the best I have read since since Snow White." *DT*, March 18, 1940.
220   "it soon . . . in a war." DM, 40, pp. 6–7.
221   "purported rifts . . . government." JPK Jr. to JPK, March 17, 1940, JPKP. HTF, p. 410.
221   "ardent proponent of intervention." KK Diary, p. 75.
221   "Kick . . . got unpleasant." JFK to JPK, Spring 1940. Box 4B, Correspondence 1933–50, Gene Schoor, "Young John Kennedy folder," JFKP.
221   "I am sure . . . so important." HTF, p. 409.
221   "usual gracious self . . . peace plan." DM, p. 40, pp. 12–13.
222   "appreciation . . . anything upon it." DM, 40, p. 12.

CHAPTER 18

223   "Chamberlain is convinced . . . against him." DM 40, p.16.
223   "sat . . . It was weird." DM, 40, p. 26.
224   "if the Allies . . . Europe?" DM, 40, p. 29.
224   lacked "confidence" DM, 40, p. 37.
224   "It was . . . considerable wit." Sumner Welles letter to FDR, quoted in Benjamin Welles, *Sumner Welles: FDR's Global Strategist*, p. 253.
224   "to thousands . . . drier and drier." DM, 40, pp. 32–33.
225   "There seems . . . devastation." DM, 40, p. 36.
225   "under the cloak . . . eat my hat." Hooker, Moffat Diary, March 13, 1940, p. 303. Also in DK, p. 244.
225–226   "I thought . . . later anyway." KR, p. 205.
226   "It is not an English . . . rather big." JPK to REFK, March 14, 1940. HTF, p. 409.
226   "There is nothing . . . the children." Ibid.
226   "Knowing myself . . . I'm just *nuts!*" JPK to REFK, March 17, 1940. HTF, p. 415.
226   "You would never . . . all the more." JPK to REFK, March 20, 1940, HTF, pp. 410–411.
226–227   "Joe dear . . . hearts of the British." AS, p. 35. Quoted in LL, p. 299.
227   "It's easy . . . difficulty is—what?" Ibid.
227   "a little fatter . . . still great." JPK to REFK, March 14, 1940. HTF, p. 409.
227   "I really. . . . real difficulty. " JPK to REFK, March 20, 1940. HTF, p. 411.
227   "Mother says . . . fat you . think—"RK to JPK, April 4 (?), 1940. JPKP. Also in HTF, 412.
227   "scant . . . lasting peace in Europe." RD, p. 194. Langer and Gleason, *Challenge to Isolation*, p. 375.
227   "started me out on the job." NH, p. 307.
228   "Rush . . . Becoming a Pacifist!" HTF, p. 232, and FO/24251x 9191.PRO.
228   "England . . . prepared for war." JFK, *Why England Slept*, p. 17.
228   "more work than I have ever done in my life." Michael O'Brien, *John F. Kennedy*, p. 105.
228   "Jack rushed . . . very good." JPK Jr. to JPK, March 17, 1940. Series 3.5, Family Correspondence, File 1910–1994, Box 56, "Joseph P. Kennedy, 1924–49," REFKP.
229   "amateurish in many respects," Krock Oral History, JFKP.
229   "three girls . . . of glory." HTF, p. 417.
230   Bullitt rescues FDR. CB, p. 545.
230   "that they were . . . once they went in." RD, p. 195.
230   "an unbalanced . . . world peace." JPK Diary notes, March 10, 1940.
230   "I wasn't . . . White Paper." JPK to REFK, April 5, 1940: JPKP/ "Kennedy, Mrs. Joseph P." Also HTF, p. 413.
230   "We continue . . . unheard of power." NC to Ida Chamberlain, March 30, 1940. NCDL, p. 514.

230–231 "Nobody . . . once and for all." JPK to REFK, April 5, 1940: JPKP/ "Kennedy, Mrs. Joseph P." Also HTF, p. 413.

231 "in bedroom all morning." CBL diary, April 2, 1940, CBL papers, Library of Congress.

231 Affair with Daye Eliot and gynecological operation. Burton Hersh, *Bobby and J. Edgar Hoover*, p. 70.

232 "one thing . . . missed the bus." Graham Stewart, *Burying Caesar*, p. 402.

232 Admiral Kirk report. DM, 42, p. 2.

232 "oratorical feat . . . every pore." DM, 42, p. 5.

232 "Far from . . . bus stop." Graham Stewart, *Burying Caesar*, p. 403.

232–233 Cryptography reading British naval signals. Martin Gilbert, *A History of the Twentieth Century*, p. 301.

233 "The Norwegian . . . fight over here." JPK to REFK, April 26, 1940. Series 3.5, Family Correspondence, File 1910–1994, Box 56, "Joseph P. Kennedy, 1924–49," REFKP.

233 "The situation . . . very rapidly." JPK to FDR and CH, April 26, 1940. DM, 43, p. 2.

233 "England . . . one can imagine." JPK to FDR and CH, April 26, 1940. SD 841.00/1464. DK, p. 246.

233 "These are . . . difficult days." FDR to JPK, May 3, 1940, in *F.D.R. His Personal Letters, 1928–1945*, ed. Elliott Roosevelt, vol. II, p. 1020.

CHAPTER 19

234 "The English blundered. . . . a lot of damage." JPK Jr. to JPK, May 4, 1940. Series 3.5, Family Correspondence, File 1910–1994, Box 56, "Joseph P. Kennedy, 1924–49," REFKP.

234 "like the script of a West End play." HF, p. 196.

234 "Have you missed . . . a mastery of the facts." DM 43, p. 4.

234–235 "we must . . . name of God, go." Leo Amery diaries quoted in Roy Jenkins, *Churchill*, p. 579.

235 "These . . . friend and colleague." WM, p. 650.

235 "runaway jury . . . Commons." WM, p. 647.

235 "I say . . . *friends in the House*." WM, p. 653.

235 "conventional . . . personal friendship," RS, p. 425.

235 "The issue . . . from any quarter." DM, 43, pp. 7–8.

236 "Go in the name of God, go." HF, p. 197.

236 "dissuade Churchill from disastrous over-reactions." HF, p. 199.

236 "very respectable . . . Such is life!" EK to JPK, TTR, p. 262.

236–237 "her bloomers . . . at the games." REFK to JPK, May 8, 1940: JPKP/ "Kennedy, Mrs. Joseph P." HTF, p. 421.

237 "You would . . . I finally did." EK to JPK, TTR, p. 262.

237 "singularly uninformed." DM, 43, p. 11.

237 "tearing his hair." Alan Kirk oral history at Columbia University, cited by DK, p. 251.

238 "I hope . . . do our best." Cited in NM, p. 91.

238 "I cannot . . . as P.M." Sarah Bradford, *The Reluctant King*, p. 312.

238 "[H]ence Norway, hence Prime Minister." DM, 43, p. 12.

238 "walking with destiny." GS, pp. 526–527.

238 "How grateful . . . fear of that." WC to NC, May 10, 1940, quoted in RS, p. 431.

239 "tumbled to bits in a moment." NC to Hilda, May 17, 1940, NCDL, p. 531.

239 "ghastly . . . broken man." JPK Diary, May 16, 1940.

239 "constantly . . . of my life." JPK to NC, May 18, 1940. Series 8.2.1., Box 104, Neville Chamberlain, JPKP.

239 "always imbued . . . of doom." Violet Bonham Carter, *Winston Churchill: An Intimate Portrait*, p. 178.

239　　"I have nothing . . . no survival." Winston Churchill, *War Papers, Vol. II*, p. 22.

239　　"absolute virtue . . . forces of evil." WM, p. 683.

240　　"ill-conditioned . . . not deter them." JPK Diary, May 15, 1940.

240　　"You know . . . what we could do?" DM, 44, pp. 9–10.

240　　"We all . . . based on the facts." JPK Diary, May 16, 1940.

240　　"It isn't fair . . . our own use." DM, 44, p. 9.

240　　"never give up . . . fight on." DM, 44, p. 10.

240–241　"I think . . . message to you." JPK to CH, May 15, 1940, FRUS, 1940, III, pp. 29–30.

241　　"Former Naval Person . . . withheld too long." Warren Kimball, *Churchill and Roosevelt: The Complete Correspondence, Vol. I*, p. 38.

241　　"a toughness of moral and physical fiber." CB, p. 552.

241–242　"Everyone is unanimous . . . their backyard." JPK Jr. to JPK, May 18, 1940. Series 3.5, Family Correspondence, File 1910–1994, Box 56, "Joseph P. Kennedy, 1924–49," REFKP.

242　　7.7 percent favored immediate entry, 19 percent favored going in if the Allies appeared headed to defeat. Langer and Gleason, *Challenge to Isolationism*, p. 507; quoted in Jon Meacham, *Franklin and Winston*, p. 55.

242　　"The President . . . Allied debacle." JPK to CH, May 15, 1940, FRUS, 1940, I, pp. 224–225.

242　　"who . . . to the German will." Jon Meacham, *Franklin and Winston*, p. 53.

243　　"it would . . . heart or courage." NM, *19 Weeks*, p. 112.

243　　"Each day brought new disasters," DM, 45, p. 3.

CHAPTER 20

244　　"even . . . smoke gases." Mollie Panter-Downes, *London War Notes*, p. 65.

245　　"require persons . . . their property." NM, p. 131.

245　　"Various . . . in Brixton prison." Mollie Panter-Downes, *London War Notes*, p. 66.

246　　"This is quite . . . very interesting." Document declassified for this book. Secret Correspondence, Kent, May 20, 1940, F790009–1327, SD.

246　　"played up . . . forget about him.'" FF, pp. 310–311.

247　　Official file doctored. Transcripts of the Kent trial in the public domain have two different indexes with disparities. Bryan Clough, *State Secrets: The Kent-Wolkoff Affair*, p. 248.

247　　"Don't you think . . . I don't know." Document declassified for this book. Secret Correspondence, Kent, May 20, 1940, F790009–1327, SD.

248　　"secretly and unconstitutionally plotting with Churchill." Farago, *The Game of the Foxes*, as quoted in Joseph E. Persico, *Roosevelt's Secret War*, p. 23.

248　　Tyler Kent affair, secret diplomatic codes, and British government motivations: Thorough coverage and review of literature in Bryan Clough, *State Secrets: The Kent-Wolkoff Affair*. British deportation order, p. 167.

248　　"The interrogation . . . further detention." DM, 44, pp. 14–18.

249　　"threw . . . all of Europe." DM, 44, p.18.

249　　M–138 military cipher. Bryan Clough, *State Secrets: The Kent-Wolkoff Affair*, p. 249.

249　　"since this case . . . complete story." JPK telegram to CH, May 22, 1940. NCW 76–1, Declassified, March 30, 2006, SD.

250　　"The English . . . near the finish." JPK to REFK, May 20, 1940. HTF, pp. 432–433.

250　　Rosemary unnerved by British agents. CH, p. 215.

250　　"to continue her art studies." *Boston Globe*, June 2, 1940.

251–252　"swell job . . . pinches that survives." JPK to JFK, May 20, 1940: JFKL/1979–93 Exhibit Book. HTF, pp. 433–435.

252　　"I and . . . Is Billy all right?" KK to JPK, May 21, 1940, TTR, p. 263.

252 "I do . . . superiority in numbers." JPK to CH, May 24, 1940, FRUS, III, pp. 31–32.

252–253 "I was learning . . . tell them." DM, 45, p. 7.

253 "a human being . . . useless sacrifice." GB, p. 190.

253 "It could . . . do-or-die." FRUS I, p. 233.

253 "avoid . . . slippery slope with France." John Lukacs, *Five Days in London: May 1940*, p. 149.

253 "They seem . . . a great hustler." DM 45, pp. 11–16.

254 "[w]ars . . . liberation of the Old." NGI, p. 218.

254 "will quit and quit soon." DM 46, pp. 2–4.

254 "a note . . . of elegant phraseology." Mollie Panter-Downs, *London War Notes*, p. 60.

254 "Many people . . . to blame." DM 46, pp. 2–4.

255 "a jackal . . . the picture." DM, 46, pp. 5–6.

255 "lodged in prison . . . other countries." Quoted in Michael Lind, *The American Way of Strategy*, p. 105.

255–256 "the hand . . . not unhopeful hour." NM, pp. 166–167.

256 "America . . . continued to fight." JPK Diary, June 14, 1940.

256 "Churchill hated him from then on." Private memorandum by Herbert Hoover, April 19, 1945, in Hoover papers, quoted in KR, p. 208.

257 "these poor people . . . in the war." JPK to FDR and CH, June 14, 1940, HTF, pp. 440–442.

257 "[t]hen . . . awaited salvation." NM, p. 174.

CHAPTER 21

258 "down in cap-card . . . graduoin." EMK to JPK, June 20–21, 1940, TTR, p. 265.

258 "He . . . got a wonderful smile." REFK to JPK, June 24, 1940: JPKP/ "Kennedy, Mrs. Joseph P." Also in HTF, pp. 446–447.

258 "a swell guy." JPK telegram to JFK, May to June 1940, Box 4B, JFKPP, in Michael O'Brien, *John F. Kennedy*, p 106.

259 "We are . . . curtain to go up." JPK to REFK, July 23, 1940, JPKP. Also in HTF, pp. 451–452.

259 "6 feet 7, Straight from Heaven." RFK to JPK, July, 1940, HTF, p. 448.

259 "The chief . . . you are doing." EK to JPK, June, 1940, TTR, p. 265.

259 "The people . . . tear me to pieces." DM, 44, p. 37.

259 "I expect . . . 'their finest hour.'" Roy Jenkins, *Churchill*, p. 621.

259 "London . . . watchful hush." Mollie Panter-Downs, *London War Notes*, p. 69.

259 Britain . . . a house in which the girders [the French] had fallen. DM 28, p. 12.

260 "We cannot give . . . too soon." HTF, p. 445.

260 "everyone seemed . . . favorably of you." REFK to JPK, June 24, 1940: JPKP/ "Kennedy, Mrs. Joseph P." Also in HTF, pp. 446–447.

260 "Everything looks good to me tonight." DM 47, p. 1.

260 "everyone . . . end of the month." Ian Macleod, *Neville Chamberlain*, p. 279. Also in RD, p. 210.

260 "the only solid basis . . . for optimism." DM 47, p. 1.

261 "While people . . . a little gayer." DM 48, p. 6.

261 "We have got . . . drain together." DM 47, p. 1.

261 "Germany's fast . . . exports." JPK to JFK, August 2, 1940, HTF, p. 454.

262 mixed signals from the U.S. embassy. NM, p. 250.

262 Cordell Hull's cable to Kennedy about Donovan, State Department to Kennedy, July 11, 1940, SD 740.011.

262 "height of nonsense . . . out of joint." Joseph E. Persico, *Roosevelt's Secret War*, p. 65.

263 "I am happy . . . hideous evening with Joe." *Ibid.*, p. 67.

263 "This . . . United States." JPK to CH, July 31, 1940, SD, 740.0011.

263   "Donovan . . . attitude in Washington." NM, p. 251.
263–264 "once more . . . democratic statesmen." DM, 47, p. 6.
264   "millions . . . they will do." JPK to REFK, July 23, 1940, in HTF, pp. 451–452.
264   "has had . . . invade it." JPK to JFK, August 2, 1940, HTF, p. 454.
264   "to bomb . . . this week." JPK to REFK, July 23, 1940, HTF, pp. 451–452.
264   "with great respect . . . common cause." DM 47, p.7.
264   "Confucious . . . a helmet." DM, 47, pp. 6–7.
265   "president . . . new in my life." DM 48, pp. 3–4.
265   "I am not . . . were to leave." JPK Diary, August 1, 1940.
265   "I am not . . . ash can." JPK to REFK, August 2, 1940, in HTF, p. 455.
265   "I think my poor old friend is finished." JPK to REFK, August 2, 1940, in HTF, p. 457.
266   "I didn't . . . you oppose." JPK to JPK Jr., July 23, 1940. Series 3.5, Family Correspondence, File 1918–1994, Box 56, "Joseph P. Kennedy, letters to family members," REFKP.
266   "So, whether . . . years to come." JPK to JFK, August 2, 1940, in HTF, p. 453.
266   "thoroughly aroused . . . national preparedness." Henry Luce introduction to JFK, *Why England Slept*, pp. 13–14.
267   "young man's . . . for older men." *London Times Literary Supplement*, October 12, 1940.
267   "Thinking . . . admission to it." Laski quoted in Michael O'Brien, *John F. Kennedy*, p. 108.
267   "a great argument . . . strength at all times." FDR to JFK, August 27, 1940, JFK Pre-Presidential Papers, JFKL.
267   "I thought . . . met Joe Kennedy." RD, p. 214.
267   "so many things going on." JPK to JK, August 2, 1940, TTR, p. 269.
267   "the survival . . . getting those destroyers." DM, 48, p. 10.
267–268 "on which . . . might well depend." DM, 48, p. 11.
268   "give people . . . in muddy waters." Ibid.
268   "My God . . . sack cloth and ashes." DM, 48, p. 18.
268   "If we . . . some time." DM, 48, p. 9.

CHAPTER 22

269   Kennedy's prognostication about air attacks. Halifax to Lothian, July 31, 1940, FO414/277, p. 20. Also in DK, p. 256.
269   "The defense . . . within a month." Tim Clayton and Phil Craig, *Finest Hour*, p. 237.
270   "Never . . . better days." MG, p. 671.
270   "Snoopers' room." GB, p. 188.
271   "Not to tell . . . is bad organization." JPK to CH, August 7, 1940: JPKP / "1940, August to Dept." Also in HTF, pp. 458–459.
271   "people would say . . . no value." JPK Diary, August 23, 1940.
271   "is very . . . the Air Force fight." Memorandum for the Ambassador's Diary, August 23, 1940, JPKP.
271   "is going . . . important company." JPK Diary, August 23, 1940.
272   "The least . . . get out." JPK to CH, August 7, 1940: JPKP / "1940, August to Dept." Also in HTF, pp. 458–459.
272   "I have . . . being a dummy." JPK cable to FDR, August 27, 1940: JPKP/ "1940, August to Dept." Also in HTF, p. 463.
272   "There is no . . . details here." FDR to JPK, cited in KR, p. 212.
272   Roosevelt's sadistic treatment of JPK. Correspondence with Conrad Black, April 2007.

272 "gloom personified . . . before the firing squad." Michael Beschloss, *Presidential Courage*, p. 166.

273 "and I . . . homeland." NGI, p. 249.

273 "riding . . . a mystery." JPK Diary, September 6, 1940.

273 "made me plenty homesick." JPK to JFK, September 10, 1940, HTF, p. 468.

273 Labor Day weekend sailing competition and trophies. *NYT*, September 4, 1940, and FF, p. 327.

273–274 Joe, Jr.'s visit to "Wyntoon" and Hermosa Beach. LP, p. 165.

275 Rose raising funds for ambulances. CH , p. 218.

276 "The people . . . to the ground." IK, p. 309.

276 "the fires . . . blood-red." Edward R. Murrow, *This Is London*, p. 171.

276 "There's hell to pay here tonight." JPK to FDR and CH, September 7, 1940, SD 740.0011 European War 1939/54801/2. Also in DK, p. 258.

276 "just when . . . the next 72 hours." DM 49, p. 7.

277 "has never . . . his method." JPK to REFK, September 11, 1940, in HTF, pp. 469–470.

277 Roosevelt invasion scare. JPK Diary, September 22, 1940.

277 "a people . . . will be." NGI, p. 253.

277 "the wealthy . . . their homes." Tim Clayton and Phil Craig, *Finest Hour*, p. 295.

277 "[w]hen the siren . . . with white faces." Martin Gilbert, *The Second World War*, p. 124.

277 "It is . . . in great shape." JPK to EMK, September 11, 1940, in HTF, pp. 470–471.

278 Joe almost killed by anarchist. Ron Chernow, *The House of Morgan*, p. 212.

278 "I don't think . . . slightest bit." JPK to REFK, September 10, 1940, HTF, p. 467.

278 "Haven't . . . to break down." JPK to JFK, September 10, 1940, JFKPP 1933–1950, Box 4A, JFKL.

278 "underneath . . . sapped." Harold Nicolson, diary September 19, 1940, in Nigel Nicolson (Ed.), *The War Years*, p. 116.

278 "You could see . . . adding to." JPK to REFK, September 10, 1940, in HTF, pp. 466–467.

278 "When they drop . . . good place." DM 49, p. 6.

278 "an extraordinary . . . unity was exhilarating." NM, p. 322.

278 London a run-down city covered in dust. NM, p. 335.

279 "bit holes." Robert Self kindly researched what these were. See Angus Calder, *The People's War*, p. 138.

279 "frightfully nervous . . . in a million." JPK to REFK, September 10, 1940, in HTF, pp. 466–467.

279 "they are dropping them all 'round 14 Prince's Gate." JPK letters to JK and EK, in TTR, pp. 272–274.

279 "I can't tell . . . gone mad." JPK to EMK, September 11, 1940, in DKG, p. 609.

279 "one of my best . . . more frequently." JFK to JK, September 11, 1940, in TTR, p. 272.

279 "I am sure . . . in London." JPK to EMK, September 11, 1940, JPKP, in HTF, pp. 470–471.

279 "My sons . . . strong there." JPK to JFK, September 10, 1940, JFKPP 1933–1950, Box 4A. Also in HTF, pp. 469–470.

280 "dove . . . dull thud." JPK to REFK, September 10, 1940, JPKP. Also in HTF, pp. 466–467.

280 British planes lost and Lord Beaverbrook's aircraft factory production. Tim Clayton and Phil Craig, *Finest Hour*, p. 247.

280 Kennedy believed that Hitler had not yet used one-twentieth or one-thirtieth of German air power on England. GB, p. 213.

281 "no one . . . seemed to care less." DM 49, p. 6.

281 "a trouble-maker . . . out of sympathy." Israel's *Long Diary*, quoted in DK, pp. 258–259.

281 "a bitter pill . . . a Prime Minister." DM 49, p. 10.

281 "I cannot . . . this war." DM 49, p. 11.

281 "a struggle . . . bad underneath." JPK to FDR and CH, September 11, 1940, SD 740.0011 European War 1939/54801/2, Section Four. Also in DK, p. 265.

281–282 "production . . . be getting." DM 49, p. 10.

282 "And for the United States . . . battle are." JPK to FDR and CH, September 11, 1940, SD 740.0011 European War 1939/54801/2, Section Four. Also in DK, p. 265.

282 "That one . . . don't count." *NYT*, September 24, 1940. Also in FF, p. 322.

282 "military suspicion . . . of the conflict." DK, p. 258 and footnote, p. 556.

282 "by inches." HTF, p. 474.

282 "We read . . . buttons on his coat." REFK to JPK, n.d., HTF, p. 474.

282 "I could see . . . get back." JPK to CBL, October 1, 1940, CBL papers, Library of Congress.

282 "If you ride . . . part of the show." JPK to REFK, September 10, 1940, JPKP, in HTF, p. 477.

CHAPTER 23

283 "The gent . . . utmost vigilance." DM 50, p. 2.

283 244 raids. *NYT,* January 22, 1941. Also in FF, p. 322.

283 "unenviable . . . protracted peril." *NYT*, October 8, 1940.

283–284 "to be . . . the life of England." DM 50, pp. 5–6.

284 "the old . . . Totalitarianism." DM 50, p. 7.

284 "Of course . . . come in." DM 50, p. 8.

284–285 "the Pres. . . . could not take." REFK to JPK, October 7, 1940, in HTF, p. 474.

285 "gloomy . . . consequences." Arthur Krock, *NYT,* October 8, 1940.

285 "the grass roots of a thousand country clubs" Steve Neal, *Dark Horse*, p. 99, as quoted in Jean Edward Smith, *FDR*, p. 453.

285–286 "I don't want . . . see each other again." JPK Diary, October 19, 1940.

286 "So perhaps . . . take me soon." JPK Diary, November 9, 1940.

286 "few cases . . . my disappointments." NC to JPK, October 19, 1940. Series 8.2.1., Box 104, Neville Chamberlain, JPKP.

286 "real worth while . . . world of our hopes." JPK to NC, October 22, 1940, JPKP, in HTF, p. 477.

286 "mentally exhausted . . . just an ordinary man." GB, pp. 239–242.

287 "I did not . . . in reverence." Kennedy quoted in *Time*, November 4, 1940.

287 Joe carrying air-raid siren. KR, p. 215.

287 "Tears of joy . . . on the back." *Boston Post* report cited in LL, p, 307.

288 "Ah, Joe . . . talk to you." KR, p. 215.

288 "You would . . . resign now." KR, p. 216.

288 Frank Murphy tells of Supreme Court Justices' strategy meeting. DM 52, pp. 1–2.

288 "shaking . . . hands." Series 1, Box 3, "Visit to Washington," October 29, 1940, REFKP.

288 "acting . . . great influence on me." DM 51, pp. 3–4.

289 "not . . . get away from me and loaf." JPK: Notes dictated for his diary, November 4, 1940.

289 "Joe did most . . . snapping his eyes." Series 1, Box 3, "Visit to Washington," October 29, 1940, REFKP.

289 "Since it doesn't . . . American government." DM 51, p. 6.

289 "Somebody . . . the president." DM 51, p. 5.

289 "the right . . . 3,000 miles away." DM 51, p. 6.

289   "I stand . . . political office." LL, p. 311.

289   "But . . . what I wish." KR, p. 219.

290   "Please remember . . . is true!' " CBL to JPK, October 28, 1940, JPKP, cited in Michael Beschloss, *Presidential Courage*, pp. 187–188.

290–291 "Even . . . concern to us all." *NYT*, October 20, 1940.

291   "the most effective vote-getting speech of the campaign." *Life*, January 27, 1941.

291   "hitting . . . in the 9th inning." DM 52, p. 1.

291   "Listened . . . effectively with Big J.P." David Pitts, *Jack and Lem*, p. 76.

291   "Proud . . . Love, Jack." JFK telegram to JPK, October 30, 1940: JPKP/ "K." Also in HTF, p. 489.

291   "boys are . . . any foreign wars" CB, p. 595.

292   "welcome . . . Kennedy." *NYT*, November 1, 1940.

292   "the Pres . . . 4th hostage." KK to JPK, October 30, 1940: JPKP/ Unmarked File. Also in HTF, p. 489.

292   "with great sorrow . . . fair and brave." JPK Diary, November 9, 1940.

293   "Democracy . . . would be gone." *Boston Globe*, November 10, 1940.

293   "We can forgive . . . championship of freedom." London *Daily Mail*, November 12, 1940. Also in KAW, p. 175.

293   "had created . . . all parties." *News Chronicle*, November 13, 1940.

293   "she bothered us . . . at the embassy." KR, p. 224.

294   "[Y]ou're going . . . in your life." NH, p. 213.

294   "reconcile itself . . . lives accordingly." KR, p. 226.

294   "had never seen . . . out of here." Interview with Gore Vidal, May 14, 2007.

294–295 "Never before . . . your own skins." KR, pp. 232–233.

295   Cabinet meeting Roosevelt mention of Kennedy. Ickes Diary cited in DK, p. 307.

295   "He did not . . . as focal points." RFK on JPK in FB, p. 213.

295–296 "a chance . . . it would be OK." JPK Jr. to JPK, November 2 (?), 1940, in HTF, p. 490.

296   "I am gloomy . . . meet it successfully." JFK to JPK, December 6, 1940, HTF, pp. 498–505.

296   "It is easy . . . heartrendingly unsuccessful." David Dutton, *Neville Chamberlain*, p. 220.

EPILOGUE

297–298 "It would leave . . . could straighten it out." DM, 52, pp. 7–8.

298–299 "The saddest feature . . . 'the real defeatists.'" JPK NBC Radio Address, January 18, 1941. Series 9.2., Kennedy Urges America to Stay Out of War radio address, 1–18–41, folder 1 of 2, JPKP.

299   "wonderful . . . we Catholics are." RFK to REFK, undated, RFK Pre-Aministration files, JFKL. Also in Evan Thomas, *Robert Kennedy: His Life*, p. 33.

299   "The American people . . . possess the earth.'" Kennedy Oglethorpe University address. Series 9.2. Private Citizen Speech, 5–24–41, JPKP.

299   "Let us . . . by force or otherwise." DK, pp. 312–313.

300   "We are all in the same boat now." Doris Kearns Goodwin, *No Ordinary Time*, p. 290.

300   "Name . . . I'm Yours to Command." JPK to FDR, December 7, 1941: JPKP: "White House." Also in HTF, p. 533.

301   "dedicated his life . . . anything to hurt him." KR, p. 260.

302   "He had . . . a wonderful one to live." JFK epitaph on JPK Jr., in *As We Remember Joe*, p. 5.

302   "You had . . . Not all of us." JPK-Churchill exchange. JPK memo on Churchill conversation, JPKP. Also in BL, p. 184.

302   "I am so anxious . . . hardly sit still." KK to JPK, October 20, 1941, in HTF, p. 532.

302   "No one . . . better that minute." JPK on KK's death, HTF, p. 636.

303   "by doing . . . the hell with it." RFK on JPK. FB, pp. 211–214.

303   Rose's bitterness about Rosemary's operation, DKG, p. 643.

304   "Beneath . . . needed assistance." RFK on JPK, FB, pp. 211– 214.

304   Kennedy made a Knight of Malta. *Boston Herald*, January 3, 1942.

304   "Pat is . . . mind to it." Patricia Kennedy Lawford, Wikipedia, June 26, 2007.

306   Joe's love and loyalty important to Jack. Interview with Ted Sorensen, June 13, 2007.

306   "had to placate . . . independent." James MacGregor Burns, letter to author, June 11, 2007.

306   Joe helped arrange Jack's appointment to the House Education and Labor Committee. Robert Dallek, *An Unfinished Life*, p. 141.

306   "there was many . . . feeling rather down." Ibid., p. 124.

306   "his courage . . . war, war." And Rose's favorite phrase. Interview with Ted Sorensen, June 13, 2007.

307   "Don't buy . . . a landslide." www.thinkexist.com, Joseph P. Kennedy quotes, p. 1.

307   "as both an obligation and a joy." Interview with Ted Sorensen, June 13, 2007.

307   One of Rose Kennedy's favorite quotes. Ibid.

307   "And so . . . freedom of man." Ted Sorensen, Editor, *"Let the Word Go Forth,"* p. 14.

307   "For only . . . never be employed." Ibid., p. 13.

308   Khrushchev sizing up Jack as weak. BL, p. 312.

308   "both gave as good as they got." Interview with Ted Sorensen, June 13, 2007.

308   "a real statesman." David Talbot, "A Warrior for Peace," in *Time*, July 2, 2007, p. 50.

308   "always believed. . . . from the walls." Interview with Ted Sorensen, June 13, 2007.

308   "We must face . . . every world problem." David Talbot, "A Warrior for Peace," in *Time*, July 2, 2007, p. 50.

308   "almost as bad as the appeasement at Munich." David Talbot, *Brothers*, p. 165.

309   "We all inhabit . . . all mortal." Ted Sorensen (Ed.), *"Let the Word Go Forth,"* p. 286.

309–310 "We are confronted . . . American Constitution." Ibid., p. 194.

310   General Edwin Walker's crusade against Kennedy's "defeatist" foreign policy. And "He kept the peace." David Talbot, "A Warrior for Peace," in *Time*, July 2, 2007, p. 50.

310   "Few men . . . painfully to change." RFK Speech at the University of Capetown, South Africa, Day of Affirmation, June 6, 1966. www.mtholyoke.edu/acad/intrel/speech/rfk-sa.htm.

310–311 "But we can . . . once again." RFK, "The Mindless Menace of Violence Speech," April 5, 1968, Cleveland, Ohio. Politics and World Affairs, World Press.com.

311   "be remembered . . . tried to stop it." Evan Thomas, *Robert Kennedy*, p. 393.

311   "a rare . . . beautiful rose of all." CH, p. 430.

311   "I hope . . . as war does today." JPK to EMK, September 11, 1940, in HTF, pp. 470–471.

311   "[H]e had amassed . . . in the country." *Time*, April 14, 2006.

312   "No matter . . . read me stories." Interview with Senator Ted Kennedy, June 5, 2007.

313   "Each time . . . oppression and resistance." Evan Thomas, *Robert Kennedy*, p. 322.

Bibliography

Ackroyd, Peter. *London: The Biography*. New York: Anchor Books, 2000.

Bailey, Thomas A. *The Art of Diplomacy*. New York: Appleton-Century-Crofts, 1968.

Baring, Sarah. *The Road to Station X*. York, England: Wilton 65, 2000.

Barrow, Andrew. *Gossip: 1920–1970*. New York: Coward, McCann and Geoghegan, Inc., 1979.

Berg, A. Scott. *Lindbergh*. New York: Putnam, 1998.

Beschloss, Michael. *Kennedy & Roosevelt: The Uneasy Alliance*. New York: Norton, 1980.

Presidential Courage: Brave Leaders and How They Changed America 1789–1989. New York: Simon & Schuster, 2007.

Bilainkin, George. *Diary of a Diplomatic Correspondent*. London: George Allen & Unwin Ltd., 1942.

Bjerk, Roger Carl William. *Kennedy at the Court of St. James's: The Diplomatic Career of Joseph P. Kennedy, 1938–1940*. Ph.D. dissertation. Pullman: Washington State University, 1971.

Black, Conrad. *Franklin Delano Roosevelt: Champion of Freedom*. New York: Public Affairs, 2003.

Blair, Joan, and Clay Blair, Jr. *The Search for JFK*. New York: Berkley Publishing Corp., distributed by Putnam, 1976.

Bloch, Michael. *Ribbentrop*. London: Abacus, 2003.

Blum, John Morton (Editor). *From The Morganthau Diaries: Years of Crisis, 1928–1938*. Boston: Houghton Mifflin, 1959.

Bonham Carter, Violet. *Winston Churchill: An Intimate Portrait*. New York: Harcourt, Brace & World, Inc., 1965.

Bradford, Sarah. *America's Queen: The Life of Jacqueline Kennedy Onassis*. New York: Penguin, 2000.

———. *The Reluctant King: The Life and Reign of George VI, 1895–1952*. New York: St. Martin's Press, 1989.

Bullitt, Orville H. *Personal and Secret: The Correspondence Between Franklin D. Roosevelt and William C. Bullitt*. Boston: Houghton Mifflin, 1972.

Calder, Angus. *The Myth of the Blitz*. London: Pimlico, 2004.

The People's War: Britain 1939–1945. London: Jonathan Cape, 1969.

Cameron, Gail. *Rose: A Biography of Rose Fitzgerald Kennedy.* New York: Putnam, 1971.

Cecil, David. *The Young Melbourne.* New York: Bobbs-Merrill, 1939.

Chernow, Ron. *The House of Morgan: An American Banking Dynasty and the Rise of Modern Finance.* New York: Touchstone, 1990.

Chisholm, Anne, and Michael Davie. *Lord Beaverbrook: A Life.* New York: Alfred A. Knopf, 1993.

Churchill, Winston S. (edited by grandson). *Never Give In! The Best of Winston Churchill's Speeches.* New York: Hyperion, 2003.

Churchill, Winston. *The Second World War, Volume II.* London: Cassell & Co., 1964.

Clayton, Tim, and Phil Craig. *Finest Hour.* London: Coronet, 2001.

Clinch, Nancy Gager. *The Kennedy Neurosis.* New York: Grosset & Dunlap, 1973.

Clough, Bryan. *State Secrets: The Kent-Wolkoff Affair.* East Sussex, England: Hideaway Publications, Ltd., 2005.

Collier, Peter, and David Horowitz. *The Kennedys: An American Drama.* New York: Summit Books, 1984

———. *The Roosevelts: An American Saga.* New York: Simon & Schuster, 1994.

Costello, John. *Ten Days That Saved the West.* London: Bantam Press, 1991.

Dallek, Robert. *An Unfinished Life: John F. Kennedy, 1917–1963.* New York: Little, Brown and Company, 2003.

Davis, John H. *The Kennedys: Dynasty and Disaster, 1848–1983.* New York: McGraw-Hill, 1984.

deBedts, Ralph F. *Ambassador Joseph Kennedy, 1938–1940: Anatomy of Appeasement.* New York: Peter Lang, 1985.

de Courcy, Anne. *1939: The Last Season.* London: Thames and Hudson, 1981.

———. *Society's Queen: The Life of Edith, Marchioness of Londonderry.* London: Phoenix, 2004.

Devonshire, Andrew. *Accidents of Fortune.* Norwich, England: Michael Hall, 2004.

Dutton, David. *Neville Chamberlain.* London: Arnold, 2001.

Enright, Dominique (Editor). *The Wicked Wit of Winston Churchill.* London: Michael O'Mara Books Ltd., 2001.

Feiling, Keith. *The Life of Neville Chamberlain.* Hamden, England: Archon Books, 1970.

Ferguson, Nial. *The War of the World: Twentieth-Century Conflict and the Descent of the West.* New York: Penguin, 2006.

Fuchsner, Larry William. *Neville Chamberlain and Appeasement: A Study in the Politics of History.* New York: W.W. Norton and Company, 1982.

Gellman, Irwin, F. *Secret Affairs: FDR, Cordell Hull, and Sumner Welles.* New York: Enigma Books, 1995.

Gilbert, Martin. *A History of the Twentieth Century, Volume Two: 1933–1951.* New York: HarperCollins, New York, 1998.

———. *The Appeasers.* London: Phoenix Press, 1963.

———. *Churchill: A Life.* New York: Henry Holt & Company, 1991.

———. *Churchill and America.* New York: Free Press, 2005.

———. *The Second World War: A Complete History.* New York: Henry Holt and Company, 1989.

———. *Winston S. Churchill, Volume VI: "Finest Hour," 1939–1941.* Boston: Houghton Mifflin, 1983.

Goodwin, Doris Kearns. *The Fitzgeralds and the Kennedys.* New York: Simon & Schuster, 1987.

Hamilton, Nigel. *JFK: Reckless Youth.* New York: Random House, 1992.

Herman, Dorothy. *Anne Morrow Lindbergh: A Gift for Life.* New York: Ticknor and Fields, 1992.

Hersh, Burton. *Bobby and J. Edgar Hoover: The Historic Face-off Between the Kennedys and J. Edgar Hoover that Transformed America.* New York: Carroll & Graf, 2007.

Hersh, Seymour M. *The Dark Side of Camelot*. Boston: Little, Brown, 1997.

Heymann, C. David. *RFK: A Candid Biography of Robert F. Kennedy*. New York: E. P. Dutton, 1998.

Higham, Charles. *Rose: The Life and Times of Rose Fitzgerald Kennedy*. New York: Pocket Books, 1995.

———. *The Duchess of Windsor*. New York: McGraw-Hill, 1988.

———. *Trading with the Enemy: The Nazi-American Money Plot, 1933–1949*. New York: Barnes and Noble Books, 1983.

Ickes, Harold L. *The Secret Diaries of Harold L. Ickes, Volume III: The Lowering Clouds, 1939–1941*. New York: Simon & Schuster, 1954.

James, Lawrence. *The Rise and Fall of the British Empire*. New York: St. Martin's Griffin, 1994.

James, Robert Rhodes. *Anthony Eden: A Biography*. New York: McGraw-Hill Book Company, 1987.

———. *A Spirit Undaunted: The Political Role of George VI*. London: Abacus, 1999.

———. *Churchill: A Study in Failure*. New York: The World Publishing Company, 1970.

——— (Editor). *Chips: The Diaries of Sir Henry Channon*. London: Weidenfeld & Nicolson, 1967.

Jenkins, Roy. *Churchill: A Biography*. New York: Farrar, Straus & Giroux, 2001.

Kee, Robert. *1939: In the Shadow of War*. Boston: Little, Brown and Company, 1984.

Kennedy, John F. (Editor). *As We Remember Joe*. Privately printed—1945.

———. *Profiles in Courage*. New York: Harper, 1956.

———. *Why England Slept*. New York: Wilfred Funk, Inc., 1961.

Kennedy, Rose. *Times to Remember*. New York: Doubleday & Co., 1974.

Kennedy Family. *Her Grace Above Gold*. Privately printed memoir of Rose Kennedy. Copy in the John Fitzgerald Kennedy Library.

Kershaw, Ian. *Fateful Choices*. New York: The Penguin Press, 2007.

———. *Hitler: 1936–1945 Nemesis*. New York: Norton, 2000.

———. *Making Friends with Hitler: Lord Londonderry and Britain's Road to War*. London: Penguin Allen Lane, 2004.

Kimball, Warren. *Churchill and Roosevelt: The Complete Correspondence, Volume I*. Princeton, N.J.: Princeton University Press, 1984.

Klein, Edward. *The Kennedy Curse: Why America's First Family Has Been Haunted by Tragedy for 150 Years*. New York: St. Martin's Press, 2003.

Koskoff, David E. *Joseph P. Kennedy: A Life and Times*. Englewood Cliffs, N.J.: Prentice-Hall, 1974.

Krock, Arthur. *Memoirs: Sixty Years on the Firing Line*. New York: Funk and Wagnalls, 1968.

Lambert, Angela. *1939: The Last Season of Peace*. New York: Weidenfeld & Nicolson, 1989.

Langer, William L., and Everett S. Gleason. *Challenge to Isolation, 1937–1940*. New York: Harper & Row, 1952.

Leamer, Laurence. *The Kennedy Men: 1901–1963*. New York: William Morrow, 2001.

———. *The Kennedy Women: The Saga of an American Family*. New York: Villard Books, 1994.

Leaming, Barbara. *Jack Kennedy: The Education of a Statesman*. New York: W. W. Norton & Company, 2006.

Lind, Michael. *The American Way of Strategy: U.S. Foreign Policy and the American Way of Life*. New York: Oxford University Press, 2006.

Lindbergh, Charles A. *The Wartime Journals of Charles A. Lindbergh*. New York: Harcourt Brace Jovanovich, 1970.

Lovell, Mary S. *The Sisters: The Saga of the Mitford Family*. New York: Norton, 2001.

Lukacs, John. *Five Days in London: May 1940*. New Haven, Conn. and London: Yale Nota Beta, 1999.

———. *Remembered Past: John Lukacs on History, Historians, and Historical Knowledge.* Wilmington, Del.: ISI Books, 2005.

Macleod, Ian. *Neville Chamberlain.* London: Muller, 1961.

Manchester, William. *The Last Lion: Winston Spencer Churchill: Alone, 1932–1940.* New York: Dell Publishing, 1988.

Maier, Thomas. *The Kennedys: America's Emerald Kings—A Five-Generation History of the Ultimate Irish-Catholic Family.* New York: Basic Books, 2003.

Margetson, Stella. *The Long Party: High Society in the Twenties and Thirties.* Westmead, England: Saxon House, 1974.

Martin, Ralph G. *A Hero for Our Time: An Intimate Story of the Kennedy Years.* New York: MacMillan, 1983.

———. *Seeds of Destruction: Joe Kennedy and His Sons.* New York: G. P. Putnam's Sons, 1995.

McCarthy, Joe. *The Remarkable Kennedys.* New York: Dial Press, 1960.

McTaggart, Lynne. *Kathleen Kennedy: Her Life and Times.* New York: Dial Press, 1983.

Meacham, John. *Franklin and Winston: An Intimate Portrait of an Epic Friendship.* New York: Random House, 2003.

Milton, Joyce. *Loss of Eden: A Biography of Charles and Anne Morrow Lindbergh.* New York: Harper Collins, 1993.

Mitford, Jessica. *Hons and Rebels.* London: Victor Gollancz, 1960.

Morrow, Lance. *The Best Year of Their Lives: Kennedy, Johnson and Nixon in 1948.* New York: Basic Books, 2005.

Moss, Norman. *19 Weeks: America, Britain, and the Fateful Summer of 1940.* Boston and New York: Houghton Mifflin Company, 2003.

Muggeridge, Malcolm (Editor). *Ciano's Diary, 1939–1943.* Melbourne, Australia: William Heinemann Ltd., 1950.

Murrow, Edward R. *This Is London.* New York: Simon & Schuster, 1941.

Nicolson, Nigel (Editor). *Harold Nicolson: Diaries and Letters 1930–1939.* New York: Atheneum, 1966.

The War Years 1939–1945, Volume II of Diaries and Letters. New York: Atheneum, 1967.

Nunnerley, David. *President Kennedy and Britain.* New York: St. Martin's Press, 1972.

O'Brien, Michael. *John F. Kennedy: A Biography.* New York: Thomas Dunne Books, St. Martin's Press, 2005.

Panter-Downes, Mollie (edited by William Shawn). *London War Notes.* New York: Farrar, Straus & Giroux, 1971.

Perret, Geoffrey. *Jack: A Life Like No Other.* New York: Random House, 2002.

Persico, Joseph E. *Roosevelt's Secret War.* New York: Random House, 2001.

Pitts, David. *Jack and Lem.* New York: Carroll and Graf Publishers, 2007.

Pryce-Jones, David. *Unity Mitford: An Enquiry into Her Life and the Frivolity of Evil.* New York: The Dial Press, 1977.

Reeves, Thomas C. *A Question of Character: A Life of John F. Kennedy.* New York: MacMillan, 1991.

Renehan, Edward Jr. *The Kennedys at War.* New York: Doubleday, 2002.

Reynolds, David. *In Command of History: Churchill Fighting and Writing the Second World War.* New York: Random House, 2005.

Roberts, Andrew. *Hitler and Churchill: Secrets of Leadership.* London: Phoenix, 2004.

———. *'The Holy Fox': The Life of Lord Halifax.* London: Phoenix, 1997.

Roosevelt, James (with Bill Libby). *My Parents: A Differing View.* Chicago: Playboy Press, 1976.

Rose, Norman. *The Cliveden Set: Portrait of an Exclusive Fraternity.* London: Pimlico, 2001.

Rosen, Robert N. *Saving the Jews: Franklin D. Roosevelt and the Holocaust.* New York: Thunder's Mouth Press, 2006.

Rubin, Gretchen. *Forty Ways to Look at Winston Churchill.* New York: Random House, 2003.

Saint, Andrew, and Gillian Darley. *The Chronicles of London*. New York: St. Martin's Press, 1994.

Schlesinger, Arthur M., Jr. *A Thousand Days: John F. Kennedy in the White House*. Boston: Houghton-Mifflin, 1965.

———. *Robert Kennedy and His Times*. New York: Houghton-Mifflin, 1978.

Schoor, Gene. *Young John Kennedy*. New York: Harcourt, Brace & World, 1963.

Schwarz, Ted. *Joseph P. Kennedy*. Hoboken, N.J.: John Wiley & Sons Inc., 2003.

Searls, Hank. *The Lost Prince: Young Joe, the Forgotten Kennedy—The Story of the Oldest Brother*. New York: World Publishing Company, 1969.

Self, Robert. *Neville Chamberlain: A Biography*. Hants, England: Ashgate, Aldershot, 2006.

——— (Editor). *The Neville Chamberlain Diary, Letters, Volume 4: The Downing Street Years, 1934–1940*. Hants, England: Ashgate, Aldershot, 2005.

Shirer, William L. *Berlin Diary: The Journal of a Foreign Correspondent, 1934–1941*. London: Hamish Hamilton, 1941.

———. *The Rise and Fall of the Third Reich*. New York: Simon & Schuster, 1959.

Smith, Amanda (Editor). *Hostage to Fortune: The Letters of Joseph P. Kennedy*. New York: Viking, 2001.

Smith, Jean Edward. *FDR*. New York: Random House, 2007.

Smith, Sally Bedell. *Grace and Power: The Private World of the Kennedy White House*. New York: Random House, 2004.

———. *Reflected Glory: The Life of Pamela Churchill Harriman*. New York: Touchstone/Simon & Schuster, 1996.

Soames, Mary. *Clementine Churchill: The Biography of a Marriage*. Boston: Houghton Mifflin, 1979.

Sorensen, Theodore C. (Editor). *"Let The Word Go Forth": The Speeches, Statements, and Writings of John F. Kennedy, 1947 to 1963*. New York: Laurel, 1988.

Spaulding, E. Wilder. *Ambassadors Ordinary and Extraordinary*. Washington, D.C.: Public Affairs Press, 1961.

Stafford, David. *Roosevelt & Churchill: Men of Secrets*. Woodstock, N.Y.: Little, Brown & Company, 1999.

Stewart, Graham. *Burying Caesar: The Churchill-Chamberlain Rivalry*. Woodstock, N.Y. and New York: The Overlook Press, 2001.

Strawson, John. *Churchill and Hitler*. New York: Fromm International, 2000.

Swift, Will. *The Roosevelts and the Royals*. Hoboken, N.J.: John Wiley & Sons, Inc., 2004.

Sykes, Christopher. *Nancy: The Life of Lady Astor*. Herts, England: St Albans, 1979

Talbot, David. *Brothers: The Hidden History of the Kennedy Years*. New York: Free Press, 2007.

Thomas, Evan. *Robert Kennedy: His Life*. New York: Simon & Schuster, 2000.

Thompson, Robert Smith. *The Complete Idiot's Guide to Nazi Germany*. New York: Alpha, 2003.

Vickers, Hugo. *Elizabeth, The Queen Mother*. London: Hutchinson, 2005.

Vieth, Jane Karoline. *Joseph P. Kennedy: Ambassador to the Court of St. James's, 1938–1940*. Unpublished dissertation, Ohio State University, 1975.

Warwick, Christopher. *King George VI & Queen Elizabeth*. London: Sidgwick & Jackson, 1985.

Welles, Benjamin. *Sumner Welles: FDR's Global Strategist*. New York: St. Martin's Press, 1997.

Welles, Sumner. *The Time for Decision*. New York: Harper & Brothers, 1944.

Whelan, Richard J. *The Founding Father: The Story of Joseph P. Kennedy*. New York: New American Library, 1964.

Wheeler-Bennett, John W. *King George VI: His Life and Reign*. London: MacMillan & Co., Ltd., 1958.

Willis, Clint. *Kennedys: Stories of Life and Death from an American Family*. New York: Thunder's Mouth Press, 2001.

Wills, Garry. *The Kennedy Imprisonment: A Meditation on Power.* Boston: Little, Brown, 1982.

Wilson, A. N. *After The Victorians: The Decline of Britain in the World.* New York: Farrar, Straus & Giroux, 2005.

Wise, Stephen. *The Challenging Years: The Autobiography of Stephen Wise.* New York: G. P. Putnam's Sons, 1949.

Wofford, Harris. *Of Kennedys and Kings: Making Sense of the Sixties.* New York: Farrar, Straus & Giroux, 1980.

Wyman, David S. *The Abandonment of the Jews: America and the Holocaust, 1941–1945.* New York: The New Press, 1984.

Index